# Evaluating Leisure Services
## Making Enlightened Decisions

### (Third Edition)

# Evaluating Leisure Services
## Making Enlightened Decisions

## (Third Edition)

Karla A. Henderson, Professor

North Carolina State University


M. Deborah Bialeschki, Professor Emeritus

University of North Carolina–Chapel Hill

Production Manager: Richard Yocum
Manuscript Editing: Richard Yocum and Daniel Threet
Cover Design: StepUp Communications
Library of Congress Catalogue Card Number: 2010925046
ISBN-10: 1-892132-88-5
ISBN-13: 978-1-892132-88-8

Dedicated to

H. Douglas Sessoms and Betty van der Smissen

# Table of Contents

# List of Tables and Figures

# Preface

To say we live in an information age is an understatement. As Alvin Toffler (1970) warned many years ago, people can become drowned in information but starved for knowledge. Professionals in any field of human services must have the means to access and assess information. Having information is not enough, however, unless that information can be applied and used. To organize and manage recreation services (i.e., all elements related to the various specialties in the field such as parks, tourism, sports, arts, therapeutic recreation, camping, event management), information is needed about people's preferences, needs, and behaviors and the programs, administrative structures, and resources that comprise the organizations. To build a body of knowledge and to document the value of recreation, systematic processes are needed. Evaluation and research can provide information that will enable "enlightened decisions."

Evaluation is a process that each of us uses every day. You probably made a judgment about what you liked or didn't like when you saw the cover of this book and began to thumb through these pages. Although this type of intuitive evaluation is important, this book is about systematic evaluation and research that focuses specifically on identifying explicit evaluation criteria or research questions, collecting evidence or data, and making judgments about the value or the worth of something applied to service improvement or knowledge development.

Unfortunately, evaluation and research strike terror in the hearts of some students and professionals. People are often afraid to do evaluations and afraid of what they might find. Research seems overly complex. Doing evaluations or research does not consist of any magic formula. Further, learning to do evaluations or research cannot be done overnight. The two of us have been doing research for well over 30 years and we feel we are always learning something new, as we hope to show in this third edition of *Evaluating Leisure Services*. The more you learn about evaluation and research procedures, however, the easier they become. We hope you will see how assessment, evaluation, research, and statistics can be valuable in making enlightened decisions as well as generating important knowledge.

This text will not make you an expert. It is intended, however, to provide an awareness and understanding of the need for evaluation and research in our profession. This book aims to provide a basic overview and working knowledge of procedures. Knowing basic steps in evaluation research and having some familiarity with evaluation and research tools can help you to begin a process of lifelong learning about systematic inquiry. Thus, this book will provide a primer that will enable you to use evaluation and research to become more experienced as you practice and apply the concepts and techniques.

This textbook is designed for upper-level undergraduates, beginning graduate students, and practitioners who wish to apply evaluation and research to their efforts. The text is written for students, but students are defined as anyone who is in a learning situation. Many professionals find that what they have learned makes the most sense once they are in the "real world" where they need to apply text material immediately to their situations.

This book consists of a discussion of the three main elements of evaluation divided into four logical units. The three parts are the thesis or the "trilogy" of a systematic process for evaluation or research—criteria (research questions), evidence (data), and judgment (interpretation).

Since the evidence section is mainly oriented to techniques, strategies, and research methods, we have divided it into two units on collecting data and analyzing data. Because evaluation uses a number of conceptual ideas and specific research applications, we have organized the chapters around specific topics. Sometimes it is useful to read about a particular concept and technique and reflect upon it before moving to the next idea. Other times you may want to turn to a particular chapter that will give information to address a specific problem.

We have taken the *USA Today* approach to writing this text. *USA Today* uses short articles that can be read and comprehended fairly quickly. Unlike *USA Today,* we have tried not to oversimplify the ideas but we have structured chapters that we hope will be easily read. The number of chapters in this book may seem a bit overwhelming but none of them is particularly long and we have tried to organize the reading by outlining key points and providing examples.

We have also made the assumption that most readers are in the recreation field, broadly conceived. We have tried to use examples related to therapeutic recreation, youth agencies, community recreation, commercial businesses, tourism, sports, and camping and outdoor recreation. Although not all of these examples will be directly applicable to your interest, we believe that in a field that shares the common goals of enhancing the quality of life for people through recreation and leisure, that we can learn from each other. In most cases the implications of evaluation to any one area of recreation can apply to other applied areas as well.

A number of people have influenced the writing of this textbook. We are most indebted to Pat Farrell and Herberta Lundegren (Penn State University) for the excellent evaluation book that they wrote many years ago. We used their model in the first edition of this book and have tried to build upon their framework with the inclusion of more examples of evaluation based on qualitative data. Other individuals in the field of parks, recreation, and leisure studies who have contributed to our understanding of evaluation are too numerous to mention here but are acknowledged throughout this book.

This book has evolved from our teaching evaluation and research methods to students over the past 30 years as well as our experiences as researchers and evaluators. We are indebted to all students and colleagues who have helped us learn how to teach these topics.

We hope that you as students and readers will evaluate this book favorably because you set criteria that valued a readable, understandable, and useful text and because you found evidence that supported those criteria.

# Unit ONE—CRITERIA

\*\*\*

# *Foundations for Evaluation and Research*

## 1.0 Introduction to Criteria

Beginning a text is not easy. Beginning a research or evaluation project isn't always easy either. Because your anxiety may already be high, we dislike beginning on a theoretical note. Yet a certain framework needs to be presented to provide a foundation for any type of systematic inquiry, such as evaluation or research. In discussing evaluation and research, we are systematic with the procedures that we outline for you. It is sometimes more tempting to start in the middle of the process than at the beginning. For example, people sometimes draft a questionnaire before they have thought about the overall design of the project, the theoretical framework, or who will use the information.

To explore any type of systematic inquiry effectively, we as authors and you as readers must be on the proverbial "same page." Therefore, we start by providing a conceptual background. As a reader, of course, you can start wherever you would like, but we encourage you to ground yourself in a basic understanding of evaluation and research processes before you begin to collect data.

The goal of systematic evaluation and rigorous research is to make reliable, valid, useful, and enlightened decisions and interpretations. Of course, all of us are continually involved in a process of evaluation. How many times have you stuck your toe in a swimming pool to test its temperature before jumping in? Simplistic as it may be, dipping your toe is a form of evaluation that will lead to a judgment or a decision about whether and how to enter the water. If only formal evaluations and research were as easy as sticking one's toes into the water and making a decision! Unfortunately, most evaluations in recreation are (and should be) more systematic and complicated than this intuitive example. In this book, we provide a process for systematic inquiry leading to effective evaluations and rigorous research.

This first unit sets a framework for evaluation and explores the aspects of **determining criteria**. In research, this aspect might be called developing research questions. We will use the term 'criteria' to encompass the broad range of considerations necessary for establishing the purpose of the inquiry. In plain terms, **what is it you want or need to know?**

Although Unit One ("Criteria") is not the most "action-packed" unit, it is one of the most critical. One major problem with any type of inquiry is that sometimes evaluators do not take time to plan and ascertain the appropriate criteria to use. For example, by putting your toes into the swimming pool, you were using your sense of the water's temperature as a criterion, but many other criteria, such as water quality or depth, could have been measured by using some other process. Perhaps the pH level in a swimming pool is a more appropriate criterion to measure than temperature before you go swimming. Measuring the pH level with one's toes would not be appropriate if the criteria included a chemical balance check. Thus, an essential dimension of any project is making sure you are collecting evidence using the appropriate criteria or research questions.

Evaluation refers to making decisions based on identified questions or criteria and supporting evidence. Evaluation research includes the processes used to collect and analyze data or evidence. Research studies are described in relationship to evaluation projects in the text, but the major focus is on evaluation scholarship and its use. Since this text is primarily aimed at undergraduate students who are more likely to conduct evaluation projects in entry-level jobs, we refer to you as the evaluator. Research, however, shares many of the common techniques used in evaluation, so we discuss both in this book. Recreation services are the human service organizations and enterprises related to:

- parks
- recreation
- tourism
- commercial recreation
- outdoors
- education
- sports
- therapeutic recreation

Other specific terms will be defined throughout this book. In addition, we include a glossary of terms to assist you as you read the text.

In this first unit, we examine what evaluation is, its purposes, its relationship to research, and how the aspects of criteria, evidence, and judgment are defined and interrelated. We explore areas of evaluation within recreation services and the types of evaluation that might be done. Within these types we examine approaches and models that can be applied to evaluation or research. Further, we consider how evaluation systems, as well as evaluation and research projects, are designed. Finally, we address legal and ethical issues that may be encountered in conducting evaluations.

## 1.1 The Basic Question: What is Systematic Inquiry?

Most of us wish we lived in a perfect world. We want to get all 'A's because our schoolwork is of the highest quality. As leisure service professionals, we want participants to experience many benefits from recreation programs. We want staff to perform their duties enthusiastically and appropriately, budgets to reflect cost-effectiveness, and people to flock to our programs. We don't want people to complain or doubt our abilities as recreation professionals.

In reality, however, our lives and our student or professional situations don't run perfectly all the time. We need to use the resources available to improve ourselves and make our organizations more effective. None of us will ever be perfect, but we can use the processes and techniques of systematic inquiry, in the form of evaluation and research, to help us make enlightened decisions and improve what we do, whether as practitioners or as scholars. We want to understand the world better through this systematic inquiry. We need logical and informed processes for using evaluation and research to improve something or add to a body of knowledge.

For the purposes of this text, we define evaluation as the systematic collection and analysis of data to address criteria and make judgments. Effective evaluation means making decisions based on identified questions and supporting evidence. Other definitions exist that have slightly different interpretations. Generally, however, the goal of evaluation is to determine "what is" compared to "what should be." Similarly, research is the systematic collection and analysis of data to answer a theoretical question and contribute to a broad body of knowledge.

Doing evaluation or research is a bit like solving a mystery. For example, when a robbery occurs, detectives use elements of criteria, evidence (or data), and judgment (or decisions). The criteria would be questions that they wish to answer: what was stolen, who stole it, and what was the motive. The evidence would include information such as statements from witnesses, an inventory of what was missing, and physical clues such as fingerprints. Based on what they want to know and what evidence is collected, a judgment can then be made about what was stolen, who took it, and probable cause. With those judgments, an arrest can be made and justice can prevail. If detectives do not have enough evidence, the judgment or arrest is difficult to make. These same principles apply to evaluation and research.

# Systematic (Formal) Evaluations

We are all continuously engaged in a process of intuitive evaluation. We say things to ourselves like, "the room is too hot," "I'm too tired to think," or "I wish I hadn't eaten so much for lunch." The evaluation we do in recreation agencies, although it may be intuitive on an everyday basis, can be more trustworthy when it is systematically designed. A camp director told us once, "I don't use evaluations. I just watch and listen and talk to campers and staff and I find out all that I need to know." We acknowledge these important means for evaluation, but we also believe that formal systematic evaluations that are purposeful, reliable, and valid need to be conducted within organizations from time to time.

A systematic evaluation process takes greater effort (in time and money) than informal evaluations which rely on intuition or expert judgment. Systematic or formal evaluation, however, provides a rigor when outcomes are complex, decisions are important, and evidence is needed to make "enlightened" or informed decisions or interpretations.

The major purpose of evaluation is, therefore, to make decisions. We want to make the best possible decisions based on systematically gathering evidence related to a particular purpose or standard for decision making. Evaluation provides information that can lead to decisions, interpretations, and action. Through evaluation, we try to improve or show the value of various aspects of recreation. We generate this information through the application of evaluation research methods and techniques.

Research and evaluation share common methods and a similar framework for making decisions. The differences between evaluation and research projects are described in more detail in the next chapter, but for now keep in mind that the methods and tools for evaluation and research are the same. Methods and tools for systematic inquiry are used for data collection and analysis, regardless of whether evaluation or research is undertaken.

Thus, evaluation, as well as research, requires the systematic use of a framework of procedures and methods that include: **criteria** (also known as hypotheses, research questions, guiding questions, working hypotheses, purposes, measures, or objectives), **evidence** (or data that are collected and analyzed using appropriate designs and methods), and **judgment** (or interpretations expressed in conclusions and recommendations). Therefore:

*Criteria + Evidence + Judgment = Evaluation*

# Evaluation Today

Evaluation ranges from habits of everyday living to formal systematic studies, all of which help to assess where we are, where we want to be, and how we can reach desired goals. Thus, evaluation might entail intuitive feelings and thoughts, expert judgments, descriptive qualitative and quantitative analyses, quasi-experimental designs, or experimental designs.

Nothing is wrong with intuitive evaluation, but it is generally not enough if professionals want to make sure organizations are effective. Expert judgments are frequently used in the recreation field when consultants provide information or accreditation teams visit facilities and make recommendations. Descriptive analyses include summaries of "what is" in an organization. These descriptions provide a basis for recommended changes. Quasi-experiments and true experiments are means to measure changes that occur because of a program or intervention. Figure 1.1 provides a pictorial example of how evaluation might look as a continuum ranging from intuitive to formal systems. Each of these methods on the continuum for doing evaluations will be discussed in more detail in Unit Two.

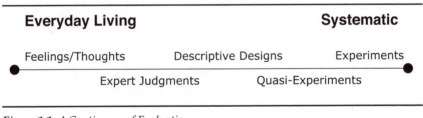

**Everyday Living**　　　　　　　　　　**Systematic**

　　Feelings/Thoughts　　　Descriptive Designs　　　Experiments

　　　　Expert Judgments　　　　Quasi-Experiments

*Figure 1.1* *A Continuum of Evaluation*

Developing a system for evaluation, gathering resources, and conducting formal evaluations may be the basis for more efficient and effective operations, staff, and programs. This, in turn, results in increased recreational, educational, and personal benefits for children, youth, and adults. Effectiveness relates to changes or the results of a program or intervention. Efficiency implies how changes or results happen. To focus on evaluation for improving effectiveness and efficiency in the conduct of all aspects of recreation services, several important characteristics of evaluation should be kept in mind:

1. Evaluation is a process. It consists of three dimensions: determining criteria, collecting and analyzing evidence, and making judgments and decisions.

2. The goal of evaluation is to make decisions by ascertaining value or worth. Decisions should be based on sound judgments and not just on personal biases.

3. The most common way to evaluate is to measure and judge how well objectives are met. As you will see later in this text, however, this model is only one of many ways to conduct evaluations.

4. The results of evaluation should lead to decision making about and for a specific situation or context. The results of research should lead to a contribution to the body of knowledge that has some generalizability.

5. Evaluation may be informal or formal. Systematically and formally gathered data, however, are necessary for making the best decisions within most recreation organizations.

6. Evaluation within an organization should be ongoing with evaluation systems in place to address aspects of personnel (staff), program improvement, policy (administration), places (areas and facilities), and participant outcomes. Within these evaluations systems, particular evaluation projects may be undertaken.

7. Evaluation is continuous and does not necessarily occur only at the end of an event or activity. Evaluation may occur as an assessment to determine "what is" versus "what should be," formatively to examine processes, or summatively, to ascertain outcomes.

8. Responsive evaluation is based on the premise that evaluation should respond to issues and concerns within an organization. Evaluation should have relevance to an organization and those people who make decisions in the organization. Research should help understand the world better.

9. No magic formulas for evaluation exist. Each evaluation or research project undertaken will be different than the previous and ought to reflect the particular context within an organization.

Each of these ideas will be revisited throughout this unit and will be applied in the process of doing evaluations by using criteria, evidence, and judgment. As you will see, research also has many of the same purposes, but the primary focus of this book will be centered on evaluation as systematic inquiry.

## From Ideas to Reality

In any professional situation, you have the choice of whether you want to evaluate or not. Most of us are continually engaged in a process of intuitive evaluation about staff, programs, facilities, policies, and participants, whether we are consciously aware of this or not. Many times this intuitive evaluation is not enough. Intuition is helpful but may not be unbiased or detailed. Often colleagues, participants, or other stakeholders in an organization want some type of systematic proof about something. It may be documented information concerning the performance of a staff member or it might be numbers that describe the average rating of satisfaction concerning a certain program activity. Thus, we need to collect these data based on criteria that will provide information to make judgments about something's worth and the need for improvement.

Now that you have studied this chapter, you should be able to:
- Write definitions of "evaluation" and "research," regarding their commonalities
- Describe the importance of systematic formal evaluations
- Identify the characteristics of evaluation and research that lead to enlightened decisions

## 1.2 Evaluation and Research: Viva la Difference

This book is primarily about evaluation and the evaluation research methods used to make decisions in recreation organizations. Anyone using this book, however, might also be interested in research projects as well. Frequently we see the words "research" and "evaluation" used together. Although many similarities exist in the processes of evaluation and research, differences exist in the outcomes of each.

Evaluation is defined as the systematic collection and analysis of data to address some criteria of judgments about the worth or improvement of something. Research is generally defined as systematic investigation within some discipline undertaken to establish facts and principles to contribute to a body of knowledge. The goal of research is not necessarily to assist in practical decision making, but to generate facts that might be generalized to a broader knowledge base. Both use scientific principles and methods to examine something. Both evaluation and research are characterized by a clearly delineated protocol in collecting, processing, and analyzing data. Evaluation, however, is a specific form of applied research that results in the application of information for decision making.

Therefore, we emphasize that evaluation and research use the same methods but have different purposes and outcomes. The scientific method, or the way that systematic inquiry is undertaken, is not bound by purpose, so it can be applied in both evaluation projects and research studies. Evaluation projects use research methods but they do not have unique methods. Models of evaluation should apply some variation of the basic rules of the scientific method. In this chapter we discuss the differences between evaluation and research as well as aspects of theory and literature review that are usually connected to research rather than evaluation.

## Differences in Objectives or Purposes

The objectives or purposes of evaluation and research projects need to be discussed because they constitute one of the major differences between evaluation and research. First, research tries to prove or disprove hypotheses, whereas evaluation focuses on improvement in some area related to programs, personnel, policies, places and facilities, or participant outcomes. Researchers are usually concerned with increasing understanding, satisfying an inquiring mind, or finding scientific truth. Evaluators are concerned with problem solving and decision making in a specific situation. The aim of research is new knowledge that may or may not be applicable immediately. This aim does not mean that research projects do not address problems and offer data for application, but these direct applications are not necessarily the outcome of the research project undertaken. Direct application is the purpose of doing evaluation projects.

Second, evaluation projects generally compare the results with organization goals to see how well the latter have been met. Research, by definition, applies scientific techniques to testing hypotheses or research questions focused on findings related to tests of theory or theory generation. Theory is the process of giving order and insight to what has been observed. Theory allows for an explanation of findings that may be generalized beyond a particular context. Evaluators usually focus at the applied level for a particular situation and usually do not get into theory questions that might be generalized beyond a specific situation. Research involves inquiry based on a desire to know something in a theoretical and generalizable sense. Thus, research is theoretically grounded whereas evaluation is problem-based.

Third, evaluators are not interested in generalizing results to other situations, although sometimes that possibility is relevant. Research, by using theory and sampling techniques, should be generalizable to other situations. Evaluation uses specific information for making decisions about a particular situation. Similarly, in evaluation the questions or criteria emerge from the decision makers who will use the information and not necessarily from the personal interest of the evaluator. In research, the hypotheses may come from the researcher's interests and goals or from previous research.

Fourth, evaluation projects should be undertaken when a decision needs to be made or the relative worth of something is unknown. Research is conducted to develop new knowledge. Stated again, research leads to theoretical conclusions whereas evaluation leads to decisions for solving problems. As was discussed in the previous chapter, evaluation must lead to judgment about the worth of something; the value of evaluation lies in making valid judgments that result in enlightened decision making.

Fifth, the results of research are usually published because their purpose is to add to the body of knowledge about a particular topic or theory. Publications and presentations are the way this purpose is accomplished. Although evaluation reports are generally written and presented formally to decision makers, the information is not necessarily shared publicly or broadly. We find some exceptions regarding applied research in some of the major journals of the leisure services field such as the *Journal of Park and Recreation Administration, Tourism Management, Sport Management Review,* and the *Therapeutic Recreation Journal.* Editors of these journals sometimes publish evaluation studies that serve as models for research methods or provide insights for other professionals to use in their organizations.

## Sharing of Common Methods

In the broadest sense, research includes elements of evaluation, and evaluation requires the use of research techniques. We frequently see separate chapters in research texts (e.g., Babbie, 2006) that focus on evaluation research. Research and evaluation projects, nevertheless, share common methods. If you have a good grasp of the repertoire of methods as well as data collection and analysis techniques available for evaluation, you will have a sound methodological foundation for conducting research. The use of methods may be applied differently, however, because research relies on theory as its building blocks and evaluation relies on application and decision making. Figure 1.2 shows how evaluation and research share common methods such as surveys, observations, and experiments but have different applications.

## A Comparison of Evaluation and Research

In some cases, either an evaluation or research project could be undertaken depending on how the data are used. For example, suppose you wanted

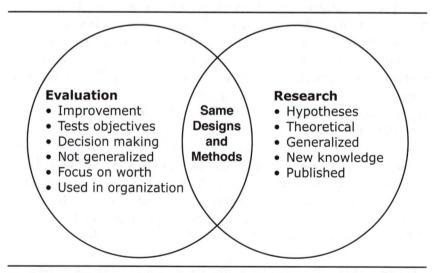

**Evaluation**
- Improvement
- Tests objectives
- Decision making
- Not generalized
- Focus on worth
- Used in organization

**Same Designs and Methods**

**Research**
- Hypotheses
- Theoretical
- Generalized
- New knowledge
- Published

*Figure 1.2* *A Comparison of Evaluation and Research*

to know how adolescent girls experienced a recreation activity. In an evaluation project you might develop criteria to determine how self-esteem changed as a result of participating in an activity. You could measure these changes using a pre- and posttest to see what the girls experienced before they started the activity and then again after the activity. From a research perspective, you might do the same thing but you would be interested in examining a theory such as learned helplessness as a theoretical framework for understanding how self-esteem changes. The difference between evaluation and research also relates to how you explain what the changes or lack of changes mean. In the judgment phase, the evaluator would be concerned with ways to make sure that these positive changes continue to happen through the recreation program. The researcher would be interested in tying the findings to theory and building the body of knowledge about girls and a theory such as learned helplessness in general that may or may not be directly applied to a particular recreation program.

Doing evaluation and research at the same time is possible, but the criteria phase will need to include research questions linked to theory and the judgment phase will need to include a discussion of how the body of knowledge based on a literature review can be enhanced with this research information. Evaluation is generally, but not always, easier to do because it relates to addressing specific criteria for making decisions about programs, places, participants, policies, or personnel. Most people who develop evaluation skills can also develop research skills. Keep in mind that the reasons and applications are the major differences between evaluation and research.

Evaluation should not be sloppy research! The same protocols and rules of methodology that apply to research apply to evaluation. Good evaluations rely on sound research methods. The process for evaluation and research is similar and even the first two aspects of the trilogy are necessary (i.e., criteria and data), but the major differences lie in the purpose of the research and how the evaluation or research results are used. The use of theory and literature reviews is more often associated with research than with evaluation projects.

## A Word About Theory

One of the major differences between research and evaluation lies in the use of theory as an aspect of criteria and judgment. Many excellent books have been written about research, theory, and leisure sciences that you may wish to consult. This chapter simply introduces some of the aspects of theory to consider.

Two of the primary aims of research are either to fit data to a theory or to generate a theory from data. Theory gives order and insight through explanations to what can be, is, or has been observed (Henderson, Presley, & Bialeschki, 2004). In other words, theory provides a "road map" (Tinsley, 1984). Research is sometimes criticized in leisure studies because it lacks theory or has poor theoretical quality. Although not all research that lacks theory may be classified as evaluative, it is generally more like evaluation than research if theory is lacking.

Conceptual frameworks are the basis of all research, regardless of whether theory is confirmed or tested. Conceptual frameworks precede theories and describe the assumptions from which the researcher is operating. In evaluation projects, concepts are often key dimensions that also provide direction for the evaluator in understanding the relationship among variables. In evaluation, however, the focus is not necessarily on linking the concepts into a framework but using the concepts to collect data and ultimately to make decisions. Concepts are always used in evaluation projects, but they are not necessarily linked into conceptual frameworks.

The use of theory in research projects ranges from theory testing and confirmation to theory development. In theory testing, a known theory is stated prior to beginning a research study. The study is then conducted to see whether or not that theory helps to explain "what is" related to the topic. In theory development, a theory is generated after the research to aid in explaining what happened. This theory emerges from the data and is frequently tied to other similar or related theories. Closely associated with theory is the use of models for illustrating theory in leisure research literature.

Theories are generally associated with hypotheses in research projects. Hypotheses reflect the researcher's "guess" about what the outcomes of a research study might be. Hypotheses are like criteria in evaluation projects, and they are useful because they set out goals regarding the research outcomes. These hypotheses may be stated as relationships between variables or as research questions. For example, one hypothesis stated as a relationship might be, "organized camping programs will enhance the prosocial behavior of youth." Stated as a question, the hypothesis might be, "Do organized camping programs enhance the prosocial behavior of youth?" These hypotheses should be based on theory or evidence, should be testable, and should be brief but clear.

Frequently, theory is tested and confirmed in research projects. Theory, however, might also be grounded or developed in a research project, particularly when qualitative data are collected and the researcher does not have a preconceived idea of what he or she might find. This theory, sometimes referred to as emerging theory, can then become the basis for other studies that might test it in other ways.

A number of theories are used in leisure research. Some of these theories are borrowed from other fields such as business and psychology. For example, researchers have used marginality theory to explain the lack of participation of people of color in recreation programs. Social exchange theory has been used to analyze the reasons why people choose or do not choose to become involved in Advisory Boards. Carrying capacity has been used to determine how much use an outdoor area can take before the resources and recreational experiences of participants are diminished. We have also developed conceptual frameworks and theory specifically related to leisure sciences. For example, travel cost models are used to examine why and how people make vacation choices. Conceptual constraint models have provided a plethora of information about why people do not participate in recreation activities to the full extent they would like. Journals such as *Leisure Sciences, Journal of Leisure Research, Annals of Tourism,* and *Journal of Sport Management* contain numerous examples of how theory and conceptual frameworks have been applied in the field of recreation and leisure research.

# Using Literature Reviews

The review of literature involves finding other studies related to the proposed research study. "Reviewing the literature" includes finding sources of information in books, journals, or reports, and reading and evaluating them to see how they fit with the proposed research questions. An individual undertaking an evaluation project might also use literature to assist in conducting a project, but not necessarily. Since evaluation projects are usually not published within the scientific community, they are often not as easily accessible as research projects.

The review of literature undertaken for a research project is usually extensive, thorough, and aimed at trying to uncover as much as possible about previous studies regarding the research topic. This review is important because it provides a way to find out what others have done so the researcher can contribute to the existing body of knowledge by building on this previous work. The literature review provides the foundation for the interpretation of research if the researcher has gained insight into the meaningful results obtained by others. Doing a literature review helps to delimit the research problem, provides insight into possible methods, and uncovers the most current thinking about theories or conceptual frameworks.

With the myriad of resources available in libraries and on the Internet, finding sources for the literature review should not be difficult.

The difficulty lies in sifting through all the literature to critically examine what can be learned to strengthen a proposed research study. The researcher must also have a means for organizing the information so the best ideas can be put together to create the foundation for the pending research project. This literature review will also provide a touchstone when the data are collected and analyzed to show how the research project contributes to what information already exists. Doing the literature review is a central task for any research project. A literature review may be helpful for an evaluation project but is not mandatory, as it is for a research study.

Some of you reading this book may be more interested in research and theoretical applications than in evaluation. If you read this book and study Units Two and Three, as well as portions of Unit Four, you will have a solid background in research methods. If you want to do research, however, we suggest you do additional reading from texts designed specifically to address research issues and from journals that report the most recent research in the field. Doing evaluation projects does not mean that you shouldn't also know this research literature, but doing evaluation requires a different point of beginning and a different point of application in the end.

# From Ideas to Reality

Evaluation and research are closely linked because they share common methods. As indicated previously, we find it most useful to think of research and evaluation as two separate approaches to finding answers. Regardless of whether you are conducting research that uses theory and a literature review or constructing an evaluation project, methods such as surveys, observations, unobtrusive measures (that might include historical research), or experiments are possible. Similarly, both researchers and evaluators will need to be concerned about sampling, measurement, and analysis. The major differences between evaluation and research are in the purpose and in the interpretation of the results.

Now that you have studied this chapter, you should be able to:
- Describe the differences between research and evaluation
- Explain when a research study would be desirable and when an evaluation project would be more appropriate
- Identify the types of research that you might see in recreation journals
- Describe the importance of theory and literature reviews

# 1.3 The Trilogy of Evaluation and Research: Criteria, Evidence, and Judgment

The premise of this book is that three components must be present for evaluation to aid in decision making: criteria, evidence (data), and judgment. Expressed in a slightly different way related to research but with the same elements might be the components of research questions, evidence (data), and interpretation. If any part of this trilogy is missing, successful evaluation or research will not occur. In other words, we might say:

*Criteria + Evidence + Judgment = Evaluation*
and
*Research Questions + Evidence + Interpretation = Research*

The purpose of this chapter is to define this trilogy. It would be wonderful if we could offer a magic formula that showed how to use the evaluation and research trilogy for any given project, but that is not possible. Every project in every organization and setting is going to be different. An infinite number of combinations exist for linking criteria, evidence, and judgment. Regardless of the project, the importance of the trilogy for systematic evaluation and rigorous research lies in our ability to link and logically use the three elements.

## Criteria

Criteria refer to the standards or the ideals upon which something is evaluated or studied. Criteria are the basic organizing framework for evaluations, similar to how hypotheses or research questions are used in research. Further, criteria will determine to a great extent what method would be best to use. To determine criteria is to determine the purpose of an evaluation, the models that might be applied, the levels of evaluation needed, and the specific evaluation questions that will be explored. In many ways, criteria are directly tied to planning because to develop criteria is to set a framework or a road map to follow from the beginning to the end of a project.

All of us always have criteria in our heads, but they may not be appropriate in all situations. For example, when people disagree over how good a restaurant might be, we must be careful that the same criteria are being applied. If someone dislikes a restaurant because the servers are slow and rude, a different criterion is being applied than if the criterion is the price of the food or how it tasted. Of course when we eat at a restaurant we expect all criteria to be met or exceeded, but depending on the definition of criteria, our judgments might vary depending on what criteria we use. Some criteria may be more important than others. For example, if the food at a restaurant is extraordinary, you might be willing to downplay slow service.

Developing criteria often appears to be the easiest aspect of the inquiry process, but in reality it may be the most difficult. Depending upon the purpose of the evaluation or research project, the criteria or research questions may be self-evident. For example, if a program has a set of good goals and objectives to serve as the criteria, the evaluator can then decide how best to gather evidence. If, however, you are not sure what needs to be evaluated, determining criteria may be more difficult. You can't evaluate or research everything, so you will have to choose what can be examined based on the time and resources you have as well as who wants the information. For any project, measuring everything with any degree of depth is unlikely. Criteria must be intentionally chosen.

One of the major pitfalls of evaluation is not stating the criteria specifically enough so that they can be measured. The evaluator must be able to articulate what to measure. A great difference exists between determining how many people participated in a program and identifying their satisfaction with the program. Sometimes data are collected without a specific set of criteria in mind. If you are lucky, the data may answer the critical evaluation questions, but chances are they will not unless a plan was made. Sometimes we collect data believing we are addressing one set of criteria only to find out this assumption was not the case. Sometimes the evaluator has one set of criteria that she or he thinks should be measured while stakeholders (e.g., Boards of Directors or parents) may have something else in mind. Thus, clearly identifying what questions you wish to address or what criteria to evaluate before data are collected for an evaluation or research project is essential.

Many people struggle with how to design evaluation systems, as well as specific projects, because they do not have a sense of the criteria that need to be evaluated. To skip over the step of identifying criteria, or to skip over this unit, will not be useful in the long run if good decision making and/or contributions to the body of knowledge are to occur. The more time spent determining what you want to evaluate, the more time will be saved later when you are collecting reliable and valid information and making decisions about what the data mean.

# Evidence

Evidence means data. Data are pieces of information that are collected and analyzed to determine whether criteria are met. In gathering evidence the timing, type of data, sample size and composition, and techniques for handling data must be determined; these aspects of evidence will be discussed in greater detail later in this book.

The two major types of data are qualitative and quantitative. Quantitative data in the simplest form refer to numbers from measurements that result in some type of statistics. Qualitative data refer to words used to describe or explain what is happening. Many evaluation designs and research methods can be used to collect these two types of data ranging from experimental and descriptive designs to the more specific methods related to surveys, observations, and unobtrusive measures. All of these methods will be discussed in detail in Unit Two.

Evidence must relate directly to the established criteria or research questions. If poor criteria were set up, designing instruments that will measure what you really want to measure will be difficult. Applying data collection, analysis techniques, and research methods are not difficult processes, in themselves. Applying them appropriately based on criteria is what requires effort.

# Judgment

Judgment is the interpretation of the value of something based on evidence collected from predetermined criteria. Judgments refer specifically to the conclusions and recommendations that are made for any project. Judgment is one aspect of evaluation that frequently gets left out. You can have excellent criteria and evidence laid out for an evaluation project. However, the final step of the evaluation process is lacking if judgments, in the form of conclusions and recommendations, are not made about what the data mean.

Judgment is not a matter of learning a process that can be applied each time. Each set of criteria and method of gathering evidence will result in a number of possible conclusions and recommendations. Conclusions, however, must relate back to the hypotheses, objectives, research questions, or criteria of the project, as well as to the data. Recommendations are proposed courses of action to be followed based on the conclusions. These conclusions and recommendations generally are articulated in the form of reports, presentations, or journal articles before a project is complete.

# Putting It All Together

The steps to evaluation and research involve more than just stating criteria, managing evidence, and making judgments. Useful and rigorous projects use the trilogy as the framework for the entire process. Table 1.3 provides a summary of how the trilogy relates to the process of evaluation and research. The use of the trilogy of evaluation is a simple way to be sure that evaluation is being conceptualized appropriately. We find it a useful and straightforward way of thinking about and moving through the evaluation and research processes.

# From Ideas to Reality

Several brief examples may help to illustrate how the evaluation process works. If we wanted to examine what the outcomes to individuals were of participating in a particular kind of activity, we might decide to use satisfaction as the criterion. We would then find an instrument or develop one to measure satisfaction with an activity. We would select an audience or a sample and collect evidence (data) by using that instrument. We would then analyze the data using descriptive statistics to develop conclusions and make recommendations about how satisfied people were with participation in a recreation activity and what might be done to improve satisfaction.

---

*Table 1.3* *Summary of How the Trilogy Works*

---

Criteria
  • Determination of a problem and a reason for doing evaluation or research
  • Examination of goals and objectives (if they exist)
  • Development of broad evaluation questions or a research problem statement to be addressed (for example, "What are the motivations for involvement in an activity?" "What job-related expectations should be used to evaluate a staff member?")

Evidence
  • Method selection, including instrument design and pretest
  • Sample selection
  • Actual data collection
  • Data analysis (i.e., coding and interpretation)

Judgment
  • Presentation of findings
  • Development of conclusions
  • Development of recommendations (for improvement, applications, or further research)

---

Perhaps we were interested in determining if the riding area of a horseback program for children with disabilities was safe. We would have to determine the criteria that describe a safe riding area. Standards developed by other groups might provide the criteria to examine. Using those criteria and developing a checklist, we would observe the area where children with disabilities are riding. Based on the results we would then draw conclusions and make recommendations for how to improve an area so it will be safer for the participants.

We might be interested in whether the administrative policy we have for refunds is appropriate. The criteria will be to determine how often the policy has been used and what the situations are surrounding its use. The data would be collected from existing records that we would examine and tabulate. On the basis of those records, we would make judgments concerning how much and how often the policy was used, and we could offer possible recommendations for how it might be improved in the future.


Now that you have studied this chapter, you should be able to:
- Describe the value of using criteria, evidence, and judgment together in an evaluation or research project
- Design a project showing how the trilogy of evaluation or research would be linked

## 1.4 You Don't Count if You Don't Count

The title of this chapter is a play on words, obviously. Further, not all evaluation or research requires numbers or counting as you will see later in this book. However, evaluation and research are important. The goal of evaluation is to determine the value or worth of something so that good decisions can be made. The goal of research is to get information that will contribute to the body of knowledge about a field and lead to an enhanced quality of life. Evaluative research enables us to gain information or feedback by developing criteria to be used to gather data (e.g., count) to make proactive, enlightened decisions. "Why evaluate" is the focus of this chapter.

Many reasons exist for doing evaluations and research. Each evaluation or research project conducted will likely have different purposes associated with it. Regardless of the purpose, formal systematic inquiry and data collection must be done using criteria, reliable and valid evidence or data, and an open perspective for understanding phenomena and examining how programs, facilities, staff, and administrative procedures in leisure services can be improved.

Some professionals are afraid of evaluation because they fear what they might find. If everything appears to be going all right, evaluation seems like more work on an already overburdened schedule just to find that everything isn't perfect. The adage "don't fix it if it ain't broke" comes to mind. But evaluation is not meant only for crisis situations when changes *have* to be made. When evaluation is done systematically, crisis situations can often be avoided.

The new century offers many opportunities for decision making. Some societal trends are making evaluation and research imperative. Many organizations are seeking to show that what they do really makes a difference. Further, new emphases are being placed on determining what constitutes quality as well as outcomes in evaluation. One of the required standards from the Council on Park and Recreation Accreditation (CAPRA; the group that accredits community park and recreation departments) is that "there shall be a systematic evaluation plan to assess outcomes and the operational deficiency and effectiveness of the agency."

## New Concepts in the 21st Century

New concepts are also associated with evaluation in the 21st century. One notion is *"best practices."* A best practice is an aspect of an agency, process, or system that is considered excellent. These practices are always evolving, but some determination, presumably through evaluation, has to be made that these practices are indeed superior in some way. Sometimes the idea of best practices has been criticized for allegedly promoting practices because they work well in one organization, without having done a systematic assessment of how the practices might work elsewhere. Evaluation can counter that type of criticism.

Another emerging term is *benchmarking*. It is often considered a way to identify best or promising practices because it is a standard of operation that enables an organization to compare itself to others' performance or to some standard or average. Benchmarking is used to determine who is the best, who sets the standard, and what that standard is. In basketball, for example, you could argue that many consecutive NBA Championships made the Chicago Bulls the benchmark. We can do the same thing in recreation services. Who has the best organization? Who has the most inclusive program? Who gets the greatest return on investment? Once a professional decides what to benchmark, and how to measure it, the object is to figure out how the "best" got to be there and how others might also reach that standard. Evaluation is central to benchmarking.

Another emerging concept related to evaluation and research is referred to as *evidence-based practice*. It refers to a decision-making process that integrates the best available research, professional expertise, and participant characteristics. Evidence-based practice has been largely used in clinical settings, but it has great potential in communities. It is an approach to assuring that the programs conducted in recreation have the potential to make a difference in people's lives. Evidence-based practice helps to determine what works best regarding issues such as how organizations can encourage people to be more active, or how youth programs should be conducted to obtain positive youth development. It moves beyond just intuition to gathering evidence about how and why those practices work and how they can be used in different settings. The focus is on assessing effectiveness after an effort such as a therapeutic recreation intervention or the conduct of community recreation program.

Further, staff in many organizations need to justify how resources are being used to achieve realistic results from their programming and management efforts. Calls for good decision making and accountability are coming from participants including clients and consumers, from the professionals' desire to improve services, an awareness of good management practices, a recognition of society's limited fiscal and human services, and legislative mandates such as requirements of the Americans with Disabilities Act.

Since evaluation is so important for recreation service, the rest of this chapter focuses directly on reasons for evaluation. In the broadest sense, professionals evaluate for several reasons: because it's compulsory and they have to evaluate, for defense and/or offense to determine the worth or lack of worth of an aspect of the organization (e.g., program or a staff member or area/facility), or to improve or validate an aspect of the organization. More specifically we believe the major purposes for evaluation can be described with eight broad and not necessarily mutually exclusive reasons:

1. To determine accountability

2. To assess or establish a baseline

3. To assess the attainment of goals and objectives

4. To ascertain outcomes and impact

5. To determine the keys to successes and failures

6. To improve programs

7. To set future directions

8. To comply with external standards

These reasons overlap one another a great deal. Evaluation usually does not occur for only one reason, but occurs for a combination of reasons that enable decision making. Research, as juxtaposed with evaluation, generally focuses more on theory confirmation or development that may also relate to any of these broad reasons.

## Accountability

Accountability, as one dimension of decision making, is often mentioned as a primary purpose of evaluation. We might think of accountability as being more reactive than proactive, although it can be used for proactive decisions. It assures people that the organization is behaving in a responsible manner. If an organization or program is not showing accountability, then a decision may be made about whether that organization or program should continue to operate.

Accountability is a relative term that describes the capability of a leisure-service delivery system to justify or explain the activities and services provided. According to Connolly (1982), accountability reflects the extent to which expenditures, activities, and processes effectively and efficiently accomplish the purposes for which an organization or a program was developed. Often projects are evaluated for accountability when some external unit, such as a city manager or hospital administrator, requests the evaluation. Accountability, however, should be an ongoing concern of staff in any organization, regardless of who is "watching," and especially if tax dollars are used to support the program.

Accountability results in determining legitimacy. It is also applied to see if a recreation program is meeting the needs and desires of people in the community. A by-product of the evaluation is that the agency may be seen in a better light in the community, but the bottom line is that accountability should result in avoiding unnecessary expenditures of money.

## Establishing a Baseline

Evaluation may be done to set a baseline or to benchmark. This reason for evaluation usually results in an assessment or a needs-assessment (defined later in this Unit), depending upon the context evaluated. An assessment is the gathering of data or the measurement of phenomena that is then put into an understandable form to compare results with objectives. Assessing a baseline can also provide a starting point for measuring change and a plan for future action, by comparing an organization to a standard. Community needs-assessments, as well as clinical assessments of people with disabilities, are frequently used to establish a baseline in leisure services.

## Assessing Goals and Objectives

One common reason for doing evaluation is to assess whether goals and objectives have been met. As indicated earlier, goals and objectives have been the backbone of many evaluation efforts, although some approaches to evaluation don't take goals and objectives directly into account. Assessment of goals and objectives, for example, may help to determine how programs and areas/facilities are designed to reach those goals. A good deal has been written recently about the "intentionality" or "purposefulness" needed to assure that goals are reached. The logic model, which will be discussed later in this book, is based on determining goals and objectives, designing programs to meet those goals, and then measuring the outputs and outcomes, as well as the processes used.

An example of a research study that examined outcomes related to intentionality was an analysis of camper outcomes. One finding of the study was that camp directors promoting spirituality at camp were much more likely to see gains in spirituality measures of campers at the end of camp than those directors that did not have this goal (Henderson, Bialeschki, Thurber, Whitaker, & Scanlin, 2007).

Judgments from assessing goals and objectives result in determining if stated objectives are operating and/or whether other objectives are more appropriate. Thus, evaluation also can allow us to redefine the means for setting objectives and to determine exactly what goals our organizations ought to be setting and striving to accomplish.

## Ascertaining Outcomes and Impacts

Determining the impact, effects, outcomes, and results of a program, area, facility, or administrative procedure is the bottom line of evaluation. By ascertaining the outcomes of a staff member's efforts, the expenditure of money, or the changes that occur in participants as a result of a program, decisions can often be made about value and impact.

Impact evaluation asks what differences a program has made, how it has affected people, and how it will in the future. Outcomes are defined as the benefits or changes that occur. Outcomes and impact are not always easy to measure, but they are the essences of program planning, in particular, within leisure service organizations. If what we do in any area of leisure services does not have a positive effect on people, then it may not be worth doing whether the activity is done through therapeutic recreation, sports programming, or park planning. The use of the logic model described later has had great influence on addressing outcomes.

## Explaining Keys to Success and Failure

Some evaluations are undertaken to document processes that are used to obtain certain objectives. In other words, evaluation is undertaken to see what works and what doesn't. This idea is akin to evidence-based practice. In addition, determining what contributes to a successful program, as well as what might create problems or failures, is useful. An important element in program evaluation is a newly applied term called fidelity. In other words, how can the presentation of a program be consistently presented so that the outcomes may occur in other situations? Fidelity refers to "exactness" as well as the idea of "faithfully" doing what you say you will do. The value of fidelity in evaluation and research is to assure that best practices can be analyzed and the keys to success or failure can occur over and over if the program is faithfully executed.

Success can be determining in many other ways. For example, weighing benefits against costs is one way to describe success. Other aspects of whether a program has worth relate to determining inputs such as staff effort, expertise, or leadership that might affect a program. This reason for evaluation allows professionals to increase the utility and probability for successful programs that they conduct in the future and also allows individuals to share procedures, processes, and best practices that might be useful with other professionals in similar situations.

## Organization Improvement

Organizational improvement related to quality control is a key practical reason for evaluation. Professionals evaluate staff, programs, policies, and participants to make revisions in their existing programs. In the starkest way, one might decide whether to keep programs or staff members or whether to let them go—a "go/no go" proposition. Sometimes the evaluation of staff, for example, results in promoting professional growth and education by appraising personnel quality and qualifications. The organization can also be improved by gauging public sentiment, attitudes, and awareness that provide information to enable professionals to improve and/or maintain high quality in the organization. Further, evaluation for improvement provides a way for two-way communication with participants, staff, and the public.

Improvement might be sought by appraising existing facilities and physical property as to adequacy, accessibility, safety features, attractiveness, appropriateness, availability, and utilization. The evaluator tries to seek out and eliminate any detrimental features that could create risk or prevent the best recreation experience. Evaluation for improvement might also result in replacing outmoded concepts and invalid ideas about how a recreation program ought to be run. Summative evaluations can lay a basis for new projects and can point a professional towards how to program more effectively in the future. When we know what worked and didn't work and how people liked a particular program, it is easier to set objectives, improve programs, and implement plans for the future.

## Set Future Directions

Setting future directions has been mentioned in the previous reasons. Ultimately all evaluation should result in changes for the future. In some cases, the rationale for putting money or additional resources into future programs needs to be considered. Evaluation can provide information for making decisions that will affect the future of any organization.

## Complying with External Standards

Some organizations are required to do evaluations to comply with external standards set by the government or by some other funding agency or professional body. These evaluations often are done for other purposes that directly aid the organization, but this evaluation may be done simply to meet accreditation or licensing requirements. The current procedures done by organizations like the American Camp Association (ACA) and the National Recreation and Park Association (NRPA) use a standard evaluation whereby a camp or a recreation organization can become accredited by showing that they have complied with certain standards. The accreditation process of these organizations is meant to be a guideline for helping organizations evaluate themselves by using the external standards as a beginning point. "Experts" then assure that the organization's evaluation is accurate.

If you are interested in a career in public parks and recreation, you may want to be aware of the Commission on the Accreditation of Parks and Recreation Agencies (CAPRA) that provides standards for agencies including a specific set related to evaluation (www.nrpa.org). These standards include a mandate that "there shall be a systematic evaluation plan to assess outcomes and the operational deficiency and effectiveness of the agency." In addition, the standards recommend that there "should be" involvement in research in the organization as well as personnel on staff or a consultant with expertise in directing the evaluation/research process. The standards also recommend in-service education for professional employees about conducting quality evaluations.

## Other Reasons to Evaluate

As you can see, reasons for evaluation are numerous and overlapping. Seldom would a professional only have one specific reason for evaluating. In fact, a problem may exist when the evaluator is so single-minded that he or she does not see all the possibilities for learning that can result from doing an evaluation project. For example, the initial purpose of an evaluation might be to assess goals and objectives, but the process can also highlight keys to success and expose areas that can be improved.

Evaluation experts such as Weiss (1972) have suggested some other reasons for evaluating that may not be as positive as the previous examples and may be detrimental to an organization if they are the sole reason for evaluating. Examples of these "not so good" reasons to evaluate include: to postpone decisions or avoid responsibility, to further public relations only, to only meet funding requirements, to justify programs, and to eliminate staff.

Sometimes professionals use evaluations to postpone decisions or to avoid responsibility. Sometimes evaluation will "buy" time until something else can be figured out that has no relationship to the evaluation. If a supervisor or a manager has a tough decision to make, for example, she or he might decide to evaluate in hopes that some magic solution will occur. Sometimes this answer emerges, but usually not. Evaluation still requires that necessary third element of judgment. Ultimately the supervisor or manager will have to "bite the bullet" and take responsibility.

Evaluating solely for the public relations impact may not help to improve a program. It looks good to see an organization doing evaluations, but if nothing ever changes or the evaluations are not used, the public will not stay impressed for long. Related to this idea is conducting evaluations just to increase prestige either within departments, in an organization, or with one's peers. Evaluations will only increase prestige when they are appropriately used.

Evaluations done solely because of grant or funding requirements are often not as effective as those in which the stakeholders or the participants really care about how the feedback can be used for decision-making. When funding sources require an evaluation, the evaluator ought to consider carefully what can be learned that may be helpful. In other words, staff should address not only the "letter of the law" but also the "spirit of the law." Evaluations can be helpful if we expect them to be helpful and not just another chore that has to be undertaken. A required evaluation is a wonderful opportunity to explore other reasons for evaluation that can assist in decision making.

Evaluation done only for the purpose of program justification or to eliminate staff may not be appropriate. An evaluation may result in program justification, but a great deal of bias may be built into something that has program justification as its sole purpose. Further, an evaluation may give some ideas about what needs to be done to improve an organization, but using it solely for the purpose of getting rid of people is probably not going to be beneficial to the morale of the organization or the way that employees view the value of evaluation in the long run.

# Fear of Evaluation

Many professionals are afraid of evaluation for good and not so good reasons. Some people associate evaluation with statistics, which is often a scary subject. If good goals and objectives have not been written, evaluations are frequently difficult to do. In other cases, people do not know how to measure the information that they would like to know. Some professionals disregard evaluations because their prior experiences with formal evaluations didn't tell much more than they already knew. Others have done evaluations but then have not used the data so the evaluations were seen as simply a "waste of time." Still others are afraid of what they might find out if they evaluate—negative results are not always easy to take. Finally, some professionals fear evaluations because they can be very time-consuming and most professionals already feel too busy. Each of these fears, however, can be countered by paying attention to planning evaluation projects based on carefully determined and appropriate reasons for undertaking them.

# When *Not* to Evaluate

Although evaluation is important and can be extremely useful, Theobald (1987) suggested that a professional must also know enough about when *not* to evaluate. The first rule is to not evaluate unless you are sincere about making decisions to improve your program. Secondly, you may not want to evaluate if you know your program has serious organizational problems. The wise plan would be to try to fix those problems rather than think that evaluation is going to provide you the magic answer. Evaluation can expose problems, but is not necessarily the panacea for fixing them.

Along with these concerns, make sure that you have goals and objectives that can be measured. You do not always need to have specific objectives, but you need to be clear and purposeful about what you think your program ought to be doing. If you do not have any goals and objectives, it is best to get those written and then do the evaluation. Usually it is not best to evaluate when something is just getting started—give the program or staff member a chance to get started or use a formative approach to make the evaluation more useful.

Further, don't evaluate if you already know the outcome—it will be a waste of time, unless of course some stakeholder needs to see written documentation of the results. Finally, don't evaluate if you know the disadvantages will outweigh the advantages. If you know that an evaluation will be too time-consuming or too costly for what you will get, then don't do it or use a different evaluation design.

## Knowing How to Evaluate

Although excuses may be valid for not evaluating, we suspect the major reasons that evaluations are not systematically conducted are because professionals do not know how to set up an effective evaluation process, how to analyze the data, and/or how to interpret the data in useful ways to assist in making decisions.

The bottom line is that evaluations must be used for decision making. If the data are not interpreted or if conclusions and recommendations are not used, the evaluation project or research is useless. Evaluation is not necessarily a panacea for solving the problems in an organization, but the process can provide important information. We will address more specific ways to implement and use evaluation results in an organization in a later chapter, but you should consider the "whys" of evaluation before you begin to evaluate any aspect of a leisure-service system.

The best evaluation in the world cannot provide a definitive picture of the future, reduce the costs of goods and services, or decide the most desirable course of action. Those goals and decisions are still up to you as a professional. You make this decision, however, based on the data you obtain from evaluations. Hopefully, as an evaluator you make good decisions because you have the best possible data collected for the most appropriate reasons, just as you undertake research as a way to add to the body of knowledge to better understand human behavior and how the world works. If you don't count (i.e., evaluate in some way), you just may not count!

## From Ideas to Reality

Suppose someone on your Park and Recreation Advisory Board suggests that she or he is not sure that the summer playground program is really meeting the needs of youth in your community. You believe that a systematic examination of that program may be useful to determine if the program is meeting children's needs. A number of reasons might be examined for doing this systematic evaluation: to determine if funds are being appropriately spent (accountability), to see if the goals and objectives for the program are being met, to determine if the inputs as far as staff and leadership are adequate to meet the program goals, to improve the program so that it better meets the needs of children, and to determine exactly what outcomes are happening to children because of the program. All of these reasons will result in determining future action concerning the program. As you can see in this situation, the reasons for undertaking the evaluation are multiple. These reasons are important to consider before an evaluation is undertaken. Further, it is important to make sure that staff, board members, and participants are in agreement concerning why an evaluation should be undertaken and how the results will be used.

Now that you have studied this chapter, you should be able to:
- List the reasons why an evaluation might be undertaken given a particular situation
- Describe the concerns and fears that some people have regarding undertaking evaluations
- Determine when it is best to undertake an evaluation project and when evaluation may not be to the advantage of an organization

# 1.5  Approaches to Evaluation: Models and More

Thinking about doing evaluation and research can be overwhelming. Approaches or models for evaluation provide a framework for conceptualizing and planning evaluation projects. No one model is specific to recreation services. Professionals in the recreation field have borrowed heavily from education evaluation principles as well as from business management and operations.

The lack of specific models for recreation creates both challenges and opportunities. Having so many choices based on the models designed in other fields can be challenging. On the other hand, these examples offer opportunities in that we can choose the best model for the specific criteria that we want to measure for any of the areas (described as the five Ps later in this book) discussed in this text.

In determining how recreation services might be evaluated, we discuss six approaches that may provide helpful frameworks. Intuitive Judgment is a pseudo-model with five other systematic models: Professional Judgment, Goal-Attainment, Logic Model, the Goal-Free Model, and Systems or Process Approaches. No one model of evaluation will work everywhere and every time. Further, for an evaluation project, more than one model might work. The evaluator, therefore, must choose the best model for the situation. We simply cannot apply a standardized model across organizations or even across all the areas that might be evaluated. The value and applicability of any of these models lie in diversity and adaptability, not in uniformity and rigidity (Patton, 1978). All of these approaches have some relation to one another and offer a framework for organizing evaluation systems and planning projects.

# A Pseudo-Model: Intuitive Judgment

A traditional component of evaluation is gut-level judgment. After you have conducted some type of program, you have a good sense of whether or not it went well. With the development of the scientific method applied to evaluation, more systematic models have evolved beyond these intuitive feelings. However, do not ever doubt the importance of intuition in developing more formal models.

The pseudo-model, Intuitive Judgment, has importance but does not supplant a systematic approach. This form of evaluation relates to day-to-day observations made that provide information for decision making. For example, if in a casual conversation a staff member sensed that potential participants had not heard about a special event to be held even though a promotional plan had been implemented, something probably should be done immediately. Even without a systematic evaluation, changes could be made right away to better promote the event. Many changes and improvements can occur in organizations based primarily on Intuitive Judgment and experience. Personal and collective reflection within an organization is important. Sometimes this intuitive evaluation is most useful when it is written down, so that during the next program or intervention, you remember the observations made.

Intuitive Judgment is useful, but reliable and valid evaluations that use systematic approaches to determine criteria, collect evidence, and make enlightened decisions are also necessary. We acknowledge the value of "gut-level" evaluations but they should not be the *only* means of evaluation if leisure services are to be accountable and based on a commitment to improvement.

# Professional Judgment

Evaluation by Professional Judgment or expert opinion is commonly used in the recreation sectors. The approach often relates to two common strategies: (a) hiring an external evaluator or a consultant, or (b) using a set of external standards. Even if an external consultant is hired, she or he may use one of the other models to obtain information in addition to her or his expert judgment.

Howe (1980) talked about evaluation by Professional Judgment as being like an art criticism model, where someone other than the artist critiques the artwork. Using the Professional Judgment of an external person may be a good idea when a high degree of objectivity is required, money is available, and an expert is available. Many community recreation and park departments hire private consultants to assist in long-range or strategic planning. The pros and cons of using a consultant or an external evaluator are discussed in more depth in the chapter on competencies.

Another common way that Professional Judgment is used is in evaluation by standards, generally through some type of accreditation process. Essentially, evaluation by standards involves a critical review by an individual or individuals who are experts because they have had training in judging established predetermined minimum criteria.

A standard is a statement of desirable practice or a level of performance for a given situation. Standards are an indirect measurement of effectiveness.

People evaluating by using standards assume that if stated desirable practices are followed, the program will be effective. Standards are not maximum goals but minimal goals and should be used as a guide, not necessarily a quality rating.

Standards change and must be reviewed regularly and revised as conditions change. Standards ought to reflect the needs of the patients, clients, participants, or campers in the specific area being served, must be reasonably attainable, and must be acceptable and usable to the professional who will apply them. Standards should be based on sound principles and the best information available about practice. They should stand the test of time, although they also should be revised to reflect changing societal conditions.

Accreditation is common in recreation services. For example, the American Camp Association has the *Accreditation Process Guide* (2007a), which has existed and been updated in numerous ways for over 60 years. Table 1.5(1) shows an example of one of the standards from the camp accreditation process. The National Recreation and Park Association have been accrediting recreation and leisure curricula in universities for over 30 years and municipal park and recreation agencies for over 15 years. Quality

*Table 1.5(1)*  *Sample of Standards (adapted from American Camp Association Accreditation Process Guide, 2007a, p. 196)*

PD-24 PROTECTIVE HEADGEAR MANDATORY (ALL)

Does the camp require that helmets be worn by all participants (staff and campers) when engaged in:

PD-24A: Activities involving bicycling?   YES   NO
PD-24B: Activities involving any kind of motorized vehicle?   YES   NO

INTERPRETATION: PD-24A requires helmets to be worn in any program activity that involves bicycling on any surface provided by the camp, the camper, or a vendor. This standard does not apply to riding four-wheeled pedal bikes. If bicycle riding occurs outside of a program activity, helmets are not required to be worn, but all riders are encouraged to wear helmets as a way to model good safety practices. Standard PD-24B includes any program activity involving motorized vehicles such as motorcycles, motor bikes, go-karts, ATVs, etc. Helmets should be appropriately sized and designed specifically for the activity being conducted, given that helmet construction standards vary for different activities. Helmets may be supplied by the camp or by a staffed public facility or vendor.

COMPLIANCE DEMONSTRATION: Visitor observation of activities; staff and camper description of helmets required.

assurance standards within therapeutic recreation have been related to the Commission on Accreditation of Rehabilitation Facilities (CARF) and the Joint Commission on Accreditation of Healthcare Organizations (JCAHO).

The process used for accreditation or evaluation by standards is generally to have an organization (e.g., hospital, public recreation department, or a camp) do a self-evaluation, make changes and improvements to comply with the minimum expectations or guidelines established by the accrediting body, and have trained outside experts, who are usually volunteers, confirm that particular situations exist that meet the standards.

The standards used for accreditation traditionally have been criterion referenced. That is, evaluations are based on some standard level of performance. They also may assess whether standard objectives have been met. In criterion-referenced evaluation, the subject evaluated is not compared to any other organization but simply is held up to a pre-defined standard for measurement. In the case of the above examples, the standards usually exist in a checklist, to which the evaluator responds "yes/no" or "fully met/partially met/not met." In some situations, such as the NRPA accreditation of universities, qualitative comments are added to explain the responses to the checklist.

Norm-referenced standards might also be applied in some situations for evaluation. These measures tell the relative position of a person or thing in reference to another person or thing using the same measuring tool. Persons compared to a norm of performance such as physical fitness tests would show the relationship of an individual to others in her or his age group. For example, if an individual was in the top quartile, she or he would be among the top 25% of those who took a particular test. The meaning of the score lies in the comparison to others. Professional Judgment is used in these measures to determine the meaning of the rank of one person in relation to others.

Some major changes, however, are occurring in professional standards in a number of fields, as professionals try to understand how to better access the quality of various recreation services and how that quality impacts a group or people or a community. The American Camp Association is exploring ways to add "quality" analyses to the accreditation standards. Howe (1980) noted a number of years ago that the implied association of standards to performance is a problem—high scores on standards do not necessarily reflect high quality or effectiveness.

Several other precautions should be noted with the current standards in most organizations. A great deal can be learned from Professional Judgment about the administrative procedures, areas and facilities, and programs, but the model is less useful for human dimensions such as personnel performance or participant outcomes or impacts. Another criticism of the Professional Judgment model related to standards is that the standards often are viewed as the maximum rather than the minimum guidelines. Lastly, evaluation based on standards assumes that all recreation organizations operate in a similar context, when this may not be the case at all. We must be careful that the use of standards does not result in homogenized programs that are the same everywhere regardless of the context and resources of an organization.

# Goal-Attainment Model

The Goal-Attainment Model, also known as evaluation or management by objectives, is probably the backbone of educational evaluation applied to recreation and leisure programs. Goal-Attainment is a preordinate model because pre-established goals and objectives are used to measure outcomes. The model works best when goals are discrete and/or objectives are measurable. Within this model, an evaluator can assess broad goals or measure specific objectives. Generally a focus on specific objectives is easiest and best when using the model. Specifically stated objectives should be easier to measure. The current focus on intentional or purposeful programs aimed at specific outcomes requires that goals and objectives be articulated.

A goal is a clear general statement about where the organization and its programs are going related to the purpose or mission. Goals may be expressed in broad general terms or may be readily quantifiable and measurable in objective terms, which are usually then called objectives. Objectives may be defined as written or expressed intentions about intended outcomes. Goal-Attainment evaluation is based on measuring the congruence between performance and objectives. For this model to work, you must have well-written objectives and good criteria.

Writing objectives may not always be the most fun activity, but it is necessary if the Goal-Attainment Model is to be applied. Goal-Attainment can be used in any area of recreation and applied to any system. It may also be used in assessment, formative, or summative evaluations. Therapeutic recreation specialists, for example, have used the model frequently and effectively in setting goals and objectives during the assessment phase of treatment.

To emphasize again, the prerequisite and bottom line for using the Goal-Attainment Model of evaluation is to have appropriate and measurable goals and objectives. This process requires setting goals at the outset preferably before a program is begun (program evaluation), before an employee begins work (personnel evaluation), or before an administrative procedure or policy is implemented (organizational evaluation). Goals and objectives can be set prior to beginning the actual evaluation, although this timing is not as desirable as prior to the beginning of delivering services.

Objectives are specific operational statements related to the desired goals and accomplishments of the organization, staff, participants or program. Many objectives may exist for an organization depending on who is setting them. Objectives may be written for participants as well as for staff and for the organization (i.e., management objectives). Objectives are the criteria, and determining the appropriate measurement of objectives is critical.

For purposes of this discussion on the Goal-Attainment Model, we will refer to two types of objectives: outcome and process. Process objectives are associated with outputs that address how an organization operates. For example, a process or organizational objective might be to recruit, train, and supervise 10 volunteers to assist with the youth athletic program. Another objective might be for a staff member to obtain a "good" or better rating on 75% of the evaluations completed by a tennis class. A process objective for a staff member also might be that she or he would oversee the publishing of a program brochure three times each year.

Outcomes are a description of the performance you want participants or staff to be able to exhibit when they have achieved the stated objectives. Often outcomes and behaviors are described synonymously, although outcomes are broader than just behavior. Outcomes usually refer to the (hopefully positive) impact on the participant as a result of your program. For example, an outcome objective might be that a participant would pass half of the skills in the swimming test. The resulting participant outcome would be that the participant become a stronger swimmer. Other outcome objectives might be that participants in a walking program will continue to walk four to five times a week after the program is completed, or that children in a camp nature program would be able to identify five animal tracks that they might find along a riverbank. The key is that the objectives provide a measuring stick for particular impacts (outcomes) from your program.

Although writing objectives has probably been covered elsewhere in your college degree program, a quick review of how to write these process objectives may be helpful. The essential components include describing a task, establishing who will do it, identifying the action that should be taken and the conditions, and stating the criteria for an acceptable minimal level of performance for the task (Lundegren & Farrell, 1985). In writing these objectives, consider using strong verbs, stating only one purpose or aim per objective, specifying a single end-product or result, and specifying the expected time for achievement. Examples of action verbs that might be used in writing objectives include: "to enjoy," "to assume responsibility," "to engage in," "to describe," "to examine," "to identify characteristics," "to change," "to develop," "to define," "to prepare," "to compile," "to visualize," and "to understand."

Within outcome objectives, several domains have been identified:

1.  Cognitive (thinking, knowledge)

2.  Affective (feeling, attitudes)

3.  Psychomotor (movement, acting)

4.  Social (how people relate to each other)

When writing objectives for a participant or a program, you need to keep in mind the area where you want to see change in performance or behavior. As indicated previously, these objectives then become the criteria for evaluation. In measuring the outcomes of a program, objectives can provide the foundation for collecting data and making judgments about the success of a program.

In summary, the Goal-Attainment Model is a useful model for recreation professionals. It requires well-written and measurable goals and objectives. One of the cautions is to make sure that you don't get so focused on evaluating the goals that you ignore other evidence that suggests good things came out of an organization, a program, or a staff member's work. Measuring objectives does not mean you cannot measure unplanned objectives. The Goal-Attainment Model must be kept flexible enough to accommodate unplanned measurement. The information received may result in more appropriate goals and objectives written for evaluation next time. Further, the application of a Logic Model—a subtype of Goal-Attainment— requires having a thorough sense of the process and outcome purposes of any program, and such flexibility allows one to maintain that broad sense.

## Logic Model

The Logic Model came into being during the 1970s and seems to be experiencing a resurgence of popularity, particularly with funders. The Logic Model is a form of Goal-Attainment, but we discuss it separately here. Yogi Berra's famous statement, "If you don't know where you are going, you will end up somewhere else" is a good way to describe the value of a Logic Model. It helps a programmer determine where the program is going. The Logic Model has emerged in recent years as a potential framework for considering how to think about program evaluation as well as an assessment of participant outcomes (Kellogg Foundation, 2001). The premise of the Logic Model is that program components should lead to program outcomes. The model provides a picture of how an organization does its work in terms of the theory and assumptions underlying a program and suggests that a logical sequence of events occurs (Baldwin, Caldwell, & Witt, 2005). The model also provides a means for integrating planned work and the intended results of that work. Stated in another way, it provides a means for examining how program planning and implementation relate to participant outcomes.

Figure 1.5(2) shows a general example of a Logic Model used in training by the American Camp Association (2007b). Although various templates can be followed, they all show the relationships among program goals and objectives, the resources to invest (inputs), the activities/strategies to carry out (outputs), and the benefits/impacts expected (outcomes). A Logic Model can be read as a series of if/then statements that connect

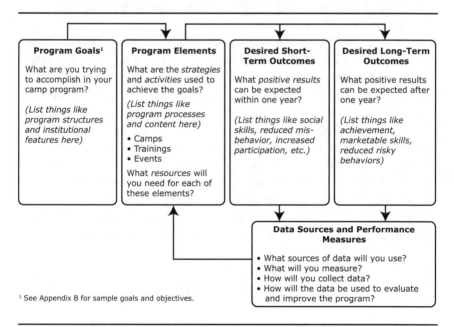

¹ See Appendix B for sample goals and objectives.

*Figure 1.5(2)* *Framework for a Logic Model (from American Camp Association* Creating Positive Youth Outcomes, *2007b, p. 21)*

the different parts of your program. For example, if you have resources (inputs), then you can carry out activities and strategies (outputs). If you carry out these activities and strategies (outputs), then you can create changes in your participants (outcomes). Outcomes are often described as proximal (short-term) and distal (long-term) outcomes that often focus on learning, skill development, and conditions. Figure 1.5(3) is an example of a simple logic model for an environmental education program.

| Goal | Activities & Resources | Proximal Outcomes | Distal Outcomes |
|---|---|---|---|
| To increase children's connection to nature | Funding for staff and appropriate materials to run after-school environmental education activities | Increase in youth environ-mental literacy | Youth become environmental stewards |

*Figure 1.5(3)  Example of Environmental Logic Model*

The Logic Model links directly to evaluation. It increases the potential for programming effectiveness by focusing on the questions that have value for the stakeholders. The model lends itself to both formative and summative evaluation questions (Kellogg, 2001). The model enables an evaluator to ask questions about the context of the program (e.g., what aspects of the program most shaped our ability to do the work? were the instructors effective?). It also addresses the implementation related to the quantity and quality (e.g., how many people participated? how did people find out about the program?). Further, the focus on outcomes includes criteria to be addressed, such as effectiveness, magnitude, and satisfaction (e.g., what is our assessment of what resulted from the arts program? how satisfied were the participants? what have we learned about doing this type of program?).

No single right way exists to construct a Logic Model. It depends on the purpose. The linkages and not just the labels of input, output, or out-come are what give power to the model. The lines and directional arrows show the action that exists. These arrows and lines are necessary, as they show the linkages that exist and the "logic" behind the model, that is, "if you do X, then Y should happen." The model can be as general or as spe-cific as needed regarding its use and the level of the program.

Ideally, a Logic Model is developed during the time that a program is designed and can be modified and enhanced as a program evolves. How-ever, a Logic Model can be created at any time that it seems appropriate in helping to better understand a program or how it might be evaluated. If you find that in using your Logic Model, you determine that the outcomes and the activities do not connect, then you may need to change the activities to reach the outcomes. Remember, the purpose of the Logic Model is to show the relationships that exist to assure that program activities achieve the desired outcomes.

The evaluation plan often is not a direct part of the Logic Model depiction. The Logic Model lays out the program and how outcomes occur. However, the evaluation questions, measurement strategies, and methods for an evaluation plan should reflect the model and are often an added component of the model (see Figure 1.5[2]).

Although the Logic Model is a useful depiction of how programs are planned and has implications for evaluations, it also has some limitations. First, the Logic Model represents what an organization intends to do—it does not necessarily reflect reality. That's why evaluation is needed. As in the case of the Goal-Attainment Model, the Logic Model reflects expected outcomes; however, in a field like leisure services, many unexpected outcomes may occur that we should not overlook in the evaluation process. The model also focuses on positive change, which is certainly what we seek in our recreation programs. However, change can be negative, so we must be aware of that possibility. Some people suggest the Logic Model oversimplifies behavior, when in reality any change is, in fact, complex and due to many factors that may influence outputs and outcomes. A Logic Model assumes that the "right" things are being done in terms of the purpose of a program. Further, Logic Models are not necessarily easy to develop and may appear to stymie the creativity and spontaneity of program development. Regardless of some of these limitations, the Logic Model is frequently used for program development and provides a roadmap for how evaluation might be focused and undertaken.

## Goal-Free (Black Box) Model

A model of evaluation that has some possibilities in the field of recreation services is what is referred to as Goal-Free or Black Box Model (Scriven, 1967). The model has been around for a long time, but its systematic value is only beginning to be realized. The basis of the model is the examination of an organization, group of participants, or program, irrespective of the goals. In other words, the intent of Goal-Free evaluation is to discover and judge actual effects, outcomes, or impacts without considering what the effects were supposed to be. The approach is the opposite of the Goal-Attainment or Logic Model. The evaluator or researcher begins with no preordained idea about what to find.

The purpose of Goal-Free evaluation is to find out what is truly happening. The value lies in discovering descriptions or explanations that may have unintended side effects. Scriven (1967) argued that if the main objective of an evaluation is to assess the worth of outcomes, you should not make any distinction at all between those outcomes that were intended as opposed to those that were not.

You must realize that to be completely goal free is impossible, because an evaluation always involves some type of question or comparison. Further, the evaluator must select only certain information out of the total information pool that she or he could collect. Data from the Black Box Model are usually qualitative (i.e., focused on words rather than numbers) and collected in relation to recognized concerns or guiding questions. Without some type of focus, however, you might be collecting data forever. Useful information emerges, therefore, from the issues identified by participants, citizens, or staff. The proponents of the model argue that the evaluator should be free to choose the range of issues to use for an evaluation and should be able to recognize concerns and issues as they arise.

The data collected in the Goal-Free Model may be either qualitative or quantitative, although the model lends itself best to qualitative approaches, as you will see when we discuss data-collection methods. In the Goal-Free Model, the evaluator will usually talk to people, identify program elements, overview the program, discover purposes and concerns, conceptualize issues and problems, identify qualitative and/or quantitative data that needs to be collected, select methods and techniques to use (including the possibility of case studies), collect the data, match data and the issues of audiences, and prepare and deliver the report. The evaluator is a detective, in a way, as she or he tries to identify the important relationships and outcomes that exist within an organization or a program. Unlike the Goal-Attainment Model, however, the evaluator does not start out with a specific plan for what criteria will be measured. Also, unlike the Intuitive Judgment Model, the data are systematically collected, recorded, and analyzed.

The Goal-Free evaluator uses logical analysis and observation as well as any other needed data collection methods. The drawback to this model of evaluation is that it may be time-consuming and some outcomes may be difficult to measure. The results, however, can be helpful in understanding in-depth aspects of recreation services.

# Process or Systems Approach

The Systems Approach, as an important model of evaluation, is commonly used in understanding how a program or place contributes to the overall mission of a leisure service organization. This model is process-oriented in general and does not use objectives. The model is used to establish a working understanding of an organization and it is capable of achieving end products such as the provision of services. An important element of the Systems Approach is the focus on outputs, which is one important component of the Logic Model. The purpose of the Systems Approach is to examine the degree to which an organization realizes its goals under a given set of conditions. The type and timing of data collected depends on the structure of the system or organization.

The Systems Approach is often used in management planning and has specific designs that are developed. Examples include Program Evaluation and Review Technique (PERT), Critical Path Method (CPM), Program Planning and Budgeting System (PPBS), Management by Objectives (MBO), and Total Performance Measurement (TPM). Data related to inputs, process, and outputs result in feedback that is used for decision making. If you were to develop an evaluation system for a recreation, park, or leisure services organization, you would likely use a Systems Approach in determining how evaluation fit into the overall operation of an organization. Fiscal evaluations also are frequently used within a systems context.

Within recreation organizations, program planning is often based on a Systems Approach with evaluation being just one part of it. The strategy and goals are the inputs, the program design and implementation are the process, and the evaluation yields information that provides a means for feedback regarding outcomes. Planning, delivery, and evaluation are related to one another. An evaluator can examine how an organization is operating to determine how effective it is. Within the Systems or Process Model, an entire organization or just components of it can be examined. An evaluation through this model results in the determination of outcomes as related to processes used by an organization. The Program Quality focus will be discussed in more detail later in this book. The model assumes that different decisions require different types of information inputs. Decisions are based on continuation, modification, or termination of the program, staff, or whatever is being measured.

These six models provide a way to frame evaluation. They offer a context for assumptions for determining how to set criteria and collect data. The models are not mutually exclusive but each has a set of assumptions that should be considered in using them. They are applied in varying degrees when conducting evaluation projects. In undertaking an evaluation project, it is essential to set the stage by determining which model best sets the framework for the evaluation.

## Strengths and Weaknesses of the Models

Table 1.5(4) provides a summary of the strengths and weaknesses of each of the models. If experts and standards exist, Professional Judgment

*Table 1.5(4)  Summary of the Strengths and Weaknesses of Evaluation Models*

| Model | Strengths | Weaknesses |
|---|---|---|
| Intuitive | • Relatively easy<br>• Day-to-day analysis | • Not scientific<br>• Lacks reliability |
| Professional Judgment | • Uses expert opinions<br>• Standards based<br>• Easy for organization<br>• Requires less time | • Must have expert<br>• Expensive<br>• Standards must be valid |
| Goal-Attainment | • Most commonly used<br>• Uses preestablished goals and objectives<br>• Objectivity | • Needs good goals and objectives<br>• Requires measurement instruments<br>• Too much focus on goals possible |
| Logic Model | • Requires assessment of goals and inputs<br>• Provides a model for evaluation<br>• Links program directly to evaluation<br>• May be simple or detailed<br>• Minimizes faulty assumptions<br>• Provides short- and long-term view | • Requires careful planning<br>• Represents intentions and not reality<br>• Focus is only on positive change<br>• May oversimplify processes<br>• May stifle creativity |
| Goal-Free | • Allows for qualitative data<br>• Examines actual effects<br>• Uses logical analysis<br>• Allows in-depth analysis | • Impossible to be goal-free<br>• Possible bias<br>• Time-consuming<br>• Evaluator-driven |
| Systems Approach | • Process-oriented<br>• Useful in management<br>• Integrates elements of an organization | • May be too broad-based<br>• Complicated to use<br>• Can't evaluate everything |

might be best. If goals and measurable objectives exist for a program, evaluating by using those goals and objectives as the foundation for Goal-Attainment or the Logic Model will be best. If you are interested in finding out what is happening without comparing actual outcomes to established goals, the Goal-Free approach may be superior. If the evaluator is examining one component of a leisure services organization in relation to the inputs, processes, outputs, and outcomes, then a Systems Approach will enable him or her to choose the elements to examine in relation to the broad mission of the organization. The evaluation model chosen will depend upon the purposes of the evaluation and the situation that currently exists.

## From Ideas to Reality

Choosing evaluation approaches or models is not the most exciting task that an evaluator undertakes, yet the approach is necessary so that appropriate decisions can be made about criteria and methods. The six models outlined here might be used in any number of ways, depending upon how an organization is set up. For example, say you wanted to find out if your older adult program was contributing to the life satisfaction of the individuals who participated. You could use the Intuitive Judgment Model and informally observe the older adults and draw conclusions. You might invite in external evaluators (Professional Judgment) to help you determine the contribution that your program is making to the lives of older adults. You could use the goals and objectives set for the program (Goal-Attainment or Logic Model) as the basis for collecting data to determine how the program affects life satisfaction. Or you might use a Goal-Free Approach and do in-depth interviews to find out how the older adult programs affect the individuals who participate. The exact model is not as important as the framework that you decide to use for your evaluation. The models simply provide a roadmap for making decisions about how an actual project might best be conducted by helping you determine criteria and ways to collect data.

Now that you have studied this chapter, you should be able to:
* Describe the differences between the six models presented
* Choose an appropriate model given a particular situation that requires evaluation

# 1.6 Those Who Fail to Plan, Plan to Fail: The Five Ps of Evaluation

Evaluation doesn't just *happen*. It requires planning. Furthermore, every aspect of recreation services has the potential to be the object of evaluation or research. As indicated earlier, some of this evaluation may be intuitive, but in most cases a systematic evaluation is needed from time to time. Whenever a new program is begun or a new staff member is hired, some plan for evaluation ought to be considered. The purpose of this chapter and the next is to introduce a discussion of the areas of evaluation in recreation services and the systems that can be developed for evaluating within an organization.

Classifications can be used to determine broad areas of evaluation in recreation organizations. Traditionally, Kraus and Allen (1987) suggested that there are program-oriented and people-oriented areas to evaluate, and Lundegren and Farrell (1985) described the four major areas as personnel, program (including people), administration/policies, and areas and facilities.

For the purposes of our discussion and to help you remember the areas of evaluation, we would like to discuss the five Ps of evaluation: program quality and improvement, personnel, places, policies/administration, and participant outcomes. You should realize, however, that these five areas are not discrete and tend to overlap. For example, a recreation program is of little use unless some kind of impact is made on a participant. The policies of an organization may affect the program. The nature of a place in terms of the area or facility will affect the job of the staff person or personnel. Seldom do we evaluate any one of these aspects alone without also acknowledging how they relate to one another. We will use these five Ps to describe the areas of evaluation within recreation organizations of all types. This chapter will describe how we develop a system for evaluation and cover three of the five P areas: personnel, policies, and places. The next chapter will address program quality/improvement and participant outcomes as essential areas of evaluation today.

## Evaluation Systems

Few recreation organizations submit themselves to a continuous and systematic program of evaluation. Those organizations that use standards for accreditation have a system in place for evaluation, but more evaluation may be needed than is done every three or five years as required. Many organizations evaluate various aspects of their program, like staff performance, but organizations should have a clear system for how evaluation fits into their overall operations.

Not every aspect of an organization needs to be evaluated every year. In fact, for available time and money, it may be more useful to determine what and when evaluations ought to be done. Rather than doing piecemeal evaluations, the development of a way that the entire organization or system can be evaluated over a period of time, for example, three years, may be more beneficial. Not every program has to be evaluated each time it is offered. Programs especially should *not* be evaluated if the data obtained are not going to be used. A system can enable you, as a professional, to make sure that all Ps are covered over a period of time. A system in place can enable you to make enlightened decisions concerning the entire organization. Let's examine how this system of evaluation might look.

To develop a system, you must know which Ps will be evaluated and how often this process should be done. A systematic plan might be developed by establishing goals and objectives, examining conclusions from previous evaluations, examining strategic plans or long-range plans that exist in the organization, and then setting a schedule. Figure 1.6(1) gives a pictorial example of how an evaluation system might be organized. You would determine the *what* (one of the Ps); the *why* (reasons

| What | Why | When | Who |
|---|---|---|---|
| Program | | | |
| Participants | | | |
| Personnel | | | |
| Physical Place | | | |
| Policy | | | |

*Figure 1.6(1)* *A System for Evaluation*

for evaluation); the *when* (timing related to how often and when during the year, which will be discussed in more detail later in this unit); and the *who* in the plan, more specifically, the resources needed to carry out the evaluation such as personnel, facilities, funds, and supplies.

You cannot evaluate everything at once. To try to assess everything usually results in poor conceptualizations of projects or failure to think about the issues involved. Further, the amount of data that you would generate would be overwhelming. Those people participating in the evaluation also can become overwhelmed by the complexity and endlessness of evaluation, unless a system is established.

Theobald (1979) offered several practical considerations for setting up a system for your organization. First, keep in mind the time and financial constraints of evaluation. On one hand, evaluation ought to be considered an investment. "Quick and dirty" evaluations, are usually not nearly as helpful as well-planned evaluation projects. On the other hand, the more money and time spent on evaluation, the less is available for program, staff, and the development and maintenance of areas and facilities.

Second, in developing a system, keep in mind that evaluations have political overtones. In determining the worth or value of something, you want to be sure that the criteria and measurement are appropriate. You also must consider the scope of evaluation and what it will cover, the size of the program, duration, program input, complexity, and span of goals. More about the political implications will be discussed later in this unit.

Third, to have a system in place means that you have established appropriate reasons for evaluating based on whether staff want the information, the funding organization requires it, or you need to make decisions about continuing or terminating a program. The remainder of this chapter will focus on systematically evaluating the Ps of personnel, policies, and places.

# Personnel

In most recreation organizations, the biggest expenditures go to staff salaries and benefits. Some of these staff are full-time, some part-time, and some seasonal. Volunteers are also considered unpaid staff. The benefits of staff evaluation include improving job performance and providing feedback for the personal development of staff, regardless of whether they are young and in paid positions of responsibility for the first time, have been a professional for 30 years, or periodically volunteer in the organization. Since evaluation is so important in the personnel process, mid-year or formative evaluations as well as end of the year, or summative, evaluations are frequently used. Most public organizations *require* yearly personnel evaluations, at least for paid staff.

The formalities of personnel evaluations are up to the organization, but generally staff personnel files are kept that provide documented evidence of the performance of staff. Staff performance evaluations are generally based on a combination of the goals and objectives found in the job descriptions and on the performance outcomes that result from doing the assigned jobs. Ideally, the evaluation should consist of an examination of the relationship between the criteria as stated in the job description and the performance of the staff member.

Thus, a well-written, accurate job description is the basis for an individual staff evaluation. The staff member ought to know from the very beginning the criteria upon which she or he will be evaluated. The staff member must also receive feedback concerning the judgment that is made by the evaluator. The feedback to staff ideally occurs on an everyday informal basis as well as during the formal process that is scheduled as part of a yearly performance appraisal.

Personnel evaluation is often called performance appraisal or performance evaluation. Most administration textbooks go into detail about this form of evaluation, but we will provide a bit of background so the principles of evaluation can be related to personnel. Personnel evaluations are generally necessary for making decisions about compensation, promotion, training, and employee development. These personnel evaluations are formal, structured, systematic ways to measure an employee's job-related behavior.

Employees at all levels ought to be evaluated at least annually and preferably more often. Regular volunteers should be evaluated from time to time as well as be asked to provide input for elements of the evaluation system. A performance evaluation is not just a single activity but takes into account observations and intuitive judgments made by supervisors and colleagues throughout the year. The criteria for personnel evaluation may vary greatly depending on the organization, but usually it is best to address aspects of the job and not an individual's personality. Ideally, the job description is the criterion. The purpose of the evaluation ought to focus on improvement and not necessarily whether to keep or fire an employee, or necessarily to give that individual a salary raise. Salaries, however, are generally based on performance in most, but not all, organizations.

The procedure used in employee evaluation is to assign duties, determine criteria for evaluation based on those duties, gather information about how the employee performs, appraise the performance, provide feedback to the employee, and make decisions and adjustments about the employee's performance. These decisions may relate to letting the employee know her or his relative value in the organization; identifying people for promotion; enhancing communication among supervisors, staff, and participants; providing directions for further continuing education and on-the-job training; and helping to establish and implement career goals. As you can see, these aspects of personnel evaluation relate to how we would incorporate the trilogy of evaluation into any of the Ps.

Glover and Glover (1981) offered four standard recommendations necessary for effective personnel evaluation. First, the appraisal for development or improvement purposes should be separated to the extent possible from appraisal for administration that results in such decisions as determining job raises. Second, the evaluation system should provide "coaching" for the employees on a regular basis. Third, professionals who do the evaluating need training in how to be effective in devising measurement criteria and recognize that personnel evaluation is an ongoing process. Finally, the evaluation should be behavior-specific concerning the job the employee performs. A concrete plan (i.e., part of the judgment phase) to address deficiencies should exist. No matter what data are collected, ultimately the supervisor must make decisions about the employee's behavior on the job and will need to help the employee to improve upon her/his behavior.

Data for personnel evaluations can be obtained from administrators, other employees, and/or participants. Table 1.6(2) shows an example of a generic evaluation form that might be used with an employee. The supervisor would use this information in providing feedback to the employee along with other information obtained about the specific job duties that might be performed.

Another popular type of personnel evaluation is known as the 360-degree evaluation. This process provides each employee the opportunity to receive performance feedback from their supervisor, four to eight reporting staff members or coworkers, and in some cases, even customers. Most 360 degree feedback tools are also responded to by each individual in a self-assessment. The feedback from this evaluation allows each individual to understand how their effectiveness as an employee, coworker, or staff member is viewed by others. The most effective 360-degree feedback processes provide feedback that is based on behaviors that other employees can see. If done correctly, the 360 degree feedback can help each individual understand their strengths and weaknesses, and contribute insights into aspects of their work needing professional development.

*Table 1.6(2)  Example of a Personnel Evaluation Form (source unknown)*

| | Outstanding | Above Average | Average | Needs Improvement | Poor |
|---|---|---|---|---|---|
| 1. Demonstrates insight and vision regarding objectives and long-range plans | — | — | — | — | — |
| 2. Possesses the physical stamina and drive to handle the rigors of the position | — | — | — | — | — |
| 3. Demonstrates pleasant personality and good communication skills | — | — | — | — | — |
| 4. Is consistent and fair; does not play favorites | — | — | — | — | — |
| 5. Solves problems rationally; can come to the heart of things | — | — | — | — | — |
| 6. Gets along well with other people | — | — | — | — | — |
| 7. Demonstrates ability to work together as a team | — | — | — | — | — |
| 8. Is approachable and willing to make changes | — | — | — | — | — |
| 9. Takes personal interest in each participant | — | — | — | — | — |
| 10. Welcomes and respects the opinions of others | — | — | — | — | — |
| 11. Is continuously alert to new ideas | — | — | — | — | — |
| 12. Is well-informed at all times regarding the total operation and how she or he contributes to it | — | — | — | — | — |

# Policies/Administration

Evaluation is used for analyzing policies, procedures, and administrative issues. Administrative aspects that may be evaluated include the way that an agency or business is organized and operated. Budget analysis is another way to examine policies and administration.

A professional might do public policy and community surveys to ascertain support for a particular activity, to measure the diversity of opinions, and gain information from the public at large. Evaluations and needs assessments can allow an organization to gain a more comprehensive knowledge of the community, its people, their needs, their opinions, and special problems. Policy and administrative decisions may be made based on community dissatisfaction, perceived lack of opportunity, the need to equalize services or upgrade services, and to meet new demands.

Cost-benefit and cost-effectiveness are econometric models that are used as a means for evaluation in leisure services. Cost-benefit analysis relates the costs of a program or an operation to the benefits realized from it, which are expressed in dollar figures. Benefits other than dollars are, however, often hard to quantify. Cost-effectiveness is easier because it is the ratio of costs to revenue generated. A program that generated enough income to pay the expenses would have a cost-effectiveness of 1:1. Per capita costs may be related to amount of cost per person. For example, we might have a Little League program that cost $20,000 for 150 children. The cost-effectiveness would then be $133 per child. The cost-effectiveness of one program could then be related to other programs sponsored by the organization.

Performance based program budgets are another common administrative method of evaluating how money is spent in relation to the outcomes of the programs. In this budgeting approach, the professional breaks down work or program activities into detailed subunits for the purpose of determining the specific costs of each of these units. These breakdowns are sometimes used to set the cost for a given program based on the expenditures. The information provided by the budget is useful to top administrators and to other policy boards who want to see the big picture. It also helps to think about programs in terms of unit costs. The bigger the recreation enterprise, the more useful this budgeting approach is for administrative evaluation.

Economic impact is a specific example of a policy/administrative area that might be measured. Economic impact relates to the amount of revenue activity generated in an area due to a particular event such as a festival or other tourist activities. For example, we might determine that for every dollar spent on tourism promotion in a community, five dollars of income might be generated in the community from tourist spending. Economic impact also expands beyond primary initial spending to secondary spending, which results in a multiplier effect in the community.

Assessments could also be useful for administrative planning. For example, Fletcher and King (1993) surveyed voters to assess how they felt about purchasing and developing recreation and park areas and facilities in the East Bay Regional Park District in California. Based on this telephone interview assessment, they learned what the people were thinking and used this information to address the policy implications that helped to guide the bond campaign. The $225-million bond measure passed.

# Places (Areas and Facilities)

The level of use of leisure services, given by measurements like number of participants, is a common way to measure outputs or how well an organization is doing. When we evaluate places, we may examine many aspects including use as well as safety and legal mandates. Pre-established standards are often helpful in evaluating risk management and safety concerns in the facilities, equipment, and landscape of an organization. Routine checks of facilities and equipment in the form of "walk-thrus" as well as scheduled maintenance procedures and the keeping of maintenance logs and checklists, can serve as a formal system of evaluation.

Master plans done for long-range planning are a form of assessment and evaluation. In these plans, one staff member might examine the distribution of areas and facilities. Table 1.6(3) shows an example of such a checklist that might be used for evaluating what exists or does not exist in a community. Carrying capacity, defined as the amount of use an area can take before recreation experiences become diminished, is another example of evaluation and research applied to places.

*Table 1.6(3)*  *Example of a Neighborhood Evaluation Checklist for Facilities for the State of Pennsylvania (adapted from Lundegren & Farrell, 1985, p. 191)*

| Recommended Component | Yes | No |
|---|---|---|
| 1. Turf for field sports | ___ | ___ |
| 2. Multipurpose, hard surface, all-weather court area | ___ | ___ |
| 3. Space for recreation sports | ___ | ___ |
| 4. Individual and dual sports | ___ | ___ |
| 5. Water facility—outdoor pool | ___ | ___ |
| 6. Winter activity area | ___ | ___ |
|     a. Ice area | ___ | ___ |
|     b. Sledding slope | ___ | ___ |
| 7. Outdoor education area | ___ | ___ |
| 8. Natural area for nonmotorized travel | ___ | ___ |
| 9. Communication space for dance, drama, music | ___ | ___ |
| 10. Building | ___ | ___ |
|     a. Multipurpose meeting rooms | ___ | ___ |
|     b. Assembly area | ___ | ___ |
|     c. Specialized activity area | ___ | ___ |
|     d. Physical recreation area | ___ | ___ |

A frequent way of evaluating places is through the application of standards. Many examples of standards exist in parks and recreation, as previously discussed. The American Camp Association offers standards for camping that relate to property risks and safety equipment as well as standards that relate to personnel and programs (an illustration of the Professional Judgment Model). Likewise, the Joint Commission on Accreditation of Healthcare Organizations (JCAHO) has standards for hospitals.

One of the newest and most exciting tools available to use in evaluating places as well as recreation services is spatial analysis, through the use of Geographical Information Systems (GIS). The GIS technique integrates spatial and demographic information (Wicks, Backman, Allen, & Van Blaricom, 1993). GIS is being used for numerous applications, including land-information systems, urban planning, land-use mapping and facilities management, environmental-impact assessment, wildlife and park management, identification of socioeconomic demographics, and geographic survey and mapping.

GIS consists of census information combined with resource data that enables a professional to pictorially display an element such as the distribution of people around a park. Based on that mapping, decisions can then be made about new landscape designs or where activity areas might best be placed. GIS also allows for an analysis of demographic characteristics in an area. For example, a map could indicate locations of community centers and the concentrations of racial groups that exist in a city, based on data obtained from census information.

GIS technology goes far beyond maps and site analysis for use in planning and policy-making. It also has immediate applications for marketing strategies. In addition, GIS is not only useful for evaluation of places and facilities but has implications for information about assessing the needs for programs, as we will discuss further in the next chapter. Regardless of whether you are a land-use planner, a parks and recreation director, or a therapeutic recreation specialist working with older adults, GIS applications will likely become a part of your evaluation process. Figure 1.6(4) shows an example of a GIS map.

## From Ideas to Reality

Obviously many aspects of organizations can be evaluated. An evaluator, however, must be able to make decisions about what can be feasibly and systematically evaluated at any given time. This chapter has provided some examples of the variety of aspects related to the five Ps that might

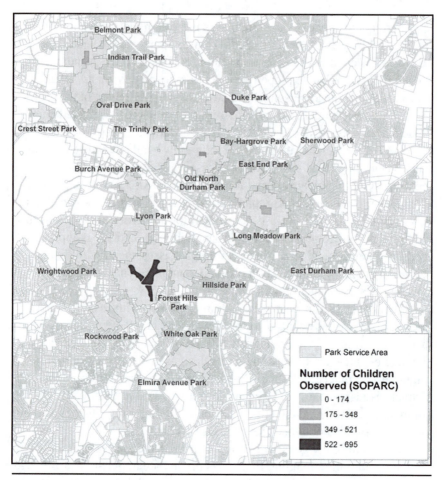

*Figure 1.6 (4)* *Example of Information from a GIS Map*

be evaluated in any organizations. Not everything can be evaluated at once, but over time and with thoughtful planning, a system of evaluation will develop. For example, many organizations have good staff evaluation systems in place that will simply need to be maintained. The professional might then focus on determining if places are being adequately evaluated. These current ideas taken in conjunction with the areas of programs and participants discussed in the next chapter can provide a basis for a sound evaluation system within any community or organization.

Now that you have studied this chapter, you should be able to:
- Describe three of the five Ps related to personnel, policies, and places and what components of each might be evaluated
- Make a plan to determine what aspects of the five Ps might be evaluated in an organization over a five-year period

# 1.7 From Good to Great: Evaluating Program Quality and Participants

Running a recreation program is not difficult. Running a quality program that results in positive outcomes for participants, however, is a challenge. Probably the most common association with evaluation that most recreation professionals have relates to program evaluation. Programs are most often evaluated regarding participant outcomes, although program quality and means for improvement have influences that can be measured relative to communal, environmental, and economic impact.

The purpose of this chapter is to describe the remaining two Ps of program quality and participant outcomes. The Ps overlap with one another. However, as indicated in the Logic Model, they have a direct relationship to one another in many ways. The underlying assumption of evaluating anything in our field is that positive outcomes should occur as a result of efforts (i.e., an investment of time and money), and no matter how good the participant outcomes are, program improvement is always possible.

## A Primer on Benefits and Outcomes

The notion of benefits or positive outcomes from recreation is not a new idea. Since the beginning of the organized recreation movement in the late 1800s, volunteers and professionals have extolled the values, importance, and benefits of recreation and associated areas such as camping and youth development. In the mid-1990s, the National Recreation and Park Association (NRPA) defined the "benefits movement" for our field and articulated the need to focus on the individual, environmental, communal, and economic benefits that occur because of recreation programs in a community. The premise is that recreation agencies must develop effective programs and services that influence the quality of life for citizens—programs, facilities, and opportunities that make their lives better. Awareness of the benefits and potential positive outcomes of recreation is essential. "The benefits are endless…" is the slogan that NRPA has used.

A benefit has been defined as anything that is good for a person or thing. A benefit might also relate to a desired condition that is maintained or changed. A benefit also equals an outcome or end result. NRPA has identified four areas of benefits. *Individual* benefits include improving health and wellness, building self-esteem, providing alternatives to self-destructive behavior, reducing stress, and providing opportunities for living a more balanced life. *Communal* benefits include building stronger families, reducing loneliness and alienation, enhancing community spirit, reducing crime, and promoting ethnic and cultural harmony. *Economic* benefits are associated with attracting business relocation and expansion, contributing to healthy and productive work forces, attracting tourism, and enhancing real estate values. *Environmental* benefits might include protecting natural resources and open space areas, enhancing air and water quality, reducing congestion, and providing and protecting wildlife habitat. All of these areas would likely be included in evaluations to determine if, in fact, quality recreation services are resulting in positive outcomes for citizens and for communities. Documenting these outcomes is the vital role that evaluation can play.

## Overview of Program Quality Evaluation

One of the chief ways that recreation organizations provide services, besides building facilities and areas, is through programs. Programs, however, are not just a bunch of activities that are planned for people. Programs should have a clear purpose and should have identifiable goals. A quality program results in activities that are designed and implemented to meet certain outcomes that address specific community needs. Quality programs should meet outcome goals.

Evaluation is seen as one of the prime components of a program system when it is examined along with the phases of assessment, objectives, and implementation. Evaluation, however, may not occur only at the end of a program but may occur throughout it and/or even at the beginning. Thus, as Howe and Carpenter (1985) illustrated in Figure 1.7(1), evaluation in recreation may occur at all stages of the program. Evaluating programs at all stages of their development may be important to assure that the desired results are obtained.

Many possibilities exist for developing program improvement evaluations. An examination of levels of program evaluation adapted from the longstanding work of Bennett (1982) may be useful in further understanding program evaluation (see Figure 1.7[2]). These are also sometimes termed a "hierarchy of effects." Four basic levels of program evaluation are suggested. The first aspect relates to the *participation* or inputs to a program. This level may include:

1. Inputs—resources available and expended such as money, paid staff and volunteer time, facilities, and equipment.

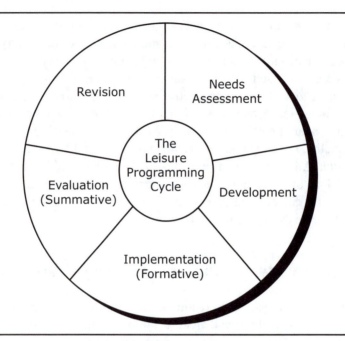

***Figure 1.7(1)*** *The Relationship Between Program and Evaluation (adapted from Howe and Carpenter, 1985)*

2. Activities—the strategies, techniques, and types of undertakings and organizational processes that are used, including publicity, actual activities, and the delivery of program.

3. People involvement—the outputs usually measured in terms of volume of activity pertaining to statistics and demographics describing the number of people, characteristics of people, frequency, and intensity of involvement.

A second broad level includes *reactions,* which can be likened to outputs:

4. Reactions—responses from the participants including degree of interest, like or dislike for activities, satisfaction, expectations, appeal, and opinions.

A third level gets into short-term and medium-term outcomes. It includes the benefits and changes for individuals or populations during or after participating in program activities. For an abbreviation, this level is sometimes called KASA:

5.  KASA outcomes include Knowledge (awareness, understanding, problem solving ability), Attitudes (feelings,
change of interest, ideas, beliefs), Skills (verbal or physical
abilities, new skills, improved performance, abilities), and
Aspirations (desires, courses of action, new decisions).

A final, and the highest functioning, level includes *actions* that result
in practice change or long-term outcomes that impact individual or community life:

6.  Practice change outcomes—adoption and application of
knowledge, attitudes, skills, or aspirations to leisure or
lifestyle.

7.  Long-term impact on quality of life outcomes—social,
economic, environmental, and individual consequences,
how people are helped, hindered, or harmed as a result of
this program.

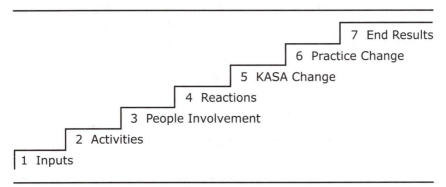

*Figure 1.7(2)* *Levels of Program Evaluation*

The objective of this illustration of the levels of programming is
to show how many different aspects might be evaluated in a program-
quality examination. Recreation professionals are frequently interested
in how well they are designing and implementing quality programs and
this information can be evaluated in the lower levels of the model. For an
organization to function efficiently and effectively, these aspects must be
considered. The outcomes and the significance of how recreation contributes to the quality of life, however, depend on the outcomes associated
with learning and actions (e.g., KASA, practice change, and impact on
quality of life). Many of the outcomes are measured as individual change,
which will be discussed in more detail a bit later. The important point
to note is that the evaluator must be aware of what exactly she or he is

measuring when any program evaluation focused on quality, processes, or improvement is undertaken.

One of the challenges in program evaluation is to make sure that you are not trying to evaluate too many criteria at once. The seven levels identified provide a framework for making decisions about what aspects of a program may be most important to evaluate. Most program evaluations do not measure, or often cannot measure, all seven levels. The evaluator must determine what the most important aspects are to evaluate and then design measurement instruments and evaluation projects to get at those.

Two examples of program evaluation forms are illustrated. Table 1.7(3) is an example of camper reactions and Table 1.7(4) shows how to measure inputs.

## An Example of Program Quality

To illustrate an example of program quality and the quality improvement process, we will examine some current work undertaken by the American Camp Association. This organization has designed two workbooks that address how to create positive youth outcomes (*Creating Positive Youth Outcomes*, 2007b) and how to design programs (*Designing Quality Youth Programs*, 2008). An important distinction between outcomes measure-

*Table 1.7(3) Camper Program Evaluation Reactions (source unknown)*

**Scoring:**
Awesome! = 5   Good = 4   Fair = 3   Yawn = 2   Boring = 1

| Activities | Score | Activities | Score |
|---|---|---|---|
| Archery | ___ | Soccer | ___ |
| Battlefield Tour | ___ | Campfires | ___ |
| Crafts | ___ | Bible Classes | ___ |
| Canoeing | ___ | Swimming | ___ |
| Cycling | ___ | Nature | ___ |
| Hiking | ___ | Physical Fitness | ___ |
| Sports | ___ | Music | ___ |
| Basketball | ___ | Meals | ___ |
| Softball | ___ | | |

ment and quality improvement is that program quality focuses primarily on "point of service" (generally the environment provided by the organization and program staff) while outcomes measurement focuses on the resulting program impacts on the participant. The combination of both is important, because you may not be able to "control" whether a measurable outcome actually occurs, but you can always control the quality of your organization and staff performance in setting the appropriate environment conducive to desired outcomes.

The value of designing outcomes and quality programs is in finding systematic ways to improve the likelihood that desired outcomes are reached. It is also a way to involve participants in shaping programs as well as demonstrating to stakeholders that an organization is committed

---

**Table 1.7(4)** *Parks and Recreation Department Program Outputs Evaluation*

---

How are we serving you? Please take a minute to complete this brief questionnaire and return it directly to our staff. We value your participation and want to serve you better. Thank you.

Location _____ Date _____

Activity _____

Please check Yes or No:                                                    YES        NO

1.  Was the staff courteous?                                          ____      ____
2.  Was the facility clean and attractive?                           ____      ____
3.  Was the activity well-organized?                                 ____      ____
4.  Was the area in a good state of repair?                          ____      ____
5.  Did the activity start on time?                                  ____      ____
6.  Did you feel safe and comfortable at the facility?               ____      ____
7.  Would you return to this facility for another activity?          ____      ____
8.  Was the activity interesting?                                    ____      ____

9.  Overall, how would you rate this activity (please check one)?
    ____ Excellent    ____ Good    ____ Fair    ____ Poor

10. What other activity would you like us to provide?

11. How did you hear about our classes/programs? Check one/or any that apply.
    ____ Mailed brochure       ____ Yellow pages      ____ TV
    ____ Picked up brochure    ____ Flyer/poster      ____ Newspaper
    ____ Friend                ____ Radio             ____ Referral
    ____ Online at Website     ____ Called facility   ____ Other

to positive human development. The approach uses evaluation as a central process to document the effectiveness of strategies in the action plan. Designing quality programs includes eight action steps:

1. Ask (assess) participants

2. Ask staff

3. Assess current practices

4. Brainstorm

5. Choose strategies

6. Take action

7. Share your plan

8. Evaluate

An important premise of program quality is to use intentional and purposeful actions to create positive change. A common approach is often to just change the activity. While you will likely see improvement in your desired outcomes, the results are greatest when spread across your program's strategies, policies, and activities. Evaluating likely builds upon the assessment of your participants and staff on how things change as a result of the process. After going through this process, success can be measured by small incremental changes, data that show where changes were made, an assessment of effective strategies, directions for future programs, and empowered staff and participants who recognize they have a role in program improvement. Remember, people are the focus of change, programs are not.

# Participant Outcomes

The goal of most recreation organizations is to produce positive end results or outcomes from involvement in recreation. Participant outcomes have emerged as a central area for evaluation. Some organizations refer to proof of these outcomes as impact research. As noted above, outcomes can refer to learning or action outcomes. Participant outcomes include what individuals know, think, can do, and how they behave or change ("learn, do, become"). Although the goal of recreation is to satisfy the participant in terms of her or his wants, or interests, we also hope that involement addresses a human need that improves an individual's life and thus, the life of the community.

We use the term "participants" throughout this book to refer to the people who receive recreation services. In applied cases, these participants might have other names such as consumers, clients, patients, guests, tourists, or campers. No matter what they are called, they all are involved in recreation endeavors and experiences. We are trying to change their lives in positive ways. The common goal of all recreation and human service programs is to make life better and more rewarding for people. For example, we may be interested in evaluating the acquisition of a certain skill level or the improvement in attitudes toward recreation or towards oneself. Self-constructs, including self-confidence and self-esteem, are frequently assessed in participant outcome research. Table 1.7(5) provides an example of some impact questions asked in a national Girl Scout study.

The value of measuring participant outcomes lies in assuring that the inputs and outputs addressed in recreation agencies really are making a difference. The Logic Model is useful in this regard because it takes into account how processes may impact outcomes. Therefore, accountability is important in measuring participant outcomes. This information, however, also results in improved services so that the outcomes are likely

---

*Table 1.7(5)*  *Outcomes-Oriented Self Questions Asked in a National Girl Scout Study (adapted from* Girl Scouts of the USA, 2000)

---

**DAL = Disagree a Lot**
**D = Disagree**
**A = Agree**
**AAL = Agree a Lot**
**DU = Don't Understand**

| | | | | | |
|---|---|---|---|---|---|
| It's okay that I'm good at doing some things but not good at doing other things. | DAL | D | A | AAL | DU |
| I know what I'm good at. | DAL | D | A | AAL | DU |
| I feel comfortable talking about my feelings with some people. | DAL | D | A | AAL | DU |
| I will let someone know if I'm afraid to do something. | DAL | D | A | AAL | DU |
| When I feel happy about something, I usually tell other people. | DAL | D | A | AAL | DU |
| My friends usually think my ideas are good. | DAL | D | A | AAL | DU |
| If I try hard, I can learn anything. | DAL | D | A | AAL | DU |
| I have good ideas. | DAL | D | A | AAL | DU |

to occur over and over again. We must keep in mind that instruments designed to measure program processes should not be used to make judgments about participant outcomes. Although quality programs and best practices ought to lead to positive changes in people, the issues cannot be measured in the same way.

To do effective measurement of participant outcomes, several steps must be employed. First, the outcomes you want to measure (i.e., the criteria) must be determined. Then you must determine what data are needed to measure the outcomes. Data must be collected and analyzed and compared to the intended outcomes. Finally, you need to use the findings in the form of conclusions and recommendations. For example, if we wanted to know if a midnight basketball program reduces the youth crime rate in a community, we would determine the desired outcome is to reduce the crime rate, measure the crime rate before the program started and then again periodically during the program, and make judgments about the value or worth of the program in relation to the outcome of reduced crime. We recognize that other good things might happen to individuals as a result of the midnight basketball program, but in this use of participant outcomes, we would focus specifically on determining goals and objectives that could be measured.

Different populations may need to be examined using different tools if participant outcome evaluation is to be effective (Sengstock & Hwalek, 1999). For example, evaluating programs for children and youth may be quite different than for adults. Youth may have a shorter attention span than adults. Measurement is also complicated by the rapid developmental stages that youth undergo. Therefore, changes in aspects such as social skills may not be the result of a recreation program as much as it might be the maturation of a child. Instruments must also be age-appropriate for children. Evaluators must be concerned that evaluation is diversity-sensitive and that evaluators are aware of their own "cultural competence." For example, youth for whom English is not their first language may understand the wording of instruments differently and may not score in the same ways as others who interpret the questions differently. People with disabilities are another group that may interpret instruments differently than the evaluator intended if their needs are not considered. More about this topic will be discussed later in this unit. Further, as we will discuss in Unit Two, pilot-testing is a way to address some of these potential problems with different populations.

Outcomes evaluation is not nearly as easy to do as evaluating inputs, activities, and reactions. There are no magic formulas. Yet, that area must be addressed because it demonstrates your commitment to a sustained evaluation process focused on program-quality improvement and impact.

# Five Ps Summary

Developing an evaluation system is not easy, but it can be exciting. As you work through this book, however, certain aspects of how the Ps can be systematically analyzed within any organization over a period of time should become evident. Table 1.7(6) summarizes a number of examples of ways that the five Ps might be used in leisure-service-organization evaluations.

# From Ideas to Reality

Recreation experiences offer many potential positive outcomes for individuals and communities. Program evaluation is a large area and the evaluator might want to focus on particular programs during different years and the myriad benefits that might occur. This program evaluation includes program quality, program processes, and program improvement.

---

*Table 1.7(6)* Summary of Components of the Five Ps of Evaluation

---

Participant Outcomes
    Motivation/Satisfaction
    Changes in Attitudes as Outcomes
    Changes in Knowledge as Outcomes
    Changes in Skills and Abilities as Outcomes
    Carry-over into Other Situations
    How Individuals Interact
    Demographic Characteristics
Program Quality and Improvement
    Effective Leadership
    Promotion of Program
    Participant Gains
    Risk Management
Place
    Safety Concerns
    Master Planning
    Adequate Facilities
Policies/Administration
    Accountability of Budget
    Cost-Benefit Analysis
    Cost-Effectiveness Analysis
    Equitable Provision of Services
Personnel
    Performance Appraisal
    Assess Training Needs
    Provide Feedback for Improvement

---

Assessing these aspects is closely linked to participant outcomes. When evaluating participant outcomes, you might want to examine an outcome such as skill development in a particular area. The possibilities are endless and the evaluator must use a system to determine the most important aspects to evaluate given the time, money, and expertise that may exist within an organization. All of the Ps are important and all can be evaluated in a variety of ways, but the undertakings must be carefully considered if appropriate and useful evaluations, which can document benefits and values of the services provided and improve on programs for the future, are to be conducted.

Now that you have studied this chapter, you should be able to:
- Determine when to use the levels of program evaluation
- Articulate how program quality, program processes, and participant outcomes relate to one another
- Discuss the value of measuring participant outcomes
- Give examples of using the five Ps of evaluation

## 1.8 Like Sands Through an Hourglass: Timing of Evaluation

The five Ps of leisure services (program quality, participant outcomes, personnel, places, and policy/administration) can be evaluated in different sequences and ways. For our discussions about evaluation, we examine the timing related to the three areas of assessment, formative, and summative evaluations. We have referred to these time-related ways of thinking about evaluation previously in this unit, but we would like to describe them further.

Timing of evaluations can profoundly affect the process, as the temporal sequence changes the evaluator's approach. Evaluation may be done at the beginning (*assessment*), during the process of a program/ course of a year (*formative*) or at the end of the program/year (*summative*). These three approaches can be illustrated through a classroom example. Some professors may want to know how much students know about a particular topic at the beginning of a semester. They may give a quiz or exam on the first day of class to assess the knowledge level or attitudes that students have about a subject. Many professors are required to give final exams, which are summative evaluations. They tell the instructor what happened at the end of the course but at that point, little can be done to change the learning or lack of learning that occurred. For this reason, many instructors give mid-term exams that might be thought of as formative evaluations. When these midterms are given, the instructor then has the opportunity to immediately improve the class if the learning has not occurred as planned. Three different timings of the evaluations or exams result in differing outcomes for those people who are using the exam evaluations. Assessment, formative, or summative evaluations may occur within any of the Ps. These three ways of doing evaluation also are based on criteria that must be determined before an evaluation project is undertaken.

Although not completely congruent, we might say that assessment always examines some type of need and is the foundation for further *planning,* formative evaluation uses an examination of the *progress or process,* and summative evaluation measures the *product* referred to as outcomes, impacts, effectiveness, and/or overall efficiency. Thus, the criteria developed for an evaluation project will depend on its timing and whether the use of the evaluation will be for planning, determining progress, or measuring the product.

# Assessments and Planning

Assessment is a process of determining and specifically defining a program, facility, staff member, participant's behavior, or administrative procedure. Needs assessments are often conducted in community recreation programs. These assessments identify the differences between "what is" and "what should be." The needs assessment can result in a process of prioritizing results to use in planning programs, places, policies, or the use of personnel. Therapeutic recreation specialists use assessment as the initial evaluation necessary to plan intervention strategies and serve as a baseline for measuring client outcomes (Stumbo, 1991).

The assessment thus serves as a set of outcomes or judgments that focus on gaps between current aspects of the Ps and desired results. Assessments provide the direction for reducing those gaps. Assessments may determine answers to such questions as "what is the socioeconomic profile of a community?" "what do citizens want?" "what are they willing to pay for?" "what forms of recreation services are needed?" Needs are complex and often hard to understand, so an assessment evaluation can help to address such aspects as the context of need, denial of need, and/or how needs can be used in program planning. Assessments can also determine the interests of individuals or their "willingness to pay" for particular services.

Assessment evaluation assumes that you want to find out where to begin. Where to begin applies to whether you are assessing a participant, the resources available in a community, or the needs for training a new staff member. To collect data for a needs assessment, for example, a plan must be devised. The plan usually includes defining what you want to know, developing a plan of action, generating goals, collecting data about "what is," analyzing data for discrepancies between "what is" and "what should be," and then developing a plan of action for the desired intervention or for the programs to be initiated. The assessment is based on determining criteria, collecting evidence, and making judgments about where any of the Ps of your organization is now, where to go in the future, and how to get there. Table 1.8(1) shows an example of a popular needs assessment and evaluation approach being used in communities and organizations across the United States. The Search Institute (1996) developed 40 developmental assets designed to be the building blocks for development for young people so they can grow up healthy, caring, and responsible. As an assessment tool, a community might examine how some of these assets are or are not being addressed within an organization of community.

The only time you do not need to conduct an assessment is when you are sure of the goals and objectives for your organization, program, participants, or staff and when that information is complete, correct, valid, and useful. An assessment may be done internally or externally, depending on the particular situation.

## Formative and Process Evaluation

Formative and summative evaluations may not be measuring different aspects of recreation services, but the timing is such that the results often are used in different ways. In general, formative evaluation is concerned more with organizational objectives such as efficiency and effectiveness, while summative evaluation is concerned with the overall performance objectives, outcomes, or "products."

When we are interested in examining the processes and progress toward goals associated with an organization, we often use formative evaluation. Formative evaluation is defined as the systematic examination

---

*Table 1.8(1)* *Examples of the 40 Developmental Assets Identified by Search Institute (1996)*

---

**Support**
1. Family support: family life provides high levels of love and support.
3. Other adult relationships: young person receives support from three or more nonparent adults.

**Empowerment**
7. Community values youth: young person perceives that adults in the community value youth.
8. Youth as resources: young people are given useful roles in the community.

**Constructive Use of Time**
17. Creative activities: young person spends three or more hours per week in lessons or practice in music, theater, or other arts.
18. Youth programs: young person spends three or more hours per week in sports, clubs, or organizations at school and/or in community organizations.
19. Religious community: young person spends one or more hours per week in activities in a religious institution.
20. Time at home: young person is out with friends "with nothing special to do" two or fewer nights per week.

**Social Competencies**
32. Planning and decision making: young person knows how to plan ahead and make choices.
33. Interpersonal competence: young person has empathy, sensitivity, and friendship skills.

**Positive Identity**
39. Sense of purpose: young person reports that "my life has a purpose."
40. Positive view of personal future: young person is optimistic about her or his personal future.

---

of steps in the development and implementation of a program, organizational structure, policy, or staff person. Formative evaluation occurs while a program or administrative procedure is in progress and is used to examine the process as it is occurring within the organization. Feedback is provided early so that revisions can be made and weaknesses pointed out while there is still time to correct them. The value of formative evaluation lies in the changes that can be made while a staff member is working, when a budget is being used, or when a program is going on. Examples of process evaluation questions that might be asked are "is the program attracting a sufficient number?" "how are staff contacting participants?" "are some media methods working better than others?" "are the participants making progress toward their individual goals?" "will the program break even or make money?"

An example of how formative evaluation might be embodied could relate to another example of university teaching by faculty. An instructor could do a formative evaluation at the midterm of the semester to determine how a class is going. She or he might ask such questions as: "what is the instructor doing that is contributing to your learning?" "what are you doing that is contributing to your learning?" "what could the instructor do to improve your learning?" "what could you do to improve your learning?" From those data, the instructor might make changes to enhance the learning process. Similarly, the use of this type of formative evaluation might result in students evaluating their behavior and making changes as well. This formative evaluation allows for changes to be made midway rather than waiting for a summative evaluation at the end of the semester that will not benefit the students who are currently taking a class.

Evaluation using standards of practice developed by professional organizations is another good example of formative evaluation. For example, in therapeutic recreation, the concept of quality assurance (QA) is frequently cited. This concept pertains to providing quality healthcare and determining what constitutes quality care within therapeutic recreation (Riley & Wright, 1990). QA is a mechanism employed to systematically monitor and evaluate the appropriateness and quality indicators of patient care activities. This system uses written criteria that directly contain structure, outcome, indicator, and process measures that can be evaluated formatively to aid in ongoing patient care.

Another example of a formative process might refer to the concept of quality of service (MacKay & Crompton, 1990). Professionals in tourism and other areas of recreation have a central interest in service quality. The intent is to use any number of methods to examine how services are provided. Tangible and intangible aspects are measured: physical facilities, equipment, appearance of personnel, reliability (including the ability to perform the promised service dependably and accurately), responsiveness (defined as the willingness to help users and provide prompt attention), assurance (indicates courteous and knowledgeable employees who convey trust and confidence), and empathy (includes offering caring and individualized attention to users). By comparing what customers expect and what they experience, an organization can make formative changes to provide better services for present, as well as future, participants.

Another common formative evaluation is done with seasonal staff. In this process, staff are evaluated after the first two weeks or midway through a summer to see how they are doing. At this point in time, changes can be made in duties or needed training can be provided to address whatever potential problems are uncovered. Rather than waiting until the end of the season to give a staff member an evaluation, the formative evaluation allows one to receive feedback that can be used to improve or to change immediately.

## Summative and Product Evaluation

When most people think of evaluation they tend to think of the final evaluation, the evaluation that occurs at the end of something that measures the outcomes or the end results. A grade at the end of the semester or the bonus/pay raise at the end of the year are examples of how a summative evaluation might be applied. Summative evaluation uses an overall examination of impact and effectiveness that is completed at the end of a program or the end of the year. A decision to continue or discontinue the aspect evaluated is imminent, although the material gained in a summative evaluation can be applied to improving subsequent programs. Formative evaluation can occur within any stage of organization process, whereas summative only occurs at the end of the year, the end of a program, or some set temporal boundary. Summative evaluation particularly is important for accountability purposes but should not be used exclusively for that purpose.

A common form of summative evaluation is outcome or impact evaluation, which ascertains if a program produced the intended effects. In particular, one might be interested in reactions to a program but in the end, learning or practice change is the most important. Sometimes, immediately after a program is not the best time to evaluate long-term outcomes. Some studies of outcomes of youth at camp, for example, were not measured only as a pretest before camp and a posttest on the last day or camp, but also measured as outcomes six months later to see if the changes that occurred in camp had remained over the long term (Thurber, Schuler, Scanlin, & Henderson, 2007).

In summative evaluation, we are interested in determining the net effects of a program, policy, or place/facility. The results are comparative in that you examine what happened based on where an organization began. For example as noted previously, experimental designs often are used for the purpose of summative evaluation. A pretest is given before a program and a posttest after it is over to determine the impact of a program. In another example, the bottom line of impact analysis relates to a comparison of what did happen after implementing the program with what would have happened had the program not been implemented (Mohr, 1988).

Iso-Ahola (1982) described one illustration of summative evaluation. He suggested that intrinsic leisure motivation should be the main concern of evaluation. If leisure is a state of mind, then we ought to evaluate those aspects in participants such as an outcome goal like leisure satisfaction. He defined leisure satisfaction as having feelings of freedom and control and suggested measures whereby we could determine how leisure helps people receive a degree of balance in their lives, promotes social interaction, and gives feedback about their competence. Different people prefer different leisure activities/programs for different intrinsic rewards at different times. Rossman (1982) suggested that the notion of leisure satisfaction is best measured by investigating underlying satisfaction dimensions rather than a single, all-encompassing measure of "overall satisfaction." Table 1.8(2) shows examples of some of the reactions that could be measured through a summative evaluation.

Summative evaluation, however, becomes a complicated aspect when one starts to evaluate what really happened to people. Halle, Boyer, and Ashton-Shaeffer (1991) suggested two types of impact criteria that ought to be examined: experimental and therapeutic. Experimental criteria imply that a program causes a desired effect or has a definite outcome. We also need to consider, however, the therapeutic criteria that refer to the importance and meaning of the change produced. In other words, does a particular leisure program make a difference in people's lives over the long run? Halle et al. did a study of ten ambulatory students with moderate intellectual disabilities participating in aerobic exercise paired with 14 exercise buddies. They collected data on weight, percent body fat, graded exercise, and the frequency and quality of social interaction between those individuals with and without disabilities. They found that the social value of the program was just as important as any physical change that had occurred in fitness levels. Thus, summative impact was broader than just an experimental design.

Summative evaluation may be measured related to different levels of program evaluation (e.g., participation, reactions, learning, or actions) as well as timing. For example, we might look at changes immediately after a program or examine what is occurring 6 months later or 10 years later. Similarly, outcomes may be specific to a situation or may influence an individual to change his or her quality of life. Summative evaluation can become complex as we seek to determine what criteria or levels of evidence ought to be measured.

Efficiency, as another aspect of summative evaluation, relates to inputs and activities in terms of numbers and costs to organizations. We are often concerned with examining costs in comparison to benefits. Were funds spent for intended purposes? Did a program achieve its success at a reasonable cost? Can dollar values be assigned to outcomes? Efficiency assessments, including cost-benefit and cost-effectiveness, provide a frame of reference for relating costs to program results. Inputs and outputs are measured in numerical terms. To calculate efficiency, you must look at costs to and benefit for whom. Further, costs and benefits may refer to individuals, program sponsors, or the society at large. These are all examples of summative evaluations.

We need to use a proper amount of caution in determining summative economic benefits. Not all benefits can be converted to monetary

*Table 1.8(2) Examples of Measures of Leisure Satisfaction (adapted from Rossman, 1982)*

**Achievement**
I learned more about the activity.
It was a new and different experience.
My skills and ability developed.
I became better at it.
**Family Escape**
I was able to be away from my family for a while.
**Environment**
The area was physically attractive.
I liked the freshness and cleanliness of the area.
I liked the open space.
I enjoyed the pleasing design of the facility.
**Risk**
I liked the risks involved.
I liked the chance for danger.
**Autonomy**
I was in control of things that happened.
It gave me a chance to be on my own.
**Physical Fitness**
I enjoyed the exercise.
It keeps me physically fit.
**Social Enjoyment**
I enjoyed the companionship.

terms. Cost-benefit and cost-effectiveness often are viewed more conceptually than they are technically because the required technical procedures of converting benefits to dollar amounts may be beyond expertise and resources of most evaluators. For example, an important question today is how community recreation programs can contribute to people becoming more physically active and thus healthier. How much is then saved in healthcare costs because these now-active people are healthier? Measuring prevention outcomes is complicated, but that does not mean we should not try to do such.

Political and moral controversies also exist about whether you can put value on some outcomes. For example, what is the value of a child's life if she or he is given swimming lessons so that someday she or he will not drown? These dilemmas about dollar figures may obscure the rel-. evancy of evaluations if one gets too caught up in the numbers. As a form of summative evaluation, however, measuring outcomes is essential.

# From Ideas to Reality

Timing can relate to all aspects of evaluation. Assessment involves getting potential baseline information about available inputs, what needs and interests people have, current involvement, attitudes and reactions to leisure or a particular situation, and an assessment of what knowledge, skills, aspirations, and attitudes now exist. A formative evaluation would be concerned with various aspects of efficiency and progress as leisure services are delivered. The summative evaluation would be concerned with outcomes or effectiveness. Clearly, the timing of evaluations will be closely linked to the reasons for conducting an evaluation project.

All aspects of timing are needed within organizations but not all programs, participants, places, policies, or personnel need to be evaluated within each timing sequence. Decisions will need to be made concerning the most appropriate timing to be used for a particular evaluation system and project. Sometimes in the case of personnel, you may be doing assessments or formative, and summative evaluations, whereas in other situations—such as evaluating safety procedures on a camping trip—only formative evaluation might be used. As an evaluator, you will need to decide when and how evaluations are most appropriate and most useful to aid you in making the most enlightened decisions.

Now that you have studied this chapter, you should be able to:
- Describe the differences between formative, summative, and assessment evaluations
- List some possible applications for each of the timing aspects of evaluation

## 1.9 Designing Evaluation and Research Projects: Doing What You Gotta Do

Data for an evaluation or research project should not be collected until a solid plan has been carefully identified. Once you have determined what to include in your organization's evaluation system, you can then plan a specific evaluation project or conduct research. Once you know what burning questions you want to answer in your research, you can begin to design the proposal. Planning a project includes choosing a model to guide you, determining the timing of evaluation and the area (Ps) within recreation services that you will evaluate, and then selecting specific methods to use. A research proposal requires the initiation of a literature review, the identification of the role of theory, and design and methods selections. In this chapter, we examine how to design an evaluation project as well as how to develop a research proposal. Both tasks share some commonalities, but each also is unique.

Sometimes the design for a project, such as a performance appraisal for staff development, is a tool that will be used over and over again. Other times, each individual evaluation or research project will be designed anew. Generally small-scale, highly focused, and manageable studies are more useful than large, broad evaluations. Sometimes more complex projects will be necessary, and cutting a major project or study into manageable portions may be needed to complete it successfully. Regardless of the magnitude of the undertaking, keeping the evaluation or research project focused and on target is essential.

A design for evaluation or research is a plan for allocating resources of time and energy. The design must be carefully considered for each project, depending on the specific context of the situation. You always have many choices. Various constraints, however, are associated with every plan and you must do the best you can, given the financial, time, and human resources that exist. In addition, for any evaluation or research endeavor, many designs may be proposed, but no single plan is necessarily going to be perfect. Thus, you will have to make decisions about what is likely to be the best approach.

Taking time to plan is important in any project or study. Careful planning saves time in the long run and can result in better research and evaluation. You will need enough lead-time to plan the entire process for evaluation or research before you begin to collect data.

# Developing Plans for a Specific Evaluation Project

We have found planning guidelines to be a most useful framework in developing individual evaluation projects and in doing research projects. In general, when planning a project, you will be examining several basic questions:

*Why* (e.g., for what reason or purpose is this project being done, is it worth the effort, and what use will the results have);

*What* (e.g., which aspects of the Ps will be evaluated; what issues need to be addressed; what goals and objectives are to be evaluated; what level of evaluation will be used, and what criteria are to be measured);

*Who* (e.g., who wants the information and in what form, who will actually conduct the evaluation, and who has the information);

*When* (e.g., timelines and timing);

*Where* (e.g., sample size and composition); and

*How* (e.g., how to collect and analyze data, methods, techniques, and ethics; how the final report with be presented; and resources, financial and time, needed).

These questions resemble what was asked in setting up an evaluation system, but in the evaluation project design you will get more specific about how a project will actually be conducted from the beginning to the end. The design of the actual project is the "nitty gritty" of evaluation.

Theoretically, you will consider the *why, what, who, when, where* and *how* together, but practically, each will build upon the others. Smith (1989) suggested avoiding two types of error in initial planning: measuring something that does not exist, and measuring something that is of no interest to management and policymakers. Thus, the first three steps of determining *why, what,* and *who* are essential.

The *why* of doing evaluations has been discussed extensively in Chapter 1.4 but the evaluator must always keep in mind the purpose of the project to stay focused and on track. The why has implications for *what* and *who*.

The *who* often refers to the stakeholders or who wants the information. Stakeholders are those individuals who are personally involved in the organization, who derive income from the organization, whose future status or career might be affected by the quality of the organization, and/or who are the clients or potential recipients of the organization's services. Arranging a meeting of the stakeholders for a proposed evaluation project is often useful before you begin. Staff members are usually more involved in the organization than either sponsors or clients, so they need to have input about how an evaluation will be conducted. Many aspects of the evaluation plan, such as the type of evaluation, the availability of resources, and the reasons for evaluating can be determined early in the project by talking to stakeholders. Further, clarifications should be made specific about *why* a project is being undertaken and *what* the project is.

A second part of the *who* question is to determine who has the needed information. In some cases, documents may already exist that can help to address the evaluation criteria. Existing research/evaluation literature may be used as well as organizational records. You may want to find out what has been done elsewhere if possible, and "borrow" or adapt their approach and/or instruments whenever possible and appropriate. *Who* also relates to the general population to be asked. For example, will it be parents of children who attend a program, the children, their teachers, or a combination?

A third part of *who* is to determine who will be in charge of the evaluation. Although one person may do an evaluation project, a team approach is often desirable. The more people involved in an evaluation project, the more likely they are to have ideas that can help to make the evaluation recommendations usable when completed. You may want to use a citizen advisory committee or a Board of Directors, for example, depending on the type of project undertaken.

*What* relates to the model to be used and the criteria to be measured. Is it possible to measure the criteria desired? Do the resources exist to do an appropriate evaluation project? Are the level of evaluation and the timing of the evaluation consistent with what the stakeholders want and need? These answers represent critical aspects in developing the evaluation plan because now is the point that an initial decision should be made about whether to attempt a particular evaluation project or not. If the Goal-Attainment Model is to provide the framework, for example, you must be certain that measurable goals and objectives exist or can be written. At this point in time, you will also determine which model is going to be best to use.

*When* refers to the timing and timelines. Should the evaluation be assessment, summative, or formative? If the evaluation is summative, when is the best time to collect information: immediately or several weeks after a program? How long will the project take to complete? When are the results of the evaluation needed? When is the best time during the program or the year to do the evaluation? To some extent, these answers will depend on the criteria used. You must try to be realistic about how long a project may take to complete. Keep in mind that it takes time for proper pretesting of instruments, training of data collectors, getting related material from other books and journals, analyzing the data to draw conclusions and make recommendations, and writing the report. It is possible, but very unlikely, that someone could administer and analyze a survey in 2–3 weeks if it is brief and done on the Internet or by telephone. Also, think about the unforeseen problems that might be encountered, such as an inadequate sample size, that could slow down the data collection. All of these issues will be discussed further in Unit Two, but the conscientious evaluator will consider the possible problems in the planning phase to try to prevent them from happening when the evaluation is actually implemented.

*Where* the evaluation is conducted will depend on the recreation area examined, the sample used, and the timing. The particular aspect of the five Ps will also determine the *where*. Usually the *where* question is not difficult to answer once other components of planning have been carefully considered.

The final task is to determine *how* to do a project. *How* relates primarily to data collection and analysis. Such decisions include sampling, research design, data collection administration, choice of statistics, and how the findings will be reported. Once the preceding questions are answered, these *how* questions will likely fall into place, although decisions about *how* will still need to be made as you go along. The problem with some evaluations is that researchers decide they are going to use a particular technique, like mailed or e-mailed questionnaires, before determining any of the other aspects of the evaluation project plan's design. The *how* aspect of the plan, however, has to be realistic because one must also assess the resources available for the project. The evaluator must be careful to avoid "data addiction." That is, you should plan to collect only the data that are needed, not everything that would be interesting to ask. If criteria are appropriately delimited, data addiction should not be a problem.

The *how* also includes considering costs such as:
- Staff time for planning
- Labor and material costs for pretesting
- Copying and software/computing costs
- Supervisory costs for interviewer hiring, training, and supervising staff or use of volunteers
- Labor and expense of data administration and entry
- Cost of preparing codes and mailing/telephoning/personal/e-mail contact
- Cost of cleaning the data if mistakes are made when entering it
- Labor time and material costs for analysis and report preparation
- Telephone charges, postage, reproduction, and printing

A good evaluation is not always inexpensive, and some projects are more economical than others. The costs will obviously increase with the complexity of the project and analyses needed.

After these *why, what, who, when, where,* and *how* decisions are considered, a brief proposal or written plan will be useful to make sure that all people involved in your organization agree with what will be done in the evaluation project. Sometimes when you see things written down on paper, possible mistakes or problems are easier to see. The following planning framework outline (Table 1.9) is offered as an example and a model that can be used in doing small-scale evaluation-project planning.

Several other items might be considered in designing an evaluation project. First of all, baseline data about a program, participant, staff member, or place may be needed before the data collection begins. You may want to know the state of affairs that existed up to the present time. This information might provide a standard of comparison for measuring the outcomes.

Second, evaluators also need to be aware of their agendas and biases as well as those of the stakeholders or audience. Possible conflicts should be discussed ahead of time and negotiated. The goals of the project should be agreed upon and the possibility of unexpected consequences, such as what happens if undesirable effects are found, should be anticipated. All parties in the evaluation should be aware of how the evaluation is to be conducted and how the data will be presented.

Third, an evaluation that works in one situation may not be appropriate for another. "Borrowing" evaluation instruments that other agencies have used may be a good idea, but they should not be used wholesale without considering the specific context of your organization. You can use someone else's evaluation as a starting point, but make sure that it addresses the criteria that you have determined and that the instrument is aimed at the same level of evaluation that you wish to address. An instrument that is used, for example, to get reactions to a program may be helpful but not if you are interested in skill changes.

Finally, usefulness for enlightened decision making is the primarily focus of evaluation. As Patton (1978) suggested, evaluations are not a panacea for solving problems. For an evaluation project to be useful, criteria must be addressed to answer questions for decision makers. Avoid questions that decision makers do not want answered. Avoid questions that already have known answers. If the problem is a disorganized organization, one should organize it rather than try to evaluate it. Unless a lack of knowledge and information is a part of the disorganization problem, evaluation research will not help. Further as Hudson (1988) suggested concerning community needs assessments, evaluation projects must be comprehensive, customized, versatile, flexible, and efficient. They take a commitment of time and resources and often have limitations. They must be designed, however, to provide the greatest potential to get useful information for making the best possible decisions.

# Developing a Research Proposal

Many of the principles that apply to designing an evaluation project plan also pertain to a research proposal. Criteria necessary for theory testing or development, along with the use of a literature review data collection,

---

**Table 1.9** *Evaluation Project Planning Framework Example (adapted from the work of students: Ginna Millard, Sara Shope, and Amy Bryan)*

---

**Agency:** University of North Carolina Hospitals (Pediatric Play Room)

**Why?**
  *Background:* Problems exist trying to keep track of the toys, videos, and other resources that are available to use and check out in the Pediatric Play Room.
  *Purpose:* To describe the process (success and failures) in the present system, set a baseline, and to provide for organizational improvement in the future.
  *Cost-effectiveness:* The administration of the project can be done by volunteer undergraduate students who will provide a report to the CTRS responsible for the play room.

**What?**
  *Model:* Goal-free.
  *Criteria:* What are the problems, what policies currently exist, how are they enforced, how willing are staff and volunteers to enforce policies.
  *Data Type:* A combination of qualitative (field observations) and quantitative data (questionnaires to staff and volunteers who supervise the play room)

**Who?**
  *Who Wants the Information:* Director of Therapeutic Recreation Services at UNC Hospitals and CTRS in charge of play room.
  *Who Will Do the Project:* Undergraduate TR students in an evaluation class.
  *Who Will Provide Data:* The evaluators will observe the play room and survey all individuals who have responsibilities for supervising the play room.

**When?**
  *Timing:* Formative evaluation.
  *Timelines:* March (observation) and April (surveys and analysis) 1994.

**Where?**
  *Sample Size and Composition:* Random sample of observations during various hours that the play room is open; a population sample will be done of supervisors in the play room.

**How?**
  *Method(s) to Use:* Field observations and quantitative questionnaires.
  *Time and Money Resources Needed:* Time to plan, conduct, and write report is volunteer time from students; supplies for printing from hospital budget = $10; computer analysis free.
  *Special Considerations:* Gaining cooperation of supervisors in the play room.

---

(Note: More detail will be added to each of these as the specific plans for data collection are solidified.)

and analysis issues, result in conclusions that add to the body of knowledge. The research proposal should include as much detail as possible. This plan is important to clarify thinking and give focus and direction to the work. The value of a research plan or proposal, just like the evaluation plan, is to state your ideas so that others might react to them and improve upon them. Planning may prevent serious problems in implementing a study.

Most research proposals (including many grant proposals) include the following sections:

- Introduction
- Statement of the theory and hypotheses
- Initial review of the literature
- Description of proposed sample
- Methods and techniques to use in carrying out the study
- Plans for how data analysis will be done.

The *general introduction* identifies the area to be studied and how it will contribute to the body of knowledge that already exists. The need for the study and the statement of the problem addressed is generally included in this introduction.

The statement of the *theory and/or hypotheses* gives a framework for the study. This framework tells the reader what is being addressed and the possible questions or relationships that will be examined. Theory is the foundation for any research undertaken. For studies that focus on generating theory, the guiding research questions serve as the framework for this part of the research design.

In a proposal, an initial *review of literature* should be described. More may be added to the literature review as the study is undertaken, but the researcher needs to determine what literature currently exists and what methods have been employed to address these topics in the past. The most important and recent literature is usually included in this brief review.

The researcher will also want to identify the *sample* to be used and how it will be selected. This description will include the characteristics of participants in the study as well as the number needed. Sampling procedures and rationale would be determined as well as the source of the data to be collected.

The *methods and techniques* for data collection in carrying out the project will need to be identified. This aspect is also referred to as the research design. The methods and techniques should be consistent with the theory or hypotheses that are used. This section may also contain information on how the rights of your research subjects will be protected.

Related to the procedures of data collection is a plan for *data analysis*. The analysis may influence the number of participants needed as well as the way the instruments are used or designed. The analysis must also result in being able to answer the hypotheses and research questions that are generated.

A research proposal is generally longer than an evaluation plan but both are critical to designing studies that will address the questions that need to be answered for decision making or for contributing to the body of knowledge in a field such as leisure services.

# From Ideas to Reality

Planning evaluation projects and research studies beyond the idea stage is often not the most exciting endeavor. Many times it is more fun to actually begin collecting data. Some evaluators and researchers, particularly when they are novices, have a tendency to want to begin to collect data and later work out the "bugs" of a study. We encourage you to consider drafting an outline for each phase of your evaluation or research study before you begin to collect data. It will set a course for you that can provide direction as you move through the undertaking. As you can see by the examples given in this chapter, the plan or proposal does not need to be elaborate at this stage, but it at least can give you a path to follow. It may be modified slightly as the project or study develops but a plan provides a foundation upon which to build. Once you have more information about methods such as questionnaires or observations and techniques such as sampling and analysis, you can develop a more sophisticated plan to follow as you complete your evaluation or research project, and write the final report.

Now that you have studied this chapter, you should be able to:
- Write an evaluation project plan including the why, who, what, when, where, and how
- Describe the elements that are part of a research proposal. How are they alike or different from the evaluation project design?
- Determine the considerations that should be made in planning any type of evaluation or research project
- Analyze whether an evaluation plan or research study is feasible and has the potential for producing usable results

# 1.10  To Be or Not to Be:
# Competencies and the Art of Systematic Inquiry

Most recreation professionals are pretty good intuitive evaluators but education, training, and practical experience are necessary to become confident and competent at systematic formal evaluation. As indicated in the preface, reading this book is not necessarily going to make you an expert evaluator or a skilled researcher. That learning will take years of experience. You do, however, need to have some basic skills and background to conduct and evaluate your own projects and improve upon your abilities as a systematic inquirer.

A critical aspect of learning is that when one acquires knowledge about a few things, one often finds out about all the things that one *doesn't* know. We have learned as professors over the years that sometimes the value of a college education is not in what you learn, but how a person comes to appreciate what she or he doesn't know. We are all lifelong learners and getting good at evaluation or research requires continually learning new skills. For example, when the first edition of this book was published, no one had ever heard of Internet surveys. Now, as you will see later in this book, they are a common means of collecting data. Thus, one important aspect of developing competencies for evaluation in recreation evaluation is to learn the limitations of one's own skills, as well as the limitations of what evaluation can do for an organization. It also means keeping up on what is "new" related to evaluation and research!

Sometimes understanding how to judge the merits of evaluations or to critique research is just as important as being able to actually conduct studies. Some organizations rely on external evaluators or consultants who come from outside the organization to conduct evaluations. Other organizations use only internal evaluators who are professionals within the organization whose job responsibilities include evaluation. Whether you are actually the internal professional who conducts the evaluation or the scholar who does the research, or whether you use the information obtained from an external evaluator or you read research articles, you still need to know the terminology and the components that must be considered in a process of systematic inquiry.

## Internal versus External Evaluations

The ideal situation for an organization is to have both internal and external evaluations conducted appropriately within the evaluation system. The decision whether to use internal or external evaluators may depend on a variety of factors. Table 1.10 provides a summary of the advantages and disadvantages of internal or external evaluators.

Certainly many advantages exist with using internal evaluators. The professional who is an employee in the organization ought to know a lot about the organization. Less time will be needed for the evaluator to become familiar with the ins and outs and the intricacies of the organization. An internal evaluator will also be more accessible to colleagues and will likely not be as obtrusive as an external evaluator. Once the evaluation is complete, the internal evaluator may be in a better position to make changes and to use the results of the evaluation for decision making. When internal evaluators are used, they receive their regular salary so the costs would likely be lower. Further, because the internal evaluator knows the organization, realistic recommendations that can enhance the efficiency and effectiveness of the organization might be more easily offered.

Obvious advantages also exist to using an external evaluator. These consultants may have more objectivity due to the remoteness they have to the situation and the freedom from responsibility for the organization or the services. Their objectivity is also based on a professional commitment to the field and not the individual organization. Further, they have credibility based on their professional experience and competency. With more experience, they may have access to a greater variety of methods and techniques. They may also know more about how other organizations address some of their evaluation concerns and may be better able to assist in benchmarking. Consultants may have resources, such as sample

*Table 1.10* *Advantages and Disadvantages of External and Internal Evaluators*

**Internal**

| Advantages | Disadvantages |
|---|---|
| Knows the Organization | Pressure to Have Positive Results |
| Accessible to Colleagues | Difficult to Criticize |
| Realistic Recommendations | May Lack Training |
| Can Make Changes | |

**External**

| Advantages | Disadvantages |
|---|---|
| More Objectivity | Threat to Employees |
| Competence | Must Get to Know Organization |
| Experience | May Disrupt Organization |
| More Resources | May Impose Values |
| Less Pressure to Compromise | Expensive |
| Lower Costs | |

measurement instruments or computer programs for data analysis, that are not available to internal evaluators in an organization. Since external evaluators have less investment in a program, they may feel less pressure to make compromises in their recommendations. In addition, if staff conflicts are a problem in an organization, outside evaluators may be able to mediate them better than someone who is involved within the organization. Their objectivity will likely be unencumbered by knowledge of personal issues and conflicts. A further advantage is that they may have data from other organizations that would make for comparative evaluations.

A downside exists to using only internal or external evaluators. The internal evaluator may feel pressure to have positive results. Her or his job, or the jobs of colleagues, may be on the line if evaluations are not good. It is generally easier for an internal evaluator to focus on strengths rather than weaknesses. An internal evaluator may find difficulty in criticizing certain aspects of a program. Further, an internal evaluator that does not have extensive training in evaluation may not be as competent as someone who specializes in evaluation.

The external evaluator may also have disadvantages. This outside individual may be seen as a threat to employees. Employees may be on their best behavior and the organization may not appear as it really is. The external evaluator must spend a great deal of time just getting to know an organization and may miss some of the nuances that go on within a particular organization on a day-to-day basis. The outside evaluator may take valuable time away from staff or may disrupt the normal functioning of an organization. As is true in any situation, the external evaluator may impose her or his value system on an organization that may not hold the same values. Further, to hire an external evaluator often is expensive and many recreation agencies do not have those resources.

Decisions will have to be made about who is the best person to conduct an evaluation. Some decisions are obvious. For example, one's immediate supervisor usually conducts personnel evaluations and bringing someone from the outside does not usually make sense. On the other hand, when standards are applied through an accreditation process, external reviewers are required. Some programs may be evaluated easily "in-house" whereas hiring someone to conduct a more thorough evaluation may be useful every once in a while. We would hope that all recreation majors would be good internal evaluators and would also possess some of the skills to be external evaluators too. The development of these skills, however, takes education and practice. Just as important is knowing when you see a well-done evaluation that is useful to an individual or an organization. Performing evaluations and studying others' are both important.

# Developing Competencies

Regardless of who conducts the evaluation or research project, every recreation professional ought to have some utilizable training in systematic evaluation. The more individuals who have evaluation and research training, the better off the organization will be. Even if an external evaluator is hired, the professionals in the organization have to know how to formulate criteria for the project and will need to determine the reliability and validity of the judgments made by external evaluators.

In hiring an external reviewer or conducting a research project, several specific competencies ought to be required:

1.  The individual conducting the evaluation or research should have some knowledge about the topical area to be evaluated. If the adult sports league is to be evaluated, for example, the evaluator ought to know something about recreation programming for adults and about sports programming. In addition the basic terminology of evaluation should be understood.

2.  An individual ought to know something about designing evaluation systems, developing planning frameworks for individual projects, and writing goals and objectives. Knowing why and what to evaluate are necessary prerequisites for writing different types of objectives. The evaluator must be able to judge how measurement can be conducted in relation to these goals and objectives.

3.  The individual ought to know all the possible evaluation research methods from which to choose. He or she should know how to determine the best way to collect data, how to choose a sample, how to choose appropriate instruments that will result in accurate information, and the appropriate techniques for analysis.

4.  The evaluator or researcher should be able to interpret the data and relate those results to the criteria. An understanding of the trilogy of evaluation and how the parts fit together are essential.

5.  The individual should know what to look for in analyzing both qualitative and quantitative data using the most appropriate strategies or statistics. As you will see later, professionals may be partial to qualitative or quantitative data.

These preferences, however, do not preclude knowing the basic assumptions about each type of data so that sound evaluative judgments can be made.

6. An evaluator must understand how to use evaluation results in decision making, regardless of what area of the Ps are evaluated. This competency will involve knowing how to organize, write, and present reports so that the information can be communicated effectively to those individuals (e.g., staff, Board or Commission members, parents) who want and/or need the information.

7. An evaluator or researcher needs to be able to address the political, legal, moral, and ethical issues that may be encountered in doing an evaluation. Certain legal and ethical concerns must be addressed, as well as how evaluators can be politically responsive to those users of the evaluation information. More detail will be given about these issues in the next chapter.

8. Although most of the above competencies relate to conceptual and technical skills, certain personal skills are an additional aspect needed to be a successful evaluator or researcher. Personal qualities are necessary, such as an interest in improving programs, places, policies, participant experiences, and/or personnel. The evaluator must be worthy of the trust of her or his colleagues as well as of the administrators and the decision makers of organizations. She or he must be as objective as possible, although one's personal biases cannot help but enter into any undertaking. The effective evaluator must be able to see and respond to sensitive issues and situations as they relate to the uniqueness of organizations. The effective systematic inquirer must possess good "people" skills.

When you begin to assess the competencies needed to conduct evaluation or research projects, they may appear to be a bit overwhelming. These competencies are not that rigorous, though, if you see evaluation and research as a system of linking criteria, evidence, and judgment. Conducting these projects or examining evaluation information should not be feared. The best way to learn is to "just do it" and the only way to get started is to begin. Some aspects of evaluation are technical but not so difficult that they can't be used by an enthusiastic and committed recreation professional.

# From Ideas to Reality

As indicated earlier, to become a good evaluator or researcher requires a combination of education, training, and practical experience. All recreation professionals ought to have a basic background in methods that will enable them to do projects and judge the merit of projects done by others. No magic formulas exist to teach one how to be a competent evaluator or researcher, but by learning the basics and trying them out, evaluating your own work, and practicing, you can become effective and successful. You will also know if others have displayed the competencies needed to do reliable, valid, and useful projects.

Whether to use internal or external evaluations is a decision left up to an organization. Both have advantages and disadvantages. Many times organizations do not have the funding necessary to hire outside consultants, so they rely on internal evaluators. It is better to go outside the organization for some types of criteria that may need to be measured. The professional will need to determine when it is most appropriate to do internal or external evaluations and how that relates to the entire evaluation system.

Now that you have studied this chapter, you should be able to:
- Describe the advantages and disadvantages of using internal versus external evaluators
- Determine when it is best to hire an outside evaluator or use an internal evaluator
- Describe the competencies needed to be a good evaluator or researcher

## 1.11 Doing the Right Thing: Political, Legal, Ethical, and Moral Issues

Research and evaluation books often include a chapter or a section on legal and ethical issues toward the end of the text. You may not have enough information about data collection at this point to fully comprehend this chapter, but we believe that the political, legal, ethical, and moral questions surrounding evaluations and research ought to be put in the forefront. Hopefully you will not have to confront many such problems if you carefully consider the design of your project. You will likely have to make some decisions about a project or study based on these issues.

Regardless of the project, the bottom line is to consider how you will treat subjects and organizations with dignity. If you are honest with yourself and the people with whom you work, you will likely have few problems. How to treat people with dignity and keep your own integrity is easy to articulate but often challenging to implement without careful consideration.

## Political Issues

Politics deal with practical wisdom related to the beliefs and biases that individuals and groups hold. Evaluation systems and projects can be political in that they may support or refute the views that people hold. The simple fact that people are involved in evaluation projects makes them political. As the saying goes, "All politics are local."

Politics encompasses personal contacts, value-laden definitions, controversial recommendations, subtle pressures to please, and advocacy for certain results or outcomes. According to Patton (1978), to be innocent of politics in evaluation is to become a pawn. Value orientations and the collection of empirical (observable) data make evaluation projects, as well as research, political whether we like it or not. Because criteria, evidence, and judgment are used, evaluation and research are political. Further, politics affect the utilization process. By their nature, evaluations are political when the information is used to "manipulate" other people, even though the manipulation may be positive.

As an evaluator or a researcher, you may want to be aware of several considerations that can make the evaluation process less politically biased.

- First, you must understand an organization or a group of people well before a project is undertaken. This suggestion means understanding the strengths and the limitations of organizations and their participants, clients, or consumers.

- Second, before claiming any conclusions about the evaluation or research, you must provide evidence. Thus, the judgments must be directly linked to the criteria and the evidence. Sometimes generalizations and recommendations are made without paying attention to the data. Evaluators and researchers, however, must be careful not to go beyond the actual findings in drawing conclusions.

- Third, the purpose of the evaluation must be made clear to all involved before it is undertaken. That purpose must also be kept clear throughout the research process.

Essentially, the only way that evaluation and research studies are not political is if they are not used and even nonuse may make a political statement. Not understanding the political ramifications may be a reason why evaluations do not get used. What a waste of time, however, if the recommendations from a project are never even considered. If we acknowledge that evaluations and research are often political, then we can use those politics to our advantage and not resist or ignore them.

# Legal Issues

In the vast majority of evaluation and research projects, you will probably encounter no legal concerns. If you were collecting information about an illegal behavior and its cessation due to a recreation program, however, you might run into legal issues. For example, if someone admits to you during an evaluation interview that they are drinking at the recreation center, are you obliged to "turn them in"? The answer is probably "no," but if this illegal activity has safety implications, you should consider your responsibility carefully. You also might be careful that you do not associate any names directly with your data in the event that a legality must be addressed. Your evaluation or research data can be subject to subpoena, so it is usually best to make sure that you cannot directly connect data through coding with people's names. Issues of coding are described further in the next section, which is about ethical issues.

# Ethical Issues

Ethics have to do with what is right and wrong and how you conform to the standards of a given profession. In this case, certain "rules" must be considered when doing evaluation and research projects. Ethics involve primarily being as open as possible about a project within the constraints of privacy. This statement means that people (participants or personnel) have the right to know that they or their programs are being researched. In addition, they also have some right to privacy and confidentiality concerning the information that they wish to divulge.

As an evaluator, you have ethical obligations to the people with whom you work. First of all, you must be careful not to promise too much from an evaluation and should be realistic about an evaluation project's value and limitations. An evaluator must assure loyalties to the profession and to the public before the program evaluated.

Privacy is a second ethical issue. Evaluators and researchers also have the responsibility to assure anonymity and confidentiality if that is needed in the evaluation. Anonymity means that no one, including the people collecting the data, will know the names of the participants in a project. Confidentiality says that the evaluator or researcher will know who participated, but no one else will. Some projects do not require this assurance, but others may require confidentiality or anonymity. For example, you may want to use only code numbers to identity respondents instead of people's names. Those codes must be kept separate from questionnaires and the codes should be destroyed once all data are tabulated, so even the evaluator will not know who provided information. The evaluator may also want to present statistics by broad enough categories that no one can figure out how a particular individual might have responded. You should realize that people answer differently sometimes depending if their name goes on the survey. Sometimes the person's name makes a difference and you will want to use it, but that person *must* give you permission to do so.

Coercion is a third ethical concern in some projects. People should never be forced into participation unless involvement is a necessary prerequisite that is understood. For example, staff evaluations are required in most organizations. A staff member knows when she or he takes a job that a performance evaluation is required, so the person should not feel any coercion. In other evaluation and research situations, however, participation in data collection should be optional. As evaluators, we need to make a project interesting and important enough that people *want* to participate.

Related to coercion is the fourth area of written consent. Written informed consent is not necessarily required in most evaluation projects, but evaluators need to be aware of its potential use. Most research studies (and many grant proposals) require Institutional Review Board (IRB) approval and the use of informed consent. Written consent is a way to assure anonymity or confidentially to individuals by having them sign a form indicating that they are aware of how data will be collected and used. For some types of extensive evaluation involving children in particular, informed consent may need to be obtained from parents or guardians as well as from children.

A fifth ethical question raised in evaluation relates to how someone may be harmed by evaluation or research. If any harm is possible as a result of a project, you should make sure that the harm does not occur. This ethical concern refers to physical or psychological harm in doing an evaluation or in *not* getting a treatment. For example, if we want to find out if some new activity in therapeutic recreation really works, we may design an experiment where half of the clients will get the treatment and half will not. In this situation, we have to ask what possible harm could be incurred to the group not getting the treatment. After considering the possible negative physical and psychological effects, the ideal experimental design may not be possible in some cases, if harm would be caused. Most recreation professionals will not be in situations where these concerns of possible harm will arise, but one must always be aware of them.

A final ethical aspect that might be considered relates to how much participants have the right to know about the results of a project. People who contribute data should be given the option to see the results. They may not be interested, but you at least owe them the opportunity. Sharing results with participants as well as other professionals is the best way to assure that good evaluation and programs are developed. You may want to offer to send the results to participants or have a meeting to explain what you learned from an evaluation project. Sometimes this procedure is referred to as "debriefing," but it need not be that formal. People, however, who have been involved in giving you information, should have access to that information. That information should also be accessible in that it is written or presented in a "nonacademic" way so that it can be easily understood. In other words, many people are not interested in statistics but would like to know, for example, a summary of the most important findings and what they might mean.

# Moral Issues

Moral issues are closely related to ethical issues. We will address them separately, however, as they relate to what the evaluator might do that could be construed as right or wrong in conducting a study. Moral concerns relate to biases and mistakes made in conducting an evaluation project that may affect the outcome of the project. For example, the choice of an inappropriate or inadequate sample may affect the outcomes of a study. If we wanted to know how effective a program was, we might need to survey dropouts as well as those individuals who completed the program. If the evaluator is aware of a concern such as this and does nothing to compensate for it, that person has acted in a morally inappropriate manner.

Cultural and procedural biases may also cause evaluation problems. The careless collection of data by using an inappropriate instrument for the respondents or poorly written questions are moral concerns. As an evaluator, you must be honest about your skills and either get help or do an evaluation project that is appropriate to your competence and skill level.

Allowing bias, prejudice, preconceived perceptions, or friendship to influence the evaluation outcomes, or being a patsy to the stakeholders, are further moral issues to avoid. The evaluator or researcher must also be careful not to be predisposed to any particular outcome. For example, you may be faced with a situation where your agency may want an "evaluation" to prove a particular position. As the evaluator, you must conduct the evaluation with impartiality.

When the evaluator actually gets to the judgment phase and writes the report, several aspects must be considered. For example, not publishing negative results is a problem as is discounting some findings or not letting all the information out. All the details of the study need to be reported, including procedures that may not have gone particularly well. The possibilities of negative results should be discussed and addressed ahead of time with the stakeholders of an evaluation to avoid moral conflicts and embarrassment arising from the evaluation situation.

Taking too long to get results out also has moral implications. Since evaluation is oriented toward problem solving and enlightened decision making, most people need that information just as soon as possible. Although not morally wrong, an evaluator has a responsibility to get an evaluation project completed in a timely manner. Data that are "old" are generally not helpful.

Morally the evaluator or researcher is bound to do the best possible evaluation. Thus, shortcuts must be avoided. Improper sampling procedures and the use of a convenience sample rather than a probability sample may not be appropriate and may affect the results of a study. Further, procedures need to be pre-tested to assure that they are appropriate.

Quality control must be instituted throughout the project. The evaluator must also be able to address the possibility of what are called, in research, Type I and Type II errors. Type I are false positive errors (e.g., the discovery that a program really makes a difference when it does not). These errors may be compared to Type II errors, which are false negative and assume that a program makes no beneficial difference when it really does. In evaluation, Type I errors are more likely, but you have to consider the possibility of both and what they mean from a moral perspective. These explanations may seem complex overall, but if you are running a program that is evaluated and a Type II error is made, you might be out of a job when, in fact, the results did not affect the program.

# A Word About Institutional Review Boards (IRB)

Most evaluation projects that will be used internally do not require an external review. However, universities require all research projects that use human or animals as subjects to go through a rigorous process to assure that ethical, moral, and legal problems are clearly addressed. The process differs somewhat from institution to institution, but the ultimate goal of all Institutional Review Boards (IRB) is to protect the subjects of research. They exist to assure that participation in studies is voluntary and that no harm comes to individuals who participate.

If you are required to get IRB approval for a research project, you should consult your university's website for full details. Follow those guidelines. In some cases, especially in the fields of recreation, the paperwork is completed and the project is exempt, which means that it poses no harm to participants. Sometimes a project might be considered expedited, which means there are particular populations (e.g., youth or people with disabilities) that must have assistance in giving informed consent to participate in a project. Other studies, particularly those that might be medical in some way, may require a full review with extensive protocols written regarding how data will be collected. The purpose of the IRB is to protect the participants in a study. If all evaluators and researchers were ethical, we would not need such reviews. However, we must continually remind ourselves of the duty that we owe to the people involved in our evaluations and research.

# Avoiding Problems in Evaluation and Research

Posavac and Carey (1992) have offered several key ideas to consider in addressing legal, ethical, political, and moral issues in evaluation.

- First, humility does not hurt. You must realize what can and can not be done, be able to admit your limitations, and adjust.

- Second, evaluation is not easy and it is not a "slam-bam" proposition. Patience is necessary and impatience may lead to disappointment and problems. Planning is essential to avoid pitfalls.

- Third, the evaluator must focus on practical questions and feasible issues. The evaluation or research questions must be well-focused and the criteria clearly defined. Get other staff to support you, and make sure they know what is going on and are able to monitor the quality of your project as well.

- Finally, adopt a self-evaluation orientation in your own work. You as the evaluator are ultimately the one who knows whether you have made the appropriate moral, political, ethical, and legal decisions. You must be the one to continually monitor yourself to do the right thing.

# From Ideas to Reality

Political, legal, ethical, and moral issues will be different in each project or study. Hopefully none of these will be a problem for you, but they are always a possibility. If you are honest with yourself, your colleagues, and the individuals associated with any aspect of the evaluation or research project, you will probably not face major dilemmas. If you do run into problems, it is best to face them squarely and try to adjust to overcome them. Covering up problems or deceiving people in any way is likely not to be the way to find success in conducting evaluations or research.

One of the safeguards that you may need to address is obtaining consent to do your evaluation or research. Many institutions like hospitals, schools, camps, and residential facilities have formal procedures that ensure the safety and privacy of their participants. In these situations, you may be required to submit your plan or proposal with the ways that you will address the issues described in this chapter. This proposal may require formal approval by the organization. Until you gain the support and approval, you will not be able to begin your evaluation project or research.


Now that you have studied this chapter, you should be able to:
- Identify possible political, legal, ethical, and moral dilemmas that you might face in doing an evaluation or research project
- Avoid possible problems by being honest with all involved in a project
- Understand the necessity of following procedures required by Institutional Review Boards

# Unit TWO—EVIDENCE

## ✱✱✱

# *Data Collection*

## 2.0  Introduction to Evidence

You should now have a fundamental background in the way that criteria are identified and/or developed and how people use systematic inquiry to plan evaluation and research projects. After the criteria are determined, the possible ways to gather evidence, usually referred to as **data collection methods**, can be examined. Once the methods are determined, you can develop procedures and strategies for obtaining that data. As mentioned previously, the possible methods, techniques, and tools used for gathering evidence for evaluation projects are the same as those used in research. The ways that these methods are applied and the use of theory determine the differences between evaluation and research.

Unit Two explores the differences between quantitative and qualitative data. In addition, we examine the options available for methods. We talk about the actual techniques and procedures used in developing questionnaires, conducting interviews, designing experiments, and doing observations. Further, we examine the specific application of some types of evaluation tools used in recreation and leisure services. Sampling, triangulation, and trustworthiness are discussed. These applications will tie to the second phase of evidence, data analysis, described in Unit Three. Evidence relates to both data collection and data analysis but considering them separately may be less overwhelming.

In this unit, we move into the technical part, known as the "how-to's" of doing evaluation and research. Methods have particular rules, guidelines, and protocols associated with them that we describe. We hope this unit provides the information needed to address most of the evaluation and research questions that you will encounter as a recreation professional. We believe these second and third units will give a sound background that can be used in conducting any research project or evaluation study.

# 2.1 Qualitative and Quantitative Data: Choices to Make

Data come in different forms. Generally we talk about qualitative and quantitative data. Before making decisions about method, you must understand the differences and the similarities between qualitative and quantitative data used for evaluation and research. In simplest terms, quantitative data are based on collecting and using numbers, numerical calculations, or statistics. Qualitative data refer to the use of words for data collection and result in patterns ascertained through the content analyses of people's words.

Some individuals are purists who believe that evaluation or research can best be done using only qualitative or quantitative data. We believe that different situations may call for particular types of data. We also believe it is possible to collect and use both qualitative and quantitative data in a single study, if the criteria are such that this combination would be helpful. In this chapter we describe both types of data and why they might be used either separately or together in collecting evaluation and research evidence.

## Worldviews and Data

The relationship between worldviews and data used in evaluation or research is important to clarify. Worldviews are also called "paradigms," and they represent broad assumptions about data and how projects ought to be undertaken. Data are the evidence. Methods are the tools for data collection.

Because people see the world from different worldviews or paradigms, various methods of inquiry are typically used. Patton (1980a) described how paradigms are linked to methods such that allegiance to a paradigm is usually the major, but not the only reason, for making decisions about methods. For example, if the purpose of an evaluation is more closely related to gathering facts than gaining a broad understanding, you probably would favor methods that are linked to a quantitative data. Further, qualitative and quantitative data are ideal-types and real-world choices usually vary. The use of methods will typify more closely the attributes of one of the paradigms. Methods will depend on measurement options, including kinds of data, evaluation design opportunities, personal involvement, and analysis possibilities such as inductive analysis (i.e., moving from specific to general—using data to understand theory) versus deductive analysis (i.e., moving from general to specific—using theory to understand data).

Most models of evaluation imply a *positivist* worldview that purports facts and truth can be found and articulated. This view is most often associated with the traditional scientific method and generally results in quantitative data. For example, the Goal-Attainment Model is usually closely related to the positivist paradigm. Positivist approaches to data usually result in the use of statistics to make decisions or to confirm theory. Because evaluation requires that judgments be made, however, all quantitative data are always going to call for a certain amount of subjective interpretation.

A second paradigm, the *interpretive* paradigm, suggests that not one answer, but many multiple perspectives and truths may exist within any evaluation project or research study. The Goal-Free Model is often used in this case to collect qualitative data to gain a broad understanding of a problem or question. An interpretive approach to an evaluation project assumes that the realities of a program are multiple, and that different perceptions, descriptions, and interpretations can be found in the same program when data are collected. For example, programs sometimes have outcomes broader than initially intended. In an evaluation of an exercise program for older adults, the gains made in cardiovascular fitness might be secondary compared to the positive social experience that older adults experienced as a result of an organized walking program.

The reality, especially in evaluation projects, is that a *post-positivist* perspective is more likely to be used than a pure interpretive paradigm. This post-positivist approach allows for creativity in data collection and the possibilities of broadening understanding of something, yet it also stays closer to the traditional scientific method with a relatively narrow focus on a topic of interest. Time is often limited, and we do not have the luxury to allow the answers to problems to evolve slowly. We need specific information, which means we must narrow a topic. However, we also recognize that many tools exist for addressing that topic. A post-positivist approach enables us to focus on a problem while also being open to obtaining information beyond specific criteria that we had in mind.

# Evaluation Data Types

We do not wish to debate whether one paradigm or one type of data, qualitative or quantitative, is better than another. An approach may be better given a particular evaluative situation and the criteria that are to be examined, but you must make that determination. Much has been written about qualitative and quantitative data in the past several years, but a discussion of which one is better is not useful, as each has its place in research and evaluation projects. How to use the data to make the best decisions or conclusions is the most important question.

We want to emphasize that no such thing as a qualitative or quantitative *method* exists. You can do an interview and collect either type of data, quantitative data or qualitative data, depending upon the design of the interview and the types of questions asked. The same is true of observations and even questionnaires. The nature of the data provides the framework for whether a project uses qualitative or quantitative approaches, not the methods that are used.

Either of the two types of data may be collected depending on the questions asked and how data are collected. The simplest distinction between the two types of data is to suggest that quantitative data use numbers or easily convert words to numbers such as 1="yes" and 2="no." Qualitative data use words almost exclusively. The meanings of these differences, however, are more complicated than this simple explanation implies.

Qualitative data invite individuals to describe experiences in their own words. Open-ended questions that allow for elaboration on the part of the respondent result in qualitative data. These data are usually highly useful in providing in-depth understanding about issues that may be impossible to acquire through quantitative procedures related to scales or yes/no questions. Ellis and Williams (1987) suggested that questions about outcomes and change across time, the context within which change occurs, and the nature of the causes or conditions associated with outcomes are often asked in evaluation projects. Questions about the context in which change occurs, as well as the use of Goal-Free Models of evaluation and research make qualitative data useful. Rather than provide a list of pre-established responses to questions about a particular activity or program, the evaluator or researcher using qualitative data will solicit responses in the actual words of the participants.

Depending upon the criteria measured, either or both quantitative and qualitative data may be useful in measuring any of the five Ps. You will need to determine how best to collect the data to assist in decision making.

# Describing Differences in Data

A number of contrasts can be made between projects that rely on collecting quantitative or qualitative data. Table 2.1(1) gives an example of some of those differences.

Quantitative data usually follow standard procedures of rigor related to the instruments used and to statistical data analysis. Quantitative data

*Table 2.1(1)* Making Choices about Quantitative and Qualitative Data (adapted from Henderson, 1991)

| Quantitative | Qualitative |
|---|---|
| Rigor in Techniques | Relevance of Techniques |
| Reductionist Stance | Expansionist |
| Verification Purpose | Discovery |
| Paper/Physical Instrument | Inquirer as Instrument |
| Usually Systems or Goal-Attainment | Goal-Free Model |
| Experimental | Natural Setting |
| Stable Treatment of Data | Variable Data Treatment |
| Variables as Analytic Unit | Patterns as Analysis |
| Fixed Methods | Dynamic Methods |
| Product-Oriented | Process-Oriented |
| Reliability Based | Validity-Based |
| Uniformity | Diversity |
| Deductive | Inductive |
| Results in Facts | Results in Understanding |
| Preordinate Designs | Emerging Designs |

are deductive in that particular evaluation questions or established theories serve as the start, and data are reduced to measure those questions. Quantitative data are often associated with Goal-Attainment, Logic, or Systems Models, with verification as the purpose. The instruments used for data collection in quantitative are paper and pencil tests or surveys. Preordinate designs are used. Preordinate refers to having a specific plan laid out ahead of time concerning the data to be collected and sticking to that plan. Once the data collection begins, nothing changes with the preordinate design. The treatment of quantitative data is stable with specific statistical procedures. Variables or analytic units are used in analyzing quantitative data. Statistics are used to determine averages and relationships among variables. Quantitative data are generally highly controlled, as in experimental designs. Fixed procedures and specific rules are common in collecting quantitative data.

Qualitative data, on the other hand, are concerned with the relevance to the context or the situation. Qualitative data are generally part of a Goal-Free Model and are concerned with discovery. Qualitative data are expansionist in that they try to capture all the causes or reasons for something. The logic of generalization for qualitative data is to examine individual cases to determine a number of conclusions that fit the data. The inquirer (i.e., evaluator or researcher) is the instrument in the qualitative data collection, as she or he interprets the meaning of the words and tries to find patterns. Data collection and design are likely to emerge together as data are uncovered in projects using qualitative data. In an emerging design, the evaluator may follow ideas that flow from the data such that the questions and answers about a project occur simultaneously. Dynamic and evolving procedures are used to collect these data.

In general, quantitative data usually measure the most common results of an intervention, a program, or of testing a theory, whereas qualitative data are used to describe what happened or how people perceived their experiences. In other words, quantitative data tend to be more focused on the products of an evaluation whereas qualitative data more often reflect the process. Reliability (i.e., the data's consistency) is paramount in quantitative data, and validity (i.e., the data's relevancy) is central for qualitative data. Finally, quantitative data are quantifiable and concerned with facts whereas qualitative data provide a means for understanding phenomena within their context.

# Choosing Qualitative and/or Quantitative Data

As indicated previously, one approach to data collection is not superior to another. The dominance of quantitative data, however, sometimes has limited the evaluation and research questions asked and the way that criteria are applied to projects and within organizations.

Different situations and criteria may require different types of methods. Table 2.1(2) provides a checklist that may be useful in determining what type of data to collect. If, for example, we want to know how many people with and without disabilities attended a program, counting them generates quantitative data and statistical procedures may be appropriate. If we want to understand whether the attitudes of people without disabilities have changed due to a recreation program offered, and what the interaction is between people with and without disabilities, then some form of qualitative data, such as interviews or observations, might better allow the evaluator to obtain that information.

Qualitative data, however, are not always seen by some stakeholders as useful compared to quantitative statistics. For example, qualitative data are sometimes considered too subjective. Objectivity is traditionally thought to be the essence of the scientific method. Some people think that to be subjective means to be biased, unreliable, and nonrational. Subjectivity implies opinion rather than fact, intuition rather than logic, impression rather than confirmation. The scientific community tries to control subjectivity, particularly with an emphasis on reliability. Subjectivity,

*Table 2.1(2)* Checklist for Considering Qualitative or Quantitative Data (adapted from Patton, 1980a)

|  | YES | NO |
|---|---|---|
| • Is the evaluator interested in individualized outcomes? | ☐ | ☐ |
| • Is the evaluator interested in examining the process of evaluation and the context in which it occurs? | ☐ | ☐ |
| • Is detailed in-depth information needed in order to understand the phenomenon being evaluated? | ☐ | ☐ |
| • Is the focus on quality and the meaning of the experiences being studied? | ☐ | ☐ |
| • Does the evaluator desire to get close to the participants/staff and immersed in their experiences? | ☐ | ☐ |
| • Do no measuring devices exist that will provide reliable and valid data for the project? | ☐ | ☐ |
| • Is the evaluation question likely to change depending upon how the data emerge? | ☐ | ☐ |
| • Is it possible that the answer to the evaluation question may yield unexpected results? | ☐ | ☐ |
| • Does the evaluator wish to get personally involved in the evaluation? | ☐ | ☐ |
| • Does the evaluator have a philosophical and methodological bias toward goal-free and qualitative data? | ☐ | ☐ |

If the answer is YES to any of these questions, the evaluator ought to at least consider the collection of qualitative data as a possible way to approach the evaluation or research question being addressed.

however, may never be completely possible and incorporating qualitative data enables evaluators to acknowledge how opinion, intuition, and impression cannot be divorced from understanding just how the world works.

This dichotomy between qualitative and quantitative data, however, is false. Quantitative data can be subjective and qualitative data can be objective. Subjectivity also refers to getting close to and involved with the data. It allows researchers to take into account their own position, insights, and behavior. Subjectivity involves applying critical intelligence to important problems.

The evaluator or researcher who knows the advantages and disadvantages of qualitative and quantitative data is best equipped to do projects. Making decisions about what data to collect and how to collect it is not easy. You must look at the criteria and determine which type of data or combination is most appropriate.

# Using Qualitative and Quantitative Data Together

Qualitative and quantitative data can be used together and may complement each other. Later in this unit we address triangulation and the use of more than one method or data set. Purists say you cannot mix interpretive and positivist approaches, but post-positivism allows for many ways to collect and analyze data, as long as it is systematic. For some projects, mixing data and mixing methods may be necessary. The pursuit of good evaluation or research should transcend personal preferences for numbers or words. Further, recognize that quantitative data may become qualitative when explanations are needed for unexpected results. Qualitative data can become more quantitative as evaluation criteria become more focused and specific within a particular project.

# From Ideas to Reality

Choosing the type of data that you will use will depend on a combination of determining the criteria that need to be measured and your personal preference and skills. One type of data is no better than the other if the data provide the answers to your evaluation or research questions. A combination of the two may also be appropriate in some situations. For example, suppose you wanted to know what visitors do when they come to a park. You could design a quantitative questionnaire and let them respond. You could personally interview people at the park to see what they thought was important. You could also do observations or quantitative checklists (e.g., situate evaluators at different places in the park and record what people do). You will need to decide what type of data will be most useful to you.

Decisions about data will need to be carefully considered as a project is planned. Therefore, you need to know as much as possible about the options so that you can make enlightened decisions regarding method choices and the type of data you will collect.

Now that you've studied this chapter, you should be able to:
- Describe the differences between qualitative and quantitative data
- Describe general differences between the interpretive, positivist, and post-positivist paradigms
- Explain the link between paradigm, methods, and data type

- State why one type of data might be preferable to another, given a particular project
- Make a decision, given evaluation criteria and a particular situation, about which type of data or combination of data is best to collect

## 2.2 Choosing Designs and Methods: The Big Picture

If we were to classify the types of research designs used in recreation, we might talk about two broad categories: experimental and descriptive designs. Within those two designs we could construct a continuum, as was done in Chapter 1.1, that ranges from the most sophisticated double-blind experiment on one end to an intuitive judgment on the other end, with quasi-experimental, empirical descriptive studies, and expert judgments in the middle. Within descriptive studies, possibilities exist for collecting quantitative or qualitative data. Experimental designs are concerned almost exclusively with quantitative data.

Some texts refer to experimental and nonexperimental as the two major categories of evaluation or research design. This dichotomy puts more focus on the value of "experimental" by referring to its opposite as "non." Thus, we will refer to experimental and descriptive/evocative designs to highlight the value of both. In this text, we use the idea of descriptive/evocative designs to try to encompass the breadth of possible explanations that include all empirically focused, nonexperimental projects conducted in real-world situations. True experiments have an associated control group that descriptive/evocative projects seldom have.

Experimental designs are empirical investigative techniques employed to assure control so that the evaluator or researcher can feel confident that the results of the experiment conducted represent a true intervention. Experimental studies or projects focus on a randomized sample and a controlled setting and are probably the classic example of evaluation or research. However, these designs are not commonly used in recreation services. Within the category of experimental designs falls true randomized experiments and quasi-experiments, which are discussed in more detail in the chapter on experimental methods.

True experimental designs require that an independent variable (e.g., a program or an intervention) be controlled and manipulated. When we refer to quasi-experimental methods we mean research designs that are "seemingly" experimental but do not have all the qualities of true experimental designs and that are more closely related to descriptive than experimental approaches. Many important variables like skill development, aptitudes, integrity, and characteristics of recreation leaders, however, cannot be controlled and manipulated within experimental designs. Further in the evaluation of personnel, places, and policies, true experimental designs are frequently impossible to apply, so we use quasi-experimental and descriptive approaches.

As suggested, descriptive/evocative designs are more commonly used in recreation, park, leisure, sport, and tourism organizations. They do not require matching or comparison, but are concerned with gathering empirical data. Empirical data are data that you can observe or see. Empirical data may be qualitative or quantitative and are logical and practical.

The purpose of descriptive/evocative designs is to determine existing conditions. These studies might include quasi-experimental designs, group surveys, needs assessments, and interpretive explanatory projects. The major methods that are employed are surveys, observations, and unobtrusive measures. These designs can be further divided to include specific techniques such as questionnaires and interviews (including focus groups), checklists, field observations, document analysis, and nonresearcher contact tools.

An evaluator or researcher will need to determine how to make choices based on the two broad categories of experiments and descriptive/evocative designs. You will further need to choose specific methods and techniques to use. Each of the major evaluation methods will be discussed in more detail later in this Unit, but Table 2.2 provides a comparison of the possible methods that might be chosen. In the use of all methods, the relationships between the criteria, data, and judgment will be considered together in making a method selection. Ethical considerations also must be taken into account with each method that is chosen.

# From Ideas to Reality

Having design options presents both opportunities as well as challenges for an evaluator or researcher. No one, best way exists to do any project, and the creativity of the individual as well as the context of the evaluation or research question must be considered in developing projects. On the other hand, the options can also seem a bit daunting. As you get more experience and practice in doing evaluation and research projects, the options will make more sense and the best choices will become easier to make. Keep in mind that usually more than one way exists to do a project and you will need to choose the best design based upon the project and the resources available to you.

**Table 2.2** *The Advantages and Disadvantages of Selected Designs and Methods*

| | | Advantages | Disadvantages |
|---|---|---|---|
| **Experimental Designs—Method** | True Experiments | • Assures control<br>• Randomized sample<br>• Pretest used<br>• Represents what happened<br>• Generalizable | • Manipulation required<br>• Lab setting sometimes best<br>• Control may be difficult<br>• Sample sometimes difficult<br>• People feel like guinea pigs |
| | Quasi-Experiments | • Some qualities of experiments<br>• Control some outside variables<br>• May be appropriate to situation | • Nonrandomized<br>• Threats to validity |
| **Descriptive/Evocative Designs—Method** | Surveys | • Most commonly used<br>• Generally inexpensive and easy<br>• May allow face-to-face encounter<br>• Determine existing conditions<br>• Discovery of quan/qual relationships<br>• Useful for validity checks, triangulation<br>• Uses methods protocols and statistics<br>• Perspectives from participant | • May be obtrusive and reactive<br>• Dependent on instrument quality<br>• Misinterpretation possible<br>• Requires skill and training<br>• Requires respondent cooperation<br>• Evaluator effects<br>• Highly dependent on evaluator's abilities |
| | Observations | • Face-to-face encounter or not<br>• Large amounts of data obtained quickly<br>• Low/high interaction with respondents<br>• Can allow for *a priori*/emerging designs/data<br>• Wide range of data possible<br>• Many possibilities for sample<br>• Discovery of possible relationships<br>• Useful in triangulation<br>• Data on nonverbal, unconscious, and communication behaviors | • Missed data such as attitudes<br>• Misinterpretation possible<br>• Lack of respondent's words<br>• Success may depend on data collector<br>• Bias by evaluator possible<br>• Possible observer effects on those observed |
| | Unobtrusive | • Data often easy to analyze<br>• Wide range of types of data<br>• Usually efficient to administer<br>• Often easily quantifiable<br>• Good for nonverbal behavior<br>• Measuring devices may exist<br>• Provides for flexibility<br>• Wide range of types of data<br>• Good for documenting major events<br>• Often uses natural setting | • Possible misinterpretation<br>• May be expensive<br>• Depends on evaluation model<br>• Dependent on evaluator's investigative ability<br>• Minimal interaction |

Now that you have studied this chapter, you should be able to:
- Describe what constitutes an experimental design and a descriptive/evocative design
- Specify the methods most often associated with each design
- List some of the advantages and disadvantages of each of the methods that might be used to collect data

# 2.3 Trustworthiness:
# The Sine Qua Non of Data Collection

A great evaluation or research project idea can have wonderful criteria and research questions, but if the tools you use aren't appropriate, your project may be doomed to failure. Trustworthiness is the indispensable and essential action, or the sine qua non, necessary for data collection and then making enlightened decisions. You should always be concerned that data collected for any project are trustworthy, or of high quality. Evaluators and researchers want to make sure that measurement instruments possess characteristics of reliability and validity. Thus, trustworthiness is a foundational aspect of data collection. If a data collection instrument fails to do what it is supposed to do, everything else fails in an evaluation or research project.

Error can exist in any measurement strategy. To be completely reliable or valid would mean no sources of error, a feat that is next to impossible. The goal in data collection is to minimize the errors as much as possible. We will examine three areas of trustworthiness as they relate to aspects of data collection for any type of design: reliability, validity, and usability. Reliability is concerned with the replicatability, consistency, and dependability of scientific findings. Validity addresses relevance and the meaningfulness of data and addresses the question of "does the instrument do what it should" related to credibility and transferability. Usability refers to collecting data efficiently and effectively as well as finding application for the results.

# Reliability

Reliability is also known as dependability. Reliability relates to whether a measure consistently conveys the same meaning to readers. It addresses the degree of stability or consistency that a scale yields. A test is reliable to the extent that virtually the same scores from an individual occur in retesting. In other words, a reliable measure of behavior will perform in the future the way it did in the past.

In collecting qualitative data, we refer to dependability as meaning something similar to reliability. To be dependable, the evaluator must keep a record of how data were collected. This process is sometimes referred to as an audit trail. To audit means to examine. Reliability is strengthened when similar results would occur if the same process or procedure were followed. Dependability "depends" on documenting exactly how data were collected and how conclusions were drawn. This audit process will become clearer when in-depth interviews and field observations are discussed later in this unit.

For some quantitative instruments, a reliability correlation or coefficient is given as a statistic that tells just how likely the instrument is to measure consistently. Correlation refers to the similarity between two sets of scores for one person. In other words, when the score for one test remains in the same relative position on the re-test, the reliability will be high. Test-retest is one way to measure the stability with a comparison between the two test administrations.

Statistical reliability coefficients range from 0 to 1.00, with the scores closest to 1.00 being the best because they indicate the test has less error variance. The acceptable level depends on the nature of the evaluation done. Most instruments should have reliability coefficients higher than 0.60. The higher the reliability, the more consistently the instrument measures what it is supposed to measure. Reliability coefficients may be obtained by measuring consistency through correlation statistics, by giving alternative forms (i.e., rearranging the item order) of the same instrument, or by test-retest procedures.

Inter-rater reliability is another factor that you should address if more than one person is making observations. Inter-rater reliability is a measure of the consistency from rater to rater rather than from time to time. Comparing the ratings generated by two or more observers who have observed the same event or behavior produces the reliability coefficient. The two are compared by correlation. High correlations indicate a high amount of agreement. Observer training and a clear delineation of the behaviors rated can improve this inter-rater reliability. The higher the correlation is (i.e., generally over 0.80), the more dependable the observations. With a low inter-rater reliability, too much error may be associated with an observation.

Without reliability or dependability, a measurement instrument's usefulness is in doubt. As we discuss questionnaire development in the next chapter, you will note ways that reliability can be improved. For example, items that do not communicate effectively should be eliminated. Items on a questionnaire should be clear, unambiguous, and appropriate in length and difficulty. To improve reliability, one can lengthen the survey form although extreme lengthening may produce a fatigue or boredom effect. Further, suppose we wanted to know what was good about a particular recreation program. A questionnaire with only one item would be highly unreliable. A participant might have liked a lot of aspects of a program but not have liked the one aspect that you asked about in the questionnaire. A one-item test is subject to a number of chance factors and therefore is not usually reliable. The bottom line is that to improve reliability, an evaluator has to try to reduce as much error as possible and try to assure that an individual would respond the same way to the same questions time after time.

# Validity

Validity concerns whether or not the instrument measures the intended criteria or what it is supposed to measure. Other synonyms for validity might be accuracy, authenticity, genuineness, and soundness. In other words, the respondent must understand the question the way that the evaluator asked it and must provide the information in a manner that is consistent with the criteria or purpose the evaluator established. Validity refers to the results of the measurement, not the test or questionnaire itself. An instrument is valid only if it is appropriate for the group and the evaluation criteria measured.

Reliability is important for validity to occur. Data, however, can be reliable without being valid. People can be consistent in their responses but an instrument can be measuring the wrong information. Therefore, if an instrument is not valid, it doesn't make any difference how reliable it is. If we wanted to know the changes in attitude about art that result from a crafts program, but ask participants their reactions to the instructor's teaching techniques, we may get reliable responses but the measurement is not valid for the issues we are analyzing. Figure 2.3(1) shows how validity and reliability might be pictured.

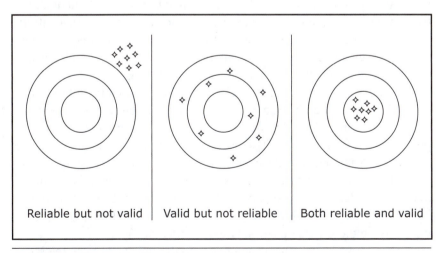

| Reliable but not valid | Valid but not reliable | Both reliable and valid |

*Figure 2.3(1) Illustration of Reliability and Validity*

Several types of validity are frequently mentioned in evaluation research. Validity may refer broadly to internal and external validity depending upon how it is applied. Internal validity is how well the instrument measures what it is supposed to measure for a particular study or project. It also shows whether a difference exists in any given comparisons. Lincoln and Guba (1985) referred to credibility in qualitative approach as the equivalent of internal validity. One type of internal validity is known as concurrent or criterion-related validity, which simply asks whether the scores on a particular instrument correlate with scores on another existing test.

The most important type of internal validity for evaluation is content validity. Content validity reflects the contents or the theoretical or practical aspects that you wish to measure in a project. Subjective judgment, sometimes called face validity, is often used to determine whether the instrument appears to measure the content intended. The evaluator must define the criteria or the research questions and then collect content to establish relevance. Further, levels of evidence (i.e., participation, reactions, learning, or actions) play heavily into content validity. For example, you may think you are measuring how attitudes change toward a particular activity when you are really measuring satisfaction with the process. Content validity requires a careful analysis of what you want to measure and how the items you select and the data you collect actually contribute to that measurement. You must make sure the instrument you select or develop and the data collected do, in fact, measure the criteria you have identified.

External validity refers to how well the measures can be generalized to other situations. External validity is also called transferability in qualitative data collection. Predictive validity is associated with external validity and is used to examine the way an instrument can predict some behavior. A common example of predictive validity is the fact that the high performance on SAT tests usually predicts success in college.

Validity must be a concern early in the use or development of any evaluation or research instrument. As an evaluator you will be responsible for content validity, but frequently others can be involved in the process to confirm that validity exists. For example, expert panels may be used to confirm content or face validity. Experts are asked to judge the instrument's ability to measure the desired content. Or it might be desirable to involve colleagues or a supervisor to examine the instrument. Those individuals can be asked if what you say you are evaluating is really coming across in the way the instrument is constructed.

The more adequate the planning time in designing a project involving surveys, the more likely that reliable and valid measures can be used. To improve reliability or validity, don't rush into developing an instrument. Take time to make the instrument clear and write the explanation of it at an appropriate reading level for those respondents who will be using it. Items need to relate to constructs, enough items to measure the constructs must be presented, and no identifiable pattern or response should be evident. Further, the evaluator needs to keep in mind that you can't necessarily use the same instrument for every evaluation situation. Some instruments work better with some groups than do others. The evaluator or researcher must develop the reliability and validity of an instrument in a particular setting for the specific audience that is using the instrument.

In collecting qualitative data, credibility can be improved by prolonged engagement in interviews or observations, persistent observation, and/or by using more than one data source or method. One can also pay attention to negative cases (i.e., cases that are not like the others) as well as use member checks (i.e., go back and talk to people) to see if the way you interpreted the interview data or observation is the way the participants intended. Transferability can be enhanced by using examples from the data and by using "thick description." Qualitative evaluators use "thick description" to mean using the direct quotes and words of respondents about what happened or how they felt in a given situation. Those words should reflect the content you are trying to measure.

## Usability

Usability relates closely to reliability and validity but has particular significance for evaluation and research. If the instrument cannot be effectively administered and if the data collected are not analyzed and applied, the project is a waste of time. For example, although an instrument might be highly reliable and valid, if data collection cannot be efficiently managed, the measurement tool may be of little use to an evaluator or a researcher.

Several issues must be considered in assessing the usability and quality of data. The administration of an instrument can affect reliability and validity. An instrument should be easy to administer whether as a self-administered test or as one given by a tester. The time required should be reasonable for the situation and for the population being studied. The instrument should be easy to score and should be able to be interpreted. Directions should be consistent. Providing a good atmosphere for testing is necessary. Dunn (1987) used the example of not giving program satisfaction surveys in a pool where people don't have a dry place to write. You need to always ask yourself if the evaluation procedure is appropriate for the setting and be aware of the subject's situation and attitudes when administering any test or questionnaire. Further, the costs should not exceed the potential benefits that might come from using a selected measurement instrument.

Usability also relates to qualitative data, but it is assumed that these data would not be collected unless they were usable in some manner. Competent evaluators who have training in qualitative methods are needed. One becomes best at collecting qualitative data by practice. Further, to ensure that data are usable, the qualitative evaluator or researcher must devote adequate time to the data collection and analysis. As one looks for a range of responses and attempts to explain the variance between individuals or situations, a time commitment is necessary. Finally, triangulation may make an evaluation project more useful if data come from more than one method or source.

Table 2.3(2) provides a summary of some suggested ways to improve the trustworthiness of your evaluation and research projects. After reading subsequent chapters, you may want to review this table again.

Trustworthiness is essential to the collection of data. Data are only as good as the means used to collect them. To have a trustworthy project, the evaluator or researcher attempts to eliminate error as much as possible. This error may be from respondents, the investigator, or the

**Table 2.3(2)** *How to Improve Trustworthiness of Data Collected*

|  | Quantitative | Qualitative |
|---|---|---|
| Reliability | • Well-written items<br>• Lengthen the test<br>• Pilot-test/planning<br>• Clear directions<br>• Appropriate to group | • Use audit trail |
| Validity | • Subjective evaluation<br>• Predictive<br>• Choose appropriate model<br>• Pilot-test/planning and level of evidence<br>• Clear directions | • Prolonged engagement<br>• Use range of cases<br>• Use examples<br>• Thick description<br>• Effect of evaluator described |
| Usability | • Easily administered<br>• Reasonable time required<br>• Easy to score/interpret<br>• Appropriate cost<br>• Explain link between criteria and data collected | • Competent evaluator<br>• Time commitment<br>• Triangulation<br>• Explain all variance |

sampling procedures. For example, a respondent may feel the guinea pig effect whereby she or he is aware of being tested. That person may also demonstrate other kinds of behavior, such as hostility or indifference, that would also affect the results of some measurement instruments. Further, sometimes participants are aware of the social desirability associated with some instrument and will respond the way they think society would. Some of these errors are difficult to avoid, but you must be aware that they can exist and try to minimize them if the evaluation project is to be useful. If the data are not reliable and valid, they will have little benefit for any project.

# From Ideas to Reality

Unless the evaluator or researcher can "count on" the data and the design, a project may not be helpful. Reliability, validity, and usability are the keys to conducting good evaluations. In this chapter we presented ways to make projects trustworthy. You will need to refer to these suggestions continuously while conducting any study or project to make sure that you are on the right track. No magic formulas exist but the strategies suggested together will help to assure that you are doing the most trustworthy undertaking possible.

Now that you have studied this chapter, you should be able to:

- Describe the factors considered in determining whether an instrument used in an evaluation project or research study is reliable and valid
- Design or select an instrument that has high reliability and validity
- Explain how the selection of criteria is related to validity
- Assess evaluation or research instruments to ascertain that they are reliable, valid, and usable

# 2.4 What are the Chances? Choosing a Sample

No matter how great the criteria or how reliable the instrument, an appropriate sample must be selected. Sampling procedures vary depending on the methods used and the resources that are available. Sometimes an evaluator may not select a sample, but use the entire population. For example, if we wanted to find out the reactions about a pottery class that had 10 enrollees, we would likely survey the entire population of 10 people in that class. We would not need to choose a sample. Similarly, if we were evaluating staff performance, we would evaluate all staff and not just a select few. Other times, however, evaluators and researchers will choose a smaller group that represents a larger population.

A population refers to all the people who might comprise a particular group. For example, when talking about the population of a city we refer to all the people that reside there. When we talk about the population of intramural sports participants we are referring to all who played during a given period of time. Many times, however, we do not have the ability and the resources to have all individuals, the entire population, participate in an evaluation project, so we have to select the sample carefully to reflect the population. A sample should represent the population so results can be generalized to the total population.

Sampling can be divided into three categories: *probability, nonprobability*, and *theoretical sampling*. Probability sampling means that everyone within a population has the same potential of being selected as part of a sample. Nonprobability samples are samples where not everyone has an equal chance and the likelihood of getting selected from a population is unknown. Theoretical sampling is used primarily with qualitative data and refers to sampling until the evaluator reaches a point of data saturation. Saturation is reached when no new data that contribute to the emerging themes are evident. Each of these categories will be discussed in greater detail in this chapter.

## Keys to Appropriate Sampling

Several key points about sampling require emphasis. First, do not confuse size of sample with representativeness. The sample size required for a survey will depend on the reliability needed, which in turn depends on how the results will be used. A large (e.g., several thousand people) sample is not necessarily better than several hundred and often does not make economical sense. On the other hand, too few responses is also problematic if the response rate is low. No simple rule for sample size can be applied to data collection. A moderate sample size is sufficient for most needs. For example, national polls usually use samples of 1,500, which is appropriate for a representative sample of a country such as the U.S. with over 350 million people. A properly selected sample of only 1,500 individuals can reflect various characteristics of the total population with a small margin of error.

Second, you can select the sample size in various ways. Table 2.4(1) shows an example of the sample size needed for various populations. For example, if you had 500 campers, you would need to randomly select a sample size of at least 217 people. You can also calculate the approximate sample size by using statistical procedures, but we will not get into that

**Table 2.4(1)** *Table for Determining Sample Size (adapted from Krejcie & Morgan, 1970)*

| Population | Sample | Population | Sample | Population | Sample |
|---|---|---|---|---|---|
| 10 | 10 | 220 | 140 | 1200 | 291 |
| 15 | 14 | 230 | 144 | 1300 | 297 |
| 20 | 19 | 240 | 148 | 1400 | 302 |
| 25 | 24 | 250 | 152 | 1500 | 306 |
| 30 | 28 | 260 | 155 | 1600 | 310 |
| 35 | 32 | 270 | 159 | 1700 | 313 |
| 40 | 36 | 280 | 162 | 1800 | 317 |
| 45 | 40 | 290 | 165 | 1900 | 320 |
| 50 | 44 | 300 | 169 | 2000 | 322 |
| 55 | 48 | 320 | 175 | 2200 | 327 |
| 60 | 52 | 340 | 181 | 2400 | 331 |
| 65 | 56 | 360 | 186 | 2600 | 335 |
| 70 | 59 | 380 | 191 | 2800 | 338 |
| 75 | 63 | 400 | 196 | 3000 | 341 |
| 80 | 66 | 420 | 201 | 3500 | 346 |
| 85 | 70 | 440 | 205 | 4000 | 351 |
| 90 | 73 | 460 | 210 | 4500 | 354 |
| 95 | 76 | 480 | 214 | 5000 | 357 |
| 100 | 80 | 500 | 217 | 6000 | 361 |
| 110 | 86 | 550 | 226 | 7000 | 364 |
| 120 | 92 | 600 | 234 | 8000 | 367 |
| 130 | 97 | 650 | 242 | 9000 | 368 |
| 140 | 103 | 700 | 248 | 10000 | 370 |
| 150 | 108 | 750 | 254 | 15000 | 375 |
| 160 | 113 | 800 | 260 | 20000 | 377 |
| 170 | 118 | 850 | 265 | 30000 | 379 |
| 180 | 123 | 900 | 269 | 40000 | 380 |
| 190 | 127 | 950 | 274 | 50000 | 381 |
| 200 | 132 | 1000 | 278 | 75000 | 382 |
| 210 | 136 | 1100 | 285 | 100000 | 384 |

detail in this text. (For more information, see a statistics text). Generally the statistical dividing line between moderate and small samples is 30 people. Further, data are usually considered "fragile" if you get less than 60–70% of a sample to respond.

Third, methods of sampling are grounded in statistical theory and theories of probability. Regardless of whether you are doing an evaluation or a research project, the sampling theory is the same. The sample used depends on the objective and scope of the method used, including the overall budget, the method of data collection, the subject matter, and the characteristics of the respondents needed.

Fourth, the relevant population to be sampled must be clearly identified. From there, a sample can be selected based on the method used and the data desired. In other words, you must decide whether you will sample participants, parents, staff members, or board members, depending upon the program that you wish to evaluate. The number for your sample should be dependent on the number in the population.

Fifth, in sampling we seek to survey as few people as necessary to get an accurate probability representation. Crompton (1985) used the example of having a barrel with 100,000 red and white marbles from which you take 400. According to probability, the proportion of red and white marbles would be the same whether you took 400 from a barrel or took 10,000.

## Sampling Errors

Sources of errors related to sampling and nonsampling must be addressed. Sampling error is the difference between the characteristics of a sample and the characteristics of the population from which the sample was selected (Babbie, 2006). The larger the difference, the larger the error. If you have a sampling error of + or -4 points it means that if 50% of the sample say they did something, then the true percentage, accounting for error, would be somewhere between 46% and 54%. The smaller the error range, the more accurate the survey. We can allow error in sampling for evaluation and research projects, but we must be careful about how much we allow. If you want to look at subgroups within a sample, you will have to draw a larger sample.

Good survey practice includes calculating sampling errors, when possible, so that you know the percentage points above or below an item. The formula for the calculation of the standard error can be found in statistics books. If in doing the calculations, for example, we found that 60% of the participants were satisfied with a program and 40% were not and we had a total of 30 participants, the standard error would be 0.089 or, rounded off, 9%. Thus, we would conclude that the true approval rate lies somewhere between 51% and 69%. Also keep in mind that the standard error is a function of sample size. As the sample size increases, the standard error decreases. In the sample above, if we had 60 participants, the standard error would be 6% so the actual approval rate would be somewhere between 54% and 66%. Therefore, the standard of error can be decreased with larger samples.

A second type of error is called nonsampling error. Nonsampling errors have no simple and direct method of estimating. Nonsampling errors concern the biases that may exist due to who answers a survey or who responds compared to those people who did not. Errors also may be created by biases. These biases come from sampling operations, noninterviews, participants not understanding the ideas being measured, lack of knowledge by the respondents, concealment of the truth, loaded questions, processing errors, and interviewer errors. For example, according to Rossman (1982), a nonsampling error might occur in giving out evaluations during the latter part of a program, when dropouts and absentees would not get included. The dropouts are probably dissatisfied, but you don't know that, so nonsampling error could be a significant problem. Therefore, to avoid nonsampling error, you need to try to sample all registered people in this case, not just those in attendance. Only then can you be sure that high satisfaction was not the result of poor sampling because the dissatisfied people left an activity. The data collector controls as much nonsampling error as possible by designing good projects and using appropriate methods and measures.

## Sampling Theory

Probability sampling theory suggests that all units must have a known chance of being included in the sample, and sample design must be explained in sufficient detail to permit calculation of sampling errors. When these guidelines are followed, you can draw inferences from the sample to the appropriate population. The types of samples range from simple random samples to highly complex sampling procedures. Quantitative data collection usually involves probability or nonprobability samples, which will be discussed first. Qualitative data collectors are more likely to use theoretical sampling. Table 2.4(2) gives a summary of the types of sampling that an evaluator or researcher might choose.

*Table 2.4(2)  Sampling Types that May Be Used*

---

**Probability:**
Simple Random Sampling
Stratified Random Sampling
Systematic Sampling
Cluster Sampling

**Nonprobability:**
Purposive Sampling
Convenience Sampling
Quota Sampling
Expert Sampling
Snowball

**Theoretical**

---

## Probability Sampling

Every unit or person who makes up a population has a chance of being selected in probability sampling. *Random sampling* is the most common type of probability sampling and is superior to nonprobability sampling. Compared to haphazard or convenience samples (nonprobability), a simple random sample is almost always the best *if* you know the entire population. Sometimes you do not have access to an entire population, so you cannot do random sampling. For example, once we wanted to do a study about the leisure constraints of women with disabilities. However, we did not have a list of all the women in our community, so it was impossible to do a random sample.

If you have a population available and do a good job in selecting a random sample, the sample will resemble the population in demographics and background. You can select the sample using the table of random numbers or literally put all numbers or names from a population into a hat, shake them up, and draw out the number of individuals needed.

Selecting from a table of random numbers may be the most unbiased and useful tool to use in random sampling. The basis of the number configurations on the table is completely arbitrary. For example, if you had a known population of 500 people and you were going to select 217 people (see Table 2.4[1]), you would first number each of the people from 1 to 500. You then would determine the number of digits needed. Since 500 has three digits, you would use three digits. Turn to the table of random numbers found in the back of this textbook (Appendix A). Notice several rows and columns of five-digit numbers. You can decide to select a five-digit number but use only the first three numbers. Deciding where to start is a matter of choice. Most people close their eyes and point a finger. This assures that no biases existed in choosing the number. From that starting point, you would move either across or up and down, however you initially decided, but consistently. You would ignore any number outside the range of 500 and go to the next. You would keep on with the procedure until you had selected 217 different numbers out of the 500 with which you started.

A *stratified random sample* is used when proportionate representation from particular groups is sought. It might be based on age, sex, or activity involvement. For example, an evaluator might want the number of African-Americans surveyed in the evaluation project to represent the number of African-Americans in the population. Or, he or she might want to stratify a sample so that a proportionate number of boys and girls are observed. If you knew the population consisted of 70% male and 30% female, you would randomly draw 70% of the sample from the list of boys and 30% from the list of girls. Stratified random sampling requires that you draw samples from separate lists. Thus, you have to be able to know what strata you want and the proportion of each stratum in the population.

*Systematic sampling* determines a rationalization for some kind of routine sample. It is somewhat easier to do than simple random sampling and individuals have a somewhat similar probability of being chosen. All selections are determined by the first selection and then you choose every "nth" one after that. If you knew there were 2,000 members of an organization and you had enough money to sample 200, you might go through and pick every tenth name on the organizational list until you had 200 names drawn. An important point is to choose a random starting point by taking a number from the table of random numbers or by closing your eyes and pointing to a random spot on the list. Systematic sampling is easier and less cumbersome than some other sampling strategies.

*Cluster sampling* subdivides a population into groups or units rather than individuals such as geographic areas, city blocks, or recreation centers. These subgroup units would be listed and the evaluator would then choose subgroup units randomly and collect data from the people within those groups. This method is a time saver, but you must be sure that the units or groups are somewhat homogeneous. For example, if a community had 10 recreation centers but you only had resources to collect data from 4 of those centers, you could put the names of the centers in a hat and randomly draw out the first 4 center names as a way to do a cluster sample.

## Nonprobability Sampling

Using probability samples is most desirable but not always possible in evaluation or research projects. Nonprobability sampling includes the procedures used when the sample is not drawn by chance from a population. We do not know the probability of selecting a single individual so we have to "assume" that potential respondents have an equal and independent chance of being selected, although this assumption is never true. Biases may occur and caution is suggested in making generalizations to the broader population, although evaluators frequently do generalize. Several types of nonprobability sampling might be rationalized in an evaluation or research project.

*Purposive sampling* is arbitrarily selecting a sample because you believe evidence supports that the sample represents the total population. In using this sampling process, you will need to be able to justify clearly why you believe a particular sample is representative. Purposive sampling also may be used for not only deciding what people to observe and interview, but which activities to observe, what locations, and what time periods. For example, we might want to sample first-year university students' attitudes toward building a new campus recreation center so we select students from classes in English composition because we believe they represent all first-year students.

*Convenience sampling,* or incidental sampling, refers to a sample that happens to be available for a project. This haphazard sampling technique has weak generalizability and external validity. Convenience sampling is generally not recommended, although it may be justified if no other sampling techniques are possible or affordable. Convenience sampling is easy because the audience is captive and available and may be representative, but you don't know the latter for sure. You are taking a chance in drawing conclusions for a larger population. If we wanted to survey students on a college campus, a convenience sample would be to pass out questionnaires to the courses that you (as a student) are taking as a means for easy access.

*Quota sampling* is based on dividing the population into subgroups and drawing a sample to fulfill a specific quota. For example, you may wish to survey an equal number of men and women, even though that may not represent the population of an aerobics program. In quota sampling, you would simply choose an equal number of males and females until you reach the number that you wanted. For example, if a data collector wanted to get the opinion of the public, she or he might go to a mall and give a questionnaire to the first $x$ number of people that pass by a given area. The problem in quota sampling is that the evaluator does not know if the people chosen represent the population. Further, once the quota is reached, no one else has a chance of being selected. A bias may exist toward individuals who are willing to cooperate with such a sampling procedure. Quota sampling is not a bad strategy, but one can never be fully sure that error does not exist.

*Expert sampling,* or judgment sampling, is a process where people are chosen on the basis of an informed opinion that they are representative of a population that has needed information. This "best guess" form of sampling is similar to purposive sampling but is based on a good deal of prior knowledge. Case studies are frequently selected on the basis of the expert judgment of individuals whom you know have information or data that you want.

One might also get a sample by using the *snowball approach.* The evaluator gets people she or he knows to recommend others to be the sample for a project. The researcher may ask friends, go to an agency and ask for suggestions, or advertise for volunteers just to get the process started. The initial respondents are asked to recommend others who might get involved. For example, if you wanted to know the constraints to why people with disabilities did not participate in community recreation programs, you might contact several individuals with disabilities to survey and then ask them to recommend others whom they know might be willing to participate. Obviously a bias exists in this form of sampling, but if you do not know the make-up of an entire population, a sample can be obtained in this way.

## Theoretical Sampling

A third form of sampling frequently used in collecting qualitative data is different than either probability or nonprobability samples. Theoretical sampling does not focus on numbers of respondents, but the contribution each person makes to address the evaluation or research purposes. Theoretical sampling includes the selection of informants through the stages of the interview or field observation process. In some ways it may resemble purposive, convenience, or snowball sampling, but the focus is not on the individuals but on the data collected. The evaluator or researcher makes decisions on who and how many to sample as information begins to unfold and as it becomes apparent that certain views are or are not being represented to address the evaluation criteria or research questions.

Theoretical sampling, in the context of collecting qualitative data, means deciding what group of people you want to study. Further, it involves realizing that you cannot observe everything, so you can only address certain aspects related to people, settings, events, and social processes. In other words, the evaluator using interviews and/or qualitative observations is not concerned about adequate numbers or random selection, but is trying to present a working picture of the broader social structure from which the data are drawn. Within qualitative approaches, the evaluator is interested in sampling so that the observations made or data collected are representative of the more general class of phenomena. The evaluator is also interested in whether the observations or interviews reflect all the possible observations or interviews that could have been conducted.

The exact number or type of informants is not specified ahead of time in theoretical sampling, although the evaluator may have some sense of what those numbers might be. In some cases, the evaluator or researcher may need to spend more time in the field or interview more people than was originally proposed to get data that are trustworthy. In other cases, the data may be grounded more easily and quickly than was initially planned. After the first few cases, the evaluator may select the sample purposely to get a variety of perspectives. Toward the end of data collection, she or he will focus more on interpretation and verification of data with the respondents. The more variability in responses or observations one uncovers, the more sampling one will need to do.

Samples used for qualitative evaluations are usually small and purposive. About 10 to 20 people is the usual number. Theoretical saturation is reached with simultaneous data gathering and analysis. It occurs when the evaluator realizes that the themes or patterns are coalescing and no additional new patterns are being uncovered. In any sampling done to collect qualitative data, you should consider how each respondent or situation contributes to an understanding of the evaluation criteria that have been established.

## Other Aspects of Sampling

Several other sampling strategies are frequently used in evaluation projects. One example is random digit dialing as a random phone sampling method. Random digit dialing is based on identifying all working telephone exchanges for an area, generating the last four numbers from a table of random numbers, and calling. The nonworking numbers reached are discarded and the interview is administered to numbers reached. A lot of wasted effort results in this process because of missing phone numbers, but it is a way to get a representative sample from a population. Since mobile phones are not listed, however, and many people no longer have "land lines," this form of random digit dialing may not be as reliable as it once was.

Another form of sampling for the telephone is sampling from telephone directories. The same problems exist with this approach as well since mobile phones are not listed. Random numbers might be used, however, to locate a starting page and then another random number used to locate a name on the page. It is convenient while still allowing for randomness but should be used carefully.

No matter how hard we try, we are unlikely to get a sample that perfectly represents the population. We can use an entire population, which is often done in smaller evaluation projects, and then we don't have to worry about sampling. We do, however, have to be concerned about both sampling and nonsampling error.

## From Ideas to Reality

Sampling is obviously an important aspect of evaluation and research projects. Sometimes we do not need to be overly concerned about sampling because we use an entire population, but at other times it is important if our projects are to be trustworthy. The possibilities for sampling described in this chapter should provide a basis for the sample decisions you will need to make in your projects. If you follow the suggestions, you should be able to choose an appropriate sample and justify why it is appropriate given a particular situation.

Now that you have studied this chapter, you should be able to:
- Describe the differences between probability, nonprobability, and theoretical sampling
- Draw a sample from a population using one of the strategies for probability sampling
- Explain what sampling and nonsampling error means
- Use the Table of Random Numbers to draw a sample
- Determine the appropriate sample size based on the population studied and the data that will be collected

## 2.5 Choosing the Right Stuff: Measurement Instruments

Once the criteria to examine are determined and a research design has been selected, you will need a measuring instrument or device. To collect qualitative data, the evaluator or researcher is most often the instrument used (i.e., the individual asks unstructured questions or makes observations). The relationship between qualitative data and the evaluator will be discussed later in this unit.

For most quantitative studies, however, a paper-and-pencil instrument, observation checklist, questionnaire, or test of some type is used. If a reliable and valid instrument already exists that you can use, you will save yourself time and effort by using that instrument. Unfortunately, not many instruments exist in recreation services that have been standardized and tested for reliability and validity. Further, evaluators must look at their particular situations to decide what type of instrument can best measure the criteria desired. Thus, you must be able to do two things well:

1. Evaluate existing instruments to see if they are reliable, valid, and usable.

2. Develop instruments that are reliable, valid, and usable to address evaluation criteria specific to a situation.

When we talk about measurement instruments, we are referring to tests, checklists, or questionnaires that might be developed. Some measurements might refer to observing behaviors, while others will refer to opinionnaires, attitude, or performance. When a set of questions is written specifically for an evaluation project with the assumption that respondents will answer honestly, the instrument is commonly called a questionnaire rather than a test. Instruments may be used to collect qualitative or quantitative data, but measurement instruments usually refer to quantitative surveys and observations.

## Tests

Tests are standardized ways (i.e., they usually have been scrutinized and used before) of asking for information. Tests have additional features such as scores and inferences from scores. They usually involve questions about the respondent's ability and/or willingness to answer accurately, honestly, or completely. When you take a test in a course, the instructor is using a standardized way to measure your knowledge or achievement.

Tests given to individuals are usually divided into four types: ability, achievement, attitude, and personality tests. Ability tests are supposed to measure what a person is capable of doing. For example, a physical fitness test is a way to measure the level of physical ability. Achievement tests show what a person has learned. Attitude tests attempt to measure some opinions or beliefs of the test-taker about an object, person, or event. They refer to some internal state of mind or set of beliefs that is stable over time and that can be compared to other people's. Personality tests refer to most anything else related to characteristics of an individual that have been standardized such as the Myers-Briggs test of psychological types of individuals (e.g., Introverted-Intuitive-Thinking-Judgment).

## Locating Existing Instruments

Assessment instruments are probably most abundant in the field of recreation services, as many communities have conducted needs assessments, and therapeutic recreation specialists use a number of assessment instruments in their work. Fewer "already developed" instruments exist for formative and summative evaluations.

Several resources exist for finding already-existing instruments. In the field of therapeutic recreation, researchers have compiled lists of such instruments (Burlingame & Blaschko, 1997). The *Mental Measurements Yearbook* (Impara & Plake, 1998) is available in most libraries and describes various personality and achievement instruments, including their reliability and validity.

Often we borrow instruments from other professionals to use in recreation settings or we seek permission to use instruments developed by other researchers. Using an instrument from someone else may save time because you don't have to develop your own instrument, but you must be careful to assure that the instrument is really a reliable, valid, and usable measurement that will work for your project.

## Standardized Measurements

Most students are familiar with standardized tests such as the Scholastic Aptitude Test (SAT) or the Graduate Record Exam (GRE). A standardized test is one that has been previously used for a relatively large group of subjects. Many standardized test results have provided information about the answers or scores to expect from similar subjects. These standardized tests usually come with elaborate and complete instructions about how to administer the test so that your results are comparable to results from other testers. You can be sure that major question-design problems have been resolved as these tests have been improved and standardized.

If you want to compare the results you obtained from using a standardized test, however, the tests must be given exactly as the instructions suggest. You should not even give additional explanations. The standardized test may be reliable and valid in general. However, as was discussed in the previous chapter, the test must be valid for the particular audience involved and evaluation criteria that you are using. For example, just because a test worked for adults does not mean that the test is appropriate for children. To develop your own standardized tests is difficult, complicated, and goes beyond what we can discuss in this book. If available and appropriate, however, you may use standardized tests developed by others. Personality tests such as the Tennessee Self-Concept Scale, for example, might be used if you were interested in determining if self-concept changed as a result of participating in a summer camp program.

## Making Instrument Choices

Dunn (1987) suggested some guidelines for using published assessment evaluation procedures that might also include standardized tests. She noted that personally or organizationally developed assessments may be good, but the confidence may not be as high in them as in previously published tests. All standardized instruments have specific instructions that give time limits, oral instructions, preliminary demonstrations, ways of handling inquiries, and other details for the testing situation. They also may have norms or averages established from previous testing done. The instrument chosen should provide evidence of validity and should have been validated on a representative sample of sufficient size. The relationship of subscores to total scores should be evident. Further, information about reliability should be provided. The manual and test materials should be complete and have appropriate quality indicators such as what high and low scores mean. The assessment should be relevant to the participants served by the agency and finally, the instrument should be relevant to the decisions made based on evaluation or assessment results.

An assessment or evaluation instrument should be revalidated when any changes are made in procedures, materials, or when it is used for a purpose or with a population group for which it has not been validated. The instrument should be selected and used by qualified individuals and should be used in the intended way. The published instrument might be combined with other tests, but it should maintain its integrity. The administration and scoring should follow standardized procedures. During the administration, care should be taken in providing a comfortable environment with minimal distractions. The administrator of the instrument also must be aware of the importance and effect of rapport with respondents. Additionally, the security of materials must be protected if confidentiality is guaranteed. Specific test results should not be released without the informed consent of the test-taker. Data regarding patients' assessment in therapeutic recreation, for example, should be kept in a designated, usually locked, file.

Many advantages can be found in choosing existing instruments rather than developing your own measures. As you can tell from this discussion, however, many considerations must be weighed thoughtfully in choosing instruments. In summary, you as an evaluator or researcher might want to ask several questions about any instrument being examined:

- Do measures exist for reliability and validity?
- Does the instrument measure the factors or traits desired to be measured?
- Is the instrument appropriate to the participants who will be completing it?
- Is the instrument reasonable in time and cost to administer?
- Are the directions clear, concise, and unambiguous?
- Is the instrument easy to score or are specific directions for how to do scoring included?
- Does it provide the best way to measure the data that we wish to measure?

If the answer to any of these questions is "no," then perhaps you should look for another instrument or consider developing your own.

## From Ideas to Reality

In quantitative studies, you will generally choose or develop instruments to collect empirical data. Using existing instruments often saves time but you must be sure they are reliable and valid for the group with whom you wish to use them. Before undertaking data collection, ascertain if any existing instruments might be available. If they are reliable, valid, and usable for your criteria, then use them. As you will see in the next chapter,

# 2.6 On Your Own Again: Developing Measurement Instruments

Developing your own instrument(s) for an evaluation or research project may be appropriate if another instrument does not already exist. Developing good measurement instruments and questionnaires, however, is an art that requires care and practice. Fortunately, many guidelines exist to help you develop good instruments. These guidelines can be applied to the development of checklists, survey questionnaires (i.e., paper-and-pencil or Internet), or test items. Several basic steps are consistent in the development of any questionnaire or test:

1. Define the problem (i.e., revisit your criteria or research questions for the project).

2. Determine the contents and ideas to be examined.

3. Identify and categorize the respondents.

4. Develop items, structure, and format.

5. Write directions.

6. Pilot-test, revise, field test, and revise.

7. Ensure response.

This chapter focuses on determining the contents of surveys, developing items and structures, and designing formats and directions. We divide the development of instruments into several components: types of questions (determining the contents), question structures and wording tips (developing items), and instrument design (formats and directions). Sampling and identifying respondents are covered in the next chapter on sampling. Pilot-testing, field-testing, and ensuring responses will be addressed in the chapter about surveys.

As a note of interest, the words 'survey' and 'questionnaire' are often used synonymously. 'Survey' can also be a verb suggesting that something is being examined. Surveys are a method because they describe a way to actually collect data. The questionnaire is the actual physical form used to conduct a survey. In other words, we conduct a survey using a questionnaire. People know what you mean regardless of the word used, but we just want to point out the subtle difference.

# The Process of Instrument Development

We also want to say a little about the overall development of instruments. To develop a questionnaire, you must know what you want to find out or what criteria are to be evaluated. Orthner, Smith, and Wright (1986) gave an example of a process used for developing a needs-assessment survey for the Navy. Figure 2.6(1) shows the process used to develop a measurement instrument for research about recreation services. Although most of the projects you undertake may not require such an elaborate plan, the diagram is helpful in understanding how a survey problem is defined and how a questionnaire is refined.

Orthner et al. (1986) first got a panel of Navy and recreation experts together and asked them to examine and review a list of possible issues and questions. From this procedure, prototypical questionnaires were developed. The items were then revised, the questionnaire tested in a real situation, revisions to the questionnaire were made, a panel once again reviewed it, the questionnaire was pilot-tested in a focus group and revised again, presented to headquarters for review, field-tested on eight bases, revised, field tested for a final time, and the final questionnaire was then completed.

It is *not* necessary to go through all of those stages unless the questionnaire is going to be standardized and/or completed by thousands of people. Several parts of this model, however, are particularly important to consider. First, you must make sure you know what it is you want to find out and that this information may be obtained from some source whether it is participants, colleagues, or organizational leaders. Second, you will need to go through several revisions of the questionnaire. Even people who have been designing surveys for years cannot write a perfect questionnaire the first time. Third, you will need to pilot-test the questionnaire with a small sample to make sure that it is doing what you want it to do. Fourth, even after you use the questionnaire, some flaws (hopefully, all minor) may be discovered that you can correct if the questionnaire is administered again.

Ask only necessary questions. Sometimes evaluators and/or researchers think that they can ask many questions and then determine later on what information to use in the final report. This endeavor is a waste of paper and a waste of the respondents' time. Know exactly what criteria are being measured at the start, and then develop questions to get that information. By using a systematic process, you should be able to develop the most reliable, valid, and usable questionnaire possible.

# Contents of Questionnaires

Questionnaires are used as a common survey technique. The questions asked will have great variability, depending on the nature of the evaluation or research project, the design used, and the criteria measured. Specific questions may be addressed followed with peripheral questions to get in-depth information.

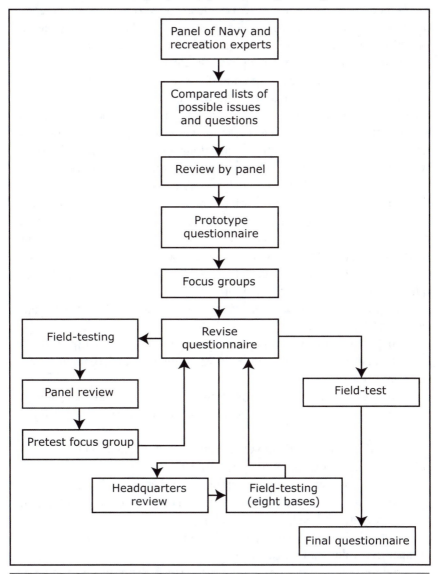

***Figure 2.6(1)*** *Navy Model of Instrument Development (adapted from Orthner, Smith, and Wright, 1986)*

A result of designing good instruments is that people will respond honestly. Questions may be asked in the time frame of past, present, or future. For most recreation, park, and leisure service organizations, questions are likely to address one or all of these five areas: *experience/behavior*, *opinion/values* (needs and interests), *feelings* (emotional responses), *knowledge/facts*, and *background/demographics*. The questions may be open-ended (i.e., no set responses) or close-ended (i.e., answer choices are given), although most of the discussion in this chapter will be based on writing objective, close-ended questions. No matter what type, good questions should be neutral, singular, and clear.

Let's talk about the information that you want to obtain in a survey. The questions are going to pertain to the level of evidence you are addressing. For example, if you wish to determine the reactions that individuals had to a particular recreation activity, you would likely use opinion/value or feelings types of questions. On the other hand, if you wanted to find out what people learned as a result of an activity, you might ask questions about knowledge or facts.

In a single questionnaire, you might ask several different content questions and you might ask them in different time frames. You must be clear, however, as to what criteria you are trying to measure. If you want to know what people will do in the future, you must be sure to write questions that pertain to the future. Let's look at a few examples of possible questions to address the five categories above:

**Experience/Behavior Questions**—what a person does or has done. For example:

(past): How many times did you swim in the XYZ pool in 2001?

(present): For what program did you register at the community recreation center?

(future): On the average, how many times do you anticipate any member of your family swimming at the XYZ pool during the coming summer?

**Opinion/Value/Attitude Questions**—cognitive and interpretive processes held by the individual. For example:

(past): What did you like about last year's volleyball league?

(present): When you call the recreation office, are the receptionists usually very helpful, helpful, or unhelpful?

(future): Do you favor the development of both a recreational and a competitive volleyball league next year?

**Feeling Questions**—emotional responses (past or present) of people to their experiences. For example:

(past): Did the trip make you feel happy?

(present): How does volunteering with this youth group make you feel? [Note: Sometimes questions are erroneously worded, as in "How did you feel about X?" when the focus is not on emotions but on opinions—be aware!]

**Knowledge Questions**—what factual information the respondent has, usually at the present time. For example:

(present): What is your target heartbeat during aerobics classes?

(present): How many fouls does a basketball player get before she or he fouls out?

**Background/Demographic Questions**—*current* personal characteristics. For example:

(past): In what state were you born?

(present): How old are you?

# Question Structures

A number of structures can be used in questionnaire design. The structures used will depend to some extent on the content and criteria that you wish to address and the statistical techniques you want to use. Writing good questions and using the best structure takes practice.

Three major structures and the scales that can be used with each include:

1. Open-Ended Questions

2. Close-Ended Quantitative Questions with Ordered (Forced) Choices and Unordered Response Choices

3. Partially Close-Ended Questions

## Open-Ended

Open-ended questions are directed with no pre-formed answers. The respondent supplies her or his own answer(s) with no restrictions on the content of the response. In paper-and-pencil tests, respondents often use lists or short essay responses. Responses to verbal open-ended questions can, and hopefully do, result in the respondent providing anecdotes and examples.

Open-ended questions are most often used when a variety of information is needed and the evaluator is unsure of possible responses. In this way, open-ended structures also provide diagnostic information. These structures are used to collect qualitative data and to develop specific questionnaires from broad information. As you develop questionnaires, you will have to ask yourself if all the information is currently available so that categories of responses can be written in advance, or whether open-ended questions will provide responses not currently known. Open-ended questions are easy to ask, but tallying the results is not always as easy, as you will see when we discuss qualitative analysis in the next unit.

The advantages of open-ended structures are evident when the population characteristics are not known and when the evaluator does not wish to overlook any possible answers to a question. From initial open-ended questions, it is possible to draft more specific close-ended questions, especially if the open-ended structure is used as the first step in developing a more quantitatively oriented questionnaire.

A further advantage to open-ended structures is that the answers are less influenced by the evaluator writing the question. In addition, a variety of responses, which may include many that are unique to an individual's situation, can be elicited. Open-ended structures can help to introduce new topics or allow respondents to summarize what is on their minds. These structures can provide valuable background for interpreting results from other questions and can add "richness" to the data because of the potential for depth of response.

The disadvantages of open-ended responses include a lack of uniform responses that may not be easy to code or tabulate. Further, this structure is affected by a respondent's verbal ability and written communication skills. The data obtained are sometimes more useful when the respondents have a higher educational level. When using open-ended questions, problems of definition and vocabulary may occur and fewer questions can be asked. Open-ended questions typically take longer to complete and people may not take as much time with them if they require lengthy writing responses. In our experience we have found that people who are really positive or really negative about an experience are the ones most likely to elaborate with their answers—this possibility can be good, but it also may not be representative of all other respondents. In addition, problems with coding or organizing the data for interpretation may emerge and some responses may be irrelevant to the criteria or information that you desire.

An evaluator or researcher who is writing open-ended questions must be careful to be asking genuinely open-ended questions. A question such as "Did you enjoy playing in the soccer league?" may appear to be an open-ended inquiry when, in fact, it potentially calls for a close-ended "yes/no" response. A useful open-ended question to get at this information might be "What was it about the soccer league that you enjoyed?" Sometimes evaluators ask a question such as "Did you enjoy playing in the soccer league?" and then follow with a "Why or why not?" The use of "why" can sometimes be threatening, since the respondent assumes there ought to be a definitive answer. The best open-ended questions are those that the respondent feels competent and comfortable in answering and that invite people to be honest, descriptive, and forthcoming.

In summary, open-ended structures are easy to write and are usually straightforward. The data collector, however, must also be prepared for the volume and variability of information that may be provided by respondents.

## Close-Ended

Specific responses are provided for the respondents to select in close-ended quantitative questions. These responses may be of two types, depending on the nature of the question: a) ordered with a forced choice or b) unordered. Close-ended structures that use ordered responses include Likert scales, Semantic Differential scales, and rankings. Unordered close-ended questions are typically used as multiple-choice checklists and are unique to the specific evaluation criteria being measured.

Several issues must be kept in mind in developing close-ended, forced-choice question items. First of all, response categories should not overlap. The answer categories should be mutually exclusive so the answer falls into one category only. For example, if you ask someone her or his age and give choices, make sure the categories are listed as "younger than 19 years," "20–29 years," "30–39 years" and *not* "younger than 19 years," "19–29 years," and "29–39 years." Second, the responses should be exhaustive and cover the gamut of possible answers. Third, the responses also must be appropriate to the questions asked and consistent in focusing on the same dimension being measured. Finally, remember that the same question may be asked in many ways using a variety of close-ended choices. The data collector has to choose what is going to be best.

The advantages of close-ended responses are that they are uniform and can be easily coded for data entry and analysis in a computer. If you want a quick analysis, then close-ended question structures are the easiest to administer and analyze. For example, if you asked, "Overall how satisfied were you with the organization of the crafts fair?" you might provide forced ordered choices of "4=very satisfied, 3=satisfied, 2=dissatisfied, 1=very dissatisfied." Tallying the results to find out the mean or average score for this question would be fairly easy to do.

The disadvantages of close-ended structures occur if you do not provide the most appropriate choices for response. If the "true" or "right" (i.e., from the perspective of the respondent) answer is missing from the list of choices, you will get only partially valid answers or no answers at all. In the example concerning satisfaction with the organization of the crafts fair, an individual might have been satisfied with some aspects but not all aspects. A disadvantage to the close-ended response is that the respondent does not have an opportunity to explain anything about the response.

As indicated, two types of close-ended questions exist:
- unordered close-ended responses
- ordered forced choices (commonly called scaling devices)

Close-ended questions with **unordered responses** are structures used with items that have no particular value associated with them in the statistical analysis. You may want to know as many possibilities for a question, or the one best answer. For example you could ask someone to choose the best thing about an aerobics program or you could ask him or her to check all of the items that apply. An example of an unordered response would be the following question:

What did you like best about the aerobics class? Check one item.

\_\_\_\_\_Becoming more physically fit

\_\_\_\_\_Getting out of the house or job for a while

\_\_\_\_\_Meeting other people

\_\_\_\_\_Having fun

\_\_\_\_\_Moving to the music

As indicated above, this same question could be asked in another unordered form by allowing individuals to check all of the items that applied about what they liked about an aerobics class.

"Yes/no" or "true/false" questions are another form of unordered close-ended question structures. These responses are appropriate to use and easy to write. You, however, must keep in mind the limited amount of information that may be obtained from yes/no questions. Some people can clearly answer yes or no for a given situation, particularly knowledge or experience/behavior questions. Many times, however, yes/no responses require qualification. In using close-ended yes/no questions, the data collector must consider the information that may not be evident in these responses.

Scaling is the major form of **ordered close-ended** questions used for measuring participation rates, attitudes, and opinions. An example would be "How often do you compete in a road race?" A scaling technique would be to use the ordered responses: a=never, b=once a year, c=3–4 times a year, d=every month, e=every weekend. Descriptive terms, or word anchors, should be used at each point on the scale so the respondent knows what the letters mean. In other words, the respondent must be clear about the choices for the ordered responses. Common forms of other ordered scaling devices include Likert scales, Semantic differentials, rankings, and self-assessments.

*Likert Scales.* Likert scales, named for the man who developed them, are a particular kind of close-ended question structure that uses a scaling system. Likert scales are most often used for attitude measurement. Usually both negative and positive statements are used with four to six responses meaning "strongly agree, agree, disagree, or strongly disagree." These scale names are referred to as response anchors. Some people will make a three- to seven-point response scale and include a middle option of "neutral or no opinion." We have found it works better to use an even number of items so respondents are forced to "take a stand." Some respondents may see "no opinion" as the "easy way out" and evaluators generally want to force people to choose one response or another. Without a neutral option, however, respondents might skip a question, which may result in unreliable data. As a questionnaire developer, you will need to decide the best way to design a Likert scale.

A Likert scale usually has a matrix-type of design with questions on the left half and anchored responses on the right half. Each response is then scored in some way, usually with the most positive response receiving the highest point value. In a 4 point scale, anything with a mean or average of 2.6 and above is usually considered positive—below that score would be negative. The Likert scale is relatively easy to construct, has moderate reliability, usually explores attitudes, involves simple computations, and is easy to score. Table 2.6(2) shows an example of a Likert scale.

*Table 2.6(2)* *Example of a Likert Scale Used to Measure Satisfaction with a Campground*

|  | Strongly Agree | Agree | Disagree | Strongly Disagree |
|---|---|---|---|---|
| 1. The entrance to the campground was attractive. | SA | A | D | SD |
| 2. Staff members were friendly and courteous. | SA | A | D | SD |
| 3. The campsites were large enough. | SA | A | D | SD |
| 4. The distance between campsites was appropriate. | SA | A | D | SD |
| 5. Restrooms and showers were clean. | SA | A | D | SD |

*Semantic Differentials.* Semantic differentials, another scaling struc-ture for close-ended questions, include a list of bipolar adjectives written in linear fashion (see Table 2.6[3]). Semantic differentials are often used to assess attitudes and responses and are assigned numbers, as is done with Likert scales. The items to be measured are selected and then bipolar adjective pairs are chosen to anchor both ends of the scales. These words should be as near to opposite as possible (such as "good/bad"), and one may or may not necessarily be the negation of the other (such as "famil-iar/unfamiliar"). Points should be anchored with numbers on the scales between the two points, so that scoring averages can be calculated later. In the listing down a page, the items should be put in opposite directions so not all the positive attributes are on one side of the scale. Semantic dif-ferentials are particularly good scales for examining the past and present attitudes and opinions about a particular phenomenon.

*Ranking.* Ranking is another form of a forced close-ended structure that is used to get a sense of how individuals might evaluate certain items. Where items fall on a ranking scale does not indicate good or bad but simply an attempt to look at the relative meaning of one item to an-other. These ranking scales are simple to use for descriptive data, but they require less commonly used statistical techniques. The biggest problem ranking has is with reliability. Too many items to rank are confusing to the respondent. Usually 10–11 items are the maximum number you will want to use. If you have more items to rank than that, you might want to divide your scale into two questions.

One of the major disadvantages to ranking as a question structure is that the directions often confuse respondents. You need to be clear and

*Table 2.6(3) Example of Semantic Differentials for Evaluating a Youth Leader*

Please indicate your perception of the leadership ability of your youth leader. Check where you believe she or he falls on the scale.

| Dedicated | 6 | 5 | 4 | 3 | 2 | 1 | Could Care Less |
| Enthusiastic | 6 | 5 | 4 | 3 | 2 | 1 | Very Low Key |
| Organized | 6 | 5 | 4 | 3 | 2 | 1 | Disorganized |
| Strict | 6 | 5 | 4 | 3 | 2 | 1 | Lenient |
| Always Late | 6 | 5 | 4 | 3 | 2 | 1 | On Time |

thorough in your directions so the individual knows exactly what to do. Be sure to say how you want the items ranked such as suggesting that a 1 is the *best* and 2 is next best and so on. The ranking is often useful but you have to realize that it is difficult to say much about what the rankings mean. For example, in Table 2.6(4), you do not know for sure whether the camper liked any of the activities. Further, she or he may have liked them all and may have seen little difference among the 10 items.

*Self-Assessments.* A further example of an ordered close-ended structure is called a self-assessment. It is not uncommon in everyday language for someone to ask you, "On a 1–10 scale, how would you rate XYZ?" In the self-assessment structure, a respondent is asked to describe where she or he is on a scale, usually scored as 1–10. For example, you might ask a question such as "After taking this class, based on a 1–10 scale (with 1 being lowest and 10 being highest), how would you rate your knowledge of the rules of tennis?" The response may be a ladder where the respondent places an "X" to show the position of the response, may be a mark on a line with "1" on the left and numbers written consecutively to "10" on the right, or you might simply ask the respondent to write down a number in a space after the question.

*Partially Close-Ended.* A final type of close-ended question structure is called partially close-ended. These questions provide some structured responses, but also leave room for people to write in their own answers or additional information. To assure that the response categories are exhaustive, "other" is sometimes included as an item response. Care should be taken to allow enough room to write what "other" means and

---

*Table 2.6(4)* *Example of Ranking Question About Camp Activities*

---

Rank the following 10 activities from what you like the best to what you like the least. That is, choose the activity that you like best and give it a 1. Choose the second best activity and give it a 2. Continue through all the activities until each has a number from 1 to 10. The number-10-ranked activity will be your least favorite from the list.

_____ horseback riding
_____ swimming lessons
_____ free swimming
_____ evening programs
_____ free time in the afternoon
_____ arts and crafts
_____ overnight camp-out
_____ mealtimes
_____ cabin activities
_____ afternoon rest period

that the respondent knows that "other" replies are acceptable. An example of a partially close-ended question is:

How did you hear about the Sunday hike at the Nature Center?

_____ Announcement on the radio

_____ Flyer at the recreation department

_____ From a friend

_____ Other (please explain)_____

Partially close-ended questions often provide important information but the evaluator is better off to try to anticipate the most common responses rather than letting the respondents do all the thinking. Although partially close-ended responses may improve the validity of a question, reliability problems can exist. The evaluator must make sure she or he is as informed as possible in developing any type of close-ended question.

## Wording Issues

Writing questions seems fairly easy at first, but often mistakes are made. Many of these mistakes could be avoided by paying careful attention to the wording of each and every question. Here are some considerations to think about:

1. **Use only one idea per question.** Make sure the question is straightforward and that you are asking an individual to respond to one construct or idea.

2. **Clear, brief, and simple are the rules for good question writing.** Make questions as simple to answer as possible. You may want to begin with a major question and then break it down into several additional questions, but the respondent must always know how to proceed. You get better information from two or three simple questions than one complex one.

3. **Avoid leading questions that suggest that you want a particular kind of response.** (For example, a leading question would be "Most young people learn great leadership skills when they serve as an officer in a club. Were you ever an officer?")

4. **Avoid asking people to make estimates.** Try to force them to answer as honestly as possible to assure reliability.

5. **Think about trying to formulate a question from the respondent's viewpoint.** Use words that are familiar to the respondent. Doing a pilot study, which will be discussed in another chapter, is often a good way to double-check that you are using words that respondents understand.

6. **Avoid advanced language and technical jargon that is familiar to you but that the respondent may not understand.** Avoid the use of acronyms (i.e., abbreviations such as ADA that may be common for you but meaningless to the general public). As recreation professionals we use many words such as "programming," "multiple use," and "therapy" that may be misunderstood by the public. People are reluctant to admit they don't understand words, and this attitude may affect the reliability of measurement instruments.

7. **Be clear about what is being asked.** Don't say, "Should the P & R Department be more active with environmental education?" Respondents may misunderstand the question because they do not know the words or what "more active" means. Every question should have a time frame. Phrases such as "more active" should be explained by saying what is already occurring. For example, "The Nature Center currently offers two bird identification workshops each year. Is this number of offerings too many, adequate, or too little?"

8. **Avoid negative questions that may confuse the reader.** For example, don't say "Why would you not want the bond issue to be defeated?" A better phrase would be, "What are the advantages of passing this bond issue?"

9. **Avoid the use of "iffy" words like "often" or "seldom."** These words may mean different things to different people, so they need to be defined if used. For example, a response to a question about "How often do you walk on the American Tobacco Trail?" might be labeled as "never," "seldom (once a month)," "often (once a week)," or "regularly (every day)."

10. **Do a pilot study.** As will be explained further, a pilot study is given to a handful of respondents who are similar

to the people who will eventually receive your questionnaire. These respondents are asked to complete the questionnaire and give you feedback regarding what questions arose as they filled it out. Examine every comment made in the pilot concerning wording. Don't take anything for granted about a questionnaire and work to keep the wording as simple as possible.

11. **State the alternatives precisely.** "Should the government put more money into recreation or not?" is a poorly worded question. Make clear what you are asking. Put options into the question if you are asking for options or else explain what those options are going to be. For example, a good question might be, "The current greens fee for 18 holes of golf is $30. Should the greens fees at the public golf course be higher, lower, or remain the same?" People, unfortunately, will often tend to choose the middle of the road if they are unsure about a response.

12. **Some questions may require several stages to get adequate information.** These staged questions require several questions to assure a valid answer. Shafer and Moeller (1987) suggested, for example, that a complex question might require up to five questions: first determine awareness by a free-answer question concerning knowledge, next inquire about uninfluenced attitudes on the subject with another open-ended question, record specific attitudes through multiple-choice, then find out the reasons through another open-ended question, and finally determine the intensity with a multiple-choice question. An example of this process can be seen in Table 2.6(5).

# Formats and Instrument Design

Clearly worded questions and an aesthetically pleasing instrument will often invite a respondent to complete a survey. Too often, no more time is given to the layout of a questionnaire than to creating a grocery list. General appearance, however, may be critical to the success of a survey. All instrument developers should be concerned with overall effects and a motivational design. Simple graphics are often important, as is the amount of "white space" on the page. Fortunately, options for online surveys now automatically format questions in a pleasing manner and

*Table 2.6(5)* *Example of a Question Asked in Stages*

---

1. Have you visited Rivers Bend County Park?
   ___ Yes (go to question 2)
   ___ No (go to next section)

2. What did you like about Rivers Bend County Park?

   _____

3. How satisfied were you with your visit to Rivers Bend County Park?
   _____ very satisfied
   _____ satisfied
   _____ somewhat satisfied
   _____ dissatisfied
   _____ very dissatisfied

4. What do you look for when you visit a county park?

   _____

5. How likely are you to visit Rivers Bend County Park in 2002?
   _____ very likely
   _____ somewhat likely
   _____ not likely

---

often do not overwhelm a respondent because only a handful of questions appear on each page. Nevertheless, at first glance a potential respondent will form an opinion about the importance, difficulty, and apparent length of a questionnaire. From this first impression, she or he is likely to decide whether or not to complete the questionnaire.

The sequencing of the questions is important. Always begin with questions that have a direct relevance to the purpose of the evaluation. These questions may also provide a context for determining attitudes and knowledge. Choosing the first question should be done carefully. Although demographic questions may be easy to answer, they are seldom directly related to the purpose of the evaluation or research. Save the demographic questions until last. If a respondent doesn't get to them you will still have the important information collected at the beginning. Put questions of less importance later in the questionnaire. Controversial items should be grouped with less controversial ones. If you think you may not get a response for something because it is really controversial, put it at the end of the questionnaire. Questionnaires usually start with general questions and proceed to more specific ones or may begin specific and proceed to more general questions. The choice depends upon the nature of the criteria or research questions.

Group the questions together according to content. Also, use the same types of question structures (e.g., Likert scales) together as much as possible if content is appropriate. It is easier to fill out an instrument when similar question structures are grouped. Build ties between the questions. If you have different content being collected in the instrument, you may want to head sections with titles such as (a) Attitudes, (b) Participation, and (c) Background (Demographics). This format may help divide a long questionnaire into manageable sections and allow the respondents to move through the questionnaire more easily.

You want to design the instrument layout so that respondents don't get confused or miss an item. It usually helps to maximize white space on the questionnaire so that an individual does not feel overwhelmed with questions. Again, questions designed to be answered on the Internet can be structured such that a respondent cannot move to the next page without completing all data responses requested. Design staged questions or questions that require the respondent to "go to" another item with easy-to-follow directions. For example, if answering "yes" leads to another question, make sure the individual knows where to go in the question-naire to answer the next question. Similarly, if "no" means that one skips questions, make that clear as well. Some questionnaires use exclusively verbal instructions such as "If NO, then skip to Question 10. If YES, then go to the next question." Some questionnaires make use of heavy lines and directional arrows that indicate where to go next. Again, online surveys can automatically move a respondent to the next appropriate question. Whichever technique is used, establishing a vertical flow (i.e., up and down) through the instrument is essential to motivating a respondent to continue to the end.

Several other formatting issues might be considered. With a paper-and-pencil questionnaire it is often useful to use lower-case letters for questions, uppercase letters for answers. An individual could also design a questionnaire using different font sizes or by using bold-face, under-lined, or italics to show the differences between directions, questions, and responses. Using numbers to identify answer categories rather than boxes to check or letters to circle will be easier later in the coding of responses into numbers that can be entered into the computer. Try to make sure the responses to a question fit all on one page or else move the whole question to the next page. In the case that a series of Likert responses are used that move onto another page, put the scaling anchors at the top of the next page so that the respondent does not get confused about how to answer the questions. Layout should include enough space in-between questions and consistent spacing. Table 2.6(6) shows an example of a possible questionnaire layout. This example was adapted from the original work of Dillman who now has several editions of his updated book (Dillman, Smith, & Christian, 2009) that present state-of-the-art information about mail, telephone, and Internet surveys. The formatting in the example is designed for a paper-and-pencil test, whereas the format may look quite different in an electronic survey format.

The way that the paper-and-pencil questionnaires are put together physically is important. Colored paper is often more interesting than plain

---

*Table 2.6(6)  Example of Questionnaire Layout for Demographic Questions*

---

Q1    What is the number of children living in your home in each age group? (If none, write "0")
\_\_\_\_\_ Under 12 Years
\_\_\_\_\_ 5–13  Years
\_\_\_\_\_ 14–18 Years
\_\_\_\_\_ 19–24 Years
\_\_\_\_\_ 25 Years and Over

Q2    What is your age? \_\_\_\_\_ Years

Q3    What is your present job status? (Circle Number)
1. Employed
2. Unemployed
3. Retired
4. Full-Time Homemaker

Q4    What was your approximate net family income from all sources, before taxes, in 2009? (Circle Number)
1. Less than $19,999
2. $20,000 to 29,999
3. $30,000 to 39,999
4. $40,000 to 49,999
5. $50,000 to 59,999
6. $60,000 to 69,999
7. $70,000 to 79,999
8. $80,000 to 89,999
9. Over $90,000

Q5    Which is the highest level of education that you have completed? (Circle Number)
1. Completed grade school
2. Some high school
3. Completed high school
4. Some college
5. Completed college (specify major _____)
6. Some graduate work
7. A graduate degree (specify degree and major
_____)

white. A subdued color, such as yellow or light blue, is usually good for most instruments. The more professional an instrument looks, the better people will respond. Using a booklet with saddle stitching is desirable for lengthy surveys, although it is also more expensive. The front page should include the title of the questionnaire, some type of graphic (optional, but interesting), the time of year it is being administered (e.g., Fall 2009), any needed directions, and the information (name, title, and address) of the sponsor or evaluator who is conducting the project. The back cover may include a "thank you" and allow space for individuals to write further comments.

Whatever you do, make sure the instrument looks professional and that there are *no* typographical mistakes or anything else that might raise questions about the credibility of the instrument or the data collection process. Also, make sure the items can be easily read. Smaller print allows one to get more on a page, but may be difficult to read for some people.

The length of an instrument also is important to consider. Instruments should be long enough to get the needed information, but not too long. Shorter questionnaires reduce fatigue and are more likely to be completed. You may get a higher response rate with a 2-page than a 6-page questionnaire. On the other hand, a well-designed six-pager is better than a poorly designed one-pager. Let people know about how long it will take to complete an instrument so they can plan their time (e.g., 10 minutes—but be honest and realistic). As stated before, the better the layout and design, the easier the questionnaire will be to complete and the more likely that you will get a high response rate.

Clear directions throughout the instrument are essential, but are often overlooked. On a paper-and-pencil questionnaire, tell people if you want them to check a response or circle numbers. Tell them if you want the *best* response or more than one. On Internet questionnaires, these issues can be controlled but they need to be in the program you are designing. Give complete directions, especially if you have a series of questions. Explain the directions for each scale each time it is encountered in a questionnaire. Most instruments have an introduction that tells the respondent what to do and how to do it. The instructions should be clear, concise, and adequate to explain what is expected, but you may need to remind respondents as they proceed if the questionnaire is lengthy.

Electronic surveys are often used today. More detail is provided about these instruments later in this unit. Regardless, however, instructions, question content, and appropriate wording are needed no matter what format is used.

# From Ideas to Reality

This chapter is full of suggestions regarding developing instruments. Developing your own instrument can be a lot of fun but it also can be time-consuming, as you can see by the myriad details that you need to address. Any instrument that is developed should be just as reliable, valid, and usable as any pre-existing instrument that might have been chosen. The instruments must also be practical and simple—easy to use, easy to understand, and easy to code and analyze. Whether you use existing instruments or develop your own is up to you. As usual, the criteria that are set likely will determine the choice that you make.

Now that you have studied this chapter, you should be able to:

- State the basic procedures used to design questionnaires
- Write questions representing the five question types using past, present, and future tenses where appropriate
- Describe the differences between open-ended, close-ended, and partially close-ended question structures
- Evaluate the difference between a well-worded, formatted questionnaire and one that is not
- Develop a questionnaire to measure criteria that uses different content types and questionnaire structures

# 2.7 Surveys:
# The Winner of the Popularity Contest

The most common type of method found in the evaluation of recreation and leisure program services and in research in parks, recreation, tourism, sport, and leisure studies is the survey. Surveys are generally easy regarding administration and can provide information from the people's perspective related to most aspects of a program such as reactions, learning, and perceived behavior changes. Many people are familiar with filling out questionnaires. Further, many professionals are more accustomed to using surveys than observations or unobtrusive methods. Just because surveys are so popular, however, does not mean that they should be used carelessly. In this chapter, we explore the advantages and disadvantages of the various survey techniques.

Surveys refer to all types of paper-and-pencil and Internet questionnaires as well as phone, Internet, personal, and group interviews. Survey methods are designed to get information from individuals. They may include open-ended or close-ended instruments used to collect qualitative or quantitative data. The choice of the specific technique will depend on the criteria to be measured, the sample selected, the expertise of the evaluator or researcher, the needs of the organization, and the availability of time and other resources. Choosing the best method and technique is essential for any project. Surveys are often the most practical approach.

No survey technique is perfect for every situation, although ideally we are always striving to find perfect methods for specific situations. Sometimes we have to settle for "good enough" approaches to data collection. It is essential, however, that evaluators and researchers carefully consider the options for collecting data from surveys and then make the best possible choices.

## Response Rate

Response rate is an issue that must be considered in administering any kind of survey. The rate refers to the percentage of surveys received based on the number that were distributed. For example, if you gave out 25 questionnaires in a class and got 25 back, you would have a 100% response rate. If you gave out 25 and only got 20 back, it would be an 80% response rate. The simple formula for calculating response rate is:

Number of Questionnaires Distributed
(divided by) Number of Completed Questionnaires Returned
= Response Rate

Crompton and Tian-Cole (1999) examined what might be an acceptable and achievable response rate for mailed questionnaires about recreation. They found that 70% was a reasonable expectation among special interest groups (e.g., parents of youth sports programs), 60% would be desirable from professional groups (e.g., staff and volunteers), and 55% estimated from general interest groups (e.g., individual participants in any recreation program). You are always hoping for a 100% response rate, but that is not generally possible. The response rate, however, can be greatly improved by some of the suggestions in this book, including making the questionnaire the appropriate length, using incentives if possible (such as a free admission to an event), and targeting the sample you will use.

Each of the survey techniques has particular strengths and weaknesses that may influence response rate. These strengths and weaknesses are presented in Table 2.7(1) and discussed in this chapter. Self-administered questionnaires and interviews (including phone, face-to-face, Internet, and group) are the two major survey approaches used. Both require the development of questions for respondents to answer. Within these approaches, we may choose from among several techniques for gathering data: mailed questionnaires, drop-off/pick-up questionnaires, group administered questionnaires, contact ahead/send questionnaires, electronic questionnaires, telephone interviews, individual interviews, or group interviews (generally referred to as focus groups). The technique used will depend on the evidence needed to measure your evaluation criteria or research questions.

# Self-Administered Questionnaires

Self-administered questionnaires can be done by mail, drop-off/pickup, group administrations, contact ahead/mail, or on the Internet. The advantage of these written questionnaires lies in the ease of presenting questions that may require visual aids. Questions that are long or may require more complex responses, such as stage questions (i.e., questions that require several items to get a response) can be done more easily with written self-administered questionnaires. You can also ask a battery of similar questions without tiring the respondent. A high degree of anonymity is found in self-administered questionnaires, assuming no identifying information

Table 2.7 *Advantages and Disadvantages of Survey Techniques*

| Technique: | |
|---|---|
| **Advantages** | **Disadvantages** |
| **Self-Administered** | |
| • Ease of presenting questions<br>• Longer, stage questions can be used<br>• High degree of anonymity | • Requires careful wording<br>• No chance to clarify misunderstandings<br>• Reading skills required<br>• Not good for open-ended questions |
| **Mailed Questionnaire** | |
| • Low cost<br>• Minimal staff/facilities required<br>• Widely dispersed samples<br>• Time for respondent to respond<br>• Easy to administer<br>• Anonymous and confidential<br>• Weather not a factor<br>• Good for vested interest groups | • Low response rate possible<br>• No assurance right person filling it out<br>• No personal contact<br>• Nonresponse bias<br>• Can't pursue deep answers |
| **Drop-off/Pick-up** | |
| • Can explain person-to-person<br>• High response rate | • Costly for staff time and travel<br>• Access may be a problem<br>• Safety of staff |
| **Group Administered** | |
| • High cooperation rates<br>• Low cost<br>• Personal contact | • Logistics of getting people together |
| **Contact/Send** | |
| • Usually higher response rate<br>• Personal contact<br>• Time/money not wasted on nonresponses | • More costly with phone calls |
| **Electronic** | |
| • Fast response and data collection<br>• Good and easy follow-up<br>• Cost savings<br>• User convenience<br>• Wide geographic coverage<br>• No interview bias<br>• Flexible use | • No population lists available<br>• Restricted to people with access<br>• Must use a computer<br>• Browser incompatibility problems<br>• Respondents are traceable<br>• Possibility of multiple submissions |

*Table 2.7* *Advantages and Disadvantages of Survey Techniques (continued)*

| Technique: | |
|---|---|
| **Advantages** | **Disadvantages** |
| **Interviews** | |
| • Ability to probe<br>• Establish and maintain rapport<br>• Questions can be clarified<br>• Low literacy rates can do well<br>• Unplanned information possible<br>• Interviewer can be adaptable | • Time and personnel requirement<br>• Trained interviewers needed<br>• Simple questions asked<br>• Usually smaller sample size |
| **Telephone** | |
| • Lower costs than personal<br>• Random-digit-dialing sampling possible<br>• Broad geographic area covered<br>• Data can be collected quickly<br>• Control over data collection<br>• Possibility of callbacks<br>• Rapport but not face-to-face | • Sampling limitations for those without phone<br>• People can hang up<br>• Visual aids can't be used<br>• Sometimes superficial<br>• Timing is important |
| **Personal** | |
| • Elicit cooperation<br>• Probing and follow-up used<br>• Other observations to use<br>• Establish rapport<br>• Longer interviews<br>• High response rate<br>• Spontaneous reactions | • Costly<br>• Requires highly trained interviewers<br>• Long data collection period<br>• Some populations not accessible<br>• Small geographic area<br>• Possible interviewer bias |
| **Group Interviews** | |
| • Fast to conduct<br>• Same as personal<br>• Possibility of phone or Internet | • Logistics of getting people together<br>• Leader must work to get all opinions |

is requested. The respondent also does not have to share directly in a face-to-face manner with the evaluator.

Disadvantages, however, exist with self-administered questionnaires.

1. Careful questionnaire wording and layout is needed because the evaluator has no chance to clarify the questions being asked.

2. Long open-ended questions usually do not work well in self-administered questionnaires, as people do not like to

write long responses or some people may feel their writing skills are inadequate. A personal (face-to-face, phone, or focus group) interview is a better approach if you want detailed information.

3. Good language and reading skills are required to do self-administered questionnaires. All questionnaires should be directed at the appropriate age of the respondents. In general, a fifth-grade reading level is suitable for most adults. In areas with high ethnic diversity, multilanguage (e.g., a Spanish translation or whatever other ethnic group might be dominant) questionnaires may be needed.

## Mailed Questionnaires

Advantages exist for mailed, self-administered questionnaires. The cost is relatively low and data can be collected with minimal staff and facilities. A mailed survey can provide access to geographically dispersed samples and samples that might be difficult to reach in other ways. With self-administered questionnaires, the respondents typically have time to give thoughtful answers and/or look up information.

Written, mailed questionnaires are obviously easy to administer. *Anonymity* (i.e., no one knows someone's identity) or *confidentiality* (i.e., only the data collector knows the respondent's identity) can be assured in this technique, even if code numbers are used to keep track of questionnaire returns. With mailed questionnaires, you have access to high- and low-income groups, although a certain level of education is necessary to respond to the questions. Weather does not impact the response rate and you can include a range of questions. The technique of mailed questionnaires is particularly good for larger samples (over 100 cases). You can be confident with the results, especially with a 50% return rate or better. The standardized instructions should result in reliable responses if the directions are clear and the questions are well-worded.

Disadvantages of mailed questionnaires lie in possible nonsampling biases. For example, maybe a particular demographic group did not respond, or people with a particular opinion did not respond. The possibility of a low response rate exists with mailed questionnaires. People sometimes do not open an envelope if they do not recognize the return address; they may throw the questionnaire away immediately if it does not interest them; or sometimes, if the letter comes from a government agency, they may be suspicious or unwilling to respond. It is possible to miss some homeless people if they do not have mailing addresses or some people who may not be able to read or understand English. Further, you can't determine how an individual perceives the questions, and whether the person you intended is filling out the questionnaire. With a mailed questionnaire, you as the data collector have limited ability to pursue answers deeply. Questionnaires often require "accurate memory," which is not always possible. Mailed questionnaires are sometimes an ineffective way to get cooperation, because you have no personal contact. If the respondent does not know or trust you, he or she is less likely to want to "give" you information. In addition, the mailed questionnaire technique also requires time and money to collect data. Sending out a questionnaire, allowing several days to respond, and mailing the questionnaire back takes time.

You must be sure to have current mailing addresses and recognize that people without postal addresses will not be included in the survey. Mailed questionnaires are seldom used with the general public because names are not available and response rates are almost always low. It is possible, however, to obtain or purchase mailing lists from local government tax rolls, utility companies, and telephone companies, although these lists will also have limitations. If you wanted to collect data from a community or a neighborhood, you might be interested in obtaining these kinds of lists of names. Mailing companies exist that will charge you to purchase lists based on the population and sample that you want to contact.

On the other hand, mailed questionnaires are usually highly useful for particular groups that have a vested interest in an activity. For example, if we wanted to know what Girl Scout leaders thought of the training they received, a short mailed questionnaire might be a good way to receive feedback with the likelihood of a fairly high return rate. Presumably Girl Scout leaders would have a vested interest in making sure that training was done well.

In doing any kind of mailed questionnaire, an evaluator or researcher must be concerned about nonsampling error, also known as nonresponse bias. In other words, it is likely that those who do not respond to a survey may be different from those who respond. As is discussed in the chapters on sampling and administering questionnaires, the data collector must do as much as possible to assure that a high response rate is obtained and that nonrespondents are not different from those who respond.

## Drop-Off/Pick-Up Questionnaires

Dropping off one day and picking up questionnaires at a later date has some advantages beyond what has already been discussed related to self-administered questionnaires. With a drop-off/pick-up technique, you can explain the study and answer questions when the questionnaire is dropped off. If someone is unable to do the questionnaire, they can say so right away. Thus, the return rate is likely to be higher than with mailed questionnaires. Having time with the questionnaire also provides the individual with the opportunity to give thoughtful answers.

Some disadvantages exist in the drop-off and pick-up technique. Frequently the costs are as high as personal interviews, because field staff and travel money are required to do this legwork. Getting access to sites may also be a problem, as is making arrangements to get the questionnaires picked up. Sometimes you might be able to drop off a questionnaire to a group such as participants at a senior center program and ask them to bring the questionnaire back the next day or next week. This technique may be effective but sometimes people forget.

## Group Administrations

Group administrations of paper-and-pencil tests have advantages in getting a high cooperation rate. This group administration process is similar to what a teacher does in the classroom when she or he gives a test. Each respondent is given a questionnaire and can take as long as needed to respond. The data collector also has the chance to explain and answer questions about the survey. Frequently the cost for this technique is low.

Disadvantages of group administrations include the possibility of only collecting a small number of surveys because of the logistics of getting people together in groups. If people already exist in a group, however, logistics and numbers generally are not a problem. You must be sure that the group completing the questionnaire is representative of the individuals you are studying so that the group administration is not just a convenience sample.

## Contact/Send

Another technique for self-administered questionnaires is to call or e-mail people to enlist their cooperation and then mail or e-mail them a questionnaire. Once people make a commitment to you over the phone or via e-mail, they are more likely to look for the survey and complete it. This technique usually has a relatively high response rate. The evaluator can also answer any questions about the project ahead of time. Additional expense of staff time is added in making contact, but this cost may be offset with the assurance that questionnaires are not wasted on people who do not want to return them, especially in the case of mailed questionnaires.

## Electronic Data Collection

A new area of collecting survey data is emerging in the form of web-based and e-mail data collection. A new chapter in this book is dedicated to a consideration of the techniques of using electronic data collection. Many advantages exist, as do some disadvantages.

Electronic evaluation may provide a greater diversity of the sample without the need for constant monitoring. Electronic data collection also is generally low-cost, quick, and reasonably easy. It is one of the least intrusive ways to collect information. If you have e-mail lists, you can put together a questionnaire, following the tenets of good design, and ask individuals to complete and return it to you. E-mail surveys are effective because most people check their e-mail when they have time to respond and therefore may be more likely to respond at their convenience, which raises cooperation and response rates. In addition, respondents can be more objective when they type in their own responses without any interviewer influence. You can also use good formatting and graphics as a way to make the questionnaires more interesting.

Some of the disadvantages of this electronic technique include possible issues of privacy and confidentiality, although this concern can be addressed with many of the electronic services that now exist. In addition, since not everyone has access to the Internet, you may have an upper- to middle-class bias built in to your study. You may also miss some older adults who do not use the Internet. Nevertheless, these forms of electronic data collection are clearly common in many areas of the recreation field today.

# Interviews

Interviews traditionally have been divided into three categories: *telephone interviews, individual personal interviews*, and *focus group interviews*. The general advantages of interviews include the evaluator's ability to probe to a greater depth, the opportunity to establish and maintain rapport, and the possibility of clarifying questions. People with lower literacy levels can often do well with interviews, although the more articulate an individual is, the more information will be obtained. The data collector may also get unplanned or serendipitous information and may gain insight into the true feelings of respondents through time spent in interviewing. The evaluator can encourage respondents to answer questions and can be somewhat flexible and adaptable to the situation.

Weaknesses of interviews, in general, include the great amount of time and personnel that are usually required. Interviewers must have some training, and interview biases are always a concern. Although interviews may be quantitative, the questions need to be simpler than self-administered questionnaires because respondents will have to listen rather than read.

Open-ended questions provide rich information but may be more difficult to analyze than close-ended questions. In addition, interviews usually result in a smaller sample size.

## Telephone

Telephone interviewing has a number of advantages. The costs are lower compared to personal interviews and moderate compared to mailed or electronic questionnaires. Sampling processes like random digit dialing can be used. The evaluator has access to certain populations in a broad geographic area. Further, the potential exists for a short data collection period. A smaller staff is needed compared to personal interviews, but more people are generally needed than for doing a mailed or electronic questionnaire. The evaluator has a little more control over the data collected in an interview because the interviewer can explain questions if needed. It is often easier to get sensitive data over the phone because individuals do not have to see you in person. A telephone conversation sometimes seems more anonymous. You are likely to get a better sample because of the personal contact and possibility of callbacks. In some cases letters are sent ahead of time to "warn" respondents that they will be receiving a call in the next week. In some telephone surveys, an initial call is made to ascertain cooperation and to set up an appointment for a more convenient time to talk at greater length.

Disadvantages of telephone interviews include sampling limitations, particularly for those people without telephones, with only mobile phones, or with unlisted numbers. Since phone interviews rely on verbal communication, response alternatives are limited with the impossibility of visual aids and visual observations. For example, you would not be able to ask people to rank more than 3–4 items in a phone interview. Some superficiality may result because you can't probe as deeply with phone interviews. Without prior contact, telephone interviews are less appropriate for personal or sensitive questions. One must consider timing if the calls are to be successful. In addition, telephone marketing is so popular these days that people often are not willing to spend time with someone they don't know on the phone and will hang up.

## Personal

Personal interviews with individuals are useful for data collection. The data collected may be quantitative or qualitative. These interviews may be brief encounters such as someone in a shopping mall stopping to ask people four or five close-ended questions about the mall, or personal interviewing can be done at an office or in a home with in-depth oral histories/case studies that may last an hour or more.

Personal interviewing is an effective way to enlist cooperation. Most people like to be asked to state their opinions. If someone does not want to be involved, they will say so immediately. Accurate responses to complex issues are possible in personal interviews because the interviewer can probe and encourage responses. In addition to the words, you can also get additional data through observations and visual cues. Rapport and confidence building is easier when you are face to face with another individual. In addition, longer interviews can often be undertaken. The success of interviews, however, depends on the interviewer's ability to get information. Personal interviews usually result in a high response rate and allow the evaluator to control the process to address the purposes of the project.

Disadvantages of personal interviewing include the cost and the need for trained interviewers who have access to interviewees. Unless you have a great deal of money, your sample size will likely be small. Further, data collection may take a longer period of time. Some populations may not be accessible for personal interviews such as people in high crime areas or "famous" people. Logistics must be taken into account, as it is often difficult to interview over a large geographic area.

## (Focus) Group

Group interviews, commonly referred to as "focus groups," have advantages because they are faster to do, even though attention to logistics is required in getting people together. They often result in speedier results and can be relatively low in cost. Focus groups allow the moderator to probe and can be high in face validity. Krueger and Casey (2009) argued that the advantages of the focus group are its socially oriented evaluation procedures that allow the interviewer to probe. Fairly large samples can be obtained if several small groups are combined in data analysis.

The limitations of focus groups are that there is less control in a group interview, the interviewer must be carefully trained, groups may vary considerably, groups may be difficult to assemble, and the discussion must be in an environment conducive to conversation. As we will discuss in Unit 3, analyzing qualitative data obtained from group interviews may be more difficult than when close-ended questions are asked.

Focus groups can also be conducted over the phone or the Internet. Phone focus groups can be set up like conference calls. Internet group techniques allow for an immediate, permanent, and secure record of responses. Internet focus groups can be developed in the form of "real-time chat groups" or ongoing groups such as with discussion boards. The real-time chat group can be set up to allow several users to engage in a discussion with moderator control. An ongoing Internet discussion group will provide respondents time to post responses and enable post follow-up questions. Regardless, the focus groups must be focused and systematic.

# From Ideas to Reality

The survey technique you choose will depend on the object of your study and the availability of the population. Many survey options exist. The use of the right technique coupled with a good questionnaire or interview schedule will contribute to success using any survey technique. If you follow these suggestions for making decisions, you should be able to conduct the best possible survey project.

Now that you have studied this chapter, you should be able to:
- Describe why surveys are the most common method used in recreation, park, tourism, and leisure services
- Explain the advantages and disadvantages of self-administered and interview surveys
- Choose the appropriate survey technique based on the criteria and resources that are available for a given evaluation or research project

# 2.8 Surveys: Administering Questionnaires and Conducting Telephone Interviews

When using surveys, you have to consider the best way to actually get your questionnaires to the right population and sample. This chapter identifies some of the procedures to follow in administering paper-and-pencil questionnaires and conducting interviews. Another chapter will be devoted specifically to issues concerning Internet surveys. Regardless of the data collection strategy, we assume that the criteria are well-established for a project and that you have selected or developed a reliable, valid, and usable instrument.

## Pilot-Testing and Field-Testing

All evaluators and researchers should pilot-test their instruments with a sample similar to the one that will be doing the actual evaluation. Usually the pilot-test is done to see if any problems exist with the instrument or the sample. This recommendation was discussed to some extent in the chapter on choosing and developing instruments, but we cannot emphasize enough the importance of pilot-testing. Changes may need to be made in the instrument after the pilot is completed, or you may use the data obtained in the pilot-test to develop plans for sampling or for future data analysis.

A pilot-test usually consists of going to a small sample (5–30 people) that is like the individuals who will ultimately receive the questionnaire. The data collector will distribute the survey exactly as it will be administered and note the responses from the sample. In addition, people taking the pilot might be queried about whether the items on the questionnaire were clear and understandable. Some problems may be evident to you as you assess the way that people responded to the questions. As indicated previously, you must pay attention to the information you get in the pilot as it can give you insight to consider before you actually begin to collect data. At this point, changes can be made in the questionnaire to make it more usable. If major changes are made, you may need to do a second pilot study.

Some people also use the pilot to test the reliability, validity, and usability of an instrument. The pilot-test will determine if, in fact, an instrument can be successfully administered over the phone or whether another method would be better. If a standardized test is used, a pilot-test may not be necessary, but doing one may help to assure that the instrument is valid for its intended use.

Another technique that is sometimes used similar to the pilot-test is a field-test. A field-test usually refers to a testing of the process that will be used to obtain data more so than a focus on the actual instrument. For example, in a study of campers that we did, we conducted a field-test the summer before to see if the logistics of collecting pre- and post-camp data, especially from parents, would work. Based on our experience, we revised our plans for data collection.

# Implementing Mailed Questionnaires

In conducting mailed questionnaires, several aspects need to be considered, including cover letters, mailing procedures, and follow-ups.

## Cover Letters

A questionnaire, whether mailed or emailed, should never be sent without some explanation of the evaluation project or research study. This description is usually done with a cover letter. The letter should contain a clear and brief, yet adequate, statement of the purpose and value of the survey. If possible, the letter should be personally addressed to the respondent.

The cover letter should engage the potential respondent in a constructive and appealing way and should provide good reason why the respondent should take time to complete the questionnaire. The respondent's professional or public responsibility, intellectual curiosity, or personal worth are typical response appeals. The tone should be one that is inviting and not authoritarian.

The cover letter should indicate a reasonable but firm return date. Usually people need 2 weeks to respond. Make sure a deadline is given or you may still receive questionnaires for months after you have completed your project. An offer to send the respondent a report of findings is an ethical responsibility. Make this offer only, however, if you are committed to making sure that a summary is sent. The use of letterhead, signature, and organizational endorsements lend prestige and official status to the cover letter.

The cover letter should guarantee anonymity or confidentiality and explain carefully how the data will be used. The evaluator or researcher should sign the letter individually, if at all possible. It is often best to avoid using words like "questionnaire" and "study," as these terms sometimes are not perceived as positively as are words like "project" and "survey." Table 2.8(1) shows a sample cover letter that might provide a prototype to follow when designing your own letter.

*Table 2.8(1)  Sample of a Cover Letter*

---

Department of Recreation and Leisure Studies
CB #3185 Evergreen House
University of North Carolina at Chapel Hill
Chapel Hill, NC  27599-3185

December 1, 2009

Dear (name):
Summer staff salaries are an issue each of us will address shortly. For some time, many camp directors have wondered how their summer camp salaries compared to other positions in the same region and in comparable camp settings. Baseline data about summer camp staff salaries may be useful information for the camping movement in general, as well as for specific camps.

Your camp has been randomly selected for participation in this project. We are asking only a small percentage of accredited agency, religiously affiliated, and independent day and resident camps across the United States to complete and return this short questionnaire. Therefore, your participation is extremely *important*.

You may be assured of confidentiality. The questionnaire has an identification code number for mailing purposes only. This coding is done so that we may check your camp name off the mailing list when your questionnaire is returned.

The results of this survey will be made available to the American Camping Association and will be distributed at the next ACA Conference in Denver. You may receive a copy of the results in mid-February if you send us a self-addressed stamped envelope with your questionnaire.

To get the results tabulated by February, it is necessary to have the data as soon as possible. We are asking that you please return the questionnaire by December 18. Since ACA is doing this study on a small budget, you will contribute to the organization by putting your own stamp on the return addressed envelope enclosed.

We appreciate your assistance. We believe we are undertaking a valuable and useful project. If you have any questions, please call us at 919-962-1222. Thank you again.

Sincerely,


(names)
(titles)

---

# Mailing

Depending on the number of questionnaires to be sent, one may use bulk mail or first class. First class mail is faster, but more expensive. Bulk rate may take up to two weeks for delivery, but is less expensive. If an address is wrong, first class letters will be returned to the sender but not for bulk mail. Therefore, with bulk mail you do not know if a percentage of your nonresponse was due to people not receiving the questionnaires or due to respondents not taking the time to complete the questionnaire.

The higher your response rate, the more confidence you can have that your survey represents the views of the sample. You should always have a goal of getting a 100% response rate. To get a higher response, you can do such things as enclose a stamped, self-addressed envelope. A "business" envelope will also work. Business reply envelopes are usually more financially desirable, because you are only charged postage for the questionnaires returned. Response rates are generally higher if it is as easy as possible for someone to return a questionnaire. Some evaluations may use self-mailers, in which the respondent simply folds the questionnaire, staples or tapes it, and puts it in a postal box. You will need to decide the best way, but keep the mail back as easy as possible for the respondent.

Although 100% is a possible goal, for most mailed surveys you should realistically expect a 50–70% response rate. The shorter the questionnaire, the better the response rate. If the response is lower than 50%, you may have nonsampling or nonrespondent bias. As noted earlier, response rate is calculated by dividing the actual number of responses returned by the number in the sample size minus those individuals who were not reachable (such as questionnaires returned due to incorrect addresses or no forwarding address), and then multiplying by 100. The resulting number should be as close to 100 as possible.

A low response rate does more damage than a small sample size, since no valid way exists of scientifically inferring the characteristics of the population represented by nonrespondents. People likely not to respond often have little or no interest in the topic, are low-income and blue-collar workers who tend to express themselves less frequently in written form, and who lack much formal education (Michigan State University, 1976).

Sometimes you can provide incentives such as a small amount of money, gift certificates or coupons, pencils, gifts (small mementos), or a promise of a copy of the results to encourage people to respond. Providing incentives adds additional expense to the survey, but may be important in some situations. We know of one health club that offered two free guest passes to any member who returned a completed evaluation questionnaire. The best thing to do, however, to assure a high response rate is to convince people of the value of their input on a well-designed mailed questionnaire.

Many evaluators use a code number system to keep track of who and how many people return questionnaires. This code is created by giving each respondent a number associated with her or his name and address. This number is then written somewhere on the questionnaire. In the cover letter, you should explain what the number means. When the questionnaire is returned, the name can be crossed off the list so that no additional money is wasted on follow-up reminders, and the individual does not have to deal with what then becomes "junk" mail. Destroying the list of names and numbers after the data are coded and tabulated also assures the respondent of confidentiality.

Follow-up contacts should also be conducted to obtain a higher response rate. Followers of the Dillman et al. (2009) "total design" or "tailored design" method send a reminder postcard to individuals who have not returned questionnaires after the first 10 days. It is just a friendly reminder. A second follow-up letter should be sent several days after the initial due date. It should include a second cover letter with much of the same information as in the first, including a "plea" to complete the questionnaire by a new due date. This follow-up letter might suggest that the evaluator hopes the questionnaire is in the mail, while also reaffirming the value of the project. Another questionnaire and a self-addressed stamped envelope should be included with the second follow-up letter. A final contact in the form of another postcard should be mailed about 10 days after the second letter is sent to anyone who has not returned the questionnaire. If you still have not received a good response rate, a telephone call to nonrespondents might be initiated to either ask them to return the questionnaire or, if possible, complete the questionnaire over the phone.

For some studies, you may want to determine nonresponse bias. In other words, are those people who didn't respond different than those who did? You can call to get demographic data or check if late respondents are different demographically than early respondents to your survey. If you get a high response rate (high is usually 50–70%), determining nonresponse bias is probably not necessary.

## Administration to Groups

The administration of surveys to groups mainly requires getting people together to give them a questionnaire. You will need to provide them with a writing instrument and a place that is conducive to responding. Clear directions should be given about the purpose of the questionnaire and what to do once it is completed. The response rate is much higher when people are required to complete a questionnaire on the spot, although sometimes people do not want to take the time if the questionnaire looks long. Possibilities also exist to administer a questionnaire to a group via a number of computers set up in a room. If such a group administration is possible, data can be collected easily and if any computer issues exist or questions arise, the data collectors will be available.

Sometimes it may be necessary to allow people to take a questionnaire home. In that case, you may want to use a code procedure similar to what was done with the mailed questionnaire so that you can send out postcards or make phone calls as reminders to those who do not return their questionnaire. If people are asked to return a questionnaire, make sure they know where and when to do so. In some situations, mailing may be easier than a drop-off. Provide the address and a stamped envelope along with the questionnaire when you distribute it, if people are taking it away.

## Telephone Interviews

Telephone interviews may be conducted by sending a preliminary letter/email or by simply calling the interviewee on the spot—sometimes referred to as cold call. Forewarning is usually helpful if the individual needs time to consider the topic and it alleviates the suspicion that a call may not be legitimate. The advance letter or contact, similar to the cover letter, contains the details about the project and when the phone call is to occur.

Timing is often critical for telephone interviewing. The best time to catch people at home is between 6:00 and 9:00pm. This time slot is not always the most convenient time to get people to do interviews, however. Most telephone interviews are not completed during the first contact. Often several calls are required to get someone and to set up an appropriate time for the interview, if it requires more than a couple minutes on the phone. Other times of the day may work well depending on the audience you are trying to reach.

You may call from a predetermined list, use a random sample from a directory, or do random digit dialing. When making the call, the first thing to do is to confirm that the phone number is correct or that the appropriate residence has been reached. If a particular person in the household is wanted, such as the oldest adult living at the residence, that person should be requested. You should then state to the desired respondent who you are and why a phone survey is being conducted. A brief description of the project should be given (2–3 sentences). You might also want to tell how the phone number was obtained and/or remind the individual that a letter was sent previously. You should tell the respondent how long the interview will take and ask if now is a convenient time. If it is not, try to schedule another time that would be more convenient. Remember that you are interested in getting as high a response rate as possible, so do all that you can to get the interview completed. If someone hangs up on you, they are considered a nonrespondent or no return. As discussed previously, you want the return rate to be as close to 100% as possible.

Proceed through the interview on the phone as quickly as possible, but make sure you allow the individual enough time to think. If you are recording the conversation, be sure to inform the individual of the recording. If not, mark your responses to the questionnaire accurately or enter them into the computer appropriately. Many telephone interviewers now use computers that immediately enter the data and, depending upon the response, will move the interviewer to the next appropriate question (rather than having so many directions about "skipping" to the next question). Getting a "computer" to actually administer the questionnaire by asking the individual to punch numbers for responses is also commonly done today, although setting up such a protocol may be expensive. Table 2.8(2) shows an example of a telephone interview schedule that might be used. Keep in mind that if the interviewer is using a computer to input the information, the next question can be programmed to automatically appear.

Interviewers doing personal telephone interviews will need to be thoroughly trained. Sometimes you can get volunteers in an organization to do phone interviews, but often you will need to hire people. Regardless of whether paid or volunteer, the interviewers must be knowledgeable about the process and how to conduct the interview. Interviewers must also learn to read the questions exactly as they appear. They must understand the telephone system and must know how to respond to questions. It is usually best if all interviewers operate from a central location for ease of supervision. One of the best times to train interviewers is during the pilot-test, so they can practice their responses before you collect the real data.

The big difference between telephone interviews and mailed questionnaires is the need to have a third person between the evaluator and the respondent, unless of course the evaluator is also the sole interviewer. Regardless, much effort goes toward making sure the interviewer is adequately prepared.

## From Ideas to Reality

Survey administration is a necessary step for data collection. This aspect of the evaluation or research project is not difficult to do but the tips provided should help to make sure that the process goes smoothly. Pilot-tests and field-tests are almost always a useful undertaking, even though they often take time. Any kind of good research is challenging enough so you will want to do everything to try to make sure that data can be efficiently and effectively collected, whether you are using paper-and-pencil questionnaires, computers, or telephone surveys. Basic principles of administration apply to all types of surveys.

*Table 2.8(2)  Sample Telephone Interview for Recreation Trails Survey*

1. As we said, this survey is about the use of any designated recreational trails in Wisconsin. By this we mean any trail in Wisconsin that is marked and maintained specifically for recreational activities. Did you use any of these trails at all in 2009?
    1. yes (go to Q2)    2. no (go to Q1a)    7. don't know (dk)    9. NA (skip to Q46)

    1a. Is it very likely, likely, unlikely, or very unlikely that you will be a user of Wisconsin trails five years from now?
    1. very likely    2. likely    3. unlikely    4. very unlikely    7. dk    9. NA

    1b. Had you heard of these trails, or didn't you know they existed?
    1. heard (go to Q1c)    2. didn't know they existed (skip to Q46)
    7. dk (skip to Q46)    9. NA (skip to Q46)

    1c. Was there anything that kept you from using these trails in 2001 if you had wanted?
    1. yes (skip to Q33)    2. no (skip to Q46)    7. dk (skip to Q46)    9. NA (skip to Q46)

2. During 2009, about how many times did you use a designated recreational trail in Wisconsin for any of the activities I'll name?

    First: for backpacking? (Enter "0" if NONE)    #:_____
3. ...hiking without backpacks?    #:_____
4. ...biking?    #:_____
5. ...horseback riding?    #:_____
6. ...cross-country skiing?    #:_____
7. ...snowmobiling?    #:_____
8. ...driving or riding motorcycles or off-road vehicles?    #:_____
9. ...canoe trails?    #:_____
10. What other activities, if any, did you use the trails for in 2009, and about how many times did you do each one?
    0. none
    a) _____ #:_____
    b) _____ #:_____

**Interviewer: If "0" to Qs 2–10, return to Q1.**

11. In 2009, did you tend to use these trails more on weekdays or on weekends?
    1. weekdays    2. weekends    3. no difference    7. dk    9. NA
12. How many different designated recreational trails in Wisconsin did you use last year?
    #:_____
13. In 2009, did you use any nationally operated trails in Wisconsin?
    1. yes    2. no    3. no difference    7. dk    9. NA
14. Any state-operated trails?    1. yes    2. no    7. dk    9. NA
15. ...county-operated trails?    1. yes    2. no    7. dk    9. NA
16. ...city-operated trails?    1. yes    2. no    7. dk    9. NA
17. ...privately operated trails?    1. yes    2. no    7. dk    9. NA
18. Do you usually use these trails with a friend, a relative, or do you go alone?
    1. friend    2. relative    3. alone    4. both    7. dk    9. NA
19. When you used any of these trails, was it usually on outings sponsored by a club or organization?
    1. yes    2. no    7. dk    9. NA
20. Do any members of your household use designated recreational trails in Wisconsin that you do not use?
    1. yes    2. no    3. single person household    7. dk    9. NA

Now that you have studied this chapter, you should be able to:

- Conduct a pilot-test for a study that you would like to undertake
- Describe the steps in implementing a mailed questionnaire so that you will get the highest possible return rate
- Write a cover letter
- Determine the steps that need to be followed to complete successful telephone interviews

## 2.9 Surveys: Talking About Personal and Group Interviewing

The purpose of interviewing is to find out what is in and on someone's mind through oral communication. It allows data collectors to enter into another person's perspective. We assume that people's perspectives are meaningful, knowable, and expressible. Further, interviewing may be done over the telephone, face-to-face, or sometimes through Internet interfaces. Interviews may be done individually or in groups. The questions asked may collect quantitative or qualitative data. In-depth interviews are usually used to collect detailed and comprehensive qualitative data and to understand the meanings behind an interviewee's words.

The value of interviewing is in finding out the thoughts of an individual that cannot be directly observed. For example, we cannot observe feelings, opinions, and intentions. We cannot observe behavior that took place at some previous point in time. We cannot observe how people organize the world and the meanings they attach to what goes on in the world. We have to ask people questions about these things.

Interviewers sometimes feel they are imposing on people. Handled appropriately, however, what could be more flattering to an individual than to be asked to talk about her or his views about various issues? Most people like to talk about themselves and the interviewer should encourage them to talk. Nevertheless, as in all survey situations, the interviewee is giving a gift of time and emotion so the interviewee should be respected for that generosity and contribution.

## Approaches to Interviewing

Four approaches, according to Patton (1980b), may be used in conducting interviews, whether they are done one-on-one or in a group situation. The first, *structured close-ended interviews*, has already been discussed in the chapter on developing instruments. An example of a telephone interview was offered in the previous chapter. In this first approach, an interview schedule is developed ahead of time and the interviewer simply asks the quantitative questions as they appear on the pre-established questionnaire. As indicated previously, telephone interviews typically use this approach where the respondent is provided with a series of close-ended responses from which to choose.

The remaining three basic approaches are open-ended and are used to collect qualitative data. The three approaches require different types of preparation, conceptualization, and instrumentation:

1. The standardized open-ended interview (structured)

2. The general interview guide approach (semi-structured)

3. The informal conversational interview (unstructured)

## Standardized Open-Ended Interviews

In the structured approach, the interviewer must follow the questions verbatim. The standardized open-ended interview consists of a set of questions carefully worded and arranged with the intention of taking each respondent through the same sequence and asking each respondent the same questions in the same way. Flexibility in probing is limited. Sometimes you can only interview each participant once for a limited period of time. The questions are written in advance *exactly* how they are to be asked. Each question is carefully worded with the probing written into the questions. These questions are also asked to try to get as much information as possible. Therefore, wording is often used such as "tell me what you think about XYZ" or "what examples can you give that show how the recreation leader did a good job?"

The standardized open-ended technique minimizes interviewer effects by asking the same questions. Interviewer judgment does not enter into the interview and data organization is relatively easy to do. Three good reasons to use this approach are:

(a) the exact instrument used is available for inspection;

(b) variation among interviewers can be minimized; and

(c) the interview is highly focused so interviewee time can be carefully used.

In general, this approach maximizes the sense of legitimacy and credibility. The weaknesses are that the interviewer is generally not permitted to pursue topics or issues that were not anticipated when the interview schedule was written. Individual differences and circumstances might be reduced using this structured interview.

## Interview Guides

The *semi-structured* or *interview guide* approach allows freedom to probe and to ask questions in whatever order seems appropriate. In the general interview guide, a set of issues is outlined and explored with each respondent. The questions are prepared to make sure the same information is obtained from a number of people by covering the same material. The issues, however, are not necessarily covered in a particular order and the actual wording of each question is not determined ahead of time. The interview guide serves as a basic checklist during the interview. The interviewer must adopt the wording and sequence of questions in the context of the interview.

The interview guide provides topics or subject areas so the interviewer is free to explore, probe, and ask questions that will elucidate and illuminate that particular subject. The interviewer can remain free to build a conversation within a particular subject area and to establish a conversational style. The guide allows the interviewer to take as much time as needed to cover all the aspects of the guide. Interviewees can provide more or less detail, depending on their interests and the follow-up probes used by the interviewer. Other topics may emerge during the course of the conversation and the interviewer must decide whether or not to pursue those additional ideas. Interview guides are especially useful for focus group interviews. People differ from one another, and an interview guide enables the interviewer to get participants to talk by using flexible strategies. Table 2.9(1) shows an example of an interview guide used to collect data from older adults at a senior center about their involvement in physical activity programs.

## Informal Conversational Interviews

Unstructured approaches are also referred to as informal conversational interviews. These interviews have no pre-established questions but result from a conversation. In this informal approach, spontaneous generation in the natural flow of interaction results so the respondent may not realize she or he is being interviewed.

The strength of unstructured interviews is that they allow the interviewer to be highly responsive to individual differences and situational changes. The technique, however, requires a greater amount of time and conversational skill to collect systematic information. The interviewer must be able to interact easily with people in a variety of settings, generate rapid insights, formulate questions quickly and smoothly, and guard against asking questions that impose interpretations on the situation by the structure of the questions. In the unstructured approach, the evaluator gets great quantities of data that will require much time devoted to data organization and data analysis. Table 2.9(2) provides a summary of the strengths of all four interview approaches.

*Table 2.9(1)*  *Example of Interview Guide for a Project About Physical Activity*

What do you do when you come to the CSC?

What appeals to you about the programs offered by the CSC?

What has been your history of involvement with physical activity? Possible probes: Were you an active child? Involved with sports? Active as a younger adult?

How has your physical activity changed since you retired or became eligible to come to the CSC?

What keeps you from being more physically active than you already are?

How does your participation in the CSC contribute to your (quality of) life?

How did you first get involved with the fitness and wellness programs at the CSC?

Describe how you are more physically active because of your association with the CSC.

How would you rate and describe the quality of your experience when you are at CSC?

What else can you tell us that might be helpful in understanding your physical activity involvement personally or related to being a participant at CSC?

# Content of Interviews

As with any type of instrument development, you must determine and develop the content of interview questions. You must decide what questions to ask, how to sequence questions, how much detail to solicit, how long to make the interview, and how to word the actual questions. In developing questions for any survey, the evaluator may address the past, present, or future and may ask about behaviors, attitudes, knowledge, feelings, and/or background. Examples of these question types were described in Chapter 2.6.

In conducting structured and semistructured interviews, the sequencing of questions is important, although no fixed rules on how to do this exist. An evaluator usually starts with fairly noncontroversial questions to get the interviewee talking. Asking questions about behaviors, activities, and experiences is usually a good place to begin. These conversations can begin with a request such as "Tell me a little about yourself." Then you can ask about interpretations, opinions, and feelings. Questions about the present are usually easier to answer than questions about the past or the future.

*Table 2.9(2)* *Variations in Interview Approaches (adapted from Patton, 1980b)*

| Characteristics | Strengths | Weaknesses |
|---|---|---|
| **Interview Type #1: Informal Conversational** | | |
| Questions emerge from the immediate context and are asked in the natural course; no predetermination of question topics or stances. Difficult. | Increases the salience and relevance of questions the interview is built on and emerge from observations; interview matched to individuals and circumstances. Data organization. | Different information collected from different people with different questions. Less systematic wording. |
| **Interview Type #2: Interview Guide** | | |
| Topics and issues to be covered are specified in advance. Outline form. Interviewer decides sequence and wording of questions in interview. Interview is conversational and situational. | The outline increases the comprehensiveness of the data; systematic data for each respondent. Logical gaps in data can be closed. | Important and salient topics may be omitted. Comparability of responses is reduced. |
| **Interview Type #3: Standardized Open-Ended** | | |
| The exact wording and sequence of questions are determined in advance. Same basic question in same order. | Respondents answer the same questions; increased comparability of results. Reduced interviewer effects and bias when several individuals and interviewers are used. Permits decision makers to see and review the instrumentation used in the evaluation. Facilitates organization and analysis of the data. | Little flexibility in relating the interview to particular circumstances; wording may constrain and limit naturalness and relevance of Q & A's. |
| **Interview Type #4: Standardized Close-Ended** | | |
| Questions and response categories are determined in advance. Responses are fixed; respondent chooses from among these fixed responses. | Data analysis is simple; responses can be directly compared and easily aggregated; many questions in a short time. | Respondents must fit their experiences and feelings into researcher's categories; may be perceived as impersonal, irrelevant, and mechanical. Limited response choices. |

Asking open-ended questions is an art just like asking close-ended questions. You need to make the questions neutral, singular, and clear. Try to avoid "why" questions because they presume a cause and effect. Many possibilities are evident in "why" questions. Try to use words other than "why" to get at specific philosophical, economic, outcome, or personality factors you wish to explore. Instead of "Why did you join?" you might say, "What is it about the program that attracted you to it?" or "What is it about your personality that attracts you to this activity?" "Why" questions are often difficult to analyze with any comparability unless they are made more specific.

Collecting qualitative data through personal interviews requires that the interviewer use probes and follow-ups to deepen responses and to get detailed information. As an interviewer you may want to think about probes such as "who, what, where, how, and when" as you listen to someone describe their experiences. These follow-up questions can prompt the interviewee to elaborate and give more detail. Nonverbal signs such as head nodding may also elicit more information. Probes and listening responses are seldom written into a set of interview questions, but a successful interviewer knows how to use them appropriately.

The general conduct of any individual or group interview will require that both the interviewer and interviewee see themselves engaged in two-way conversation. The interviewee must be willing to talk. The interviewer must ask for the information desired, explain why it is important, and let the interviewee know how the interview is progressing. Further, the interviewer must maintain control of the interview. Encouragement should be given, but you may also want to stop an interviewee if she or he takes an irrelevant tangent. It is disrespectful to let someone go on about something that isn't appropriate for the particular evaluation or research project. It wastes everybody's time. In qualitative data collection through interviewing, however, you sometimes do not know how relevant someone's tangent might be in trying better to understand a phenomenon.

# Conducting an In-Person Interview

Contact is usually made with interviewees by mail, e-mail, or phone. The time, place, and other logistics of the interview should be described and discussed. Usually an in-depth personal interview will take 1/2–2 hours. A place should be scheduled where privacy is possible. Sufficient time and the proper place can greatly affect the nature of the interview. Let the interviewee know whether or not the conversation will be recorded when you first contact her or him. The evaluator must be clear about the study intentions and assure confidentiality to the respondents. You will probably want to explain the general topics that will be covered in your initial conversation and offer the interviewee an opportunity to receive a copy of the abstract or the final report when the study is completed.

## Recording the Data

How the data are recorded will depend upon the interview approach used. In a close-ended quantitative interview, the interviewer can mark a response sheet, much as would be done if a questionnaire were self-administered. For any of the other three approaches, the primary raw data are quotations, so the interviewer must try to capture the actual words said. Data interpretation and analysis involve making sense of what people have said, looking for patterns, putting together what is said earlier in an interview with what is said later, and comparing what different respondents have said. Since this process is necessary for analysis, you must record what is said as fully and fairly as possible during the personal interview.

A tape recorder is indispensable for in-depth personal or group interviewing. The use of tape recordings frees the interviewer to concentrate on interviewing, improves the fullness and quality of responses, avoids an interviewer's selective listening, and allows the evaluator to check up on interviewer technique. In our experience, tape recording usually does not increase resistance, decrease rapport, or alter people's responses. If a tape recorder cannot be used to get verbatim responses, then the interviewer must take thorough notes. Taking verbatim notes is extremely difficult. Not only does the tape recorder increase accuracy, but it also allows the interviewer to give the interviewee full attention during the interview.

When using a tape recorder, the interviewee must know why it is being used and how the tapes and transcriptions will be handled. To be on the safe side, sometimes it is useful to have two tape recorders going. Today's small digital recording devices are usually not intrusive, although respondents must be told such devices are being used.

Digital voice recordings last longer than standard tapes. Be sure to select a digital voice recorder that has all the capabilities you need. We recommend a digital voice recorder with transcription capabilities. Also, some digital voice recorders claim over 250 hours of recording time. However, the higher the quality of the recording, the fewer hours of recording time will be available. Always use high-quality mode so no data are lost and the transcriptions will be clearer. The amount of interviewing you will do may also influence other features you want. For example, some digital recorders have voice activation, which stops recording automatically whenever there is a period of silence. Others include cue/review features that make it easier to find the section of the recording you want to play back. Recorders with an LCD display are useful. Personal computer connectivity is a must for interviewing. Digital voice recorders should allow you to transfer voice data to a PC using a USB interface. Some plug directly into the computer's USB port, but others use docking stations and USB cables. Regardless, these devices are superior to traditional tape recorders and are a worthwhile investment, whether doing only a handful of interviews or many projects that collect in-depth interview data.

Even if using a recording device, the interviewer ought to jot notes in case of a mechanical problem. These jottings will also help to supplement the transcription. The notes that you jot while interviewing help formulate new questions and help organize information on the tape. Tape recordings should be as high quality as possible, and sometimes using lapel mikes helps further. You may want to make a back-up of the interview either with a duplicate tape or by downloading to a PC, if you will not get a chance to transcribe it immediately. Be sure to label the tapes or files and protect them so that they do not become damaged. Remember, when using qualitative data, the words are the data and you do not want to lose any of them. If you lose your data, you have no evaluation or research project.

Making a full transcription of all recorded interviews as soon as possible after an interview is highly desirable. Transcribing tapes, however, is time-consuming. The ratio of transcribing to recording time is 5:1. For most people, it takes about five hours to transcribe one hour of tape. Transcribing can be costly as well if you hire someone, but you must consider the usefulness and how the benefits may outweigh the costs. If you transcribe recordings yourself, even though time-consuming, you will have another opportunity to listen carefully to the data that you are generating. If resources (i.e., time or money) are not available for transcribing, you can work back and forth between tape and notes, although in the long run this working back and forth may be more time-consuming than doing the transcribing in the first place.

New technology is being developed every day to help make transcribing easier. If you want to be able to transcribe the voice files you record with a digital voice recorder directly into text, you can purchase software that will perform transcription. Some digital voice recorders come bundled with voice recognition software or their own proprietary transcription software; otherwise, you may want to purchase it separately. The quality of these transcriptions, however, must be double-checked as voice recognition technology is not without errors.

## Notes on Notes

As soon as an interview is complete, make notes about the interview. List proper names and any unfamiliar terminology that may have been encountered. You can make notes about anything observed that had relevance to the interview, like where the interview occurred, who was present, how the interviewee reacted, observations about the interviewer's role, and any additional information that might be important. You should also make "notes on notes" about how you felt the interview went. To do a good job of personal or group interviewing, you should spend time after the interview going over and reflecting carefully on what occurred both in terms of how the interview went and the types of data you are uncovering.

Depending on the nature of the interview, particularly if it is qualitative, you may want to follow-up for a second interview with an individual. Therefore, you will want to keep in touch with the people initially interviewed through a thank-you note or some communication. When you do the initial interview, you may want to confirm whether or not that person would be willing to do a second interview, if needed.

# Training and Supervising Interviewers

The comments in the first part of this chapter have assumed that the evaluator or researcher will be conducting the interview. You or other staff may be able to conduct interviews, and sometimes interviews can to be done by outside (volunteer or paid) people. Often organization staffs are too busy to do data collection. On the other hand, they know the participants well, and sometimes you have no choice but to use them due to financial constraints. Hiring interviewers is costly and time-consuming but may be a viable option if staff is not available.

Regardless of who does the interviews, they must have some training. Hiring or using interviewers who have experience is best, but experienced interviewers may not be easy to find. If experienced interviewers cannot be hired, extensive training must be conducted. In hiring or choosing interviewers, sometimes peoples' attitudes may make a greater difference than their actual skills. Middle-age women are often the least threatening to interviewees and it is sometimes useful to try to match race if possible. The research on the value of race matching as well as sex and age, however, has been inconsistent. Indigenous interviewers may be good in establishing rapport, but may not always have the skills unless they have extensive training.

The purpose of training is two-fold: to explain the details and objectives of the study and to familiarize individuals with the interview schedule and allow them to practice. Several key ideas might be emphasized in interviewer training. First the interviewer must learn to recognize and control any subtle or pervasive bias and become as neutral as possible. The interviewer should be told to always carry identification about the project so that any safety concerns on the part of interviewees can be allayed. The interviewer should not dress to any extreme but should look neat, conservative, and casual. The interviewer should show interest and concern without seeming to snoop into people's private lives. In general, however, the interviewer is only as good as the training she or he gets.

## Problems Associated with Interviewing

In conducting interviews, certain problems may be encountered. One problem relates to the influence of social desirability on validity. For example, people will often over-report participation because they think they should. Income is the exception to the rule, as people often underreport it. To avoid issues of social desirability, the interviewer should show complete acceptance of answers and reassure the interviewee that answers are confidential. Providing opportunities to explain rather than just answer yes/no may also encourage a respondent to answer honestly. An individual is more likely to give an honest answer if she or he understands the questions being asked.

The language used in any personal interview must also be considered. A respondent has the opportunity to ask for clarification if she or he doesn't understand a question, but an interviewer who uses the wrong language or unknown jargon may create problems in communication. People are sometimes reluctant to admit they don't understand for fear they may appear "stupid." Data collectors must also be concerned with different cultural perspectives. As interviewers we must recognize that language and speech patterns may result in different responses than initially expected. Being able to understand leisure interests and behavior through different cultural experiences, however, may be an essential value of using in-depth interviews. More information about suggestions regarding interviewing particular groups is described in the last chapter of this unit.

Some controversy surrounds the payment of respondents or offering them other types of incentives. On the positive side, some evaluators say the answers are better when people are paid, the interview is put in a commercial light, and the payment or valued incentive reflects the value of the time and energy spent giving information. Those who are against paying respondents say that it increases the cost of a project. Further, respondents may come to expect to be paid and a bad precedent may be set for other evaluators or researchers. Other opponents feel paying respondents may affect the validity because people will respond in more socially desirable ways. Many times evaluators do not have money available to pay interviewees, so payment is not an option. Other times it may be a possibility to consider. Sometimes other incentives, such as gift certificates or small souvenirs, may be appreciated by respondents as a way of thanking them.

Every evaluator should seek to minimize the degree of interview error in the evaluation or research project. Because of authority relationships, desirability of response, and the nature of the subject matter, response accuracy is always suspect. Interview error may occur due to the predisposition of respondents, such as if they are suspicious, hostile, indifferent, unmotivated, lacking information, lacking insight, or have limited language. Error may also be due to the predispositions of the interviewer, who may be uncomfortable with the people interviewed, shy, ill at ease, unable to establish rapport, lacking in an understanding of the language, or who may have stereotyped expectations. The procedures of the project are, however, under the project leader's control, and as much error as possible should be reduced through careful interview design and interviewer training.

# Specific Examples

Not only do leisure service professionals use interviews of the general public or participants such as through community needs assessments or formative evaluations, but there also may be some special clinical applications of interviews. Ferguson (1983), for example, described the components of a Therapeutic Recreation Assessment interview technique. The purpose of the assessment interview is to gather information for inferring the leisure needs of the client. An interview usually involves assessing client readiness for treatment, assessing client rationality and appropriateness, identifying leisure behavior patterns, gaining insight into personal leisure values, determining relationships between client and family, ascertaining personal strengths and assets of the client, determining needed lifestyle adjustments, analyzing available leisure systems, and examining economic factors.

Clinical interviewing techniques are not the focus of this book, but they relate to evaluation interviewing in general. For *any* open-ended interview, it is best to use open-ended and not yes/no questions, make questions short and specific, use "how" instead of "why" because it is less threatening, ask one question at a time, give the respondent time to think, ask questions that address the purpose of assessment, show empathy, use respondent's first name, and clarify mixed messages.

Staff performance appraisals are another example of regular interviews conducted each year. A supervisor can apply the principles of interviewing as she or he interacts with an employee by establishing rapport and communicating in a two-way conversation. Further, some type of structure is always needed for these performance evaluations.

## (Focus) Group Interviews

Recreation professionals may want to consider the use of meetings or group gatherings to collect data from individuals. Data for decision making can be obtained by using open public meetings, meetings for specific users, advisory committees, and focus groups. According to Krueger and Casey (2009), a focus group includes people who possess certain characteristics and who provide qualitative data through a focused discussion. It isn't just a group of people getting together to talk but is a systematic means to collect data with a purpose. Focus group interviews are used more frequently today than ever before and offer great possibilities to consider. The value of group interviews lies in the ability to stimulate new ideas among participants by allowing spontaneity and candor. It also allows the researcher or evaluator to *listen.*

Focus group interviews with 5 to 10 respondents can often save time and money. In a group interview, interviewees can direct thoughts to each other and not just the interviewer. The evaluator can also directly observe group process. The group interview can serve as a useful scouting device for other situations and is especially good for groups who have some common denominator, such as people who live in the same geographic location or who share the same activity interest. Another use of a group interview is to test an evaluator's interpretation of evaluation findings from a survey or to establish the questions to be asked for a more quantitatively oriented questionnaire.

In conducting a focus group, the evaluator will first need to arrange to get people to attend a gathering or get them together in some other way (e.g., phone focus group or Internet chat room/discussion board). Sometimes a group already exists that can be used. At other times you may need to form and assemble a group. The group should possess the characteristics needed to best supply data. A number of businesses now exist that specialize in conducting focus groups for a fee. However, with some training almost any recreation professional ought to be able to direct such a group. Focus group sessions sometimes include a complimentary meal and/or a stipend for being involved, but a monetary incentive is not necessary.

Individuals participating in a focus group need to know in advance the purpose of the group interview and the parameters including time commitment and remuneration (such as for mileage) or other compensation. As the focus group implementer, you will need to make a list of the administrative and logistic aspects necessary to conduct the group interviews or focus group.

In preparing for group interviews, just as in any data collection process, the purpose of the meeting should be clearly established. Based on the purpose, an agenda will be developed. Focus groups might be pilot-tested just like questionnaires, although those pilot-test data might be part of the data collected, since each focus group is done slightly different. Prepare the questions to ask just as you would any guided or standardized interview schedule. As is true in any aspect of interviewing, quality answers are directly related to quality questions. The questions asked are similar to a structured open-ended interview in that they should be carefully prepared, presented within a context, and logically focused. Everyone should have consistent and sufficient background information. You also will need to have the session videotaped or audiotaped, and will need to make plans for transcribing and analyzing the data.

In the actual conducting of the focus group interview, the interviewer must hone her or his moderating skills. The interviewer must be familiar with group process as well as with the topic that is examined. Having two moderators, so one person can direct the conversation while the second person takes notes and handles logistical issues, is recommended. Having nametags or name cards is useful if group members do not know one another or the leaders do not know the members.

The beginning of the focus group is crucial since the right amount of formality and informality must be established. The introduction might consist of a welcome, an overview of the topic, and a brief discussion of the ground rules. Ground rules might include such aspects as speaking one at a time, guaranteeing confidentiality, asking for negative as well as positive comments, and a statement about whether and when breaks will be taken. The first question is usually something that will help the group get acquainted. During the focus group, the interviewer will want to make sure the conversation flows and everyone gets involved. The leader should use pauses and probes. At the end of the focus group, the interviewer should thank the participants and summarize briefly what the main points were that emerged during the discussion to assure that they are accurate.

The number of focus groups that are needed for a project should be considered. Generally more than one group is important because all groups are different. If several focus groups are conducted, you can have greater confidence that the data you have collected represents the views of a broad group of people and not just the result of a convenience sample. If you want more information about focus groups, Krueger and Casey's 2009 fourth edition of *Focus Groups: A Practical Guide for Applied Research* can tell you just about everything that you need to know.

Another variation of a group interview used in public recreation services is community forums. Citizen advisory groups can reflect the interests of the community for needs assessments and evaluation. Public meetings and workshops can be used to solicit citizen input, facilitate a two-way dialogue, and share ideas and emotions. Workshops can get people into small groups to identify needs. In these situations, people come together to address particular issues that may reflect assessment, formative, or summative evaluation. The participants in community forums are often self-selected rather than chosen, which could indicate some sampling biases. The disadvantage to community forums is that these meetings may not represent the entire community. An evaluator must be careful in drawing broad conclusions from only specific individuals. The advantages of community forums are, however, the open access, low cost, and good ideas that may be generated. In these forums, audio or videotape recordings may or may not be used. If recording devices are not used, extensive notes taken by several people often provide the best type of data. These data will need to be qualitatively analyzed just as data are from other individual and group interviews.

# From Ideas to Reality

Many options exist for doing face-to-face interviewing. Individual and group interviews are useful as a way to get into "people's heads." To use interviews effectively, you must appreciate their value and train people adequately in how to collect data. We have found interviewing to be a fascinating and useful way to conduct evaluation and research projects. We encourage you to try interviewing if it seems appropriate for the evaluation or research project that you want to undertake. Focus groups appear to be offering great possibilities for recreation evaluation and research for now and the future.

Now that you have studied this chapter, you should be able to:
- Identify the four approaches that can be used to organize interviews
- Develop an interview schedule using one of the four approaches including the determination of question content, sequencing, and possible follow-ups and probes
- Conduct a meeting to train interviewers about the skills that they will need to be effective as interviewers
- Design a project that could make use of focus group interviews
- Identify possible problems that might occur when using interviewing methods

# 2.10 Electronic Surveys: The Wave of the Present and the Future

In the past decade, the fastest growing means for collecting data, especially for evaluation projects, appears to be through electronic surveys. This trend reflects a change in respondent involvement and control over the survey process (Dillman et al., 2009). Issues such as human interaction, trust, time involvement of each respondent, and special attention given to individuals has lessened over the years. On the other hand, the respondent's control over access and whether to respond have become higher. Thus, although data collection is easier for researchers today, participants in studies also have to be motivated in new ways if they are to choose to participate.

Electronic data collection has numerous advantages but also has some challenges that must be addressed. Many aspects of using the Internet are similar to any other form of data collection. You have to know your criteria or purpose of the study or project. You have to determine the appropriate *sample*. You have to construct questions that are worded appropriately. You need to provide some type of cover letter (introduction) that explains what you are doing and why. Much of what has already been discussed pertaining to mailed and telephone surveys also applies to electronic surveys. However, the mechanisms used must be carefully considered. This chapter addresses ways to collect electronic data, advantages and disadvantages, design issues, motivating respondents and use of incentives, and using mixed modes for data collection.

## Electronic Data Options

Although different people organize the ways they think about collecting electronic data in various ways, three major types of electronic surveys are email surveys, survey programs, and web-based surveys. Using the Internet for evaluation and research may provide a greater diversity of the sample without the need for constant monitoring. Generally the costs can be kept low and cooperation rates may be high because of the ease of using the technology.

Disadvantages to electronic evaluation, however, include the lack of human interaction. Some loss of control and even subject fraud, including people doing a survey more than once, might occur if you don't apply the appropriate technical controls. Some people are reluctant to respond if they are not sure of the credibility of the sender. Further, unless explained carefully, they may believe they are just part of a mass mailing and their response is really not that important or that as a result of participating they will get more spam mail. Sometimes email filters prevent the delivery of some questionnaires. Issues of privacy and confidentiality may appear more difficult to maintain. In addition, since not everyone has access to the Internet, you may have an upper- to middle-class bias built in if the Internet is used. However, with the increased popularity of computers and Internet use, all ages seem to be involved in using the Internet.

Email is a viable tool because it is low cost, quick, and reasonably easy. Email surveys are also one of the least intrusive ways to collect information. If you have email lists, you can put together a questionnaire, following the tenets of good design, and ask individuals to complete and return it to you. The respondent can hit the reply button and include the original message in the text. The respondent can then answer the questions in the space provided. Email surveys are useful if questions are relatively short and focused. Most people check their email and respond at their convenience, which increases cooperation rates. Some of the disadvantages of this email technique are that you cannot control the parameters of the responses and you do not have any multimedia capabilities. You will also need to compile the responses yourself.

Another approach is to send the questionnaire as an attachment that the respondent has to download. Once the questions are answered, the respondent can save it as a file and send it back. This technique obviously has some drawbacks because of the multiple steps involved. It also assumes that the respondent has the ability to do all the steps and that the word processor can read the document.

A third way to conduct an online survey is to send an email with an Internet hyperlink that automatically connects the respondent with a survey program. In other words, when the respondent clicks the link, the survey appears on the computer screen in an HTML format that looks just like a survey that might be sent in the mail. Once the survey is completed, a "submit" button allows the respondent to effortlessly "return" the survey. This web-based method allows for elaborately designed questionnaires and the software is often automatically programmed to provide ongoing summaries of the data for the respondent to see after completing their survey. You can even design the survey with a "progress bar" so the respondent can see the percentage of the survey they have completed. This web-based method usually has some associated costs, but the ease of replying may be worth the investment of time and money as well as the savings related to no postage and no or greatly reduced data entry expenses.

A burgeoning number of commercial programs now exist that are inexpensive for questionnaire design and offer a growing range of formats. Programs such as SurveyMonkey and Zoomerang have been popular. More products are coming on the market each day and the techniques of using them are getting easier and easier. Further, these programs can constantly monitor the response rate and provide immediate descriptive statistics. The raw data also can be formatted and downloaded easily for use with computerized statistical programs that generate complex statistical analyses.

One of the earliest applications of computer technology, popularized in the 1980s, was the computer-assisted telephone interviewing system (CATI). In CATI, a telephone interviewer follows a script and adds the respondents' responses directly into the computer (Dillman et al., 2009). Newer approaches to telephone interviewing include touchtone data entry (TDE), in which respondents provide answers to questions by pressing the telephone keypad. Another form is interactive voice response (IVR)—a computer administers questions and the respondent answers with vocal input that is keyed to the responses.

Another means to use electronic data collection is to have either interviewers or respondents sit at a computer and enter data directly. Computer-assisted personal interviewing (CAPI) occurs when an interviewer enters responses immediately into the computer as a conversation is underway (Dillman et al., 2009) Surveys can be set up so that individuals, either in a computer lab or working on laptops, can respond directly and this strategy has been called computer-assisted self-interviewing (CASI).

The use of handheld computers or personal data assistants (PDA) are proliferating and have been successful even with children. These devices are obviously highly portable and require little training to use. They can be private, allowing no one else to see the data. They provide a question format that is answered on the spot by the respondent. These devices are generally enjoyable and interactive. More questions can be completed in a given time frame than can be done with written questionnaires. These devices also save paper and data entry costs. In addition, they can reduce the potential for data entry errors and reduce the time between collection and analysis, which is true for any type of computer-assisted data collection. The disadvantages are that several PDAs are usually required that are loaded with the survey software, and the hardware can be expensive. The screens are quite small, which may make reading difficult for some populations or may require that the interviewer gets physically close to the respondent to assist with questions that might be related to a particular screen.

Even the personal cell phone can be a possible data collection tool. If the survey is simple and very short, researchers can send a text message with the question(s) to be answered. These brief polls can be taken with people able to text their answers directly from their cell phones. In the 2008 presidential campaign, Obama's organization was often able to generate almost instantaneous data by using cell phones.

The collection of data for focus groups is also possible using electronic means. Although some experts suggest that face-to-face contact or even conference-call focus groups are superior, electronic data can be collected through social networking sites, chat rooms, discussion groups, or bulletin boards (Krueger & Casey, 2009). Chat rooms are synchronous sessions of 6–8 people that last less than 90 minutes, a format that is similar to other forms of focus groups. They allow for relative anonymity and eliminate perceptions of people based on their physical appearance. They also can connect people across broad geographic areas. Chat rooms, however, tend to emphasize speed over thoughtful responses. Live exchange is important but similar to other focus groups, in that some individuals can dominate if they type fast and quickly submit—often without using spell check or editing. Krueger and Casey recommend that the moderator makes clear his or her comments and questions by using capital letters. The questions should change regularly allowing participants to comment.

Another form for collecting focus group data is bulletin boards. With this technique, a limited number of people agree to participate in a discussion over several days. They are invited and usually restricted by the use of a password. Generally people are asked to sign in each day and read the question of the day and examine what others have said. The focus group includes a series of postings by the moderator that follow a sequence similar to what would be done in a face-to-face focus group. The discussion board allows more reflection than might occur in a chat room (Krueger & Casey, 2009). Participants can think about the comments and provide more in-depth responses. A disadvantage is that people may not want to participate over a period of days and the discussion tends to be linear rather than allow for spontaneous responses. For both the discussion board and the chat rooms, as well as to some extent telephone focus groups, the moderator cannot make observations about body language or other visual cues.

A related electronic option for paper-and-pencil survey management is to use optical imaging and scanning. Data from paper-and-pencil tests can be coded onto electronic spreadsheets such as Excel. Another option is to use electronic scanning. Scanning requires that questionnaires are set up in particular ways depending on how the scanning will occur. These questionnaires designed for scanning may not be as visually appealing as others. For example, the answer spaces may need to be in a different color than the question stem (Dillman et al., 2009). Many improvements have occurred in scanning, and this technique will likely continue to get better as a use of technology for hard-copy questionnaires.

## Design Issues for Electronic Data Collection

A key aspect of using computer technology is to ensure that the population you wish to survey has the capabilities to respond. Access is an issue as a number of households in the U.S. do not have Internet connections or have connections that are very slow. Further, some individuals such as older adults do not know how to use computers. For many populations, computers may be highly useful, but developing the mode for communication should be carefully considered.

Regardless of the strategy used to collect data, every effort must be undertaken to get a high response rate. Many of the ideas discussed regarding any kind of survey apply, but some of those elements must be considered differently when using computerized data collection. For example, visual presentation is key and with computers, many options exist. Dillman et al. (2009) underlined how important visual design and layout are. They suggested that questionnaires include four types of elements for effective communication: words, numbers, symbols, and graphics. Regardless of mode, words communicate the questions that need to be asked. Numbers assist in moving through the questions and are often useful in interpreting the words (e.g., 4="strongly agree, 3=agree, 2=disagree, 1=strongly disagree"). Symbols are useful in the form of arrows or bullets to communicate emphasis. Finally, graphics such as text boxes, squares, pictures, images, and logos can be used to make questionnaires interesting and compelling so a respondent wants to reply. These visual design elements can also be presented in different ways with different sized fonts, bolding, color, or even motion. They can be used to call attention to different words or different sections of a survey. Electronic data collection obviously provides many more options for the visual presentation of your survey. Regardless of how elements are used, the questions must be clearly presented to be understandable and easy to follow.

In designing questions for electronic use, they must appear on the respondent's screen the same as on the designer's screen (Dillman et al., 2009). The compatibility of different computer systems must be considered, as should the capabilities of hardware. For example, in some rural areas, telephone dial-up is still the only way to connect to the Internet. Questionnaires with many graphics, for example, may be interesting for the instrument but may be quite difficult to download.

You will likely send a "contact letter" (the same purpose as a cover letter) preceding the survey instrument as well as provide appropriate closing screens. The respondent will need to know answers to the same issues as described in the mailed cover letter: purpose and value of the study, how the sample was selected, and a deadline for transmitting the response back. In the case of web-based survey programs, you can "close" the program at a certain date if you do not wish to receive further surveys. The deadline can be shorter (e.g., a week) since returning will include responding and hitting a send button. With the use of the Internet, you will need to establish how anonymity or confidentiality will be guaranteed. You can indicate that the results of the survey will be posted on the web on a certain date as one way to provide an incentive. The closing screen should thank the respondent in a well-written and professional manner.

Multiple contacts may be needed to get people to respond to Internet surveys, similar to what was suggested regarding mailed questionnaires. A pre-notice can be sent to inform individuals that a questionnaire is coming. Reminder emails can be sent. Individuals can be invited to receive a paper-and-pencil form if they would prefer that version over an electronic version. They can also be encouraged to ask questions about the survey directly to the sender. Each communication should be clear about why data are needed and should appear in a different format each time they are sent.

Incentives or tokens of appreciation can also be used to get a higher response rate. Since you cannot send money easily over the Internet, other possible ways to offer financial incentives might exist. Researchers can use contingent incentives or payments that are sent after a questionnaire is completed. The problem with financial incentives sometimes is that people perceive they are getting "paid" for answering questions and may not believe the incentive offered is enough to make their investment of time worthwhile. Some data collectors have used nonmonetary incentives such as packets of coffee, stamps, key rings, park passes, phone cards, or gift certificates. Donations to charities are also sometimes offered as an incentive. Others offer to enter someone into prize drawings, contests, or lotteries for gift cards or for a particular event. If you promise incentives, be sure that they are delivered to the respondents.

# From Ideas to Reality

The advantages and disadvantages of electronic data collection are many. This new way is the sine qua non of data collection for many projects. Research is still underway to determine if the response rate to Internet surveys is better than other survey strategies, but evidence seems to suggest that electronic surveys are highly effective if carefully designed and implemented. The effectiveness may improve as people become more proficient at designing these surveys and as respondents feel more secure in responding and being assured of confidentiality. Nothing substitutes, however, for choosing the right sample and for asking valid and reliable questions.

Now that you have studied this chapter, you should be able to:
- Describe when using electronic data collection might be best compared to other strategies
- Explain the options that are available for electronic data collection
- List techniques that might be used to assure the best data that can be collected from using electronic strategies

# 2.11 Observations:
# On a Clear Day You Can See Forever

Observation methods are available for evaluation and research projects, although they are not used as frequently in recreation applications as are surveys. Evaluation by judgment through accreditation and standards programs, and various kinds of checklists such as maintenance checklists, are common examples of observations. Researchers can also use observation of phenomena such as visitor behavior. For this chapter, we examine observations by addressing checklists, professional judgments, and field-work or participant observation. These methods share a commonality in using observational techniques, although they may be applied differently.

Becoming a good observer requires practice. Many of us take observation for granted or do not realize the extent to which we have learned to be selective in what we observe. To be a good evaluator, you have to watch, listen, concentrate, and interpret data apart from gathering it. Just as most of us were not blessed inherently with the ability to do math without being taught and given chances to practice our mathematical and analytical abilities, data collectors have to learn observational techniques and practice them to become good.

# Roles of Observers

The most common roles of observation include a range from outside observer to full participant. The roles can also range from unknown to known. Figure 2.11(1) illustrates these continua. Depending on the placement on each continuum, the evaluation outcomes may be influenced.

As a nonreactive or outside observer you might remove yourself completely from involvement with the group observed. An example of nonreactive observation might be someone analyzing the way the leisure behavior of women is portrayed on TV by watching the shows or viewing videos of TV programs. Outside observers usually try to be as invisible as possible and seek to elicit little or no attention from the individuals observed. The full participant or participant-observer, on the other hand, is completely involved in an activity, and observing is not her or his only role. A danger with the participant-observer role is the possibility of becoming highly involved as a participant and losing objectivity or losing concentration on the events occurring. As indicated, being a partial observer is a good option, which would combine aspects of full participant and outside observer roles.

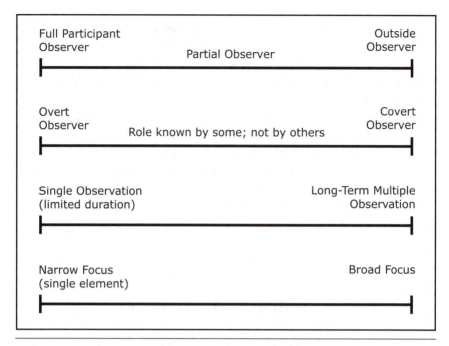

**Figure 2.11(1)**  *Dimensions of Approaches to Observation*

An unknown observer (covert) is not identifiable by the participants whereas the known (overt) observer has identified his or her role. The covert observer becomes a group member and, in essence, is posing as an "undercover agent." The overt observer is an outsider who makes her or his intentions clear. The known data collector does not try to pass as anything but an identified and recognized observer. Being in a situation where some participants know they are being observed and others do not is also possible within these continua.

Similarly, the role of the observer may range from single observations to long-term multiple observations and from a narrow focus to broad foci (Patton, 1980b). If a Goal-Attainment Model is used for evaluation and the data collected are quantitative, a single selected observation using a narrow focus may be appropriate. On the other hand, if a Goal-Free Model is being used and the researcher is not sure what may result from an observation, long-term multiple observations may be used with an initial broad focus. These observations may become narrower as time progresses. As on any continua, variations of these ranges may exist depending upon the particular evaluation criteria being measured.

No one observation role is best. Each role has value in certain situations. The evaluator or researcher may want to keep in mind the possible ethical problems discussed earlier that addressed covert observation, including invasion of privacy and what may happen to the evaluation project if you are "found out." Thus, different situations with particular evaluation criteria or research questions will require both ethical and methodological considerations.

Regardless of the roles played by observers, the basic procedure followed in any observation is the following:
- Choose a behavior or situation to observe
- Decide on mode for recording observations and collecting data (quantitative or qualitative)
- Determine sampling strategies
- Train observers or practice in the situation
- Analyze data
- Evaluate observation instrument

## Quantitative Observations

Systematic observation instruments are needed to reliably assess behaviors (Stumbo, 1983). The systematic observations usually include a checklist or a standardized form with units of analysis identified. The more structured an observation, the more likely analysis will involve coding and statistical analysis.

The most common quantitative observations use checklists and similar recording scales. These checklists are measurement instruments that the evaluator completes, not the person(s) under evaluation. Data collectors using checklists assume that *a priori* (i.e., before the observation) factors can be identified. The design of these instruments, thus, must follow the same design principles as addressed previously when we talked about developing questionnaire instruments. The criteria measured must be determined followed by the development of measurement scales.

Checklists are a technique for recording whether a characteristic is present or absent and/or whether an action is taken or not. Often a yes/ no response is used, but several checklist formats might be considered. Rating scales are used to indicate the degree of a characteristic or action. Other similar methods include frequency counts, rating scales, and duration recordings. These techniques may be useful, for example, in observing activities done during recreation instruction, in therapeutic recreation settings, or for the recording of specific behaviors in the outdoors.

Just as you can ask questions about aspects of people's lives, you can also observe many aspects of their lives. Several possibilities might be considered for quantitative observations. You might measure the affective or emotional component of what people do. How many times did they smile or act out? Cognitive observations examine intellectual components and thought processes as manifested in or exhibited by actions. What does an individual do as they seek to solve a problem? Procedures and routines might be observed. For example, you might observe in what ways a lifeguard enforces the safety rules at a pool. Often in recreation settings we observe physical environments such as space and equipment. For example, we do playground inspections or adventure course equipment inspections. Psychomotor aspects might be observed such as posture, position in relation to others, types of movement, and facial expressions. Sociological structure relates to who is talking to whom, the roles that people take on in a group, and the numbers and types of people interacting. Finally, we might observe the activities in which people are engaged.

Different coding units are also used in observation. Sometimes you will simply be counting and will use frequencies or percentages. Other times you will be using rating systems that are predetermined and defined. These systems might be scales that determine amounts or judgments of quality such as poor, fair, and good or hierarchical ratings such as not at all, seldom, occasionally, and constantly. No matter what unit, you must clearly define what each of these words means if they are used in a checklist system.

## Strategies to Obtain Quantitative Observation Information

Several checklist strategies may be used to obtain quantitative observational material. The first is *interval sampling,* whereby a series of brief intervals are observed and the evaluator notes what was observed. The interval sampling may be systematic as in doing a recorded safety check of a swimming pool every day, based on a pre-established list of criteria, or it may be used as a running account of what happened sequentially during a prescribed period of time. The running account might be a rough estimate of frequency and duration. In interval sampling, the evaluator records for a brief period of time some particular task—like when and for how long a child plays with a particular toy. Both the relative frequency and the duration of behavior are reported. The rate of behavior needs to be low enough to count, and you need to be able to determine the size of intervals and mark whether a behavior occurs.

A second strategy uses *frequency counts, event recordings, or tally methods.* The frequencies are converted to percentages. In this strategy, one counts the number of discrete events of a certain class of behavior as they transpire during a given time (minute, hour, day, week). The behavior needs to be clearly defined. This strategy is useful when determining behaviors or seeing what more than one individual is doing. An example includes counting the number of complete and incomplete tasks performed by a client in a therapeutic recreation program. You also might record the number of times a behavior is done appropriately or inappropriately. Frequency counts are relatively easy to do. In some situations, you could use a wrist-golf-stroke counter or grocery-store counter to keep track of how many times a particular behavior is happening or you could put tally marks on a paper. Systems of observation used to measure the physical activity of children include SOPLAY or SOPARC, which are described in more detail later in this unit.

Observing *duration* is another quantitative observation strategy. Duration refers to the length of time spent in a particular behavior or how long a behavior occurs. As in other situations, the behavior must be readily observable. The duration is then converted into percentages. For example one might determine the popularity of a piece of playground equipment by how long children use it. A stopwatch or other timing device would need to be used in this observation. This strategy is time-consuming and one needs to pay constant attention.

A related strategy is *latency recording,* where the time elapsed between a cue and the response is measured. For example, one might measure the time between telling a child to put away toys and when she or he actually begins the process. A stopwatch is used in measuring latency time.

Checklists might also be done using a *rating* system. For example, if you were observing an instructor in a swimming class, you might have a list of criteria that would indicate whether the individual had performed in an excellent, very good, average, fair, or poor way. In using any type of rating system, the meanings of the words such as "excellent" or "poor" must be clearly defined so that reliability exists in the ratings. Checklists like these are a common system used in personnel management. They have also been used recently to assess the quality of amenities in parks.

*Time sampling* or *spot-checking* is a way to record behavior at a particular point in time. In this strategy, the observation occurs periodically at predetermined time intervals. The evaluator specifies in advance the timing, number of observations, and type of observation within a particular context. These observations are usually done in equal intervals with a recording of the number of times something occurs. This spot-checking may include ascertaining the total number of participants using a picnic area at different times of the week, for example. You could not observe picnicking all the time, but a systematic time sampling could give you valuable information.

## Quantitative Observation Tips

For sophisticated quantitative observation systems, rigorous training periods for observers are needed. Observation systems with few categories require less training, are easy to learn, and result in greater inter-observer reliability. Most quantitative observation systems used in recreation projects fall between these two extremes.

The evaluator or researcher needs to be concerned about several aspects of doing observations or supervising others who may be doing quantitative observations. First, behaviors to be observed must be defined carefully. Since few standardized procedures exist for observations, the evaluator or researcher will often need to develop the measurement instruments carefully and pilot-test them in the situation where they will be used.

Second, the interaction between the observer and the participants must be noted. Are there reactive effects? How did behavior change because of the presence of an observer? Did the observer impose consciously or unconsciously any of his or her biases on the events so the meaning became different? Were any self-fulfilling prophecies coming true? Did the observer overidentify with the participants or a faction of them?

Third, reliable measures are needed. Thus, the observer will need to be sufficiently trained, use an instrument with clearly defined and non-overlapping categories, and use a small, manageable number of categories that can be sufficiently observed.

Inter-observer reliability is also a concern. Do all observers see the same things? If observations are to be useful, they must be reliable. The formula for reliability is number of agreements (between two observers) divided by number of observations (including agreements and disagreements) multiplied by 100, which equals the percentage of agreement:

**Agreements/Observations x 100=% of agreements
(inter-observer reliability)**

For example if two observers agreed on 24 items and disagreed on 5, we would divide 24 by 29 x 100 = 83%. This result should be as close to 100% as possible. Observers should be trained until they can reach a high agreement, which could be defined as anything over 90%.

# Professional Judgments

Professional Judgment is the direct observation and evaluation by an expert or someone familiar with a particular program. Professional Judgments are based on intuitively evaluating the quality of something based on formal and/or informal criteria.

Some evaluation procedures use Professional Judgment in conjunction with pre-established criteria. In other cases, experts may be invited into a situation to observe and use their expertise in defining the criteria. The advantages of using Professional Judgment observations are the ease of implementation and immediacy of judgment. Precautions are urged, however, in having outsiders rather than staff evaluate a program, as discussed regarding internal and external evaluators in Chapter 1.10. Value exists in having several judges, making sure the professionals clearly understand the criteria, and providing some training about the factors to consider and their relative importance for a particular situation (Weiss, 1975).

The accreditation processes used in various areas of recreation are examples of Professional Judgment observation. In cases of accreditation, certain standards are established ahead of time and are then observed. The experts answer questions or write a report concerning their responses.

Staff/personnel reviews are further examples of Professional Judgment. In performance appraisals or staff evaluation reviews, the supervisor is the professional judge. Other data besides the supervisor's expertise may be collected, but frequently it is up to the supervisor to take all input and use his or her professional judgment to make an evaluation. This process of staff evaluation works best when clear performance criteria have been set through the job description, the supervisor knows the organization well, and when the supervisor's personal biases do not enter into the evaluation.

# Qualitative Observations

Advantages exist in using qualitative observations, also referred to as field observations. These techniques may be used to collect anecdotal material and critical incidents that may not be recorded elsewhere. They might also be done systematically when an individual is a participant-observer. They are in-depth and the evaluator is able to examine the background and meanings of what may be happening in a program or organization. Flexibility exists regarding what to observe and what data to collect.

Qualitative observations are only unscientific when improper techniques are used. All of us are involved in observational activities daily, but qualitative observations must be systematic. Observation techniques are a highly valid and reliable form of data collection. To do qualitative observations, however, requires a highly trained individual or group of individuals that will expend much time and energy in field observations.

Doing qualitative observations is time-consuming. Another disadvantage of these techniques is the possible introduction of bias. Including quantitative observations along with using multiple observers, however, can reduce this bias. A further disadvantage may be that single conclusions should not be drawn, but multiple explanations, conclusions, and descriptions of a phenomenon are usually the result of qualitative observations.

Qualitative observations may be done in two major ways. One method is to keep an account of anecdotal records and critical incidents. Anecdotal records are factual descriptions of meaningful incidents and events and/or detailed accounts or running logs, often referred to as progress notes. To use these accounts for evaluation or research, the interpretation is kept separate from factual description. Critical incidents refer to unusual situations that occur that are recorded and described in detail. In analyzing critical incidents, one also attempts to describe the antecedents, behaviors, and consequences.

A second major method of qualitative observations is field observations, where the evaluator goes into a "natural" or "normal" situation such as a playground or a staff meeting, to serve as a participant-observer. Data are recorded in the form of field notes, and conclusions are then drawn about what is occurring based on volumes of descriptive notes that are taken. The process of field observation involves defining the purpose, populations, samples, and units of analysis to be included, just as is true with any other methods of evaluation or research. The data are analyzed to draw conclusions. The field observation techniques can be combined with other techniques such as interviews, case studies, or document analyses.

Prior to beginning a field observation project, the evaluator would need to become acquainted with the site or program if she or he isn't already, assume a role as known or unknown, and prepare an initial broad focus checklist of things to observe. The process is one of scheduling and becoming involved with the unit or individuals under observation. As you begin to collect data through taking extensive notes, themes will develop. In the interpretation process, these themes will be tested, refined, reinterpreted, expanded, discarded, and new data will be observed until final conclusions have been reached. This process will be discussed in more detail in the next unit about analysis.

## Note-Taking

Data are collected in field observations by recording information through note taking by the observer(s). The evaluator or researcher is, thus, the data collection instrument. Since the notes are the data, they are central to qualitative observations. Notes are taken prolifically. Even in a complete participant role, the evaluator must write down notes as often and as

206 • Evaluating Leisure Services (Third Edition)

completely as possible. The less time between an observation and recording it through notes, the more accurate the data will be. The notes are taken within the context of what is observed and will depend on the criteria measured. Often information like weather, people present, your mental state, start and finish, location, changes in environment, and formal roles observed are important to note.

The field observer should be careful to separate facts from interpretation when taking notes. The observer should be particularly careful to identify whether the idea recorded is a fact, quote, or interpretation. Observers must indicate what they knew happened as well as what they thought happened. Just as you cannot observe everything, you cannot record everything, so you must practice recording the most important observations. Table 2.11(2) shows an example of note-taking. In addition, Henderson (2006) offered several considerations in note-taking:

- Record your notes as soon as possible after making your observation.
- Write, type, or word process the notes in detail. The notes should include a running description of events, people, things heard and overheard, conversations among people, conversations with people, and incidents that occur.
- Make copies of the notes as soon as possible. If something happens to your notes, you have lost your data.
- Indicate on the notes whose language was being used. Who exactly said what? Did you? Did someone else? Include verbatim quotes, if appropriate, and always use concrete description with specific detail.
- Leave wide margins on the note sheet so you can write ideas in or note additional interpretations if they occur to you. Start new paragraphs often so the note sheets can be easily read.
- The length of field notes will differ considerably. A rule of thumb might be several-single spaced pages for each hour of observation.
- It is possible to talk your field notes into a tape recorder and then have someone else transcribe them. If this seems appropriate, the evaluator will need to review the transcriptions as soon as possible.
- Do not be afraid to record notes about what you do not understand. Something may not make sense at one time, but it will possibly become clearer later. Record your notes at will and do not be afraid of making mistakes.
- Continually monitor yourself as a data gatherer. Tiredness, emotional reactions, relationship with others, energy level, use of discrete observations, and technical problems may all affect the data collection and these manifestations should be noted.

*Table 2.11(2)*  *Sample Notes from Observation of Leisure Education Class*

| Facts | Interpretations |
|---|---|
| March 25<br>The CTRS meets with Richard in the 7th class meeting: CTRS is slouched in the chair at the table with her arms folded across her chest, waiting. Richard walks up, smiles, and fumbles as he pulls the chair out to sit down. He sits forward in the seat with his hands holding up his head. CTRS continues to look at him as he wiggles in the chair. She begins with "How are you?" He mumbles, "Fine." She says, "You look a little tired." He shrugs his shoulders. She waits a moment and then begins. She is still sitting with her arms crossed. "What did you do this weekend?" "Nothing," Richard replies. Silence for about five seconds. "Were you bored?" she asks. He shrugs his shoulders again. The CTRS pauses and then points to the decision-making board that has four words written on it: GOAL, OPTIONS, IF/THEN, DECISION. She says, "We are going to talk more about these today. Let's try to talk about leisure. What is your goal for leisure?" | Instructor looks tired<br><br><br><br><br>Both look tired<br><br><br><br>I wonder if people know when they are bored<br><br><br>I'm not sure what she is asking |

- The length of time spent in note-taking will depend on the evaluation questions being asked.
- And finally, remember, "If it is not written down, it never happened" (Taylor & Bogdan, 1984, p. 52).

## Tips on Qualitative Observation

In observation, the evaluator must be a reliable and valid measurer. As an effective observer, you must be trained to notice events and actions that are relevant to your perceptions as well as those that contradict your perceptions. Field observations take enormous amounts of energy because they require you to look beyond your ordinary day-to-day observations to apply the rigor of scientific evaluation and interpretation.

Part of good observation is learning what to observe. Everything cannot be observed, and even if you could, total sensory overload would occur. Therefore, observation becomes more focused as the data collector continues with her/his work on a particular evaluation or research project. Ultimately, the observations should result in a written report that will allow the reader to actually enter the situation and understand what was happening based on detailed descriptions from the observer.

At the observation site, it will be necessary to establish a role. You may choose to be a full participant, an outside observer, or something in between such as a staff member or a volunteer. The role may affect your ability to gain acceptance within a group, so the role should be carefully chosen. In some cases, you may be a staff member already who wants to use field observations to collect evaluation data. Adopting this observer role is possible, but you must be aware of the possible biases that you bring to the situation. No matter what role is used, an observer must be explicitly aware of the situation observed, use a wide-angle lens, take the insider/outsider perspective, be introspective, and keep good notes of both objective and subjective feelings.

Establishing rapport in the field site will be an important early aspect of the field research. Taylor and Bogdan (1984) offered several tips for establishing social interaction, including: remaining passive in the first few days, putting people at ease in whatever ways you can such as do-ing favors or helping out, collecting data as secondary to getting to know people, acting naive, paying attention to people's routines, explaining who you are to the people, explaining what will be done with the data, trying to figure out what being at the right place at the right time means, beginning with small amounts of interaction and then increasing the time at the site, and keeping your overt note-taking to a minimum initially and adjusting to more visible note-taking as you and the participants feel comfortable later. Above all, the field observer doing an evaluation should act interested and the people being observed will see that she or he is serious about them and the project undertaken.

Qualitative observation is an ongoing process of data collection and analysis. An evaluator may begin a project with some general criteria in mind, but these criteria may change and become redefined as you observe and interact with people. In other words, you will develop new insights and new ways of obtaining information as you discover new data. The qualitative observation process is one that will evolve over time. In ad-dition, your skills as an observer will improve the more that you practice systematic observation.

Field evaluation requires a high level of concentration to pay atten-tion to what is happening. If the evaluator cannot take notes immediately, concentration is required to imprint the notes in mental photography. The observer must look for key words in people's remarks, concentrate on the first and last remarks of each conversation because those are generally the most important, and be able to play back the observation or conversation easily in the mind.

A final, but not the least important, aspect of field evaluation research is the use of key informants. Respondents are people whom you observe or who answer questions with no particular rapport having been established. Key informants, on the other hand, are people who provide more in-depth information about what is occurring because the evaluator or researcher has established trust with them. This information is data that must be recorded in the form of notes similar to the notes that might be collected during an interview.

Information is usually obtained from key informants by either formal or informal interviews. One way to regard these informants is as "data collaborators." The value of key informants is in helping the observer ascertain if people "say what they mean and mean what they say." Some informants may have general information about the past and their perceptions of the present, others may be representative of a group of people, and others may serve as observers when you are not there to observe in person. Relationships with key informants will help you develop a deeper understanding of the setting being examined.

Sometimes observers run into hostile respondents. As a data collector, you need to be friendly, but not pushy. You may want to employ some additional investigative skills to determine why the lack of cooperation is occurring. The data collector will often have to talk to people that she or he dislikes or distrusts. For an effective evaluation or research project to be conducted, you must observe and talk to all types of people within the setting, and not just to the people that you like or that are friendly.

## From Ideas to Reality

In all cases, someone using observations is looking for accurate, reliable, and valid data. A reliable observation is one that is not biased by idiosyncrasies of either the observer, the subject, or by the constraints of time and place. These observations may be quantitative or qualitative depending on the pre-existing knowledge, expertise, and resources of the evaluator or researcher. Observation is not always the easiest method to use but it can provide information that will be helpful in determining what behavior is actually occurring in a particular situation.

Now that you have studied this chapter, you should be able to:
- Describe the differences between qualitative and quantitative observations
- Choose the appropriate roles that an observer will take given a particular project
- Develop a quantitative checklist using two or more of the strategies described
- Explain to an administrator the value of using Professional Judgments as a means for evaluation within an organization
- Take descriptive notes within a field observation setting
- Critique whether a field observation project has been undertaken appropriately

# 2.12 Unobtrusive Methods: Oddball Approaches

A number of years ago, Webb and his colleagues (1966) suggested that maybe too much emphasis has been placed on survey methods such as interviews and questionnaires. Sometimes researchers get so focused on written or verbal interactions with people that they forget that data can be obtained in other ways. Perhaps evaluators and researchers ought to consider methods that may not be as obtrusive or that may not infringe on people's time and privacy. Unobtrusive methods may complement methodological weaknesses in surveys such as people's socially desirable responses and the tendency to survey people who are accessible, cooperative, literate, and verbose.

Unobtrusive, sometimes called nonreactive, methods refer to observing, recording, and analyzing human behavior in a situation where interaction with people generally does not occur and people are unaware that their behavior is being observed or studied. Some aspects of observations and unobtrusive methods may overlap, but they often use different strategies. Unobtrusive methods do not require the cooperation of individuals, as is frequently needed in some way with quantitative or qualitative observations.

Unobtrusive measures are probably most often used to provide supplementary data for evaluation projects or case studies, but they may be used on their own. As in other methods, either quantitative or qualitative data may be collected.

These unobtrusive methods are also sometimes labeled "oddball" because they are unlike what is done in traditional evaluation and research projects. Their value lies in being able to address some criteria that you could not easily measure by asking or observing people directly. These methods counter the notion of dependence on language for obtaining information.

In unobtrusive methods, the anonymity of people is almost certain. Usually some activity, such as watching the behavior of individuals in a public park, or tracing activity, such as counting the types of vandalism that occur in a park, is observed. The data generally consist of physical evidence, archives, or unobtrusive and covert observations. The unobtrusive measures may be systematically identified and analyzed in a project or they may be found accidentally when other survey or observation data are collected.

Examples of unobtrusive measures that may be used to obtain data about people's behavior include observations of body language and other nonverbal behavior, shortcuts or worn grass in a park indicating where people walk most frequently, types of graffiti and where it is likely to be found, the number of beer and soda cans in household garbage, attendance records for particular events, litter frequency and type along a highway, and rental records for a business.

Sometimes these unobtrusive methods require detective-like tactics. Similarly, they offer clues to what people are doing. Some of the strengths of unobtrusive methods are the face validity, the simplicity and directness, the inconspicuous and noninterventional nature, their nonreactivity directly from people, their easy combination with other methods, the stability over time, and the independence from language (Guba & Lincoln, 1981). In evaluations of policies and administrative procedures, for example, evaluators may rely solely on records and archives.

Problems exist in using unobtrusive methods, however, because they are heavily inferential, information often comes in bits and pieces, and the situations cannot be easily controlled. Unobtrusive methods alone generally do not tell how people see and experience their activities. Additionally, if subjects are aware in some way that they are being observed, their actions may be distorted and confounded. Unobtrusive studies may also have associated biases unless appropriate random sampling procedures are used. Hardware such as hidden cameras, gauges, and one-way mirrors may be used for data collection, although some ethical problems exist in using these devices if the observed do not know they are being observed and their privacy is invaded. Although not used for research purposes, for example, most businesses use surveillance cameras in their businesses but individuals entering the store are informed by a sign, albeit quite small, that they will be observed.

The three major ways that data are unobtrusively collected include physical evidence, archives, and unobtrusive and covert observation. Each will be discussed and applied to evaluation and research in the recreation field.

# Physical Evidence

Collecting physical evidence or traces from past behavior is one way to do unobtrusive evaluations. These data may be collected quantitatively or qualitatively. For example, physical evidence might include the wear on floors in a museum as a measure of the popularity of certain exhibits (e.g., measured quantitatively in millimeters of wear or qualitatively in terms of visual scuffing). Another example would be to measure and categorize the food that is thrown away at camp to determine popularity of certain food items (e.g., tally the most common items by using a checklist). Although the number and types of books checked out (quantitative data) of a library would be an example of archival document data, the wear and tear on the books to show what was actually read would be an example of a qualitative assessment of physical evidence.

Putting a GPS device or a pedometer on individuals to follow where they go or to measure activity level and calorie expenditure is another example of quantitative physical evidence data. Asking people to wear a device is intrusive to some extent but a lot easier and more reliable than asking them to write down where they go or estimate their activity level or "count" steps, which would be quite impossible.

The advantage of physical evidence data is the lack of conspicuousness. A major drawback to the method, however, is that one gets little information about the nature of the population that is doing whatever is being measured. For this reason, physical evidence *alone* is not necessarily the best method to use for evaluation. It may be useful as data in combination with other evaluation methods.

## Archives

Archives include any records or documents that exist. Written materials can provide a past or present historical perspective for the review of patterns. Documents and records are often used to supply data for content analysis. Records are used to keep track of events and serve as official chronicles. Many documents are publicly available and in this day and age of the World Wide Web, access to numerous documents is far easier than in the past. Archives can be used for trend analysis and integration. Examples of records might be sales records (quantitative data) or minutes of a meeting (qualitative data). Documents may be either personal, institutional, or public, and often provide a historical context for a project. These documents may be letters and diaries, brochures, or newspaper articles. They may be running records or episodic. If the data are portrayed as numbers, they are generally considered quantitative and can be organized in that manner with statistical analyses. Attendance records for classes offered by a YMCA would be examples of archives and could be compared over a period of time. If the data are in the form of words such as copies of past brochures, the data will need to be analyzed qualitatively if you are interested in determining changes or trends.

Archives are generally inexpensive to access, easy to sample, and provide specific population restrictions. A great advantage in using archives is cost savings, because data collection is not needed. Sometimes it is difficult, however, for external evaluators to get access to some types of records. In addition, records are sometimes incomplete, out-of-date, and/or inaccurate. Today, however, a great deal of information that you might analyze is easily accessed on the Internet. One precaution is that often records were not collected for the same reason as how you may want to use them for research or evaluation. Further, limitations may lie in the selective deposit of certain documents or archives and how well they "survive" over time. However, in the electronic age this issue is far less a problem.

Despite possible limitations in using archives, previously collected data are often helpful to an evaluator or researcher. Records that tell information such as density of population, population distribution, age distribution, sex distribution, racial composition, education level, occupation type, per-capita income, family income, housing type, housing age, employment rate, birth rate, expenditure patterns, and crime rate and type are examples of archival records. You may want to use city maps and photos, school records, church records, real estate records, building permits, libraries, state and federal organization records, radio and TV stations, public utility records, chamber of commerce data, health and welfare records, actuarial records, large-scale social studies, voting records, weather and traffic reports, public records such as gas use or water use, sales records, institutional records, personal documents such as collections, newspaper records, tax assessments, information from scouting groups and other youth serving agencies, business and professional groups, financial institutions, planning agencies, data from state organizations and the National Recreation and Park Association (i.e., operating and capital expenditures, amount of recreation acreage, number of full-time and part-time staff, and populations served). Good sources of archives are city planning departments, Visitor and Convention Bureaus, and Councils of Social Agencies. As described earlier, Geographical Information Systems (GIS) is a new area that provides huge quantities of unobtrusive data that an evaluator might want to use. Another example of archives are blogs that people keep or journals such as those that people have posted from their thru-hiking of the Appalachian Trail.

Within recreation organizations, several sources of archives might be interesting. These include budget/financial reports, attendance rosters, trip reports, annual reports made to the recreation commission or board, and old evaluation reports. We frequently use previous records to do various evaluation procedures, such as cost-benefit and cost-effectiveness analysis. Program records and agency files are useful if good data have been kept. Inappropriate data for evaluation purposes, incomplete data, or changes in procedures may be problems in using leisure service agency archives. With the widespread use of computer systems, evaluation from agency records ought to become easier in the future. One secondary outcome in working with archives is that the evaluator learns to develop better record keeping procedures to help an agency with evaluations in the future.

## Unobtrusive and Covert Observations

Covert observations are a form of unobtrusive data collection that one must handle carefully. In the chapter on observations, we did not discuss covert observations as particularly useful. In some situations, however, they might serve a purpose.

Observations that are unobtrusive and/or covert may occur in a variety of ways. One must be careful in using this technique of data collection because it can infringe on people's privacy. People do not like to be watched if they do not know they are being observed. People usually need to give their informed consent or at least assent (acknowledgement that they know data are being collected and that observation is occurring). Contrived observation such as what is done with hidden cameras and "bugging" should be avoided, but once in a while these observation techniques can be justified. Unobtrusive observation involves the data collector being unknown and passive. These observations are often used to measure physical behavior through audiovisual analysis. SOPLAY and SOPARC are observational checklists used to assess physical activity and will be discussed later in this unit.

Physical signs and body language may be used in a group to examine simple aspects such as expressive movement including facial expressions, finger and hand movements, rituals of athletes, physical location like proximity to the leader, seating, personal space, clothing, how people sit, and how people stand. These observations might also be used to analyze linguistic behavior like the subject of conversations and with whom they occur. These data might be quantitative if they are collected in the form of a checklist or they may be qualitative if they are observations gathered in the form of notes. The values of unobtrusive observations are that no role taking is associated, measuring these activities shouldn't cause change in behavior, data collector effects should not be an issue, and data are collected first hand.

Observation in public places is one type of unobtrusive method used in studying recreation, parks, tourism, and other recreation settings. In this unobtrusive method, an evaluator uses observation and casual conversation. Observation in public places is sometimes hard to do but a researcher can get a sense of such aspects as exterior physical signs (clothes, bumper stickers, license plates), expressive movement, physical location of types of activity, conversational sampling, and time duration in particular activities. The data could be recorded and analyzed like other forms of qualitative observations or quantitative checklists.

Observations can also be recorded using tapes, films, and photos. Audiovisual aids allow the evaluator to examine a phenomenon a number of times. Audiovisual analysis can be divided into several categories. One category may refer to an analysis of media. This technique is essentially a content analysis of pictures, graphics, or words.

A second category includes audiovisual analyses that may refer to using photos and media to collect data, which can be replayed for analysis. For example, time-lapse photography may give information about patterns of movement in a park. After the photography is done, evaluators can use the data for analysis. In another example, individuals were invited to submit art to a contest about "What parks mean to me." The drawings were then analyzed to see what seemed to be the important examples that represented parks to people. See Figure 2.12 for an example of a picture drawn.

A third variation of this category is to make a photo collection or YouTube-type production and then show it to people to get their reactions. This strategy has been used in park planning where pictures of outdoor areas are taken and shown to people. They are asked to describe their reactions to what is pleasing and not pleasing about particular places.

The method of using audio-visual devices to collect and analyze data has pros and cons. Sometimes the use of audio or visual recordings presents a way to get better samples if an evaluator cannot observe everything at one time. On the other hand, there is a problem with not being able to observe everything, even when cameras or recording devices are used. Most evaluators have found that initially people may be bothered by a video camera or tape recorder, but they forget the presence of these devices after a few minutes. It appears, in general, that the use of audiovisual equipment does not affect the data that may be collected. As in the other techniques, data collection and analysis using audiovisual devices may be quantitative or qualitative, depending on how the evaluation project is designed.

*Figure 2.12*  *Example of Data Collected from a Contest on "What Parks Mean to Me"*
*(courtesy of Debra Jordan, Oklahoma State University)*

# From Ideas to Reality

Unobtrusive evaluation methods are not commonly used as primary
methods in recreation projects but they can make useful contributions
to data collection for evaluation and research projects. The value of unobtrusive techniques lies in generally not having to approach people to
gather data. The methods have great potential for analyzing history and
changes over time if you are examining, for example, how the budget
has increased or the changes in the number of participants in a particular
activity over a period of time. Less is known about the potential for these
methods than for other more commonly used methods but they are no
less reliable, valid, and useful. They also represent data, especially in the
form of physical evidence or archives that already exist within an organization. Unobtrusive techniques offer some possibilities that you may
want to consider as you undertake particular projects. These techniques
might also be particularly useful when triangulated with surveys or observations.

# 2.13 Experimental Designs: Focusing on Control and Interventions

The two major classifications of evaluation and research designs are experimental and descriptive/evocative (sometimes called nonexperimental), as introduced earlier in this unit. Experimental designs divide into *true* experiments and *quasi-experimental* designs. Quasi-experimental designs may be more descriptive than experimental, as you will see in this chapter. True experimental and quasi-experimental designs, however, share some characteristics from a methodological perspective. Pre-experimental designs are almost solely descriptive, but we talk about them as another possibility that may provide some information to consider when you want to do something like an experimental design. Pre-experimental are not experimental but *could* be with additions to the design.

When attempting to show that a summative evaluation is really the result of an intervention or a program, experimental methods are often used. For example, if we wanted to know if participation in a summer camp program resulted in increased self-esteem among young people, we would measure self-esteem scores before and after the camp session and compare those scores to before and after scores from young people who did not go to camp during that same period of time.

Experiments may be done using things as well as people. For example, you might be interested in what type of grass grows best in a playground area. You might plant half the area with one type and half the area with another. Through various observations during the summer and into the fall, you might determine which grass was greenest or held up the best in this playground situation. The type of experiment used would depend on the criteria you wished to examine and the resources that are available.

Many types of experiments exist, but the true experiments are those where a randomized sample with a control group are used. Quasi-experimental evaluation techniques, a "cousin" of experimental designs but more characteristic of descriptive procedures, do not necessarily control for a randomized sample, use a control group, or do both pretests and posttests. True experimental procedures are more valid and reliable if participants are "blind" about the group in which they are participating. That is, they know they are a part of an experiment, but they do not know to which group they have been assigned (e.g., experimental or control). Sometimes, especially in medical research, the study is "double-blind," which means that neither the participants nor the researchers doing the intervention know who has who is in the treatment or the control group.

In recreation situations, however, individuals seldom are blind to any experiment.

Thus, the purpose of the experimental design in its purest form is to control as many of the factors as possible to minimize any outside effect that might account for change due to an intervention. These experiments are modeled after laboratory work where all elements are controlled. In this way, the researcher as well as anyone using the results can be assured that the results of the experiment represent what really happened. However, when we are talking about human behavior, especially in people's everyday lives, issues of control are difficult. Nevertheless, experimental designs provide a way to measure the outcomes or impact of a program and/or what happened to individuals as a result of a particular intervention.

## Characteristics of Experimental Designs

According to research textbooks, experimental designs range from "true" techniques such as the pretest-posttest control group, to single group techniques that are essentially equivalent to one-group descriptive surveys or tests. For purposes of our discussion of experimental and quasi-experimental methods, we focus on examples that use (or do not use) some type of comparison and/or pretest. To begin, however, we discuss why experimental and control groups and randomization are important.

An experimental group includes the individuals that receive an intervention or "treatment," such as participating in a recreation program or getting a particular kind of therapy. A control group is a similar group of individuals, with characteristics like the experimental group, who do not receive the same treatment. If an experimental group was children 8–10 years old who went to camp, the control group would be children 8–10 years old who did not go to camp during the time the experiment was conducted.

When no control group is used, several threats to the results concerning internal validity (i.e., whether the procedure really measured what it said it measured) may occur. The first threat is maturation or whether a change might be due simply to a group maturing. For example, given a particular age group, basketball skills might improve naturally with practice regardless of what kind of instruction is given. Related to this threat is that history or time passing may change people's abilities or knowledge. The effects of taking a test upon the scores of a second test may be a validity threat if a participant remembers how she or he answered the first time. Changes in the measuring instruments or changes in the observers or scoring can also pose a validity problem in conducting evaluations. The Hawthorne effect can be described as the result of people improving just because they get attention. The Hawthorne effect can be mitigated by using a control group. Sometimes no changes are seen in a group because of what is known as statistical regression. This phenomenon occurs when groups have high scores in the beginning such as measured through the pretest. It is also known as the ceiling effect. On a second testing, the scores tend to move back toward the mean because they were so high initially.

To randomize means to assign people to groups by chance, as was discussed earlier in the chapter on sampling. Randomization is important because selecting or choosing experimental and control units with different characteristics may affect the results. The loss of participants must also be considered as sometimes people drop-out between the pretest and the posttest. As noted above, because of the different maturation of members of experimental and control groups, using randomization in experimental designs is desirable. Randomization controls against many threats to the validity of the findings and is highly desirable, although sometimes difficult and often uncommon in many recreation evaluation projects and research studies. Randomizing populations is difficult to do in recreational settings, where voluntary participation is the norm.

Thus, the major problem with using experimental designs is that controlled experiments are often impossible in real settings. Extra people may not exist who can serve as controls. Your professional obligations require that no one be denied services. Further, control group members may get angry if they don't get their choice about recreation activities they chose. These true experimental designs are difficult because the program must be held constant and formative evaluation isn't desirable in experimental designs. In using experiments in real life and not just in laboratories, a concern exists that evaluators often try to control too much and the recreation activity may become stale. Despite all these problems, experimental designs may still be a possible way to conduct useful evaluation and research projects.

## Using True Experimental Designs

Traditionally in research and evaluation books, certain symbols are used to indicate the procedure used for experimental design:

E = Group receiving the experimental treatment
C = Control group receiving no treatment

R = Randomized sample
O = Observation or testing done usually followed by a number
(e.g., O1 means first observation, usually called the pre-test; and O2 is the second test that might be the post-test, but may be one of a series of tests)
X = Treatment

For example, if you wanted to know if the skill level and knowledge of a group of children improved as a result of Saturday morning basketball instruction, you could set up an experiment whereby the children were randomly assigned (you could put all the names in a hat and then draw them and assign) to two groups—one for instruction and one for free play. You could give a pre-test on skills (e.g., lay-ups shot and made in a minute) and then randomly divide the group in two with a similar skill level in each group. One group could be given instruction for six weeks while the other group engaged in free play. At the end of the period, we could test the skill levels of both groups again (using the same lay-up test) and compare the differences between the pretest and posttest for each group. This **true experimental** technique would look like this:

R E  O1 X O2
R C  O1    O2

As is true in many cases in recreation, you may want to make sure that the control group does not miss an opportunity, so you should allow the group that did not receive instruction to get six weeks of instruction after the experiment is completed, especially if the treatment was successful. This procedure will assure that no ethical issues are violated in doing harm to one group because the members of another group did not receive a program or treatment. In this case the design would look like:

R E O1 X O2
R C O1    O2 X

(Reminder Note:
E = group receiving the experimental treatment
C = control group receiving no treatment
R = Randomized sample
O = Observation or testing done usually followed by a number
X = Treatment)

The only possible problem with this pretest-posttest control group technique is that the initial testing might have some effect on the results, but it is virtually impossible to control for those effects unless you eliminate the pretest.

# Other True Experiments

## The Solomon Four-Group Design

The Solomon Four-Group Design is another example of a true experimental method. The configuration looks like this:

R E O1 X O2
R C O1    O2
R E    X O1
R C       O1

In the Solomon Four-Group Design, four random groups are used. Two of those groups receive an observation or pretest at the beginning. One of those two groups then receives a treatment along with one of the other groups that was not pretested. At the conclusion of the treatment or the program, all four groups receive a posttest. This true experimental method assures that the pretest does not influence the results of the treatment of the posttest.

## Posttest-Only Control Group

The Posttest Only Control Group technique does not have the problem of a possible interaction of having had a pretest. It resembles this configuration:

R E X   O1
R C     O1

Two groups are randomly selected and one receives a treatment. Both groups are then given a posttest to see if the treatment made any difference between the groups. The only problem with this technique is that you cannot be sure that you started out with similar groups although the randomization ought to ensure that a similar baseline occurred.

# Quasi-Experimental Designs

Quasi-experimental methods do not satisfy the strict requirements of the experiment. Renowned experimental researchers Campbell and Stanley (1963) have legitimized quasi-experimental methods as possibilities to be used in any number of settings. The best techniques control relevant outside effects and lead to valid inferences about the effects of the program or treatment. Quasi-experimental methods, unfortunately, leave one or several threats to validity uncontrolled such as random selection or the use of a control group. These techniques include the following examples.

## Time-Series

In the time-series technique, observations are taken several times before a treatment is applied and then, additional observations are used. The configuration looks like this:

E O1 O1 O1 O1 X O2 O2 O2 O2

(Note:

E = group receiving the experimental treatment

C = control group receiving no treatment

R = Randomized sample

O = Observation or testing done usually followed by a number

X = Treatment)

One of the problems is the inability to control for the effects of history between measurements. Because a control group is not used, you would have to use this format in different situations to generalize the results more broadly. An example of a control-group time-series is new playground equipment at a park. To conduct this time-series quasi-experiment, you would take several visitor counts at a park. The new equipment would be installed and then you continue taking the counts at the park (Ellis & Witt, 1982). You would see if participation increased in the park compared to what it was before the new equipment was installed. Having several observations ensures that the average number is reliable for the "pre-test" and similarly for the "post-test."

## Equivalent Time Samples

The equivalent time sample is an extension of the time series technique by alternating treatment and measurement. It looks like this:

E XO XO XO XO

The procedure is useful when the effects of the treatment are anticipated to be short term. An example of its use might be in measuring how reality therapy could be used for patients with Alzheimer's disease in a therapeutic recreation program. You would do the therapy and make an observation and then do the therapy again and observe to see if repetition resulted in behavior changes. The disadvantage of this technique is the inability to generalize the findings to other subjects in other settings.

## Nonequivalent Control Group

This nonequivalent control group technique has the same structure as the standard pretest-posttest control group, with the exception that no random assignment of subjects to groups is made. It *assumes* a random assignment. Often prearranged groups are used. For example, if you wanted to compare the gains in aerobic capacity made between people in a class taking step aerobics and a regular aerobics class, you could use the two groups that exist rather than randomly assigning them. The configuration looks like this:

E O1 X O2
C O1    O2

# Pre-Experimental Designs

Pre-experimental methods are more descriptive/evocative than experimental methods, but they share some characteristics with true and quasi-experimental designs. The evaluator has to be careful, however, in referring to them as experimental methods because they result in descriptive, rather than predictive or cause-and-effect, outcomes.

## One-Group Pretest/Posttest

Although more a pre-experimental or survey-oriented technique than a quasi-experimental procedure, we will discuss the possibility of a one-group pretest/posttest design briefly because it does have possibilities in evaluation. It looks like this:

E O1 X O2

The advantage is the comparison between pre- and post-performances by the same subjects. The drawback is that no control group or randomization occurs. The subjects would be tested for knowledge, attitude, or skill level before a treatment or program begins and then again after it is over. The disadvantage is the inability to accurately determine whether the differences from beginning to end are due to the treatment or some other variables.

## Static-Group Comparison

The static-group comparison also is not technically experimental, but it has the comparison aspects of experiments in that a treatment is applied to one group of subjects. Testing or observation is then done on two groups, the one receiving treatment and another that had nothing. The technique looks like this:

E X O1
    C    O1

The value of this pre-experiment is that it can provide comparisons to evaluate a group after a treatment or program is completed. The problem is the equivalence of the groups is unknown from the beginning because randomization is not used.

## One-Shot Case Study

A third common type of pre-experimental descriptive technique is the one-shot case study, in which a treatment is given and an observation is made. The configuration is basically this:

(R) E X O

This framework is used often in survey designs, where no control group is needed. In the one-shot case study, the sample may or may not be randomized. This approach might be used at the end of a training session when individuals are asked to recount what they learned. No randomization occurred, no control group, and no assessment of what knowledge existed before the experiment was undertaken.

# Making Experimental Design Decisions

As indicated, some people raise objections about experimental designs. Some people feel uncomfortable about being "guinea pigs" and some professionals do not wish to perpetuate that idea by using experimental designs for recreation evaluation or research. In addition, the time and effort involved in planning experimental projects is obviously great. The values of using experimental and quasi-experimental procedures, however, cannot be discounted in doing summative evaluations and in assessing goal attainment. They are particularly good in assessing participant changes in learning (i.e., skills, knowledge, attitudes) and actions.

Experiments might be considered when a new program is introduced, when stakes are high, when there is controversy about program effectiveness, and when change or the value of something needs to be shown. Ultimately, experiments are best used to determine whether or not a program caused any personal or social change. Prediction and cause and effect are the most important outcomes of experimental designs.

Regardless of how an experiment is used, several criteria must be considered. Adequate control must be guaranteed so the evaluator can be assured that the results were due to a treatment and not to something else. In the field of parks, recreation, tourism, sport, and leisure studies, the results must apply to the real world. Comparisons are an essential component. Further, the measurement instruments must be sound. Thus, when you do experiments, you will either have to choose existing instruments or develop instruments for measuring the pretest and posttest information. This information has been discussed in some detail in previous chapters. Finally, the experimental methods employed in evaluation and research need to be kept simple. Figure 2.13 shows a flow chart that may be useful in deciding whether to use experimental designs.

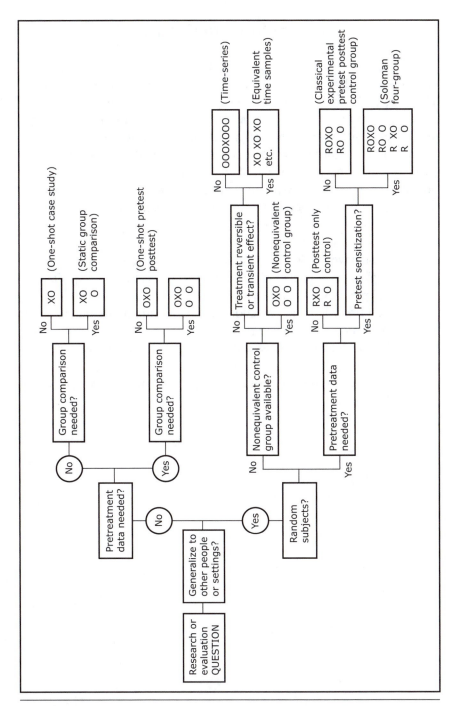

**Figure 2.13**  *Decision Matrix for Experimental Designs (adapted from Okey, Shrum &*
*Yeany, 1977)*

# From Ideas to Reality

Experiments are commonly discussed in the scientific literature and have been a respected way that research and evaluation have been undertaken. These methods, however, are not always as easy to administer as are descriptive/evocative methods such as surveys and observations. Nevertheless, experiments have much to offer evaluators and researchers. They may be the most appropriate methods to use if we want to determine whether changes actually occur as a result of controlling the programs and interventions that are conducted. Experimental designs are worth considering as options for particular kinds of evaluation and research situations.

Now that you have studied this chapter, you should be able to:

- Explain the differences between true experiments, quasi-experiments, and pre-experiment methods
- Describe why randomization and control groups are important in evaluation and research projects
- Analyze the advantages and disadvantages that are associated with using experimental designs
- Conduct a simple experiment using one of the techniques described in the chapter

# 2.14 Specific Applications to Recreation: The More the Merrier

We discussed experimental designs and the broad methods categories of surveys, observations, and unobtrusive measures. We will now examine some specific applications of techniques used in recreation evaluation and research. Each of these techniques can be used to measure aspects of the five Ps (participant outcomes, personnel, places, policies, program quality) and can be applied to assessment, formative, and summative evaluations or research projects. The steps of determining criteria or research questions, selecting methods and samples for data collection and analysis, and using the information to make judgments about practice or theory apply to all of these techniques. In this chapter we address importance-performance, case studies, single-subject designs, SOPLAY and SOPARC, economic analysis, consensus techniques, sociometrics, and several other miscellaneous evaluation techniques that have been used in the field.

## Importance-Performance

A popular technique has been the use of importance-performance (I-P) survey questionnaires to measure program effectiveness. I-P surveys are based on the notion that evaluation must be obtained from the participant. Knowing the importance is essential. People can be satisfied with performance aspects of recreation, for example, but that assessment makes little difference if the program or place has no importance to them.

The I-P technique uses a measurement instrument to quantify customer satisfaction with performance by combining importance with satisfaction. Several steps are involved in the process:

1.  Attributes (criteria) to measure are determined. These attributes can be discerned through literature reviews, focus-group interviews, and/or the use of managerial or professional judgment.

2.  Two sets of questions are developed, asking how important an attribute or amenity is to a participant and how satisfied the participant is with the organization's performance regarding that attribute or amenity.

3.  Data are collected.

4.  The responses to those two sets of questions are then matched and the means or medians plotted against one another on a two-way dimensional grid, where importance is represented by one axis and performance and/or satisfaction are represented by the other.

5.  The respondents' perceptions are then translated into management action through a facilitated interpretation. Figure 2.14(1) shows an example of the I-P grid.

Elements in Quadrant (Q) 1 are perceived as high on importance but low on performance, and they represent areas requiring managerial attention (i.e., concentrate here!). Q 2 is perceived as high on both importance and performance. The status of performance should be maintained (i.e.,

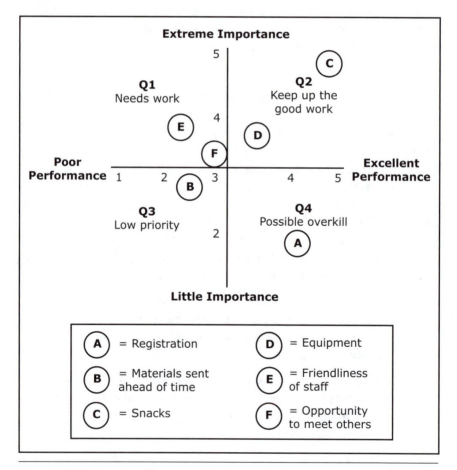

*Figure 2.14(1)* *Example of Importance-Performance Grid*

keep up the good work!). Q 3 is perceived as low importance but high on performance suggesting overcommitment of resources in these areas (i.e., possible overkill?). Q 4 is perceived as low on both importance and performance, which represent those attributes or amenities of low managerial priority (i.e., perhaps they should be reconsidered or eliminated).

Several examples exist in the parks and recreation research literature about using I-P. Siegenthaler (1994) was interested in developing and maintaining quality programs for older adults and wanted to find out what this population thought was important. She identified program features important to participants in the Austin Parks and Recreation Senior Programs and how well participants felt the agency was performing. Hollenhorst, Olson, and Fortney (1992) used I-P to examine the importance of various attributes of the West Virginia state park cabin experience and to determine visitor satisfaction with these attributes. They examined factors like cleanliness, furniture, reservation systems, appliances, location, kitchenware, linens, bathtub showers, fireplaces, open porch, deck, cathedral ceilings, and telephones. They found that the cabin design and construction didn't need to change. Visitors valued basic comforts, rustic and simple character, seclusion, natural surroundings, and access to water-based recreation.

Several tips must be kept in mind when using I-P. First, determine the attributes to measure carefully. Be sure to separate importance from performance items on the questionnaire. Finally, as is true for any evaluation, the evaluator or researcher must interpret what the data mean after they have been analyzed.

# Case Studies

Case studies are used to gather information about individuals or groups, including communities, organizations, or institutions. The difference between case studies and other methods is that they use many sources of data pertaining to a unit such as a person or an organization. A single case study or multiple case studies might be done to gather data about several units with the same goals in mind. Case studies may be the ultimate form of triangulation in that they require multiple methods and data sources such as surveys, observations, and unobtrusive data. Case studies are not as easy to do as many people think—many aspects must be considered in doing any type of case study project.

According to Howe and Keller (1988), a case study is an intensive investigation of a particular unit. It is an analytical description or construction of a person or a group observed over a given period of time. A case study may also be considered an in-depth study of the background, current status, or interactions of a given unit, which might be an individual, social group, institution, or community. Case studies are particularly useful if an evaluator or researcher is examining one situation and doesn't wish to compare it to another situation, individual, or group. On the other hand, doing multiple case studies using the same criteria could be highly useful. Case studies can be both specific and broad as they capture many variables and include descriptions of history and context. They are often longitudinal, because they tell a story that covers a period of time, and usually qualitative, because they often use prose and literary technique.

The purpose of the case study is to measure how and why something occurs. They are process-focused. In a case study, you are not necessarily concerned about generalizing the results to other situations, although case studies often give insight to other situations. You might choose a unique case or a critical case to evaluate. Further, you may collect qualitative and/or quantitative data. You might do a single case study or you might do multiple case studies. If multiple cases are used, a similar system and logic should be used in data collection for each. The important aspect in designing a case study project is to determine the unit to be examined whether it is an individual, event, or small group.

Case study techniques are frequently used in therapeutic recreation to analyze a particular client situation. For example, a Case History Review approach has been used in the *Therapeutic Recreation Journal* over the years to provide a basis for examining aspects of therapeutic recreation treatment. The *Journal of Park and Recreation Administration* also uses a similar approach with their "Programs that Work" section. Some of these descriptions are not formal systematic research, but they provide interesting "cases" for others to consider regarding how programs work.

According to the procedures used for any case study project, the evaluator or researcher will need to do the following:

1. Identify the focus of the investigation

2. Outline what needs to be studied

3. Select appropriate measurement tools

4. Develop a plan to collect the data considering effectiveness, efficiency, budget and time frame

5. Collate all the data

6. Interpret the data

7. Make recommendations from the study

For case studies, many methods previously discussed might be used to gather relevant data depending on the situation. Data included might be observations, interviews, parent interviews, and other individual interviews, review of documents, archival records, clinical or organizational record, life history profiles, diaries, and reports. Often longitudinal information in the form of unobtrusive data is collected to provide a historical context. In addition, a multidisciplinary assessment of the participant, group, or organization (i.e., using psychological, social, economic, and other information) is done with an emphasis on descriptions. These data are then assembled, organized, and condensed. The analysis for case study data consists of examining, categorizing, tabulating, and recombining evidence, just as is done in other forms of qualitative data collection. These analysis techniques will be discussed in much more depth in Unit 3. Similarly, case studies use pattern making, explanation building, and are conducted over a period of time.

Writing a case study report occurs during the entire process of collecting case study data. A final case study narrative is presented that provides a readable, descriptive picture of the unit (i.e., person, group, organization, or program) that was examined. It should make accessible to readers all the information necessary to understand the person or program. A case study may be presented either chronologically or thematically. Someone reading a case study you should get a sense that all aspects of a situation have been addressed. The final product should show the patterns that developed, explain what happened, and show information over a period of time. The boundaries of the case study should be clear with alternative perspectives offered along including evidence to support the conclusions made. The report should combine descriptive, analytic, interpretive, and evaluative perspectives.

Doing good case studies requires several competencies. An evaluator or researcher must be able to ask questions that address the criteria being examined, put ideas together as well as be a good listener, adaptive and flexible, and unbiased. As indicated above, using multiple sources helps in this process. Taking good notes, just as in field observation, is essential. All data sources need to be pulled together in a systematic order. According to Yin (2003), it is essential that multiple sources of evidence are used, a case study database is created, and that you maintain a chain of evidence concerning the data collected.

Case studies have sometimes been criticized for their lack of rigor and lack of generalization and comparisons. Sometimes they appear to be easy to do, but as you can see if they are done well they require great time and effort. Exemplary case studies are significant, complete, consider alternative perspectives, display sufficient evidence, and engage the reader in an understanding of the case being studied. The case study report must be written in such a way that people can see how their situation may or may not be like the case described. The essence of a case study is to allow the evaluator to learn the intricate details of how something is working, rather than necessarily to generalize to other situations.

## Single-Subject Techniques

A single-subject technique allows you to evaluate the effect of interventions on an individual participant or client. These techniques are somewhat like a case study, but they generally focus on a specific aspect of an individual. Single-subject techniques use an application of time-series experimental methods with subjects being their own control. Multiple and repeated assessments are used to measure intervention and its effects on an individual. Both qualitative and quantitative information can be provided.

The single-subject technique is similar to the case study, except only one person or a very small number of people are used as the sample for the evaluation. For example, suppose you wanted to know if a particular recreation technique worked with children who had autism. You might observe the behavior of a child for a period of time to establish a baseline, observe the child during the time the recreation program is administered, and then observe again as follow-up after the "treatment" is over. This approach done on individuals would show what happened and might enable you to know why some recreation experiences were more effective for some individuals and not for others. According to Datillo (1988), the single-subject technique offers a way to make informed decisions about the quality of a recreation program and provides a context for understanding behavior dynamics. The technique allows the evaluator to learn the details of how treatment is working for an individual rather than averaging the effects across a number of cases.

To reiterate, a series of measurements or observations occur over a period of time to determine how an individual may be changing as a result of a particular recreation program or as in therapeutic recreation, a particular treatment plan or intervention. Figure 2.14(2) shows an example of the way a single-subject data plot might look. The procedure used is to measure a behavior for an individual before treatment, apply a treatment, and withdraw the treatment and measure. This establishes a baseline (A). Over a period of time the treatment will be given and reinforced and then additional measures are taken (B). Subsequently after

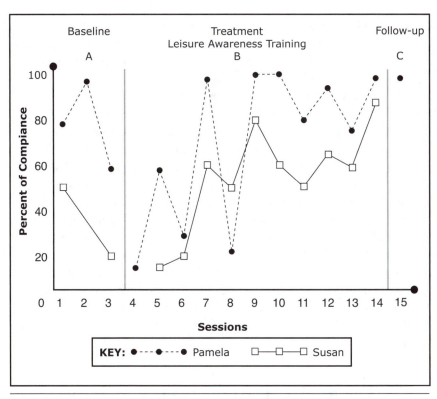

**Figure 2.14(2)**  *Example of a Plot for Single-Subject Technique*

a treatment period is over, follow-up measures (C) will be used to see if and how long the behavior continues.

The technique is precise. As in other situations, however, the results of single-subject analysis can be compromised by inadequate assessment tools, measurement procedures, or observation techniques. Although most of the studies using the single-subject technique in therapeutic recreation have used quantitative data, qualitative data could also be used. The value of single-subject evaluation techniques lie in using patterns identified in baseline and intervention conditions to determine how intervention affects an individual.

# SOPLAY and SOPARC

A system for observing physical activity has received great results in the 21st century, especially concerning childhood obesity and the overall inactivity of the population (McKenzie, 2006). Two systems have been developed, called SOPLAY (System for Observing Play and Leisure Activity in Youth) and SOPARC (System for Observing Play and Recreation in Communities). Because investigations of physical activity often require objective data about environments such as parks or playing fields where activity takes place, SOPLAY and SOPARC have become useful systems.

These observation "checklists" provide an example of time sampling techniques where periodic and systematic scans are conducted of areas (e.g., playgrounds) where individuals are—the individuals may or may not be active, which is part of the purpose of using SOPLAY or SOPARC to collect data. During these scans, for example, the observer codes each individual mechanically (with a paper-and-pencil form) or electronically (with devices such as computer notebooks for recording data) regarding behavior labeled "Sedentary" (i.e., lying down, sitting, standing), "Walking," or "Very Active." Scans may be made of females and males, differentiating by age or race/ethnicity. Summary counts include the number of people in an area and their activity levels. In addition, information may be collected about the environment such as time of day, weather conditions, temperature, presence of supervision, or equipment available. Table 2.14(3) shows an example of data collected about children and adults in parks.

# Devices to Measure Physical Activity

Other devices that are used in research and evaluation to collect objective data and measure physical activity include pedometers, accelerometers, and heart rate monitors. A pedometer is a small box worn at the hip on the clothing waistband that counts the number of steps a person takes. Most pedometers have a small, weighted internal "arm" mechanism that is suspended from a spring that moves up and down as a person walks. Each time a step is taken, the arm moves down, touches a contact, and a step is counted. Pedometers are reliable, relatively inexpensive, and easy to use. As is true of any mechanical device, some pedometers are of higher quality than others. For evaluation or research purposes, higher quality is best. Features to consider might be a large, digital display; a delayed reset button to deter accidental deletions of data; and a case that snaps shut to hide pedometer data, limit frequent checks, and prevent unintentional resets. A safety strap, or "gator clip," can help prevent the devices from falling off, especially when children or adults are active.

Some cautions might be offered in using pedometers and other electronic devices to measure physical activity. One particular concern with pedometers is the wearer reacting to the device and altering physical activ-

<table>
<tr><td colspan="2"></td></tr>
</table>

| | | | | | | | | | | | | |

School ID: __ __
Date: __ / __ / __
D8   D9   D10   D11

## SOPLAY
(System for Observing Play and Leisure Activity in Youth)

Obs. ID #: __ __   Reliability: 0. No  1. Yes

| START TIME | AREA | SUPERVISION | | | GIRLS | | | | BOYS | | | |
|---|---|---|---|---|---|---|---|---|---|---|---|---|
| | | | | | S | W | V | Act. | S | W | V | Act. |
| — — — | 1 | 0 | 1 | 2 | — | — | — | — | — | — | — | — |
| — — — | 2 | 0 | 1 | 2 | — | — | — | — | — | — | — | — |
| — — — | 3 | 0 | 1 | 2 | — | — | — | — | — | — | — | — |
| — — — | 4 | 0 | 1 | 2 | — | — | — | — | — | — | — | — |
| — — — | 5 | 0 | 1 | 2 | — | — | — | — | — | — | — | — |
| — — — | 6 | 0 | 1 | 2 | — | — | — | — | — | — | — | — |
| — — — | 7 | 0 | 1 | 2 | — | — | — | — | — | — | — | — |
| — — — | 8 | 0 | 1 | 2 | — | — | — | — | — | — | — | — |

### ACTIVITY CODES

| | | |
|---|---|---|
| 0 = No Identifiable Activity | 7 = Floor Hockey | 14 = Martial Arts/Kickboxing |
| 1 = Aerobics/Dance | 8 = Racquet Sports | 15 = Kickball |
| 2 = Baseball/Softball | 9 = Soccer | 16 = Handball |
| 3 = Basketball | 10 = Track/Cross Country | 17 = Bowling |
| 4 = Cheerleading | 11 = Volleyball | 18 = Yoga |
| 5 = Football | 12 = Weight Training | 19 = Jump Rope |
| 6 = Gymnastics | 13 = Ultimate Frisbee | 20 = None of the Above (list) |

*Figure 2.14(3)*  *Example of Data Collection for SOPLAY (System for Observing Play and Leisure Activity in Youth)*

ity patterns because of its presence. After use for a day or so, however, most people will come to ignore the devices.

Two other devices that can be used to collect data but that are more expensive are accelerometers and heart rate monitors. Accelerometers are box-like devices worn on the hip much like pedometers, but they can collect more complex data since they measure intensity of body movement. Accelerometers can record both the physical activity intensity (i.e., energy expenditure) and separate time intervals throughout the day. Accelerometers are expensive and require obligatory software to do data analysis, time commitment, and technical expertise. However, with resources and training, these devices can be a great way to measure how active people are in their daily lives.

Heart rate monitors are also an option for measuring physical activity. Heart rate monitors measure heartbeats over a specified amount of time to present the amount of cardiovascular work for an activity that an individual is participating in. They could be used to determine how intense activity is as a result of participating in a particular fitness program, for example. These devices also are expensive and may be intrusive, since straps and harnesses must be worn. Nevertheless, for particular types of study measuring exertion, they might be appropriate. More efforts are under way to use these devices to collect data about energy expenditure since people tend to overreport when they are asked about their physical activity involvement.

# Economic-Analysis Techniques

The policy and administrative application of evaluation often includes a focus on techniques for economic evaluation. Economic impact and cost-benefit analyses are commonly used, unobtrusive techniques and require a great deal more explanation than is provided here if they are to be applied to park, recreation, tourism, sport and leisure organizations. A brief description of some econometric techniques, however, may be useful.

Economic-impact evaluations might be done to measure the economic benefits of a special event on the local economy. Economic data are often difficult to gather and expensive to analyze, although standard questionnaire development and analysis can be applied. Economic-impact studies attempt to determine both the direct and indirect financial benefits of an activity by gathering expenditure data. For example, if you wanted to measure the economic impact of a sporting event, you would get expenditure data from a sample of visitors and then extrapolate to an entire group. A multiplier is used which refers to the fact that money spent in a community can be spent again and again. An increase in spending will create an indirect effect greater than the original expenditures. A multiplier of 2.0 is a conservative multiplier to use. For every dollar of income spent, two dollars circulate through a community. For example, if someone pays to stay in a hotel, the hotel owner will then pay his/her housekeeping staff who will then go out and buy groceries. The grocer will have money to pay his employees who will then spend their money on clothes for their children and so on. Therefore, the initial money spent will continue to multiply.

Economic impact can be measured along with other data like visitor satisfaction. You can find examples of economic-impact studies in the

*Journal of Park and Recreation Administration* as well as other journals like *Journal of Travel Research*. Most times, however, these studies are undertaken in communities as evaluation projects to illustrate the economic importance of recreation.

Little consensus exists concerning the best way to analyze costs and benefits. Costs are not hard to determine, but benefits are difficult to measure in either economic or noneconomic terms. In cost-benefit analysis, the evaluator has to determine the benefits in monetary terms. In cost-effectiveness you look at the cost in relation to some type of outcomes that may not be economic. Henderson (1988) has given an example of how cost-effectiveness might be determined in relation to volunteers (see Table 2.14[4]). The cost-effectiveness evaluation technique provides additional information from an economic view. However, it does not suffice for evaluating other aspects of volunteers and volunteer programs, such as the social good that volunteers may offer. You can do a similar analysis with other recreation programs to determine how much they cost. You must be careful, however, not to make decisions about programs based solely on costs. Some programs that cost more also have many more benefits that are difficult to measure.

A criticism of cost-benefits approaches is that it is hard to put a price on psychological benefits and the value of lives. The appropriate units of analysis are often difficult to determine. However, the problems associated with economic analysis should not prevent an evaluator from considering the possibilities in examining policy and administrative aspects of an organization.

# Consensus Techniques

The nominal group technique and the Delphi technique are examples of consensus strategies that can be used for evaluation and research. They may be done using questionnaires or group interviews. The Air Force, for example, used the nominal group technique (NGT) to assess future directions (Lankford & DeGraaf, 1992). The NGT is a means to identify issues, opportunities, and ways to reach potential participants. This collective decision making technique can be used for strategic planning, policy development, and goal formation. More structured than brainstorming, the data collector can obtain consensus on ideas and strategies.

Delbecq, Van de Ven, and Gustafson (1975) outlined a six-step process for NGT that has been relevant for many years:

*Table 2.14(4)* Cost-Effectiveness Analysis Worksheet *(adapted from Henderson, 1988)*

A. COSTS
  1. Direct
     a. coordinator's salary      $ _____
     b. recordkeeping/secretarial    _____
     c. recognition materials      _____
     d. expenses—mileage, meals, etc.   _____
     e. printed materials      _____
     f. office supplies      _____
     g. insurance      _____
     h. other      _____

                         TOTAL DIRECT    $ _____

  2. Indirect
     a. overhead      _____
     b. other staff      _____
     c. equipment      _____
     d. other      _____

                         TOTAL INDIRECT    $ _____

  TOTAL COSTS   $_____ (A)

B. OUTPUTS
  Activity = # of volunteers (B) x # of hours (C) x rate/hr = $ _____(D)
     a. _____   _____   x _____   x _____ = _____
     b. _____   _____   x _____   x _____ = _____
     c. _____   _____   x _____   x _____ = _____
     d. _____   _____   x _____   x _____ = _____
     e. _____   _____   x _____   x _____ = _____
     f. _____   _____   x _____   x _____ = _____

        Total (B) _____    Total (C) _____    Total (D) $ _____

C. COST-EFFECTIVENESS ANALYSIS

  Output (D) divided by Cost (A) = 1: _____ ratio
  For every $ spent, $X of service are provided

D. OTHER CALCULATIONS
  Cost (A) ÷ # of volunteers (B) = Cost per volunteer
  Cost (A) ÷ # of clients served = Cost per client
  Cost (A) ÷ # of hours volunteered (C) = Cost per service hour

1. Introduce topic and explain

2. Participants write down responses on card

3. All responses are listed

4. Items are clarified

5.  Individuals vote on the issues identified

6.  Votes are tabulated

You can go through this process twice to get additional information and you can assign value to the tabulated votes.

The consensus method that many people know is the Delphi technique. Although the data in a Delphi study are often analyzed quantitatively, they are collected initially using a qualitative process. The Delphi technique is frequently used to establish goals, determine strategies, predict problems, access group preferences, and anticipate needs similar to NGT. The critical characteristics of the Delphi technique are that it relies on the informed judgment of knowledgeable panels concerning a topic that has little known objective data. The technique is done anonymously with controlled feedback given to produce a group response.

The first step involved in the technique is to select a panel of "experts" for the topic addressed. The number of individuals is not as important as the quality of the panel. An open-ended questionnaire is then sent to the panel. The responses to that questionnaire are grouped and tabulated. A second questionnaire is sent, asking the same people to rate, usually on a Likert scale, the importance of all the initial responses received. The second questionnaire is tabulated and a final questionnaire is sent again to obtain further ratings and rankings to move toward as much consensus as possible. The final product of the Delphi generally looks like a ranking of the most important issues that the panel uncovers. For example, Anderson and Schneider (1993) used the Delphi process to identify important innovations from recreation management in the past 20 years and rated their relative importance for meeting specific management goals.

# Sociometry

Sociometrics are used to survey and analyze how groups operate by asking how people "get along" with each other. The sociogram is a tool used to identify how members of a subgroup interact and how they function. The sociogram illustrates choices made in a group by plotting them on a matrix. According to Lundegren and Farrell (1985), one merely asks, "Name three people with whom you would most like to work as a partner for the xyz group." You could ask any question, such as, "With whom do you like to play?" (for children), "With whom would you like to go to lunch?" (for adults), or "Who is most supportive of you in the work environment?" This technique is not designed for large groups. It works best with groups of less than 20.

The evaluator then sets up a matrix with each person across the top and down the side. The choices are tallied. You could analyze between sex choices if you wanted or any other category that seems appropriate. Figure 2.14(5) shows an example of a sociogram analysis. Four concentric circles are drawn representing levels of choice, with the highest in the center. Circles are labeled and entered on to the diagram. Arrows are drawn for each individual to the symbol of the person chosen. If the choice is reciprocated, a double-headed arrow for mutual choice is used. The process tells you who is most chosen and also shows the "isolates." It also tells where pairs are and shows simple choices as well as mutual choices. This technique might be useful for analyzing group cohesiveness or how a group can function better.

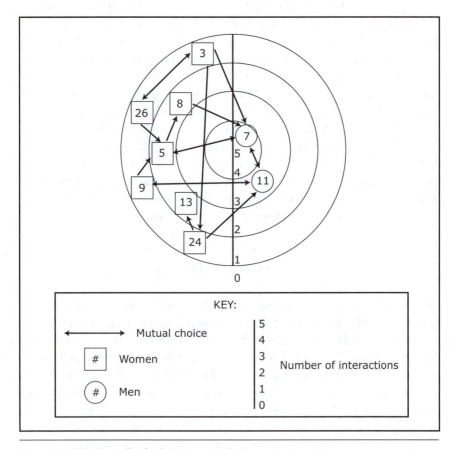

*Figure 2.14(5) Example of a Sociogram Analysis*

# Miscellaneous Techniques and Applications

A number of other techniques have been described in the recreation literature that might be of interest to evaluators. They provide further examples to consider and will be described briefly.

## Time Diaries and Time Sampling

Some research and evaluation studies have included self-report processes, in which adults and children were asked to keep records regarding their use of time or the occurrence of certain types of behaviors. Diaries or journals have been used, for example, to assess the physical activity that people undertake over a period of time like several days.

Another technique that has been used is time sampling, or what are sometimes called "beeper" studies. With this technique, people wear a pager and at certain times they receive a page asking them to write down what they are doing and other related questions such as with whom, emotions associated, or perhaps where an activity is taking place. For those familiar with Csikszentmihalyi's (1975) concept of "flow," time sampling was used to collect data to develop that original construct. Individuals were asked what they were doing and about their psychological states.

## Visual Analyses

The use of photographs and other visual media also has interesting potential for data collection. These tools can be used in a number of ways. For example, some researchers have shown photographs to people and asked for their opinion about issues such as crowding conditions in parks. Other researchers have given disposable cameras to children and asked them to take pictures of "what 'camp' means to [them]." Yet another technique was used by the Oklahoma Parks and Recreation Department when it asked children and adults to draw pictures of "what parks mean to [them]." See Figure 2.14(6) for an another example of one of the pictures that was drawn (see Figure 2.12 for the first). Visual tools are an opportunity to collect data that is generally enjoyable for participants and that can yield useful data.

## Report Cards

Report cards are a questionnaire technique that can be used to focus on indicators of satisfaction. They use items and ask people to rank them relative to grade point, with A="excellent," B="better than average," C="average," D="below average," E="poor." When used in a park, you might ask about first impression, helpfulness of staff, cleanliness of restrooms, information at park, attractiveness of the park, safety and security,

**Figure 2.14(6)** *Example of Visual Analysis Picture Drawn for "What Parks Mean to Me" (courtesy of Debra Jordan, Oklahoma State University)*

cleanliness of ground, ease of access, hours or operation, control of pets, and overall satisfaction. You can then use GPA averages to rank services: 4–3.8=A, 3.79–3.67=A-, 3.66–3.33=B+, 3.32–3.00=B, 2.099–2.67=B-, 2.66–2.33=C+. You could look at these grades over a period of time or compare one facility to another. It is usually best to include qualitative summaries with both the letter grades and the numbers. Many people relate to the notion of a GPA so if you said that people rated the cleanliness of a park as B-, then the perception would be understood in a relative manner. The question of whether a B- is a good enough score would have to be considered (the goal is almost always an A!).

## Service Quality

Service quality is a concept measured frequently in the recreation and tourism literature. The premise of service-quality evaluation is that consumers are demanding and an increased competition for customers exists. Five quality dimensions of expectations and perceptions are measured in this survey approach: tangibles, reliability, responsiveness, assurance, and empathy. The expectations are measured with a statement such as, "Tell us to the degree to which you think an excellent recreation center should have the features described in the following statements." A 7-point Likert scale anchored from "not at all essential" to "absolutely essential" is used. The perception part asks individuals to "tell us the degree to which you feel Center X has the features described in each statement," which is somewhat similar to an importance-performance evaluation. A 7-point Likert scale of "strongly agree" to "strongly disagree" is used. Features include such aspects as prompt repairs to facilities and equipment, clean and sanitary shower and lockers, good quality healthy food at snack bar, staff interested in patrons, and accurate class descriptions (Wright, Duray, & Goodale, 1992).

A Service Quality score is obtained by subtracting the mean expectation rating from the mean performance rating. Negative results indicate where a "service gap" exists. Zero implied met expectations. In using this approach, adaptations can be made in the item pool for a particular service. Similar to importance-performance, this method is proving to be useful to evaluators in all areas of recreation management.

# From Ideas to Reality

This entire chapter has been an example of how specific approaches using the methods described previously can be applied to evaluation and research in the recreation field. We can learn a great deal from seeing how others have applied methods and developed instruments. In addition to considering some of these possible techniques and applications, we encourage you to read recreation-related magazines, newsletters, and journals that give additional examples of techniques people have used in evaluation projects and research studies.

Now that you have studied this chapter, you should be able to:
- Describe how these specific techniques might be applied to one or two evaluation situations
- Analyze the possible strengths and weaknesses of any technique that might be applied to collecting data for evaluation or research

## 2.15 Triangulation or Mixed Modes: Drawing on All the Tools

As you have seen in this unit, a variety of methods choices and sampling possibilities exist for doing evaluation projects and research studies. The use of more than one method, more than one source of data, or more than one evaluator or researcher often strengthens a project. The use of more than one method, source of data, or data collector is referred to as triangulation. Elements of using more than one method is sometimes called mixed methods or mixed modes. Further, the use of more than one method or source is also referred to by some people as "linking." The notion is the same regardless of the term used. Triangulation can be a little misleading because it suggests three of something, when in reality the use by researchers and evaluators usually means two or more.

Using only one method, source of data, or data collector may be more economical, but the possibility for more reliable and valid results obtained from triangulation ought to be considered. If you think about the old adage, "two heads are better than one," you have a rationale for considering the use of triangulation.

## Triangulated or Mixed-Mode Methods

No one method is perfect, so using more than one method may give additional information to an evaluator or researcher. Triangulation can occur within methods and between methods.

*Within-method triangulation* includes the collection of both qualitative and quantitative data using the same method. The most common example would be the use of both close-ended and open-ended questions in a survey. Issues of complementariness of qualitative or quantitative data are sometimes debated, but keep in mind that methods themselves are neither qualitative nor quantitative, as was discussed at the beginning of this unit. How a method is used will produce qualitative or quantitative data, or both. Asking survey questions that may be both close-ended (quantitative) and open-ended (qualitative) is not uncommon. Different data result, depending on the use of open-ended or close-ended questions. Whether questionnaires collect quantitative or qualitative data depends on what information is currently known.

*Between-method* or *mixed-mode triangulation* is the use of two or more methods to measure the same phenomena. This form of triangulation can strengthen the validity of the overall findings. *Congruence* relates to similarity, consistency, or convergence of results obtained from two or more methods, whereas complementariness refers to one set of results enriching, expanding upon, clarifying, or illustrating the other. An independent assessment of the same phenomena results in complementary results. For example, you might observe an event and also interview a selected group of people that were in attendance at that event. Or you might use participation records from unobtrusive document analysis and then survey a sample of participants to determine their satisfaction with an activity.

Between-method triangulation can be subdivided along two dimensions. One way relates to the degree of independence of the methods used for data collection and how they might be two ways to uncover the same information. A second dimension relates to the degree to which the implementation of both methods or modes is sequential versus concurrent. Are the two modes used at the same time, or is one method used to inform the second method? The evaluator will need to decide which approach is going to be the best: to have one method follow another or to use two methods at the same time.

Evaluators and researchers often use qualitative approaches such as focus groups to get information that will then allow them to develop quantitative questionnaires. In addition, sometimes quantitative data are collected and then interviews are used to understand the meaning behind some of the numbers. Nothing is wrong with combining qualitative and quantitative data in these ways, and the combination may make for a deeper and more useful project. Howe and Keller (1988) provided a description of how qualitative and quantitative data might be used together (see Table 2.15).

Triangulated methods are becoming more common in the recreation field, especially since the Internet now exists to assist in some forms of data collection. The biggest challenge with using mixed modes is the need to collect data rigorously in all cases. The evaluator or researcher can make a case for triangulated methods by examining the congruence, as well as the complementariness, of the results desired. Further, mixed methods can reduce threats to internal and external validity.

The problem with mixed methods is that it often takes more time and money to implement two methods than one. Also, in using any method, it must be done rigorously in the development of the evaluation or research project. In other words, using two poorly implemented methods does not make for one good method (i.e., two wrongs don't make a right). The data collector must be aware of the strengths and weaknesses of methods and the resulting data when multiple methods are used.

*Table 2.15* *Summary of Benefits from Triangulating Methods (adapted from Howe &*
*Keller, 1988)*

---

**Contributions of Qualitative Data to Quantitative Data**

Qualitative data can enrich quantitative data by improving:
1. The sampling framework by using exploratory interviews and observations to confirm or rationalize the framework
2. The overall study design by prioritizing information needs and posing the right quantitative questions
3. The data collection process by developing valid instruments through using exploratory interviews and observations
4. Instrument design and interpretation as well as determining appropriate language to use
5. Verification of quantitative findings in areas where methods yield an overlap of information
6. Item construction for questionnaires, which can be generated from initial observational data
7. Clarification of quantitative findings by comparing them with field notes covering the same topics

**Contributions of Quantitative Data to Qualitative Data**

Quantitative date can enrich qualitative data by:
1. Identifying representative cases, to serve the goal of generalizability
2. Mitigating the bias or "gatekeeper" effect of highly articulate and engaged informants
3. Verifying qualitative interpretations by statistical analysis
4. Casting new light on field observations by yielding unanticipated findings
5. Helping to reduce possible measurement error

---

# Triangulated Sources of Data

Different participants or sources of data can provide insight about a topic or issue. A project often can benefit from more than one data source. For example, if you were interested in the changes that occurred in campers as a result of going to a 4-week summer camp, you might talk to campers, but you also might interview their counselors and/or parents. You would be getting data from different sources that address the same evaluation criteria or research question.

Another way to triangulate sources is to get data from different periods of time. For example, before a program begins, you might ask in-depth interview questions about expectations. While the program is going on, you might interview the same people again. After the program is over, you might ask if those expectations were fulfilled. The sources of data would be dependent on the timing of the data collection.

You could also use the decision makers for an evaluation project as one important additional source of data. For example, you might interview the Board of Directors of an organization as a source of additional data for making recommendations. Unobtrusive data such as participation statistics could be combined with newly collected questionnaire data. Other sources of data might be program records, program participants, staff delivering programs, family members and other significant relationships to participants, observations made by evaluator, and/or community-level indices. The potential sources of data are numerous for most projects. These data can be triangulated and linked to provide complementary information.

## Triangulation Using Multiple Data Collectors

Triangulated perspectives can also be obtained from multiple evaluators or researchers. If more than one person is interpreting results, developing instruments, or doing interviews, it is likely that more problems can be avoided since more than one perspective is used. "Two heads are better than one" really applies here. Many times, projects are done as a team effort and this teamwork provides the potential for the highest quality because of the variety of points of view that can be incorporated into a final product. Multiple evaluators, however, must be able to communicate with one another and must spend time clarifying exactly what the criteria are and how data are to be collected and analyzed so everyone is "on the same page."

## Cautions in Using Triangulation

Regardless of what form of triangulation is used, you must report the design and results for all triangulated aspects. It is unethical to try two different methods and then only take the data from the one that works the best. If you choose more than one method or more than one data source, you must report them in your final evaluation.

Triangulation and using mixed modes does not guarantee overcoming all biases. Be careful to not just proliferate methods, sources, or evaluators, but also see how they can be integrated. You can compound the error in a poorly designed project that lacks specific criteria if you add more methods or more sources. Problems also arise when data are in conflict due to triangulation. You have to acknowledge that possible situation and try to interpret what is meant by the discrepancies that you may uncover. You are also ethically obligated to report incongruence and inconsistencies and explain them to the best of your ability. Often different data are the result of the methods used. You need to have a good grasp of all the methods and techniques that might be available so you can make the best possible choices regarding the use of single approaches or mixed modes.

# From Ideas to Reality

Triangulation, mixed modes, and linking can add to the validity of evaluation or research, but these techniques can also be expensive in terms of time and money. Most projects involve limited budgets, short time frames, and political constraints. Using one good method or one good source of data is more beneficial than a series of poorly implemented methods or sources. If possible, however, triangulated methods, sources, and data collectors can often enhance the reliability, validity, and usability of an evaluation project or research study.

Now that you have studied this chapter, you should be able to:
- Define triangulation, mixed modes, and linking
- Give examples of how triangulation might be used between methods and within methods
- Identify possible sources for data triangulation
- Describe the problems that may be encountered when triangulating in an evaluation or research project

# 2.16 People Aren't All the Same: Considerations for Data Collection

With the ease that now seems to exist for data collection, thinking about the particular population that you are evaluating or researching may be more important than ever. Data collection is not always done with individuals who are educated, middle-class, able-bodied, and articulate. Particular groups such as youth, older adults, people with disabilities, people with low education levels, people from particular ethnic and cultural groups, and people representing other "vulnerable populations" may require some specific considerations. In some cases, their needs are no different than anyone else in the general population. But, to assure the best response rate, some specific needs should be considered as you plan your evaluation. A variety of people ought to be used in your systematic inquiry, so you get information from the diverse group of people who benefit from recreation. In this short chapter, we will raise some issues about collecting data from particular groups. If you choose to focus on a group for your study, we encourage you to use this chapter as a springboard for further reading.

## People with Disabilities

Some people with particular types of disabilities may require some special considerations. As adapting physical structures for people with disabilities or older adults facilitates access, the changes you make in your evaluation process may make data collection easier for everyone.

Some people with physical disabilities may need particular kinds of accommodations. For example, for someone using a wheelchair for mobility reasons, nothing different may need to be done to collect survey data. However, if you are interested in measuring the physical activity of people and plan to use pedometers, this data collection strategy would obviously not work with someone using a wheelchair. Devices have been developed to measure wheel revolutions, so obviously one would make that type of adaptation in data collection if physical activity was to be measured. People with severe visual impairments might need an oral administration of a survey, while for some people with less severe visual challenges, larger print would be the only modification needed.

In some cases you need to consider the cognitive abilities of your potential respondents. Malik, Ashton-Shaeffer, and Kleiber (1991), for example, described some of the aspects to consider in interviewing people with mental retardation. They believe interviewing can be successful and helpful because it de-objectifies a person and allows the evaluator to get information that couldn't be obtained some other way. Designing questions so that the individuals with mental retardation have the ability to understand and accurately convey facts and opinions is important. They suggest that considering the time, place, length of interview, and interviewer rapport can enhance an interview session. An interview should be conducted where the fewest distractions exist using a shorter length of time (e.g., no more than 30 minutes). For many people with mental retardation, yes/no and either/or questions are easiest to answer.

Obviously, various other adaptations might be made, depending on the disability. The important aspect is to recognize that not everyone is able-bodied, and if you really want to get the input of all citizens, you may need to make adaptations and modifications.

# Children and Youth

Children and youth can be characterized in a number of ways depending on their emotional, physical, social, and cognitive development. Different researchers set the definitions of childhood, youth, and adolescence in various ways that reflect different levels of ability. Children's cognitive abilities increase with age, so those developmental stages must be taken into account in conducting research with children.

In working with young people, several ideas should be kept in mind. One primary consideration is to be clear about the purpose of the study. That mandate applies to all studies but is particularly important with youth and their parents or caregivers that may need to give consent for particular kinds of projects. The social and cognitive abilities must be considered carefully when determining from whom to collect data. In some cases children are not the best sources of information. For example, if you are interested in behavioral changes in children, parents, teachers, or youth workers might be better sources for this information. As in all methods, pilot-testing should be undertaken to ensure that the data collection tools are appropriate for the age group you use. Also recognize that Institutional Review Boards in universities need to approve research undertaken with people and are particularly demanding about the protection of children and people with disabilities. While many of the research projects conducted in the recreation field pose little to no risk to the people involved, these boards are still interested in how even minimal risk (physical, psychological) is to be addressed in your project. You likely will have to show the direct benefits to participants or a worthy advancement in general knowledge.

Several tips may be useful in working with children in particular. Young people under the age of 11–12 probably will respond best if statements are simple, unambiguous, and relevant to their experiences. Responses that are numbered may be confusing to children and probably should be limited to no more than 4–5 options. Using a neutral point on a scale or a "don't know" or undecided may result in children not thinking through the response to a question. Sometimes it is most useful to "force" a decision rather than to use the "don't know" category. Children may not remain motivated as long as adults to respond to a questionnaire or interview, so especially for younger children, the data collection process should be short, concrete, and attractive. The safeguards you use with adults around social desirability will likely be similar with children. Even young children want to please or "say the right thing," so don't overlook social desirability issues.

In-person interviews also require certain considerations to be addressed with children. Minimally, the interviewer needs to be familiar with developmental stages and aware of the characteristics of the children of a particular age group. Standard interview questions can be used but should be modified to reflect children's cognitive levels. While you can obtain in-depth information from children, interviewers may often need to clarify the questions. Just as with adults, if you want children to be forthcoming, a good rapport must be developed with them. For example, they may feel uncomfortable being interviewed by a unknown adult. The interviewer may need to engage in some "pre-interview" activity with the children, so at least a minimal level of familiarity exists. Data quality must also be considered, since they do not always have the language skills to adequately articulate responses to some types of questions.

Focus groups can also be conducted with children beginning as young as 6 years old. Most children find these groups to be fun and many feel safer in these kinds of environments. Evaluators and researchers can learn about the ideas and opinions of children quite easily using this technique. The success of the method, however, is dependent on the communication skills of the children, the ability of the moderator to keep the children focused, and ensuring that all children get an opportunity to speak, including the shy ones. Some topics are better for focus groups than others, and you need to be sensitive to what children feel safe discussing in this type of setting.

# Older Adults

The number of older adults is growing in the U.S. and will continue to constitute a major population group. You may want to include them in general population studies, or you may have reason to conduct older-adult-only surveys. Similar to children, a huge range exists in the physical and cognitive functioning of older adults, often depending on whether they are 55 or 85 years old. The ability to generalize to all older people is, at best, difficult. However, researchers have gained some insight into techniques that should be considered in collecting data from older adults.

Jacelon (2007) offered a number of ideas about researching older adults that may be helpful, and some of her thoughts are summarized in this section. Jacelon suggested that older adults are sometimes neglected in research because they are negatively stereotyped, considered to lack competence, suspicious of giving "informed consent," and may require additional time to recruit. Frail older adults living in rural areas or in care facilities may be difficult to engage. However, many older adults will be as willing to participate in your projects as anyone else.

Generally the best way to recruit older adults is in a face-to-face situation. These individuals must have a positive impression of the evaluator or researcher and are more likely to participate if they have built trust and rapport with you or your project. Convincing older adults to participate may take longer for some studies. Some older adults are quite cautious and may be reluctant to sign anything, including an "informed consent," if they do not completely understand the project. Many older adults fear getting "ripped off" in some way unless they trust the data collector or the organization involved. Often if they know that someone they trust referred the researcher to them, they may be more enthusiastic about participating.

Many older adults will be glad to participate in a project if they understand its purpose. At this age, some adults value the opportunity to provide information that may be helpful and may preserve their legacy in some way. Many older adults enjoy some types of data collection projects if it allows them to socialize (particularly over a meal or snack), which is often an important dimension of older people's lives.

Any research or evaluation collected with any group requires pilot-testing. This admonition is certainly true with older adults, because they may not understand the same terminology that younger adults use. Questionnaires administered should use a large font size, be user-friendly by not overwhelming people with words, be short, and have a simple response format. Responding to a questionnaire sometimes takes older people longer than others, so they can become fatigued if you are asking them to do something that requires more than 15–20 minutes (Jacelon, 2007). Not understanding questions can also create anxiety in older adults. If you can work with older adults in groups so that you can answer questions they might have, you may cut down on anxiety and fatigue and increase your response rate. Also be aware that some physical abilities of older adults, such as vision and hearing, may not be as good as younger people so you need to plan for that possibility and be patient with this group. Make sure that the questions you ask either in questionnaires or interviews are not perceived as invading privacy, as some older adults may not be forthcoming. The bottom line for older adults, as with any group, is that you are proactive in anticipating some of the issues and challenges that might exist or evolve.

## Cultural Differences

Greater attention is being paid to considerations about collecting data from cultural groups. A term used for the results from this research is "cultural competence" or perhaps more descriptively "cross-cultural competence." Being able to interact with many cultures may be necessary in undertaking community evaluation projects. You will need to develop the skills that will make you sensitive to cultural differences and inform how to proceed in each new situation. These skills are wide ranging and will take a lifetime to develop. However, because cultural diversity is important, you will need to think about how to develop these skills. Obviously all cultures are different in terms of a range of ethnicity and religious affiliations. If you are targeting a particular group, it is important to know as much as possible about the group in order to collect the most reliable and valid data.

We are defining culture as a set of social and learned behavior patterns and beliefs. No one can ever know everything about a culture, but as evaluators and researchers, you must develop the capacity to understand how culture can influence data collection and interpretation. In some cases, something as simple as choice of language for your written or verbal communication may be an acknowledgement of a cultural difference.

Since you will likely work with more than one culture, the skills you develop and employ should include having an open mind, not making assumptions, and asking the right questions respectfully (Colorado Trust, 2007). An important point to remember is that culture is not the same as race and ethnicity. Any of the groups described in this chapter might be considered a cultural group. Culture includes visible traditions and aspects such as music, dance, food, clothing, language, skin color, and art. Other less obvious forms of culture might include factors like religion, history, social class, concepts of life, body language, and use of leisure. Even deeper areas might include the meaning of community, patterns of decision making, beliefs about health, individualism versus collectivism, and many other such issues.

The Colorado Trust (2007) has put together materials that focus on cross-cultural competency in broad ways, so we have summarized some of their information in this section. They encourage evaluators to think about a number of issues. Most of their exhortations apply to any type of evaluation or research but should be considered within the cultural context:

- Identify someone who can be a cultural translator between you and the population you wish to study
- Listen, observe carefully, and ask questions respectfully
- Learn as much as you can about the cultural group and previous studies that have been done
- Don't assume that particular terms or concepts mean the same to all people
- Pilot-test all instruments
- Set aside time and resources to build trust and relationships with the cultural group
- Be aware of the impact your study may have on people and adjust if needed
- Accept that status differences exist between evaluators and participants. Evaluators generally have power and privilege that may not be experienced by members of a particular cultural group
- Try to explain your study as clearly and honestly as possible and demystify data collection to the extent that you can
- Create comfortable settings for any evaluation or research undertaken
- Some studies may require a language other than English but make sure that cross-translation is accurate. If you are working with interpreters, make sure that they understand the project and the need to be as accurate as possible.
- Form partnerships with the group you are studying to get them involved in the project
- Although demographic differences are important to consider, pay attention to why race, for example, might make a difference. In other words, do not ignore the importance of the contextual conditions and the structural inequities that might exist.

Regardless of your research or evaluation project, you will need to consider how culture influences your results. Developing this competence is a lifelong endeavor, and you can learn best by being aware of the issues and doing projects.

# People with Low Socioeconomic Status (SES)

Populations of low socioeconomic status are considered one of the vulnerable populations that must be examined. However, people of low SES are often difficult to reach. They may not have access to certain types of facilities. They may not have a high level of education. Some of them may be homeless or have large extended families. As with the other groups, people with low SES represent a range of abilities, interests, and ages.

Gaining access to this hard-to-reach population may be a challenge. Often organizations or agencies that serve low SES people or churches might be helpful. Similar to other groups, however, these individuals may be suspicious of people that clearly represent greater power and privilege and may be especially cautious if they believe you are associated with the government. Gorin, Hooper, Dyson, and Cabral (2008) described how any research undertaken with hard-to-reach families should employ an "ethic of care." This ethic of care should reflect the pragmatic issues that exist and should be ready to deal with potential conflict and disagreement rather than trying to ignore it or eliminate it.

As in all evaluation or research, you should eliminate as much risk as possible for these participants. It is also important that evaluators, researchers, and project staff are aware of their own safety when conducting some types of studies that may have perceived threatening topics.

Further, the language used in any written material must be considered. Gorin et al. (2008) suggested that using low income was better than poverty. Poverty seems a worse term and people do not want to label themselves as living in poverty. If questionnaires are used, they should be as clear and easily readable as possible. If other methods are used, they should be carefully explained. Incentives for participation such as a gift card or a meal might be especially appreciated by people with low SES.

Working with people of low SES is a challenge, just as working with any other specific group can be. However, trying to be as sensitive as possible to the situation and anticipating issues by knowing as much as possible about a group is paramount.

# From Ideas to Reality

Because of the diversity of the American population, you will inevitably be working with a variety of groups. Understanding something about the motivations and constraints of all individuals studied is necessary, but it may be particularly important for specific groups. No magic formulas exist and you will never know everything you need to know to be completely culturally competent. However, you can be aware of the conditions that surround people's lives who might be considered vulnerable. Being as proactive as possible is essential.

Now that you have studied this chapter, you should be able to:
- Describe some of the groups that require some additional considerations that you might encounter in undertaking evaluation and research projects
- Plan ahead for special conditions that should be considered for particular groups

# Unit THREE—EVIDENCE
## ***
# *Data Analysis*

## 3.0 Introduction to Data Analysis

Thoughts about analyzing data begin as soon as a project is conceived. Project design means considering the data that will be appropriate for the analyses to be undertaken. Further, the actual process of data analysis should begin as soon as data are collected. The exception to this rule is in qualitative interviews and field observations, where the data analyses may occur almost simultaneously with the data collection. Regardless, analysis is a part of the evaluation research process where the evidence must be carefully handled. In Unit Three, we will continue the discussion of evidence, but we will specifically address what to do with data and how to manage it so judgments (i.e., conclusions and recommendations) can be made about its meanings for decision-making purposes.

Data analysis scares many people, because they associate it with statistics. In fact, when some people think of evaluation or research, they think about statistics immediately. The math anxiety that some people experience can result in a fear of undertaking projects. We do not suggest that statistics are easy to comprehend, but nor are they that complex. Understanding a few basic principles allows you to logically select the appropriate statistics for your analysis. These statistics allow you to describe your data and to make comparison among the groups that you are examining.

In this unit we discuss measurement, organization and coding data, descriptive statistics, and relationships among variables. Data analysis is an exciting aspect of evaluation and research because it helps us understand what our data mean. We will also talk about how computers make statistical analyses easier in today's high-tech society. The old adage goes, "garbage in, garbage out," however, when it comes to computer analyses. If the right applications are not selected, the results will be meaningless. You, as an evaluator or researcher, must know how to use the appropriate statistics that will be necessary to draw conclusions and make recommendations.

We also discuss how to analyze qualitative data in the following pages. Because qualitative data are not mathematical, some people assume that these types of data are easy to analyze. Qualitative analysis is different, but not necessarily easier, than quantitative analysis. When you have completed this unit, you will have a good working knowledge of data analyses that use common statistical procedures and typical qualitative data strategies.

# 3.1 Data According to Measurement

Two kinds of numbers exist in the world: continuous and discrete. Continuous data are data that can be measured along a continuum and can take on endless possibilities with intermediate values (Examples of continuous data would be weight (e.g., a woman weighs 59.6 kg), time (1:45:36 as a time for completing a half-marathon), and temperature (41.6 degrees F). Values are considered to be approximate because even though the technology applied to measuring instruments might be sophisticated, we can never be exact.

The other kind of data is called discrete data. These data are noncontinuous and finite. There can be no "in-between" numbers as there can be with continuous data. For example, the number of mountain bikers using a trail on the weekend is a discrete number (i.e., 152 bicyclers, not 152.75). With discrete data, we can count "things" that result in an exact number.

## Levels of Data

During the research and evaluation process, different types of data are collected. These data are presented as words or numbers. Measurement is the process of turning the symbolic tools of worded questions and observations into numbers that can then be used in statistical analyses. You must be able to distinguish the level of measurement obtained to make the right choices for statistical procedures. For example, data that are nominal or categorical like biological sex, will be treated differently than continuous data such as from a test score. The levels of data used for measurement are typically divided into four distinct groups: nominal, ordinal, interval, and ratio.

*Nominal*, or categorical, data are the "lowest" typology because no assumption is made about relationships between values. Each value defines a distinct category with no overlap and serves to label or name a particular group. An example of nominal data might be the biological sex of an individual. The values associated with these data might be 1="male" and 2="female," or 1="female" and 2="male." The numeric values attached to the nominal data are merely identifiers that allow the responses to be counted for later analysis. Other examples of nominal data are items such as birth state, political party affiliation, or a yes/no response.

*Ordinal* data are more sophisticated data that have some implied rank or order to the categories, according to some criterion. An example of ordinal data might be whether one placed or ranked first, second, third, or tenth in a road race. Each category has a position that is higher or lower than another, but you do not know how much higher or lower. Although the data are ranked or rated, no distance is measured. Both ranking and rating scales use ordinal data. Ratings generally define points on a scale and any number of people may be assigned a given point. In rankings, the individuals form a kind of scale with each person having a place in the ordering. Therefore, in rankings the individuals form the scale while in ratings, the scale pre-exists. An example of ordinal data used in a rating would be the classification of employees as leaders, supervisors, or administrators (e.g., Recreation Leader I, Recreation Leader II) with the ordering based upon responsibility or skills. Another example of ranked data could be the high school grade rankings of students (e.g., first in class, eighth in class). Although these data are discrete and categorical, they differ from nominal data because they have an order.

More precision is needed when you want to add scores or calculate averages. Unlike ordinal data where the distance between categories is not equal, data are needed that have equal intervals. *Interval* data result when the ordered categories have meaningful predictable size differences or distance between values. The interval scale, however, does not have an inherently determined zero point. This type of data allows you to study differences between items, but not their proportionate magnitudes. An example of interval data would be temperature. The difference between 40°F and 41°F is the same as between 80°F and 81°F but 80°F is not twice as hot as 40°F because 0°F is not by definition equal to the absence of heat. Those of us who have lived in the north know that below zero days are realities. When measuring the temperature, you will not reach a point where you can say this is as cold as it can get.

You may be wondering where Likert scales fit. The definitive answer is, "it depends." Philosophically, many statistical purists believe that Likert scales can only be treated as ordinal data, because they are discrete and categorical. Other statisticians believe that these scales can legitimately be viewed as interval data because the ordered categories have implied meaningful size differences. As you will see later in the discussion on statistical procedures, defining the data as ordinal limits the analyses to less powerful statistics. Many researchers and evaluators will choose to treat Likert scale data as interval data and use a wide variety of statistical calculations.

The most sophisticated data are *ratio* data. Ratio data have a true zero point as well as all of the ordering and distancing properties of interval data. Height is an example of ratio data, because a 6-foot tall adult is truly twice as tall as a 3-foot tall child. Ratio data always have 0 as the potential starting point. Age is another example.

Let's review these four types of data. Assume you had following variables such as age, job title, income, number of visits to a recreation center, race/ethnicity, and IQ scores. To some extent, the way that you ask questions will determine what level of data that you have. For example, you could ask someone how old she or he is and the response would usually be ratio data, such as 21 years old. On the other hand, you could ask how old and then provide a close-ended ordered response such as <17 years, 18–29 years, 30–39 years, 40–49 years, and >49 years. In this case, the level of data is nominal. Generally however, age is considered ratio as is income (they have a zero starting point), unless you are describing income categories such as low income or middle income, which are nominal data. Job title is usually nominal, as is race/ethnicity. According to the definitions, the number of visits to a recreation center is ratio data. IQ scores are also ratio data.

People using statistics must be aware of the different levels of measurement for data because each statistical procedure requires a specific level. For example, if you wanted to explore the relationship between two types of information that were categorical (nominal-level data) such as sex and job title, a chi square analysis would be appropriate. Nominal data cannot be correlated. However, if data were interval- or ratio-level data, such as in comparing self-esteem scores and age, then a Pearson Correlation analysis might be the best choice.

# Describing Variables

In preparing to analyze data, you will need to define the variables. For example, each separate item on a questionnaire is a variable that in turn, may become an element that can be analyzed. The initial selection of variables for an evaluation is made when evaluation criteria are selected and the items for a survey are drafted into questions for the respondents to answer, or when an observation checklist is developed. These variables might include demographic information such as age and sex, behavioral aspects such as the type of recreation program in which a person participates and frequency of participation, or attitudes including program satisfaction and the importance of facility amenities.

Variables are often classified as dependent or independent. In most cases, variables can be divided into *dependent* variables (ones that can be influenced or effected), and *independent* variables (ones that can exert influence or can be the cause). For example, if you were interested in how frequently men and women in your town participated in open swimming at the community center, the frequency of swimming may be dependent on the sex of the individual (i.e., independent variable) completing the questionnaire. Thus, variables like sex, age, and ethnicity are usually independent variables while variables like participation rates, scale scores, and rating scales are often dependent variables.

Several other examples can help recognize dependent and independent variables. If you wanted to examine the differences between salaries of football professionals and the teams they play on, you would conclude that salaries would be the dependent variable and team would be independent. Determining the relationship between cognitive function and age would mean that cognitive functioning would be dependent and age would be independent. In this case, cognitive functioning would be dependent upon age but age would not change just because of functioning. A final example might be a question about whether juvenile crime rates change after implementation of an after-school program. In this situation, crime rates would be the dependent variable and participation in the program would be independent. Participation or not (independent) would result in an increase or decrease in crime rates (dependent variable).

# Types of Analyses

Three types of analyses can be conducted using quantitative data. These analyses hinge on whether you want to examine the characteristics of just one variable, two variables, or more than two variables.

*Univariate* analysis is the examination of the distribution of cases on only one variable. This analysis includes the frequency distribution (the numbers and percentage) of a single variable as well as appropriate measures of central tendency (i.e., mean, median, mode). These analyses are generally used to describe a variable or a group of variables. For example, you may want to know the numbers and percentages of individuals from different ethnic groups that completed a survey about your community center programs. A univariate analysis would tell how many people and the percentage of the total that represented these groups. Another example of a univariate analysis is the scores on a midterm exam. We could calculate the mean, median, mode, standard deviation, and range on the test scores as univariate data.

*Bivariate* analysis is the simultaneous evaluation of two variables. Usually one variable is independent and the other is dependent. This type of analysis is descriptive but allows you to compare subgroups. For example, you can now compare the frequency of participation in community center programs (the dependent variable) by individuals of different ethnic groups such as African Americans, Latino/Latinas, European Americans, and Asian Americans (independent variable). Bivariate statistics can tell you if African Americans participate more than Latinos/Latinas.

The third type of analysis, *multivariate* analysis, is just like bivariate except that this analysis uses two or more independent variables and one dependent variable. For example, the frequency of participation could be analyzed by sex and ethnicity. In other words, you could tell if participation rates were different for men and women from different ethnic groups who participated in your community center programs. Both bivariate and multivariate analyses are used to explain and compare subgroups. For most evaluation projects, you will not use multivariate analysis, but these tools are available for more sophisticated analyses

# From Ideas to Reality

Types of data analysis options are important. As you will see, a multitude of statistical procedures exist for your use. You will need to determine the type and level of data measurement generated by your evaluation, select independent and dependent variables, and make the appropriate statistical choices for the analysis that will best address your evaluation or research questions. These decisions are not always easy to make, but if you have a solid understanding of the data that you are collecting, the analysis process will be easier to conduct and the results will be easier to interpret.


Now that you have studied this chapter, you should be able to:
- Identify the differences between the levels of data
- Choose the independent and dependent variables that might be used in a statistical analysis
- Determine whether a univariate, bivariate, or multivariate data analysis would be most appropriate, given a set of data you might have

## 3.2 Getting Your Data Together: Organizing and Coding Quantitative Data

A critical step in data analysis involves organizing the variables used in a measurement instrument to collect data. This step is called coding. The easiest way to think about data organization is to imagine each questionnaire as a case or observation that has a set of variables with values. Each case or respondent has only one response for each variable. The case, usually the individual who completes the questionnaire or a specific observation, becomes the basic unit upon which measurements are taken. A case could be an individual or a larger unit such as a park and recreation department or a special event.

Once a pilot study is done, the evaluator or researcher decides how to systematically organize and record information. As soon as the data are collected, the analysis begins. Data should be recorded in as much detail as possible. Specific information can always be recoded into larger groups later in the analysis process. For example, age as a value for each case could be recorded as the respondent's actual age and grouped later into age categories if desired. However, if age is originally recorded as two nominal values that encompass individuals 54 years and younger compared to individuals 55 and older, only these two age categories can ever be used in your analyses. You can go from specific coding to broad categories but you cannot go the opposite way. By reducing the number of values for a variable, you also have eliminated the possibility of getting specific statistics such as the average age of your respondents. The bottom line is you can always combine values later, but you cannot expand them beyond the values recorded from the original measurement data.

The data from a variable are assigned numbers, called values, to represent the responses. This process is known as coding. When only numbers are used, the system is numeric coding. For example, instead of entering "Agree" or "Disagree" into the computer spreadsheet, the evaluator could code an agree response as a "2" and a disagree response as a "1." When using computers for analysis purposes, this numeric coding makes the process of getting from verbal responses to statistical answers possible.

Since a coding system is often arbitrary, creating a codebook is helpful. It tells the evaluator and anyone else who might be using the data for statistical procedures how the data are coded. For a short and simple questionnaire, the codebook may not be necessary but it is usually a helpful tool for you to create. Most coding systems are easy to put together.

Codebooks that include the coding procedures can be created at any stage in the evaluation project, but we suggest you construct your codebook before you collect data to make sure you are asking the questions in the most appropriate way. Working through your coding decisions will help you anticipate the levels of data you have. As you will see shortly, levels of data will affect your choice of statistics. In setting up an electronic data collection system such as through SurveyMonkey, you can specify the way data should be coded as you devise the actual questions and the response categories.

Usually the codebook will include the variable name, the value labels for each variable, and the corresponding question from the questionnaire. If the data are to be entered into a computer for statistical analysis, the codebook can also include additional information such as the location of the data for each case. Table 3.2(1) is an example of questions from a survey that will generate data and Table 3.2(2) is the corresponding codebook.

Table 3.2(3) shows how this same information would appear when coded and the numeric values needed for computer analysis with a spreadsheet such as Microsoft Excel or a statistical program like SPSS (Statistical Package for the Social Sciences). Each row of information entered is usually the equivalent to one respondent's survey answers. The

*Table 3.2(1)  Sample Survey Questions*

| |
|---|
| 1. Do you feel that women have as many opportunities to advance in the recreation field as men?<br>____ Yes    ____ No    ____ Don't know |

2. Please indictate the extent to which you agree or disagree with these statements as they apply to the Park and Recreation field.

| | Strongly Disagree | Disagree | Neither | Agree | Strongly Agree |
|---|---|---|---|---|---|
| a. Women are often excluded from informal male networks. | 1 | 2 | 3 | 4 | 5 |
| b. There is unconscious discrimination based on gender | 1 | 2 | 3 | 4 | 5 |
| c. Women tend to work in areas that are not promotable. | 1 | 2 | 3 | 4 | 5 |
| d. Women are less committed to their careers because of family obligations. | 1 | 2 | 3 | 4 | 5 |

3. What is your age? ____ years

*Table 3.2(2)* *Example of a Coding System or Codebook from Survey in Table 3.2(1)*

| Variable Label | Variable Name | Variable Label | Questionnaire # |
|---|---|---|---|
| Opportu | Same opportunities | 1=Yes<br>2=No<br>3=Don't know | #1 |
| Exclude | Excluded from networks | 1=Strongly disagree<br>2=Disagree<br>3=Neither<br>4=Agree<br>5=Strongly agree | #2a |
| Discrim | Unconscious discrimination | (same as #2a) | #2b |
| Promote<br><br>Commit | Areas not promotable<br><br>Women less committed | (same as #2a)<br><br>(same as #2a) | #2c<br><br>#2d |
| Age | Age | 21–99 | #3 |

values of each variable appear in sequential columns in exactly the same order as the codebook. The data are then saved as a specific data file that becomes the basis for statistical procedures. In some electronic survey programs like SurveyMonkey, you can directly download the responses into a spreadsheet and do not have to manually enter the raw data.

Just a word about coding missing data. Almost every data collector will run into situations where some data are missing or where the respondent did not understand the directions and ended up with inappropriate responses. Perhaps the respondent filling out the questionnaire did not want to answer a particular question or maybe decided that two programs needed to be ranked as number one priorities. Rather than throw out the

*Table 3.2(3)* *Example of Data Screen for Coding System*

**SPSS Data Editor Screen**

| (CASE) | OPPORTU | EXCLUDE | UNCONSC | NONPROM | LESSCOM | AGE |
|---|---|---|---|---|---|---|
| 1 | 1 | 2 | 4 | 2 | 1 | 26 |
| 2 | 2 | 5 | 4 | 1 | 1 | 44 |
| 3 | 1 | 3 | 2 | 1 | 1 | 32 |
| 4 . . . | . . . | . . . | . . . | . . . | . . . | . . . |

continue to enter data until you run out of cases

entire questionnaire just because some information is missing or incorrectly indicated, you can devise a system for handling missing data. You may select a particular code to represent your missing information, or if you are using a computerized statistical package, a predetermined code may exist in the program. You always have to identify what to do with missing data. Depending on the statistical analysis system you use, different approaches are used for coding missing data.

Another fairly common coding dilemma is how to code information when your respondent did not answer the survey as directed. For example, you may have asked respondents to select just one answer, but a couple of respondents circled two separate answers to one question. You could consider that variable as having missing data, or you could make yourself a coding rule such as if the person chooses more than one answer, you will always take the first answer selected or perhaps the one with the most conservative answer. In electronic surveys, you can prevent people from multiple answers unless that is what you have specified. The main point is that you need to be consistent with your missing data and the way you code inappropriate answers. If you are not careful, your statistics may be incorrectly calculated or biased because of your lack of attention to missing information.

# From Ideas to Reality

This chapter offers some basic and practical techniques for getting data from a questionnaire into numeric forms to be used in computer data analysis. The procedures are specific and must be followed carefully if analysis is to be properly conducted. During this phase of the evaluation project or research study, you will need to carefully consider the analyses that you want to do and be concerned with accurately coding and entering the data. Once your data are coded, you will need to double-check to make sure they were coded correctly and determine what to do with missing data. Then you have to choose the right statistics.

Now that you have studied this chapter, you should be able to:
- Identify values as they relate to variables within a questionnaire
- Code data with as much specificity as measured
- Enter data into a data file in the appropriate format
- Decide how to handle missing data

# 3.3 Univariate Statistical Analyses: Describing What Is

After doing quantitative data collection, you are ready to find the answers to the evaluation criteria or the research questions you initially established by using statistics. Some answers will be fairly straightforward. For example, univariate statistics such as adding up totals for overall participation rates or figuring percentages of people who have an attitude about a community bond issue are easy with descriptive statistics like frequencies and percentages. Sometimes you want to know more complex answers, however, such as: "Are there differences in the satisfaction levels of participants based on their age?" or "Is there any relationship between neighborhood location of participants and the activities in which they participate?" These types of questions require more sophisticated bivariate and multivariate statistical analyses. To make appropriate choices about which statistics to use, you need to know your options and how to make appropriate choices about the options based on your questions and level of data. Univariate descriptive statistics are the first step toward answering more complex questions about your data.

## The Basics of Descriptive Statistics

Descriptive statistics are exactly as the name implies. They describe and summarize the characteristics of your data. These descriptive statistics are univariate (i.e., they focus on one variable) and include frequency counts, individual and cumulative percentages, measures of central tendency, and variations in data characteristics.

### Frequency Counts and Percentages

Most evaluators are interested in the actual number of responses they generate for a given question. For example, let's say you are interested in the ages of the adolescents that participated in the teen outdoor adventure program. Since one of the questions on the questionnaire instrument asked for age, you can get an actual frequency count of participants who are 13, 14, 15, and so on (see Table 3.3[1]).

You may also want to know what percentage of the total group of respondents was comprised of 13-year-olds. Individual percentages will provide this information. Percentage use can be taken a step further with cumulative percentages. These percentages are added together as you move from group to group. As illustrated in Table 3.3(1), over half of the

*Table 3.3(1)  Age of Participants in the Teen Adventue Program*

| Age | Frequency | Percent | Cumulative Percent |
|---|---|---|---|
| 13 years old | 15 | 12% | 12% |
| 14 years old | 24 | 20% | 32% |
| 15 years old | 28 | 23% | 55% |
| 16 years old | 35 | 28% | 83% |
| 17 years old | 21 | 17% | 100% |
| N=123 | | | |

participants were between the ages of 13 and 15 years old. Also note on the table that N= the total number of respondents for a particular question. When discussing any aspect of univariate statistics, the number of people described always should be noted.

## Central Tendency

Measures of central tendency (i.e., mode, median, and mean) are useful for describing a variable under consideration. The *mode* is the most frequently occurring value. The mode can be used for any level of data but is not generally the preferred measure for interval or ordinal data. For these levels of data, the mode tends to ignore too much important information. An example of the mode would be the results from asking people to check the month in which they most often participated in community center programs. If the evaluator had coded the answer 1–12 to correspond with the months, and the analysis indicated that July received the highest number of positive responses, then mode=7. In the example illustrated by Table 3.3(1), the mode is sixteen years old.

The *median* (*Mdn*) is the value above and below which one half of the observations fall. For ordinal data, the median is a good measure of central tendency since it uses ranking information. The median would be incorrect to use for nominal data, however, since ranking is not possible. In our example, we could rank the ages of the 123 teenagers, and the 62nd observation would be the age where exactly half of the respondents were above and half below. For this example, *Mdn* = 15 years old. If the sample size had been 124 (an even number sample), the halfway point between the 62nd and 63rd observation would be taken. In this age example, the *Mdn* would still be 15 since the 62nd and 63rd observation were both 15 years old.

The third type of central tendency measure is the *mean* (*M*= sample mean), also known as the average. The mean is used with interval and ratio

data. The mean is the sum of all the values of the observations on that
variable divided by the number of observations:

$$M = \sum (x)/N$$

In the age example in Table 3.3(1), the average age is 15.19 years.
Finding means for nominal data (such as yes/no responses or male/female)
are inappropriate and useless.

Several other points about measures of central tendency should also
be considered. First, these three measures (mode, Mdn, M) need not be
the same. In fact, they would not be the same except in a perfect normal
distribution. If the distribution is symmetric, however, the mean, median,
and mode are usually close in value. Secondly, the means are greatly affected by outliers while the median is not. An outlier is a score that is on
the extreme end of a scale. A good example of the effect of an outlier can
be found in salary information. Often the average salary may be quite a
bit higher than the median, because the outliers who earn high salaries
bring the average way up. Thus, the employer might point to the average
salary as a way of suggesting that salaries are at an adequate level while
the employees may use the median to illustrate that the midpoint salary
levels are considerably lower than what management may be implying
when they use the average.

# Variations in Data Characteristics

## Measures of Dispersion (How Spread Out Are My Data?)

Sometimes, two distributions can have the same mean for central
tendency and yet be quite dissimilar. For example, two basketball teams
could have their members shoot 20 free throws each:

Team A's 5 members make: 0, 1, 10, 14, and 20 free throws.
Team B's 5 members make: 8, 8, 9, 10, and 10 free throws.
Although the $M = 9$ for both teams, the teams are obviously dissimilar.

One of the easiest calculations of dissimilarity, or dispersion, is the
range. The range is the difference between the maximum and minimum
observed values. Therefore the range for Team A is 20 (i.e., 0–20 shots)
and the range for Team B is 2 (8–10 shots). The range is sensitive to ex-

tremes, which is useful with ordinal data, but does not take into account the distribution of observations within the range.

*Variance* is a dispersion measure of variation that is based on all observations and describes the extent to which scores differ from each other. In other words, variance tells you how far apart the scores are. Many times the amount that the observed scores vary from each other is critical for understanding your sample. In the basketball example above, the coach of Team A might work on free throw shooting differently than the coach of Team B. The variance (represented as $s^2$ = variance) is obtained by summing the squared differences from the mean for all observations and then dividing by the number of observations minus 1.

$$s^2 = \sum (x-x)^2/(n-1)$$

If all of the observations are identical (that is, no variation—everyone made the same number of free throws out of 20), then variance is equal to 0. When looking at the distribution curve, the more spread out, the greater the variance. For the basketball team example, the variance for Team A = 73 while the variance for Team B = 1.

The most familiar measure of dispersion is the *standard deviation*. It is the average of the degree that scores deviate from the mean and has a special relationship to the normal distribution, as you will see in the following discussion on normal distribution. The reason you should pay attention to the standard deviation (represented by *SD*) is to gain some idea about how scores are dispersed around the mean. The more the scores cluster around the mean, the more you can conclude that everyone is performing at about the same level or is answering questions similarly on an instrument. You derive the standard deviation by taking the square root of the variance. This measure is expressed in the same units of measurement as the observations while the variance is in the units squared. Thus, standard deviation is a clearer way to think of variability. In the basketball team example, the standard deviation for Team A would be *SD* = 8.5, or 8.5 free throws, and the *SD* = 1 for Team B. The SD for Team B is much smaller than Team A so you conclude that Team B is much more similar in skill level at shooting free throws. With this small example, you could have made that conclusion by "eyeballing" the data. However, with larger samples, the statistics are essential to understand issues of dispersion.

## The Distribution Curve (What Do My Data Look Like?)

The observations of many variables will cluster around the middle of the distribution, and the frequency of observations seems to decrease as you move away from the central concentration. This type of distribution is often called "bell-shaped" or a normal distribution. In society, characteristics such as height, weight, and blood pressure are thought to be approximately normal. Theoretically, if you plotted every person's weight, for example, the results would look like a bell-shaped curve.

The *normal distribution* is the most important theoretical distribution in statistics and serves as a reference point for describing the forms of distributions of quantitative data (Norusis, 1983). Let's say you ask for the weights of the people enrolled in a wellness program at your fitness center. By plotting the weights of your participants (or calculating them statistically), you can determine if your group is "normal." In other words, does your data fit the bell-shaped distribution based on the population statistics that are available? "Normal" weight, however especially in this era of obesity, does not mean the same as recommended healthy weight.

The normal distribution is symmetric with the three measures of central tendency (mean, median, and mode) theoretically coinciding at the center with gradually diminishing numbers toward the extremes (Lundegren & Farrell, 1985). In a normal distribution, you would expect to find 68% of the observations falling within approximately one standard deviation of the mean and 95% of all the observations falling within about two standard deviations of the mean (see Figure 3.3[2]). If an ob-

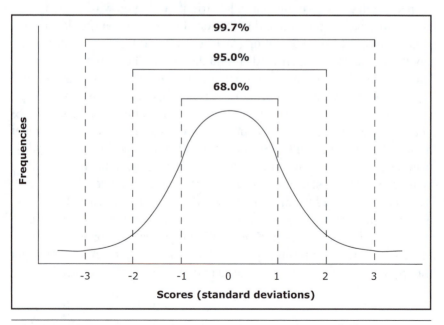

*Figure 3.3(2) The Normal Distribution Curve*

servation is outside the area covered by two standard deviations, you may want to consider that observation so unusual that it would not fit what is "normally" expected.

## Other Measures Associated With Distributions

*Skewness* is a measure used when the distribution is not symmetric and has a "tail." If the "tail" is toward the larger values, then the distribution is considered to be positively skewed. If the "tail" is toward the smaller values, it is considered to be negatively skewed. If, for example, the attitudes of parents toward a youth baseball league were measured and you found most of the responses were toward positive (larger) values, you would conclude that the responses were positively skewed. In either case, this information would indicate that the distribution of the sample was not normal, because fewer scores are on one side of the mean. Figure 3.3(3) shows an example of a skewed distribution. The issues of central tendency and distribution will be the basis for more advanced statistical procedures discussed later in this book.

# From Ideas to Reality

Univariate descriptive statistics are the most basic statistics that you will use. Many times they are used first in your analysis to describe the characteristics of the data and the general responses that have been received from a survey. They describe the information that you have. From these descriptive statistics, many other possibilities exist for data analysis.

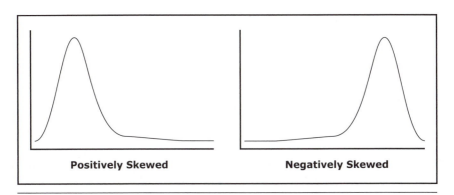

**Positively Skewed**                **Negatively Skewed**

*Figure 3.3 (3) Positively and Negatively Skewed Distributions*

Now that you have studied this chapter, you should be able to:
- Explain the most common types of descriptive statistics
- Calculate and interpret the meaning of frequencies, percentages, mean, median, mode, standard deviation, range, and variance by hand or by using a computer
- Describe why including a standard deviation statistic along with a mean is always useful
- Explain the meaning of normal distribution

# 3.4 The Word on Statistical Significance and Its Meaning

As you use univariate, bivariate, or multivariate procedures to find answers to address evaluation criteria or research questions, you will likely want to know how much faith you ought to have that the differences or relationships you find are significant and important. While a discussion of probability theory is beyond the scope of this text, a general understanding of "statistical significance" is important. Statistical significance refers to the unlikeliness that relationships observed in a sample could be attributed to chance alone. In other words, when we determine statistical significance we want to be as sure as possible that, indeed, a true relationship exists among variables. If you do not know whether or not your results are due to chance, you will likely *not* make the best decisions.

Before you begin quantitative analysis, you must decide upon a level at which you are willing to say, "If my finding exceeds this level, then I am going to consider the findings different from what I would expect due to chance." In the social sciences, statistical significance by convention is generally set at probability (p) < .05. In the simplest terms, p or the probability of less than .05 means that 95 times out of 100 you would expect to get the same results and only 5 out of 100 times the result might be due purely to chance. For example, say you wanted to see if a difference existed between women's and men's participation rates in free swim at the community center. You select the appropriate statistical test and if your results indicate p < .05, then you accept that the women and men differ significantly from each other in participation rates. You will have to examine the means (M) of each group to determine whether it is males or females who participate more or less.

There is a caution, however. Tests of significance are based on probability, so p < .05 is really saying that if you repeated this test 100 times, in only 5 times out of the 100 trials would you be wrong in thinking that the groups were different, when in actuality they were the same. In some fields like medical research, this error rate would be too great, so these researchers may set a significance level of p < .001. Thus, a medical researcher who was evaluating a new drug that resulted in statistically significant difference between the experimental and the control group would be assured that his or her finding was due to chance only 1 time out of 1,000. Most of us would rather accept the odds that one out of 1,000 times something might not work than 1 out of 100 times.

At this point you may be asking yourself, "But what if I do get a wrong answer purely due to chance?" Let's say you are interested in the effect of play in the hospital on the recovery rate of children receiving tonsillectomies. You find through the analysis of your data that the recovery rates of children involved in play therapy were faster and differed significantly at the .05 level from the children who were not in these play sessions. Given the evidence so far, group membership seems to make a difference. Maybe in reality your finding was due to chance and little real difference existed. In other words, you have made an unintentional error by assuming that the play opportunity made a difference in recovery, as indicated by your statistics. The risk you take in making this type of error, called Type I error, is the same as the level of significance (Salkind, 1991). A significance level of p < .05 means that there is a 5% chance that you will say the groups are different when in actuality they are the same, thus committing a Type I error. If you are using evaluation to determine whether to keep or eliminate a program, you must be careful that you consider a Type I error possibility so inappropriate decisions are reduced.

Another form of error is called Type II error. This error results when the data suggest that the groups are the same (no significant difference), but in actuality they are different. Ideally, you want to minimize both types of error, but Type II error is not as easy to control as Type I. In Type I situations, you as the evaluator select the significance level that you are willing to accept. Type II errors are not directly controlled but can be decreased by increasing the sample size. In other words, as you increase the sample size, you are also increasing the likelihood that the sample characteristics will more closely match or be representative of the population in a normal distribution. Therefore, you are reducing the likelihood of Type II error. You do not want to think the groups are the same when they are not.

If you try to reduce the Type II error rate by increasing the sample size, you must be careful because statistical significance can also be influenced by sample size (Babbie, 2006). For example, a large sample has the power to make everything seem statistically significant and in reality, little substantive differences may exist. Conversely, an extremely small sample may not show differences that do exist between groups. This weakness points out the importance of always determining whether or not the statistical difference is *meaningful*.

Meaningfulness is often as important as statistical significance. For example, you may ask all visitors to your parks during the summer to rate on a 7-point Likert scale their satisfaction with the available facilities. Your sample size at the end of the summer could be over 15,000 visitors. Your statistical test may indicate that statistical significance exists between tent campers and RV users at the p < .05 level, but upon closer examination of the data, you find that the means only differ by three tenths of a point. This example is a good case to illustrate the need to use your judgment when determining how meaningful the differences really are. In this case, a tenth of a point difference on a 7-point scale is probably really not important enough to justify facility changes. Sometimes, statistical procedures like "effect size" exist that will help you determine this magnitude of difference.

Effect size is an important statistic because unlike statistical significance, it is independent of sample size. Effect size is a way of quantifying the difference between groups. If one group is an experimental group and one group is a control group and a statistically significant difference is found, then the effect size is a measure of the effectiveness of the treatment. For two independent groups, the effect size relates to how much difference exists between the two groups. Generally, an effect size of 0–.20 is quite small, .21–.60 is moderate, and .61 or more is large. The greater the effect size the more important the difference may be. If you examined the differences between males and females regarding their ability to learn football rules and found that a statistically significant difference occurred but the effect size was only .12, then the difference is really of a small magnitude.

Effect size can be calculated in a number of ways. One statistic that results is the *Cohen's d*. Effect size is determined by the mean difference between the two groups divided by the standard deviation. The formula is:

$$d = M1 - M2 / SD$$

Effect size calculators are readily available on the Internet or you can easily conduct a calculation by simply entering in the means and the standard deviations for the groups. Regardless of what statistics used, however, the evaluator or researcher in the end must make the decision about what the results mean and whether they are *meaningful.*

A word of caution is reiterated regarding sample size, statistical significance, effect size, and meaningfulness. You might have a small sample (e.g., 10 people) and find no statistical significance on a variable, but large differences exist between the means. You cannot assume any meaningfulness, because if the data do not have a p-value that is significant, the difference may be due to chance. Meaningfulness only relates to data that are statistically significant, not to data that are not.

Lastly, you do not always need to find statistical significance for a result to be important. Sometimes, not finding a difference is extremely useful. For example, you may know from previous research that adolescent girls generally have lower self-concepts based on self-esteem measures than their male counterparts. You might decide to explore this idea in your teen adventure club that has been established to help teens build self-esteem and experience leadership opportunities. As a part of the summative evaluation you find that the girls' self-esteem is high and no different than the scores of the boys. The result is important and useful because it suggests that perhaps the content of the teen program is contributing to the development of self-esteem among both girls and boys. In this case, no statistically significant difference found was a really important finding.

# From Ideas to Reality

Statistical significance is one of the most helpful concepts that you will use when doing quantitative data analysis. For the evaluator or researcher, statistical significance is useful as a screening device for making subsequent conclusions and recommendations. The probability value ($p$) tells you whether or not a statistically significant difference exists between variables. Sometimes results look like differences exist, but without examining statistical significance the differences may be due only to chance. Keep in mind, however, that the meaningfulness is also important. In addition to using what the statistics tell us, we must always examine variables to see if the differences discovered are meaningful, useful, and important.

Now that you have studied this chapter, you should be able to:
- Define what statistical significance means
- Describe the difference between Type I and Type II errors
- Apply probability statistics to making conclusions about evaluation and research

# 3.5 Inferential Statistics: The Plot Thickens

Calculating and describing characteristics about data was the topic of the previous chapter. Descriptive statistical analyses give information about central tendency, the distribution of data, how varied the data are, and the "shape" of the data. Evaluators and researchers are also interested in information related to data parameters. In other words, we want to know if relationships, associations, or differences exist within data and whether statistical significance exists. Inferential statistics help to make these determinations and allow researchers to generalize the results to a larger population. In this chapter, we provide background information about parametric and nonparametric statistics and then discuss several simple inferential statistical procedures that examine basic associations among variables as well as test differences between groups.

## Parametric and Nonparametric Statistics

In the world of statistics, distinctions are made in the types of analyses that can be used by the evaluator or researcher based on distribution assumptions and the levels of data measurement (i.e., nominal, ordinal, interval, ratio) used. For example, parametric statistics are based on the assumption of normal distribution and randomized sampling, which is portrayed as interval or ratio data. The statistical tests usually determine significance of difference or relationships. These parametric statistical tests commonly include *t*-tests, Pearson product-moment correlations, and analyses of variance (ANOVA).

Nonparametric statistics are known as distribution-free tests, because they are not based on the assumptions of the normal probability curve. Nonparametric statistics do not specify conditions about parameters of the population but assume randomization and are usually applied to nominal and ordinal data. Several nonparametric tests also exist for interval data and should be used when a sample size is small and/or the assumptions of normal distribution would be violated. Evaluators will find equivalent nonparametric tests for many of the more familiar parametric tests. The most common forms of nonparametric tests are chi-square analysis, Mann-Whitney *U* test, the Wilcoxon matched-pairs signed ranks test, Friedman test, and the Spearman rank-order correlation coefficient. These nonparametric tests are generally less powerful tests than the corresponding parametric tests. Table 3.5(1) provides parametric and nonparametric equivalent tests used for data analysis. The following sections will discuss these types of statistics and the appropriate parametric and nonparametric choices.

# Associations Among Variables

## Chi-Square (Crosstabs)

One of the most common statistical tests of association is the chi-square test ($X^2$). For this test to be used, data must be at nominal or ordinal levels. During the process of the analysis, the frequency data are arranged in tables that compare the observed distribution (your data) with the expected distributions (what you would expect to find if no difference existed among the values of a given variable or variables). In most computerized statistical packages, this chi-square procedure is called "crosstabs" or "tables." This statistical procedure is relatively easy to hand calculate as well. The basic chi-square formula is:

Table 3.5(1)    *Parametric and Nonparametric Tests for Data Analysis (adapted from Loftus and Loftus, 1982)*

| Data | Purpose of Test | Parametric | Nonparametric |
|---|---|---|---|
| Single sample | To determine if an association exists between two nominal variables | — | Chi-square |
| Single sample | To determine if sample mean or median differs from some hypothetical value | Matched *t*-test | Sign test |
| Two samples, between subjects | To determine if the populations of two independent samples have the same means or median | Independent *t*-test | Mann-Whitney U test |
| Two conditions, within subjects | To determine if the populations of two samples have the same mean or median | Independent *t*-test | Sign test or Wilcoxon signed ranks test |
| More than two conditions, between subjects | To determine if the populations of more than two independent samples have the same mean or median | One-way ANOVA | Kruskal-Wallis |
| More than two conditions, within subjects | To determine if the populations or more than two samples have the same mean or median | Repeated measures ANOVA | Friedman ANOVA |
| Set of items with two measures on each item | To determine if the two measures are associated | Pearson | Spearman correlation |

$$X^2 = \sum[(O-E)^2/E]$$

where: $X^2$ = chi square
O = observed
E = expected
Sigma = sum of

## Spearman and Pearson Correlations

Sometimes we want to determine relationships between scores. As an evaluator, you have to determine whether the data are appropriate for parametric or nonparametric procedures. Remember, this determination is based upon the level of data and sample size. If the sample is small or if the data are ordinal (rank-order) data, then the most appropriate choice is the nonparametric Spearman rank order correlation ($r_s$) statistic. If the data are thought to be interval and normally distributed, then the basic test for linear (straight line) relationships is the parametric Pearson product-moment correlation ($r$) technique.

The correlation results for Spearman or Pearson ($r$) correlations can fall between +1 and -1. For the parametric Pearson or nonparametric Spearman ($r_s$), the data are interpreted in the same way, even though a different statistical procedure is used. You might think of the data as sitting on a matrix with an x- and y-axis. A positive correlation of +1 ($r = 1.0$) would mean that the slope of the line would be at 45 degrees upward. A negative correlation of -1 ($r = -1$) would be at 45 degrees downward (see Figure 3.5[1]). No correlation at all would be $r = 0$ with a horizontal line. The correlation (either $r$ or $r_s$) that approaches +1 is interpreted as positively correlated. A correlation approaching -1 means that it is negatively correlated—as one score increases, the other decreases. A correlation (either $r$ or $r_s$) of approximately 0 means no linear relationship exists. In other words, a perfect positive correlation of 1 occurs only if the values of the x and y scores are identical, and a perfect negative correlation of -1 only if the values of x are the exact reverse of the values of y (Hale, 1990).

As an example, if you found that the correlation between age and number of times someone swam at a community pool was $r = -.63$, we could conclude that older individuals were less likely than younger people to swim at a community pool. The younger the people were, the more likely they were to swim at the community pool. Or suppose we wanted to see if a relationship existed between body image scores of adolescent girls and self-esteem scores. If we found $r = .89$, then we would say a positive relationship was found (i.e., as positive body image scores increased, so did positive self-esteem scores). If $r = -.89$, then a negative

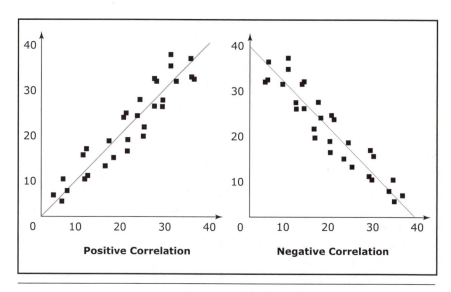

**Figure 3.5(2)** *Examples of Correlation Relationships*

relationship was found, (i.e., as body image scores increased, self-esteem scores decreased). If $r = .10$, you would say little to no relationship was evident between body image and self-esteem scores. If the score was $r = .34$, you might say a weak positive relationship existed between body image and self-esteem scores. Anything above $r = .4$ or below $r = -.4$ might be considered a moderate relationship between the two variables. Of course, the closer the correlation is to $r = +1$ or $-1$, the stronger the relationship.

Correlations can also be used for determining reliability or internal consistency, as was discussed in Chapter 2.3 on trustworthiness. Say you administered a questionnaire about nutrition habits for the adults in an aerobics class for the purpose of establishing reliability of the instrument. A week later you gave them the same test over. All of the individuals were ranked based on the scores for each test, then compared through the Spearman procedure. If you found a result of $r = .94$, you would feel comfortable with the correlation referred to as the reliability coefficient (alpha) of the instrument because this finding would indicate that the respondents' scores were consistent from test to re-test. If $r = .36$, then you would believe the instrument had weak reliability because the scores differed from the first test to the re-test. If the reliability between the first test and the second test using the exact same instrument without any intervening issues occurring was alpha = .36, then you probably better *not* use that instrument but work to develop a better one that has more internal consistency.

Two cautions should be noted in relation to correlations. First, you can *never* assume that a correlation implies causation. These correlations should be used only to summarize the strength of a relationship. In the above example where $r = .89$, an evaluator or researcher can't say that improved body image causes increased self-esteem *or* that increased self-esteem causes better body image. Either case might sound intuitively clear, but a correlation statistic does not measure cause and effect. In examining cause and effect, many other variables could be exerting an influence. You can, however, say that as body image increases, so does self-esteem and vice versa, and that finding could be important. The bottom line is that correlations address some relationship between two variables, whether it is negative, nonexistent, or positive. Second, most statistical analyses of correlations also include a probability (p-value). A correlation might be statistically significant as shown in the probability statistics, but the reliability value (-1 to +1) gives much more information. A significant p-value suggests that some kind of relationship exists, but you must examine the correlation statistic to determine the direction and strength of the relationship.

# Tests of Differences
# Between and Among Groups

Sometimes you may want to analyze by comparing two or more groups through some type of bivariate or multivariate procedure. Again, it will be necessary to know the types of data you have (continuous or discrete), the levels of data measurement (nominal, ordinal, interval, ratio), and the dependent and independent variables of interest to analyze.

In parametric analyses, the statistical process for determining difference is usually accomplished by comparing the means of the groups. The most common parametric tests of differences between means are the *t*-tests and analysis of variance (ANOVA). In nonparametric analyses, you are usually checking the differences in rankings of your groups. For nonparametrics, the most common statistical procedures for testing differences are the Mann-Whitney *U* test, the Sign test, the Wilcoxon signed ranks test, Kruskal-Wallis, and the Friedman analysis of variance. Although these parametric and nonparametric tests can be calculated by hand, they are fairly complicated and a bit tedious, so most people rely on computerized statistical programs. Therefore, each test will be described in this section, but no hand calculations will be provided. For individuals interested in the manual calculations, any good statistics book will provide the formulas and necessary steps.

## Parametric Choices For Determining Differences

*T*-tests. Two types of *t*-tests are available to the evaluator: the two-sample or *independent* t-*test* and the *matched-pairs* or *dependent* t-*test*. The *independent* t-*test*, also called the two-sample *t*-test, is used to test the differences between the means of two groups. The result of the analysis is reported as a *t* value. It is important to remember that the two groups are mutually exclusive and not related to each other. For example, you may want to know if youth coaches who attended a workshop performed better on some aspect of coaching than those coaches who did not attend. In this case, the teaching score is the dependent variable and the two groups of coaches (attendees and nonattendees) are the independent variable. If the *t* statistic that results from the *t*-test has a probability ($p$) < .05, then you know the two groups are different. You would then examine the means (*M*) for each group (those who attended as one group and those who did not as the second group) and determine which set of coaches had the higher teaching scores. Examining the standard deviation (*SD*) would tell you how dispersed the scores were and calculating an effect size would tell you how important or meaningful those results were in terms of the strength of the differences between the two groups.

The *dependent* t-*test*, often called the *matched-pairs* t-*test*, is used to show how a single group differs during two points in time. The matched *t*-test is used if the two sample groups are related. This test is used if the same group was tested twice or when the two separate groups are matched on some variable. For example, in the above situation where you were offering a coaching clinic, it may be that you would want to see if participants learned anything at the clinic. You would test a construct such as knowledge of the game before the workshop and then again after the training with the same group of coaches to see if any difference existed in knowledge gained by the coaches that attended the clinic. The same coaches would fill out the questionnaire as a pretest and again as a posttest. If a statistical difference of $p$ < .05 occurs, you can assume that the workshop made a difference in the knowledge level of the coaches. If the *t*-test was not significant ($p$ > .05), you could assume that the clinic made little difference in the knowledge level of coaches because of the clinic.

**Analysis of Variance.** Analysis of variance (ANOVA) is used to determine differences among means when there are more than two groups examined. It is the same concept as the independent *t*-tests except you have more than two groups. If there is only one independent variable (usually nominal or ordinal level data) consisting of more than two values, then the procedure is called a one-way ANOVA. If there are two independent variables, you would use a two-way ANOVA. The dependent variable is the measured variable and is usually interval or ratio level data. Both one-way and two-way ANOVAs are used to determine if three or more sample means are different from one another (Hale, 1990).

For example, a therapeutic recreation specialist may want to know if inappropriate behaviors (e.g., a scale that measured the intensity of behaviors like screaming or swearing) of psychiatric patients are affected by the type of therapy used (behavior modification, group counseling, or nondirective). In this example, the measured levels of inappropriate behavior would be the dependent variable (based on an interval scale), while the independent variable would be type of therapy that is divided into three groups. If you found a statistically significant difference in the behavior of the patients ($p < .05$), you would examine the means for the three groups and determine which therapy worked best. Additional statistical post-hoc tests, such as Bonferroni or Scheffes, may be used with ANOVA to ascertain which groups differ from one another.

Other types of parametric statistical tests are available for more complex analysis purposes. The $t$-tests and ANOVA described here are the most frequently used parametric statistics by beginning evaluators. As you get more experienced, some of the other multivariate statistical procedures such as regression, HLM, factor analysis, and discriminant analysis may be of interest to you. Most statistical programs will offer you options for these procedures as well as other advanced statistical procedures.

## Nonparametric Choices for Determining Differences

For any of the common parametric statistics, a parallel nonparametric statistic exists in most cases. The use of these statistics depends on the level of data measured and on the sample, as is shown in Table 3.5(1). The most common nonparametric statistics include the Mann-Whitney $U$, Sign test, Wilcoxon Signed Ranks test, Kruskal-Wallis, and Friedman Analysis of Variance.

**Mann-Whitney $U$ Test.** The Mann-Whitney $U$ test is used to test for differences in rankings on some variable between two independent groups when the data are not scaled in intervals (Lundegren & Farrell, 1985). For example, you may want to analyze self-concept scores of high-fit and low-fit women who participated in a weight-training fitness program. You administer a nominal scale form where respondents rank characteristics as "like me" or "not like me." Thus, this test will let you determine the effects of this program on your participants by comparing the two groups and their self-concept scores. This test is equivalent to the independent $t$-test.

**The Sign Test.** The Sign test is used when the independent variable is categorical and consists of two levels. The dependent variable is assumed to be continuous but can't be measured on a continuous scale, so a categorical scale is substituted (Hale, 1990). This test becomes the nonparametric equivalent to the dependent or matched *t*-test. The Sign test is only appropriate if the dependent variable is binary (i.e., takes only two different values). Suppose you want to know if switching from wood to fiber daggerboards on your Sunfish sailboats increases the likelihood of winning regattas. The Sign test will let you test this question by comparing the two daggerboards as the independent variable and the number of races won as the dependent variable.

**Wilcoxon Signed Ranks Test.** The Wilcoxon test is also a nonparametric alternative to the *t*-test and is used when the dependent variable has more than two values that are ranked. Positions in a race are a good example of this type of dependent variable. As in the Sign test, the independent variable is categorical or nominal and has two levels. For example, you might wish to know if a difference exists between runners belonging to a running club and those who are not members compared to their finish positions in a road race. The results of this analysis indicate the difference in ranks on the dependent variable (their finish position) between the two related groups (member or nonmember groups of runners).

**Kruskal-Wallis.** The Kruskal-Wallis test is equivalent to the one-way ANOVA. It is used when you have an independent variable with two or more values that you wish to compare to a dependent variable. You use this statistic to see if more than two independent groups have the same mean or median. Since this procedure is a nonparametric test, you would use the statistic when your sample size is small or you are not sure of the distribution. An example of an application would be to compare the attitudes of counselors at a small camp (the dependent variable) toward three different salary payment plans: weekly, twice a summer, or end of the summer (independent variable).

**Friedman Analysis of Variance.** The Friedman Analysis of Variance test is used for repeated measures analysis when you measure a subject two or more times. You must have a categorical independent variable with more than two values and a rank-order dependent variable that is measured more than twice (Hale, 1990). This test is the nonparametric equivalent to repeated measures of analysis of variance (two-way ANOVA). An example of a situation when you might use this statistical procedure would be if you had ranked data from multiple judges. For example, suppose you were experimenting with four new turf grasses on your four soccer fields. You ask your five maintenance workers to rank the grasses on all four fields for durability. You could analyze these results with the Friedman procedure.

## Making Decisions about Statistics

The decision model for choosing the appropriate type of statistical procedure is found in Figure 3.5(3). This model provides a logical progression of questions about your parametric and nonparametric data that will help you in your selection of appropriate statistics. Many other forms of statistical measures are possible, but the ones described here will provide you with the most common forms used in evaluations and research.

## From Ideas to Reality

This chapter initially may seem complex and full of terms not familiar to you. We realize that statistics are often confusing and overwhelming to some people, but as you begin to understand what they mean, they can be extremely helpful. We acknowledge that one short chapter will not make you an expert on these statistics, but we hope this chapter will at least show you some of the ways that we can gain valuable information by examining the relationships between and among variables. The more that you use statistical procedures, the more you will understand them. Thank goodness we have easy access to computers to save time and effort. Computers, however, do not absolve us from knowing what statistics to use to show associations or differences within our data. If you want more information than is offered in this short chapter, you may want to consult one of the many statistics books that exist.

Now that you have studied this chapter, you should be able to:
- Explain when parametric and nonparametric statistics should be used
- Given a situation with the levels of measurement data known, choose the correct statistical procedure to use
- Use the decision model for choosing appropriate statistical procedures for a particular set of data

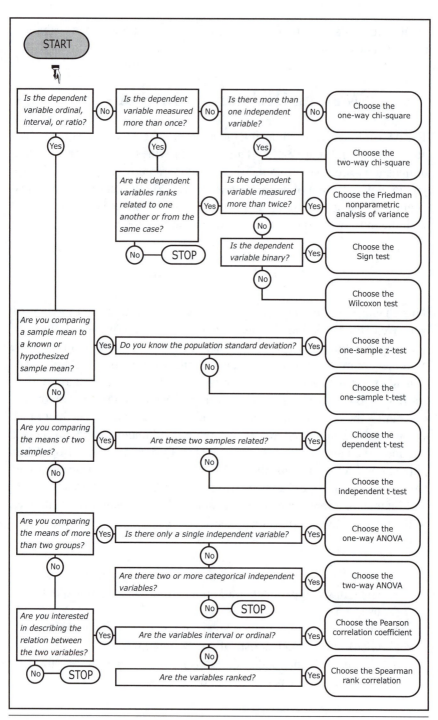

**Figure 3.5(3)** *A Statistical Decision Tree (adapted from Hale, 1990)*

# 3.6 Hurray for Computers and Data Analyses

To really understand the numeric relationships of variables for our research or evaluation projects, we have to use statistics. Descriptive statistical calculations can also be onerous with large samples. As computers have become integral in the lives of recreation professionals, the options for computerized data analyses have become common. As an evaluator or researcher, you likely will be faced with the question, "How can I best use my computer to help with my data analysis?" Most of you can meet your needs with general public software like Excel in Microsoft. Some of you may also have access to specialized software designed specifically for statistical (e.g., Statistical Package for the Social Sciences; SPSS) or qualitative (e.g., NUD*IST or Atlas.ti) analyses. Regardless of the software used, you will likely be expected to know how to use basic statistical applications for your evaluation and research projects.

Many agencies and virtually all universities have statistical software packages that are available on network systems or personal computers. Computer technology has changed so quickly that most professionals today have sophisticated and powerful applications as standard programs on their desktop or in their hand-held devices. The memory needed to do advanced statistical analysis on large data sets is usually not an issue. Almost any "off the shelf" computer will allow individuals to do many evaluation and research-related tasks such as data entry and processing, statistical analyses, reports, graphics, qualitative analyses, and telecommunications. Most of the time, you will use programs that are commercially available and widely used by evaluators and researchers. In some cases, your agency may have acquired specialized software that has been written specifically for your organization. In either case, you will have to learn how to use the software program unless your organization has a technology specialist who can run the analyses for you. Even if someone else does your analyses, you must be able to interpret the results and verify that the appropriate statistics were used.

Learning the statistical packages will require some investment of time on your part. Commercially available statistical programs such as the Statistical Packages for the Social Sciences (SPSS) have a fairly detailed set of procedures used to run the statistical package. Even statistical applications in packages like Microsoft's Excel require a learning curve. Although you can try to learn about these procedures by reading the manuals and working through the built-in tutorials, attending a workshop that will give you hands-on experiences to help you acquire the basics is usually helpful.

The advantages to using commercially available statistical programs, however, are usually worth the investment of time and energy if you will use them often. You can do virtually any type of statistical analysis desired and most of them have built-in "help" features that provide advice on everything from the correct statistics to run to troubleshooting for possible errors. Many statistical software companies also have online "help desks" that you can contact through email or phone for personalized help with more complex problems. Most programs have graphic and report options that allow you to present your results in interesting, professional formats. As a beginning evaluator or researcher, these statistical packages allow you great flexibility and sophistication in your analyses. Even if you are doing only descriptive statistics, these computer programs allow you to work easily with large data sets and use almost an infinite number of variables and values. The packages also enable you to convert data directly into figures and tables.

Some of you may not have access to specific statistical packages like SPSS. In these cases you probably do have access to more generic software like Microsoft Excel on your personal computer that will allow you to conduct statistical analyses. Spreadsheet programs like Excel, while smaller and a bit less sophisticated than specialized statistical packages, still allow you to do many standard analyses needed to complete your evaluation and research projects. Most beginning evaluators and researchers conduct basic descriptive and inferential statistics for their analyses. Software like Excel provides these basic statistics in moderately easy to learn procedures with some documentation to help you if problems arise. Many statistical packages like SPSS even allow for data to be easily imported from a spreadsheet application like Excel. This feature gives the evaluator options for ease of data entry as well as "cleaning" (i.e., making sure no errors were made in data entry) the data in a simple program like Excel, before moving into a more sophisticated program capable of running advanced analyses.

For illustrative purposes, we used the interactive version of SPSS (and in a few spots Microsoft Excel) in the following overview about computerized statistical packages. It is not within the scope of this book to teach the use of a specific statistical package like SPSS or Excel, but most packages for personal computers are not difficult to learn and use. If you know the variables that you wish to analyze and the way to enter data, almost any statistical package will allow you to do the descriptive and inferential calculations that have been discussed in the previous chapters.

# An Example of SPSS as a Statistical Program

SPSS has several formats for use but the one we are using in this section is an interactive statistics and graphics package that can compute descriptive and inferential statistics. The SPSS graphics allow the visualization of one and two-dimensional data. SPSS can handle almost unlimited numbers of cases (respondents) and variables. Spreadsheet programs like Excel may have more limitations about the numbers of cases and variables. You need to check your specific program for its parameters.

SPSS, as well as most spreadsheets, has several "windows" for performing the basic commands. For example in SPSS, the Variables window allows you to enter descriptive names and values for your data, specify particular ways to deal with missing data, and modify the parameters of your data. The Data window, meanwhile, displays your data, and the Output window allows you to see the results of your requested statistical analysis. The program also has a series of menus that allow the user to edit data and create, change, or delete variables. You can analyze data through a variety of statistical procedures and get "help" if needed. SPSS can also import files, such as those constructed in Excel. This easy exchange in files is useful to evaluators and researchers, who might initially enter data through their Excel spreadsheet for some basic calculations, then transfer the data for further, more sophisticated analyses to SPSS.

SPSS offers a broad range of statistical procedures through the Analyze menu. The option called "Descriptive Statistics" provides an array of frequencies, descriptive statistics, and even a crosstabs option. "Compare means" provides independent and paired $t$-tests, as well as one-way ANOVAs. "Correlate" computes the Pearson correlation coefficients, "Regression" computes simple and multiple regression models, and "Scale" will provide a reliability analysis. SPSS also provides selected nonparametric statistics through "Nonparametric tests" that include chi square, tests for two independent samples (Mann-Whitney $U$), two related samples tests (Wilcoxon and Sign), and K-related samples (Friedman). While these statistical procedures just mentioned are likely the ones you will most frequently use, SPSS provides an even greater menu of multivariate choices that may be applicable for some of your projects.

Excel also has a variety of analysis options available to users. Some of these options are built into the "ribbons," while others are only available after installing the Analysis ToolPak. For example, from the "Home" ribbon, you can go to the "Editing" group, and from the "AutoSum" dropdown menu, choose "Average" (Home>Editing>AutoSum). This option calculates averages for all the data selected for this analysis. Once the

Analysis ToolPak is installed, a "Data Analysis" tool will be available from the "Data" ribbon (Data>Analysis>Data Analysis). The statistical procedures available through "Data Analysis" include "Descriptive Statistics," "Correlations," several choices for *t*-tests and ANOVAs, and "Regression." Excel will also calculate chi-square statistics, but this process is a bit more complicated than in SPSS.

SPSS also has an array of graphing capabilities. The "Graphs" menu provides a choice of selections including bar, line, area, and pie graphs. You may also select plots such as box plots and scatterplots. Several other graphing options exist for more complex data. Excel also offers a variety of graphing options, but these options are generally a separate procedure and not a direct part of the analysis options.

For all of these procedures, you control the location of your statistical output. For example, while doing your initial analyses, you will likely direct the results to your screen. At the end of your computing session, you will want to save a copy of the analyses to a file on your hard drive or memory key where it is easily retrievable. You may also want a paper copy of your final results, so you can direct your output to your printer. In some cases, you may even want to create new data files based upon the results of your analyses. Further, the output produced from SPSS or Excel is easily copied and pasted directly into a word processing program like Microsoft Word when it comes time to write your evaluation or research report.

To get the most from data, every evaluator and researcher analyzing quantitative data will need to use a computer. You can learn how to run the program by reading the documentation, completing the interactive tutorial, and practicing with sample data. Learning to use a computer is a lot like learning a foreign language—the more you practice, the better you become. You can start out slowly using descriptive statistics and then move to more sophisticated analyses as you become more comfortable with the computer and data analysis.

# Interpreting Statistics

Each computer program you use will give you a slightly different output as far as how data analyses look. We will provide several general examples of how you can begin to interpret data from the analysis output.

## Descriptive Statistics

In most computer programs, the descriptive statistics will include a list of the frequencies reported for the values of the variables, the mean, median, number of cases, standard deviation, standard error, skewness, and the sum. Most people understand these statistics, and you will usually just want to choose the specific statistics that are most meaningful to your project to discuss. For example, Table 3.6(1) shows data runs from an evaluation of a Student Recreation Center (SRC). A 5-point Likert scale was used to ascertain attitudes toward select aspects of the center such as entertainment while working out (e.g., TV, music), extra equipment (e.g., towels, lockers), staff friendliness, type of equipment, and hours of operation. Each item was rated on a 5-point Likert scale with 1="terrible" and 5="outstanding."

Table 3.6(1) is the output from SPSS "Descriptives" that provides statistical information including the range (including the minimum and maximum values recorded by respondents), mean, standard deviation, and variance for these items. These descriptive statistics tell you that the respondents thought these aspects of the SRC were on average fair (3) to very good (4). The example of a frequency table for entertainment provides

*Table 3.6(1)* Examples of SPSS Descriptive Statistics

| Descriptive Statistics | | | | | | | | |
|---|---|---|---|---|---|---|---|---|
| | N | Range | Minimum | Maximum | Mean | | Std. | Variance |
| | Statistic | Statistic | Statistic | Statistic | Statistic | Std. Error | Statistic | Statistic |
| ENTERTAI | 43 | 4.00 | 1.00 | 5.00 | 3.4186 | .1341 | .8792 | .773 |
| EXTRA | 44 | 3.00 | 2.00 | 5.00 | 3.2727 | .1189 | .7884 | .622 |
| STAFF | 43 | 4.00 | 1.00 | 5.00 | 3.7907 | .1270 | .8326 | .693 |
| EQUIP | 44 | 3.00 | 2.00 | 5.00 | 3.8864 | .1309 | .8685 | .754 |
| HOURS | 44 | 3.00 | 2.00 | 5.00 | 4.0909 | .1118 | .7414 | .550 |

**Example of Frequency Table for One Variable**

| ENTERTAI | | Frequency | Percent | Valid Percent | Cumulative Percent |
|---|---|---|---|---|---|
| Valid | terrible | 2 | 4.5 | 4.7 | 4.7 |
| | poor | 2 | 4.5 | 4.7 | 9.3 |
| | fair | 18 | 40.9 | 41.9 | 51.2 |
| | very good | 18 | 40.9 | 41.9 | 93.0 |
| | outstanding | 3 | 6.8 | 7.0 | 100.0 |
| | Total | 43 | 97.7 | 100.0 | |
| Missing | System | 1 | 2.3 | | |
| Total | | 44 | | | |

additional detail regarding the percentage of distribution on each value. In this example, over 83% of the respondents (18 individuals out of the total 44) thought the entertainment was fair to very good while only 9.3% thought it was terrible or poor. This table also illustrates the use of "percent" (based on all respondents, including those who did not answer the question) and "valid percent" (based only on the respondents who answered the question).

## Correlations

A correlation shows the relationship between two interval or ratio variables. You will generally receive an $r$ score to indicate correlation. If you correlate more than two variables, you will get a matrix with a number of $r$ scores so that each variable is compared to every other variable. As indicated earlier, correlations range from -1 to +1, so you will look at a score and interpret two aspects: whether it is a positive or negative correlation and the strength of that association (arbitrarily termed as weak or strong). The $p$ value or "Sig. (2-tailed)" (the default test in all analyses is 2-tailed, but able to be changed to a 1-tailed test if desired) indicates the probability of the finding.

For example, if the correlation between how much an individual enjoyed working out and the perception of the quality of the instructors had a Pearson Correlation (sometimes called an r-value) of .394, you could conclude that a weak-to-medium positive relationship existed be-

*Table 3.6(2)* Correlations between Enjoyment and Quality Instructors

**Descriptive Statistics**

|  | Mean | Std. Deviation | N |
|---|---|---|---|
| ENJOYMNT | 4.7586 | .9124 | 29 |
| QUALINST | 4.4138 | .9826 | 29 |

**Correlations**

|  |  | ENJOYMNT | QUALINST |
|---|---|---|---|
| ENJOYMNT | Pearson correlation | 1.000 | .394* |
|  | Sig. (2-tailed) |  | .034 |
|  | N | 29 | 29 |
| QUALINST | Pearson correlation | .394* | 1.000 |
|  | Sig. (2-tailed) | .034 |  |
|  | N | 29 | 29 |

* Correlation is significant at the .05 level Sig. (2-tailed)

tween enjoyment and instructors (see Table 3.6[2]). In other words, as the quality of the instructor increased, the level of enjoyment increased. If the result had been r = -.89, you would conclude that as enjoyment increased, the perceived quality of the instructors decreased. In the case illustrated in Table 3.6(2), p = .034, so you would say that the finding was statistically significant and that a moderate positive relationship exists between the two variables. Remember, as mentioned earlier, correlations show only relationships, not causality.

For Excel users, the calculations for correlations are more challenging. Pearson product-moment correlations can be determined through the CORREL(Array1, Array2) built-in function. However, the significance of the correlation coefficient is not tested.

## T-tests

To compare the means of two unrelated groups, we do an independent t-test. The statistic that the computer will generate is a t statistic as well as a p (probability) statistic. We examine the p statistic to see if it is above or below our statistical significance standard set. For example, if the p is .23 and our standard was set at .05, we would conclude that no statistically significant difference existed between the means of two variables. If however, we were measuring the results of a basketball rules test taken by boys and girls after attending a 1-day basketball clinic, we might find that the difference between the two means was significant at .008. In that case, we conclude that a statistical difference existed between the two means. In most computer printouts, the means and standard deviations for both groups are given along with the t and p values. You will need to look at the means to determine the likely source of any significant differences.

Table 3.6(3) shows a t-test comparing opinions about the atmosphere of the Student Recreation Center with the gender of the respondents. The males' mean response was 3.00 with a standard deviation (SD) of .45 and the females had a 3.03 mean with a SD of .78. The next piece of information to check is the Levene's Test for Equal Variance, to determine if the results indicate the two groups have equal variance. If the significance standard was pre-set at .05 and was not exceeded, then you look at the t-test results for "equal variance assumed." In the example, Levene's test was .053, which does not exceed the significance level, so we look at the equal variance t-test results (p = .901). This result indicates no statistically significant differences between women and men on their perceptions about the atmosphere of the SRC. If Levene's had been less than .05, we would have looked at "equal variance not assumed" (p = .873).

Remember to look at Levene's results, because some analyses will show very different results in the *t*-tests based on the assumption of variance. You can also see from the descriptive table that the mean score between the males and the females were very similar, which further confirms that no differences based on means existed. Had the results been statistically significant, we would turn to the means of the two groups displayed in the descriptive table to determine where the difference existed.

If collecting data from the same set of respondents at two different points of time (for example, in a pre-/post-test design), SPSS has a paired *t*-test option that makes this analysis easy. Remember, when running a comparison of means that results in a significant difference, you need to report effect sizes (the meaningfulness of the statistical difference). A popular choice for this statistic is the Cohen's d or, in some cases, you can calculate the effect sizes manually as described earlier.

To run an independent *t*-test in Excel requires a couple of steps that are automatically built into SPSS. Once you define the variables of interest, you have to test the homogeneity of variance by using the F-Test tool (Data>Analysis>Data Analysis>F-Test Two-Sample for Variances). Then if the variances are equal, you select Data>Analysis>Data Analysis>*t*-test: Two-Sample Assuming Equal Variances). You then enter the appropriate information and click "OK" to run the test. Effect sizes are not calculated

*Table 3.6(3)* T-*test for Overall Atmosphere Compared by Sex*

| Independent Samples test | | | | | | | | | |
|---|---|---|---|---|---|---|---|---|---|
| | Levene's Test for Equality of Variances | | *t*-test for Equality of Means | | | | | | |
| | | | | | Sig. (2-tailed) | Mean Difference | Std. Error Difference | 95% confidence interval of the difference | |
| | F | Sig. | t | df | | | | Lower | Upper |
| ATMOSPH Equal variance assumed | 3.985 | .053 | -.125 | 41 | .901 | 3.125E-02 | .2500 | -.5360 | .4735 |
| Equal variance not assumed | | | -.162 | 31.025 | .873 | 3.125E-02 | .1931 | -.4252 | .3627 |

**Group Statistics**

| SEX | N | Mean | Std. Deviation | Std. Error Mean |
|---|---|---|---|---|
| ATMOSPH    male | 11 | 3.0000 | .4472 | .1348 |
| female | 32 | 3.0313 | .7822 | .1383 |

in Excel. However, the needed statistics needed to plug into the formula are readily available.

## Analysis of Variance

Analysis of variance (ANOVA) works the same way that independent $t$-tests do, except that you are interested in determining the differences in means between three or more groups. The statistics given on a printout are the sum of squares, mean-squares, F-ratio, and a $p$ value. The F-ratio is the actual ANOVA statistic, but the bottom line is the $p$ value. Look to the $p$ value to see whether it is above or below the standard set, which is usually .05. If the p value is above the preset level, you can say no statistically significant differences occurred among the means. If the $p$ value is below .05, a difference exists somewhere among the means. As in $t$-tests, you will need to examine the means and standard deviations of the three or more variables to determine where the difference lies. Most statistical programs provide a list of the means for each group. In other cases, you may have to run descriptive statistics to get the means for each group.

You need to know the means if you want to interpret which of the groups is different from the others. Sometimes this "eyeballing" of the means is difficult to determine the group (or in some situations, groups) that differ the most from the others. We recommend that you run a post-hoc analysis, for example a Scheffes or Bonferelli analysis, to help you determine the groups that significantly differ statistically from the others. In SPSS, varied post-hoc choices exist for this purpose. Table 3.6(4) shows an example of a "one-way" ANOVA that compares the quality of

*Table 3.6(4)  One-way Analysis of Quality of Workout by Year in School*

| Descriptive Statistics | | | | | | | | |
|---|---|---|---|---|---|---|---|---|
| QUALITY | | | Std. Deviation | | 95% confidence interval for Mean | | | |
| | N | Mean | | Std. Error | Lower | Upper | Minimum | Maximum |
| FIRST/SOPH | 18 | 3.3889 | .5016 | .1182 | 3.1394 | 3.6383 | 3.00 | 4.00 |
| JR/SR | 18 | 3.1111 | .5830 | .1374 | 2.8212 | 3.4010 | 2.00 | 4.00 |
| GRADUATE | 8 | 3.0000 | .7559 | .2673 | 2.3680 | 3.6320 | 2.00 | 4.00 |
| Total | 44 | 3.2045 | .5937 | .951E-02 | 3.0240 | 3.3851 | 2.00 | 4.00 |

ANOVA

| QUALITY | Sum of squares | df | Mean square | F | Sig. |
|---|---|---|---|---|---|
| Between groups | 1.104 | 2 | .552 | 1.610 | .212 |
| Within groups | 14.056 | 41 | .343 | | |
| Total | 15.159 | 43 | | | |

the workout at the Student Recreation Center to whether students were first year/sophomore, junior/senior, or in grad school. The significance level was p = .212, so we conclude that no statistically significant differences existed between the year in school and the quality of the workout at the Student Recreation Center.

Again, the meaningfulness of any statistical significance found in ANOVAs must be of interest to an evaluator or researcher. The most common statistic that helps with this determination is the eta squared statistic. While not automatically calculated, the formula is the sum of squares between divided by the sum of squares total. The resulting statistic provides the amount of explained variance. So for example, if the calculation resulted in .23, then you know that 23% of the variance is explained by the variables in the analysis of variance. In social sciences, anything over .10 (10%) is usually reported as meaningful.

If you want to run a one-way ANOVA in Excel, you need to define the variables, then select DATA>Analysis>Data Analysis>ANOVA: Single Factor. Unlike SPSS, no post-hoc tests are available in Excel to help you statistically determine the group(s) that differ the most from each other.

## Chi-Square

These nonparametric statistics may also be found as CROSSTABS or TABLES in different statistical packages. When you run these types of analyses, you will generally get a variety of statistics. The statistic that you are most concerned with is the chi-square statistic and the $p$ statistic. As in the other cases, you will see what the $p$ value is and then you can compare it to the standard you have set. Most computer programs that run chi-square will give you a warning if more than 25% of the cells in the computed tables have less than 5 responses in them. When this warning occurs, the results are suspect. In chi-square analysis, you will have to "eyeball" your data to determine where the associations exist if you find a statistically significant difference. Since a matrix is provided that shows the number of responses in each cell, you can usually figure out where the greatest associations are found.

Table 3.6(5) shows a 2x2 table using a chi-square statistic to show the relationship between students' participation in cardiovascular activities and their biological sex. The chi-square statistic is .201 ($p = .654$), so no relationship exists between cardiovascular activities and the person's sex. In other words, women were as likely as men to do a cardiovascular workout. The table is also useful in getting a "picture" of the specific details of the analysis. For example, the count shows 7 men and 21 women did cardiovascular workouts. For all cardio workouts, 25% were done

*Table 3.6(5)* *Crosstabs for Cardiovascular Workout and Sex*

| Crosstab | | | | | |
|---|---|---|---|---|---|
| | | | SEX | | |
| | | | Male | Female | Total |
| **CARDIO** yes | Count | | 7 | 21 | 28 |
| | % within CARDIO | | 25.0 | 75.0 | 100.0 |
| | % within SEX | | 58.3 | 65.6 | 63.6 |
| | % of Total | | 15.9 | 47.7 | 63.6 |
| no | Count | | 5 | 11 | 16 |
| | % within CARDIO | | 31.3 | 68.8 | 100.0 |
| | % within SEX | | 41.7 | 34.4 | 36.4 |
| | % of Total | | 11.4 | 25.0 | 36.4 |
| Total | Count | | 12 | 32 | 44 |
| | % within CARDIO | | 27.3 | 72.7 | 100.0 |
| | % within SEX | | 100.0 | 100.0 | 100.0 |
| | % of Total | | 27.3 | 72.7 | 100.0 |

**Chi-Square Tests**

| | Value | df | Asymp. Sig. (2-sided) | Exact Sig. (2-sided) | Exact Sig. (1-sided) |
|---|---|---|---|---|---|
| Pearson Chi-Square | .201[b] | 1 | .654 | | |
| Continuity Correction[a] | .009 | 1 | .924 | | |
| Likelihood Ratio | .198 | 1 | .656 | | |
| Fisher's Exact Test | | | | .732 | .456 |
| Linear-by-Linear Association | .196 | 1 | .658 | | |
| N of Valid Cases | | | | | |

[a] Computed only for a 2x2 table
[b] One cell (25.0%) has expected count less than five. The minimum expected count is 4.36.

by men and 75% were done by women. However, the actual number of men in the study ($n = 12$) was substantially fewer than women ($n = 32$), so the table helps look at proportions. From another perspective provided by this table, you find 58.3% of all men and 65.6% of all women did cardio workouts. Even though the actual counted numbers looked like there might be differences between men and women, this percentage demonstrates why our analysis showed no significant relationships in our testing.

For Excel users, it is important to know that Excel does not directly calculate the value of chi-square for either the test of goodness of fit or the test of independence. However, several chi-square built-in functions are available: CHIINV (inverse of chi-square distribution and returns a chi-square value for a given degree of freedom and probability level); CHIDIST (returns the *p*-level for a given value of chi square at the stated degrees of freedom); and CHITEST (compares a range of observed values with associated range of expected frequencies and reports the *p*-level of the chi-square test result but not the computed sample value of chi-square). The Analysis ToolPak has no chi-square test.

We hope this summary of statistical interpretation is useful to you. The data generated from statistical analysis initially can be rather daunting but the more you work with statistical procedures, the easier it becomes to interpret and understand your results. Do not hesitate to find someone who understands statistics to help you interpret your results. Using descriptive and inferential statistics that computer programs supply can contribute greatly to making decisions about the organizations in which we work.

# Computer Use with Qualitative Data

The computer also can be an effective tool for managing and analyzing qualitative data. More about qualitative data analysis is described in the next chapter, but we want to introduce data analyses related to computers. Although computers are not mandatory for doing qualitative analysis, they can be extremely helpful to a researcher or evaluator. Computer programs such as NUD*IST and Atlas.ti can help cut down on fatigue, save time, reduce the tedium of clerical tasks like cutting and pasting quotes from transcripts, and can allow the evaluator to have more time for data interpretation (Henderson, 2006).

Computers can be used for qualitative data collected from in-depth interviews, focus groups, unobtrusive data, or notes from fieldwork. Just as with the mushrooming possibilities for using computers to help analyze quantitative data with a myriad of statistical programs, researchers and evaluators have many possibilities for "computer help" when working with qualitative data. The technology is changing rapidly and what we write today will likely be dated by the time you read this text. We want, however, to raise some current general options that should still be considered when working with qualitative data.

One of the drawbacks to qualitative data has been the process of going from the spoken words from an interview, focus group to transcriptions that serve as the hard data to be analyzed. This process usually involves tediously transcribing tapes verbatim. With the advent of relatively inexpensive and effective voice recognition software, this process can be done easier and cheaper than the old way of hiring someone to listen and type a word-for-word tape transcription. With voice recognition, you can speak your interview data into your computer and have the text simultaneously "translated" into text that is then usable by many software programs such as Microsoft Word or more specific analysis programs. Similarly, if you record your interviews on some type of digital recorder (like an MP3 player), the audio files can be downloaded and subsequently entered into a voice recognition program. However, at the time of this writing a number of problems continue to be inherent with voice recognition technology. Transcribing manually with a foot pedal or similar machine may be the least problematic.

Good software packages exist to help with the analysis and interpretation of qualitative data. Some of the most popular current programs include NUD*IST, Nvivo, and Atlas.ti. All of these programs prepare a data file based on the transcribed data or other documents you might enter. If you are considering purchasing one of these software programs, you will want to explore carefully the options each software package offers.

All the more recent software programs (i.e., NUD*IST, Atlas.ti) offer some specific aspects you will find helpful, including opportunities to:

- Manage and search the text of multiple documents (i.e., interviews)
- Manage and explore coded ideas about the data
- Search multiple files for coded concepts
- Generate reports including basic enumeration summaries
- Index (code) text units
- Link open codes into axial coding or family units
- Link codes to construct diagrams and "theories"
- Test theories about the data

While most evaluators and researchers in recreation are concerned with qualitative textual data and document analysis, most qualitative software programs can also handle nontextual data such as maps and photographs. In addition, just as the statistical packages use varied windows for different functions, Atlas.ti, for example has editable windows for different parts of the project and the analysis. Your qualitative data are set up in two parallel databases called the document/data system and the index system. These systems help keep track of all your text files, organize your codes, and keep track of how they are indexed in your text. Both become important in the analysis functions, because they allow you to theorize about the relationships in your data and test your theories by exploring the links within the data.

# Other Uses for the Computer in Data Collection and Analysis

Rapid technological developments produce advancements that help a researcher or evaluator. Telecommunications provide access within seconds to the most updated resource materials that used to be difficult and time-consuming to acquire. Word processing and desktop publishing can help produce professional and commercial-quality questionnaires as well as final reports for an evaluation. Hand-held computers, PDAs, and GPS units can be easily taken to a site where geographic data, for example, are gathered or where interviewers can ask participants survey questions, enter the responses (often with a stylus or their voice rather than a keyboard) into a formatted data file to download (often through a wireless connection) for analysis. Information can be shared through a wireless connection between computers, and if hard connections exist, these systems of fiber optics are so quick that they may seem instantaneous.

As the public becomes more technologically oriented, data may be collected from participants through the phone/cable/satellite connections in their homes to computer networks linked to our parks, community centers, or libraries. As researchers and evaluators with similar interests, we may become part of "teams" spread across the country who collect and share data to make applications to theory and practice.

During the next few years, other discoveries certainly will be produced that will be helpful to an evaluator or researcher. As competent professionals you will want to continue to read about changing technology, attend workshops at professional meetings, and talk with colleagues who have discovered new uses for computers and technological advances. Computers have become an important part of leisure services evaluation and research. The challenge may come in trying to maximize all of the possibilities that will make your life easier!

# From Ideas to Reality

This chapter provides a broad overview of the possibilities of using technology such as computer packages in evaluation and research. We do not know what potential software packages you will have available for conducting your data analyses in the future, so it is not useful to teach any one particular approach. Most packages, however, use similar formats, and if you understand how data are coded, entered, and interpreted, you should be able to read the documentation or use the tutorial that comes with the program to determine how to run particular analyses. Once these runs are completed, the easy part is looking to see whether statistical significance exists and what the results mean. For many people, doing the data analysis is the fun part after much time has been spent collecting, coding, and entering data.

Now that you have studied this chapter, you should be able to:
- Describe the options available for using computers in evaluation and research projects
- Use basic statistical or qualitative data options available within a software package that will meet the needs of your evaluation project or research study
- Explain how to interpret whether an analysis is statistically significant and meaningful

# 3.7 Qualitative Data Analysis and Interpretation: Explaining the What, How, and Why

In projects and studies that use qualitative data, we are *not* necessarily concerned with a singular conclusion but with perspectives or patterns that describe the data. In qualitative data analysis and interpretation, the evaluator or researcher tries to uncover perspectives that will help understand the criteria being explored in a project. Professionals are interested in how and why findings are as they are rather than necessarily determining an answer regarding statistical significance.

Doing qualitative analysis is a time-consuming task, as it requires you read over notes or transcriptions, organize the data, look for patterns, check emerging themes back and forth with the data, validate data sources, make linkages, and "theorize" about the data in the case of research. These techniques are at the heart of qualitative analysis and interpretation.

As described earlier, in-depth interviews, focus groups, and qualitative observations are the most common ways to obtain qualitative data. An evaluator or researcher might also ask open-ended questions on a questionnaire that would result in qualitative data. We want to emphasize again the importance of asking open-ended questions in such a way that "yes" or "no" are not possible responses.

One of the difficulties with collecting qualitative data, however, is that it is easy to get overwhelmed with the amount of text generated. Too much data results in data management problems. Qualitative data can be coded, but not in the same sense as quantitative data. Coding in the qualitative sense is used to organize data into brief word descriptions, not numbers—as is done in quantitative coding. Further, since the qualitative data are not reduced to numbers, the interpretation of what the data mean is your responsibility as the evaluator or researcher. Thus, you become much more personally involved in qualitative analysis than in quantitative.

Analysis is the process of bringing order to qualitative data and organizing words into patterns, categories, and basic descriptive units. It can be likened to what we do with quantitative data in terms of coding and actually running statistics. Interpretation involves attaching meanings and significance to the analysis, explaining descriptive patterns, and looking for relationships and linkages within the data. In analyzing qualitative data, interpretation is like determining what statistical significance means.

An interesting and readable written summary of a project provides sufficient description to allow the reader to understand the analysis, and sufficient analysis to allow the reader to understand the description (Patton, 1980b). Analysis comes from focusing on the criteria raised at the beginning of a project and then describing how the data evolved into perspectives and conclusions. Qualitative data are often used for formative, summative, and assessment evaluations.

Qualitative analyses provide descriptions of what actually happened using word pictures and summaries. The aim is to get both the "outer" and the "inner" perspectives. The inner perspective uses the actual words of respondents. The outer perspective is the interpretation of what those words mean, as interpreted by the researcher or evaluator. Making sense of the words, however, and not having conclusions appear to be the evaluator's opinions require a rigorous process. When done properly, qualitative data analysis is as systematic as any quantitative analysis.

# Organizing Qualitative Analysis

No magic formulas exist for how to do qualitative analysis. In general, however, the data must be organized into some manageable form that is sometimes referred to as data reduction. It isn't really reduction, but you are trying to put the data into some type of form beyond the hundreds, or even thousands, of words of data that are collected. Data reduction involves the process of organizing data and developing possible categories for analysis. As soon as field notes are taken or tapes are transcribed, data reduction can begin. The procedures used may be standardized for the particular project or may be open as you begin to summarize some of the "raw" data. This data management requires judgment calls and decision rules that you will develop in summarizing and resummarizing the data.

## Qualitative Coding

The evaluator using qualitative data must consider how to organize data so that a reader can return to it quickly without having to read through reams of material. Coding is the first step essential for analyzing qualitative data. Reading, reading, and rereading of data is necessary to become completely familiar with the data. After the reading, coding can be done by reducing the words to numbers, short phrases, or to short descriptions. Evaluators are cautioned about coding to numbers because often the richness of words can be lost when this number coding occurs. Descriptive word codes may be more useful.

Coding can be done in many ways. The recommendations by Corbin and Strauss (2008) are followed by many people in beginning the coding process. Corbin and Strauss call this method "grounded theory." The analyses are *grounded* in the data. Grounded theory is the method, and emerging theory or patterns is the outcome of this approach.

Corbin and Strauss (2008) describe three major types of coding: open, axial, and selective. Open coding means to identify the ideas or concepts and to give them names. A number of potential ideas should be acknowledged at this point, so make sure that you do not become too broad. Axial coding is the process of taking the open coding and reassembling and combining to develop themes that encompass the open coding. Selective coding is then the process of integrating the axial codes and coming up with theoretical or broad conclusions about data.

The coding for qualitative data then ranges from descriptive (open coding) to interpretive (axial coding) to explanatory (selective coding), based on the stages of coding. Open codes change and expand over time as more data are collected. One way to do the data analysis process is to code the data descriptively, according to the evaluation questions or criteria that were originally conceptualized. In selective coding you can integrate the ideas. If possible, it may be useful to have two evaluators open code to assure greater reliability. Coding may be done line by line but is usually done in "chunks." The open coding also will help the evaluator or researcher become familiar with the nature of the data that are discovered and may help in focus future interviews or observations for broader or deeper information.

## Write-Ups

Field notes and transcripts can be converted into "write-ups," "memos," or "notes on notes." The write-up indicates the most important content of a study at a particular time. Draft write-ups or summaries provide a way to organize thoughts that will evolve over time. Memos or "notes on notes" are short summaries about data from the evaluator's perspective, and can also be used to highlight possible patterns and clarifications of concepts. You also might want to include memos addressing personal emotional reactions as well as any methodological difficulties that might have occurred during data collection. These memos may be "gut reactions" to what is going on, inferences about the quality of the data, new connections made, notes about what to address later, elaborations, or clarifications. Written material should be dated, titled, and anchored to particular places in the field notes or transcripts. The memos require the researcher to "think" rather than to just collect data and ideas.

## Other Organizing Strategies

A filing system can also be developed for organizing data. This system may be developed on the computer for coding chunks of data or by actually physically cutting and pasting notes and putting these edited pages into file folders. One physical technique before computers were available to assist with data reduction and analysis was to put data on note cards or Post-it notes and sort ideas into look-alike piles that could be used to organize data. Qualitative computer packages, as discussed previously, are more commonly used today with large amounts of data. The use of note cards or chunks of data organized on the computer allows one to visually examine the grouped data and to begin to visualize how data may be categorized. The computer can help in organizing data, but it is still the individual who must make decisions about the way the data are organized and ultimately put together.

## Displaying the Data

Once the data have been organized, you may then want to develop ways to display them further. Data display is the organized assembly of information that permits the drawing of conclusions and the presentation of the respondents' words. Data displays, sometimes called cognitive maps, are not required, but they may be helpful as you begin to make sense of the coded data. Displaying data as a means for organizing for data interpretation can be done in many ways. Each evaluator will find that certain display strategies work well and others do not, depending on the situation. In each case, no matter what visual techniques are used to display data, you will have to make judgments about what data are or are not important.

A matrix based on words and phrases may also be used after data are coded. A matrix can easily be viewed and compared to other matrices. Usually the evaluator or researcher will develop categories for the matrix and then fill in the matrix with words or examples from the notes/ transcripts that describe the categories. A matrix may be used to outline specific examples that fit particular themes, or it may be used for compiling the number of responses to particular analysis categories. A number of matrices for a set of data can be developed. Some people prefer to build a matrix on a huge sheet of paper with 15–20 variables (although 5–6 is usually more manageable). For example, if we wanted to examine what activities offered by a recreation program the older adults said they enjoyed most, we might make a 3 x 3 matrix with the age groups 55–65, 66–75, and over 76 across the top and then categories of physical, social, and cultural activities down the side. We would display our data by indicating within the cells what specific types of activities were described *or* perhaps what the benefits were to these older adults according to their age groups.

Visual maps and diagrams can be used to show the interrelationships that make up behavior. Diagrams are often helpful in organizing ideas, themes, patterns, and configurations of interaction. You should also make notes about how you, as the data analyst, moved from one idea to another and how you refined the data displays. Conceptual maps or flow charts can tie patterns together with arrows and directional lines. They may be useful in stimulating thinking for individuals who like to see analyses visually. For example, if you were examining how people get information about available recreation opportunities in a community, you might make a diagram showing how the ways are linked or not linked to one another.

These suggestions for displaying data are tools to be used in interpreting data. Data reduction and display are not the end products, but are techniques to assist evaluators or researchers. The reduction techniques are a means to the ultimate ends of providing a rich description and explanation of the meaning of the evaluation data.

# Techniques for Data Analysis

Once the data are organized, open coded, and possibly diagrammed, several techniques may be applied to qualitative analysis. For purposes of evaluation research, we will discuss two major techniques for developing themes/patterns: enumeration and grounded comparison. Content analysis as a means of analyzing already existing written materials may use either of these techniques. Enumeration refers to the counting of items that are similar. Grounded comparison, which is a simplified idea related to grounded theory (Corbin & Strauss, 2008) and constant comparison, is a way to analyze data that is consistent with basic approaches to developing codes and patterns as major themes emerge.

In any type of qualitative data analysis, you are attempting to account for all ideas that are presented, not just the most popular ideas. Researchers interested in using qualitative data attempt to explain all the variance. You should be interested in the outliers as well as what the majority says or does. In other words, the focus is on interpreting conclusions including pointing out contradictions that exist in the data. Further, the effort of uncovering patterns, themes, and categories is a creative process that requires carefully considered interpretations about what is significant and meaningful in the data.

## Enumeration

Enumerative strategies are often used to supplement descriptive data. In this technique the evaluator codes qualitative data and counts it. You may be interested in the number of times certain behaviors occur or the duration of behaviors. Numbers are used in this case to show the intensity and amount of interaction. These numbers may also help a researcher to be analytically honest about how much agreement and disagreement existed about particular conclusions. In enumeration, however, the numbers are only numbers and should not be converted into percentages or any other statistical data. Enumeration shows the relative relationship of ideas to one another.

In a qualitative project, the researcher usually records and uses numbers primarily as supplementary material. In open-ended questionnaires, however, numbers are frequently used because they are comparable to close-ended questions. For example, you might ask what it was about a program that individuals liked the best, provide an enumeration of number counts, and then use the words to explain the meaning of the results. Table 3.7(1) provides an example of how enumeration might be used.

## Grounded Comparison

Grounded theory is a popular systematic analysis technique for recording, coding, and analyzing qualitative data (Corbin & Strauss, 2008).

*Table 3.7(1)  Example of Enumeration Coding and Analysis*

Background about Data: An evaluation was done in a Southern university 8 months after a 4-day workweek was mandated as a measure to try to save energy costs. A questionnaire using both close-ended and open-ended questions was sent to a random sample of faculty and staff who worked at the university. These are some of the responses to a question about attitudes toward the 4-day workweek and how they might be coded using a simple enumeration process of indicating whether the attitude is positive, negative, or neutral.

I don't have the physical stamina to hold up to a 10-hour day. **(code=negative)**
There are inconveniences such as trying to cram too much into 4 days. **(code=negative)**
What is gained on the "off" day does not compensate for the stress on the other 4 days. **(code=negative)**
It causes hardships at home with trying to take care of the kids when they aren't in school early in the morning and in the afternoon. **(code=negative)**
It's great. It would be hard to adjust to going back. **(code=positive)**
I can be home on Fridays with my 4-year-old son and I like it a lot. **(code=positive)**
I am able to spend time on Fridays with friends, relatives, and I enjoy doing these things. **(code=positive)**
I don't feel I'm getting as much done during the week as I did before. **(code=negative**)
It's not good for morale because it squeezes too many expectations into too little time. **(code=negative)**
The week goes by quickly and it gives me a chance to catch up on my personal projects on Friday. **(code=positive)**
It makes sense. **(code=positive)**
I like it a lot but my older colleagues are not coping very well with it. **(code=neutral)**

Total=6 negative, 5 positive, 1 neutral, 12 total.

*The data would be reported as numbers to show the relative amount of agreement concerning how the data were coded. Percentages should not be used, as they may be confusing to the reader who is accustomed to seeing percentages related to quantitative statistics.*

The term is a little misleading, as grounded theory is not the result but the process. However, using this process results in emerging themes and potential theorizing based on the data. The results are "grounded in the data." Constant comparison is a similar idea that means that a process is used to continually compare cases to one another as well as to statements. The process of constant comparison includes reading through all data, developing open and axial codes, and reading the data again to make sure it all fits within the codes and ultimately the themes that will be summarized. Because these ideas share common techniques and describe how results emerge from data and in relationship to the data, we have coined the term *grounded comparison* for use in this text. The process is far more important than the name itself. The codes and the themes may be adjusted as you continually compare the data between respondents or even the data within a single observation. See Table 3.7(2) for an example of the first part of this process.

Obviously, qualitative data analysis takes time. The technique also may mean going to others (e.g., colleagues or respondents) to have them confirm that they see codes uncovered or that themes or interpretations are consistent.

---

*Table 3.7(2)  Example of Coding as a Means for Grounded Comparison*

---

These are some of the same responses to a question about attitudes toward the 4-day workweek and how they might be coded using an initial constant comparison approach.

I don't have the physical stamina to hold up to a 10-hour day. **(code=tired)**
There are inconveniences such as trying to cram too much into 4 days. **(code=inconveniences, not identified)**
What is gained on the "off" day does not compensate for the stress on the other 4 days. **(code=stress)**
It causes hardships at home with trying to take care of kids when they aren't in school early in the morning and in the afternoon. **(code=inconveniences with children)**
It's great. It would be hard to adjust to going back. **(code=like, but no reason)**
I can be home on Fridays with my 4-year-old son and I like it a lot. **(code=time to spend with people)**
I am able to spend time on Fridays with friends, relatives, and I enjoy doing these things. **(code=time to be with people)**
I don't feel I'm getting as much done during the week as I did before. **(code=time problems)**
It's not good for morale because it squeezes too many expectations into too little time. **(code=time problems)**
The week goes by quickly and it gives me a chance to catch up on my personal projects on Friday. **(code=personal time)**
It makes sense. **(code=logic)**
I like it a lot but my older colleagues are not coping very well with it. **(code=concern for others)**

---

*This is a preliminary coding. You would go through all the data and work with it until you saw themes emerging. For example, time is both a negative and a positive factor concerning the attitudes toward the 4-day workweek. It opens time up for some people on the weekends but also creates stress and a feeling of lack of production in some people.*

The goal of grounded comparison is to maximize credibility through the analysis and comparison of groups and data. It involves carefully examining data, data sets, documents, and the individuals and groups sampled. Different "slices of data" can also be compared. For example, one might triangulate surveys, observations, and anecdotal records and analyze how the results compare to one another. The grounded comparison technique is inductive like other forms of qualitative analysis, which means the patterns and themes emerge from the data rather than being imposed prior to data collection.

Four stages can comprise the data analysis process:

1. Open code and display the major concepts and then integrate them into themes by axial coding.

2. Go back and compare the themes to data.

3. Delimit and refine the themes and consider how all the themes work together through the process of selective coding.

4. Find examples within the data that show how the themes were derived.

First the researcher takes "pieces" of data and organizes them by identifying, reducing, coding, and displaying categories of data. If an interview guide or standardized interview guide is used, the initial stage might comprise organizing the responses based on the questions.

The second stage is to integrate the categories and their properties by comparing them to one another and checking them back to the data. In the case of the interview guide, data may appear as a response to one question that really fits better into another theme. Therefore, you must reorganize the responses according to themes. In this stage, the evaluator might also uncover and describe subthemes.

In the third stage, the categories are delimited and refined, if necessary, to further focus a "story" about the data and how it fits together with *a priori* or emerging criteria. You want to make sure that no other themes or categories might be included or that any important data are being excluded. If new themes are discovered, then the researcher must go back through the data, compare them to the new categories, and go through the analysis process once again. The evaluator or researcher must also consider the wide variety of data that might exist.

The final stage involves going back to the original data and pulling out quotes, phrases, or anecdotes that support the themes. If these data are not included, the reader does not know if the project has been appropriately analyzed.

The grounded comparison method causes you to look continually for diversity. It ensures accurate evidence, establishes the generality of a fact, specifies concepts, and verifies or generates theory. Grounded comparison does not generate a perfect theory or perfect conclusions but rather results in perspectives and conclusions that are relevant to the context in which the data were observed or recorded.

Content analysis is a form of enumeration or grounded comparison that is commonly used to analyze documents, records, transcribed conversations, letters, or any document in a textual form. It is a process for making inferences by systematically identifying characteristics of messages. It may be done in words, phrases, sentences, paragraphs, sections, chapters, pictures, books, or any relevant context. Content analysis and its many forms relate to a process of ascertaining meanings about a written phenomena studied. In this sense, the strategy is more analytic than oriented toward data collection. Like unobtrusive techniques, this method may be used with a project that stands alone or may be used in triangulation with other data analysis strategies. Field evaluators frequently use document analysis as a form of content analysis to obtain historical information about a setting or situation being evaluated.

## Making Interpretations

Drawing conclusions to make interpretations about qualitative data occurs throughout the inquiry process and is the culmination of integrating the themes. As you are reading data to organize it for enumeration or grounded comparison, you are continually reexamining the data. You will be looking for "negative evidence," which means you will be trying to make sure everything fits your categories. If not all the data fit the themes or categories, you will either have to explain contradictions or make new categories.

As stressed throughout this chapter, you will also be looking for multiple sources of evidence to draw conclusions. Sample systematically and widely and try to avoid becoming too attached to initial themes and patterns. You may need to pay attention to your own bias as you do coding and analysis. An important strategy concerning data analysis is, therefore, not to stop the analysis process too soon before you are sure you have interpreted the data as well as you can. Although evaluators and researchers are focused on the end product, you must make sure that you do not reach the end too soon or become locked too quickly into a pattern of analysis that misses other possible meanings. The emergent nature of qualitative data must be allowed to happen. Documenting your feelings throughout the data collection and analysis process is useful as your attitudes and feelings may give insights about the data and its context.

The complete qualitative data analysis process generally includes the simultaneous techniques of collecting, coding, organizing, analyzing, and interpreting data in its context. As indicated earlier, interpretation involves attaching meaning and significance to the data. With the voluminous amount of data collected in some qualitative projects, beginning the analysis during data collection helps to organize the data and make it less overwhelming. Data analysis and the development of possible interpretations should, therefore, begin as soon as possible after data collection.

Another key strategy to emphasize is that interpretations in qualitative projects come from being intimately familiar with the data. Therefore, one of the important tasks the evaluator does is to read the data over and over. The interpretation of meanings is not a task that can be assigned to someone else, like one might hire someone to enter data into a computer or to run the statistics and give the evaluator the printout. Only through interaction with the data will you become familiar enough to see the emerging patterns and themes.

When all data are collected and analyzed, however, you will need to draw conclusions and make recommendations based on your interpretation of the results of the evaluation or research project. During the final stage of data analysis, you will also double-check what data to use to support or exemplify your findings. The data will be used to illustrate how your conclusions were drawn. Two important aspects will be evident in the conclusions. You will be using examples of "emic," noted as ideas expressed by the respondents, as well as "etic," which are data expressed in the evaluator's language. As you begin to do interpretations, you will use quotations called "thick description" (Geertz, 1983), based on both the emic and etic that is uncovered in the analysis. Table 3.7(3) shows an example of a write-up that might be used. You will note that the evaluator made an interpretation and used the respondents' words to illustrate the point.

The evaluator or researcher using qualitative data will actually use quotes and anecdotes to tell the story from the data. These descriptions and quotations are essential and should not be trivial or mundane. You will want to use a balance of description with the analysis and interpretation. The interpretations from qualitative data can be fairly lengthy, but you should try to condense them to hit upon the important points. The summaries that you write let the reader know what happened in the

**Table 3.7(3)** *Sample of a Few Lines of a Qualitative Evaluation Write-Up*

The women with disabilities interviewed in this project defined leisure as free time or having time to do the things they wanted to do. They also talked about "having fun," "relaxing," "doing nothing," and "doing things at your own will and pace" as their definitions of leisure. A general distinction was made between recreation and leisure, as indicated by the 41-year-old married woman with chronic fatigue syndrome:

> To me, recreation is doing something physical. Playing softball with your child or riding a bike or something along that line. And leisure can be just doing something quietly like reading a book or even playing a game, but something that's quiet. So to me that's the difference.

Among the examples of leisure and recreation activities that the women with disabilities said they enjoyed doing were dancing, eating out, shopping, painting pictures, writing poetry, gardening, listening to music, sewing, swimming, photography, walking, church activities, watching TV, and playing games. No single activity or even group of activities was common for all women with disabilities who were interviewed. Overall the women interviewed suggested that solitary and more passive activities were done at home while going into public places to participate in a more active recreation generally required some type of assistance or companionship...

organization, what it was like from the participant's view, and how the events were experienced. The description will depend to a great extent on the criteria being addressed. In making interpretations, however, you must acknowledge that a fine line exists between description and causes. We can describe the causes, but we cannot always say the direct relationship that might exist among variables or themes. The application of this caveat will depend to a great extent on the nature of the data analyzed.

# From Ideas to Reality

This chapter has addressed analysis and interpretation related to using qualitative data for evaluation and research. As indicated throughout this text, however, it is difficult to separate the processes involved with analyzing qualitative data into distinct steps. Thus, we have described data collection, data analysis and drawing interpretations that lead to conclusions/recommendations as going hand in hand. This chapter provides an introduction for working with the qualitative data that you collect. The analysis of qualitative data is quite different than statistical procedures but no less time-consuming or rigorous. You will find that handling qualitative data effectively requires practice. You can learn best by actually working with such data.

Now that you have studied this chapter, you should be able to:
- Describe the options that are available for analyzing qualitative data
- Explain the value of being as familiar as possible with data
- Given a block of qualitative data, analyze it using the enumeration and the grounded comparison techniques

# Unit FOUR—JUDGMENT
***
# *Data Reporting*

## 4.0 Introduction to Judgment

If you don't do anything with the data you collect, then the project was most likely a waste of time. No project is complete until judgments are made, either in the form of conclusions and recommendations for evaluation projects or in the form of conclusions, theory building, and answers to the "so what?" question for research. If you don't make judgments, all your efforts will have been in vain. You lose the opportunity to use the data.

The really intensive workload of evaluation or research is over once you determine your criteria and get evidence through data collection and analysis. But the third part of the trilogy, the judgment phase, is often the real thinking part. You have to try to make sense of the findings that you have analyzed and determine how to use them. By its very definition, evaluation requires that you assess the worth or make judgments. Research requires that you try to find answers. Thus, if you do not make judgments, all your efforts may have little value.

In Unit Four we discuss how to report about your evaluation or research project by developing conclusions and recommendations. We also talk about using visuals to display data and how to write and present evaluation reports and research theses or articles. We focus on the most important part of all research and evaluations—their use. Finally, evaluation systems and projects, as well as research publications, also need to be evaluated. We discuss some of the common problems that occur in conducting projects and how you can do a self-assessment of your own work.

When you have completed this last unit of this textbook, you should be familiar with how evaluation projects and research studies are supposed to work. You will not be an expert, but at least you will have a working knowledge of how to proceed with a project and how to justify the use of evaluations and research.

# 4.1 Using Visuals: A Picture is Worth 1,000 Words

One of the most important steps in the evaluation or research process is to communicate information that you have gathered to people who will use it in decision making or for further research. Sometimes this process is simplified through the visual representation of the data findings in tables and figures. These visuals are usually incorporated into reports and presentations and offer a visual way to organize some of the findings so that judgments (in the form of conclusions and recommendations) can be made.

The old saying "a picture is worth a thousand words" is true, especially when handling complex quantitative data. A good rule of thumb is to use a visual when you find yourself picturing something as you write, or if you have several sets of numbers to compare (Robinson, 1985). You should know not only when to use visuals but the best type to use, such as drawings, charts, tables, graphs, figures, or photos.

When designing effective visuals, consider several general points. The visual should be appropriate to the audience and as simple as possible. No matter how "glitzy" you make your visuals, they will be totally useless unless the reader or audience understands them. Each part of the visual should be clearly labeled and visually pleasing with neat spacing, plenty of white space, and easy-to-read fonts.

Further, the visuals and the text should work together to provide integral documentation and support for the findings you discuss in the narrative part of your report. You should always refer to a table in the appropriate place in the text. For example, if you included a table showing the participation in various recreation centers based on race, you might show this in two ways. You might say, "As can be seen in Table 1, some recreation centers are predominated by a single racial group," or you might say, "Some recreation centers are predominated by a single racial group (see Table 1)." The following sections will address specific information about presenting tables and figures.

## Tables

Tables are the most common form of visual used for showing data. One of the primary advantages to tables is that the "number clutter" in the text can be drastically reduced. For example, instead of reading a tedious list of means used to compare two groups of participants, these data can be displayed in a table. A second advantage is that comparisons are shown more clearly in tables than with words. Tables also allow you to display data in a concise form. Do not include tables, however, if all the information on a table can be more easily included in the narrative. Tables supplement the text, but should not duplicate it.

Always refer to the specific table number in the text and usually place the full table as close as possible after its reference in the text. If the table does not follow immediately after it is referenced, place it as soon as you can on the next full page. Try not to divide a table between two pages unless it is too long. A table that covers more than a page, however, may be better placed in an appendix rather than in the body of the report.

Most publication manuals provide guidelines for the specific information and format of tables. For example, the *Publication Manual of the American Psychological Association (APA)(5th Edition)* (2001) has explicit instructions for authors on the correct format to be used with tables. Several general guidelines for tables should be kept in mind:

1. Put table number (in Arabic numbers) and title at the top of the table.

2. The title should be as descriptive as possible but not overly wordy.

3. Indicate on the table itself (either at the bottom or with the title) the source of the data, if it is not directly from your evaluation or research data.

4. Include units of measure in the headings or entries to avoid confusion.

5. Arrange data that are to be directly compared in vertical columns.

6. Arrange data in logical order, preferably by the most important characteristic.

7. Align on the decimal point columns of numbers representing the same units of measure. Numbers rounded off to the nearest whole or tenth are easier to read than long decimal numbers.

8. If independent/dependent variables are presented, independent variables should be in the row and dependent variables should be in the columns.

9. Use notes in the form of superscript letters if you need to explain anything further. You can put a superscript letter next to a heading and then explain its meaning under the table. Asterisks (*) are usually used on tables to note statistical significance.

10. For tables that have data cases, always include the number of respondents at the bottom of the table by indicating N = (the number).

Programs such as Excel, Microsoft Word, and PowerPoint as well as other software can produce tables for you with the input from the statistical analyses, but all tables should be set up considering these 10 points, regardless of how they are generated.

Tables are usually quantitative but can be used with qualitative data or examples of written material. Sometimes a table with words or phrases can help a reader understand a concept more easily than paragraphs of information can.

Whether qualitative or quantitative data are displayed, you should be able to see the significance of a table at a glance. It is usually best to use lines to separate tables and to separate related information within tables. A number of examples of tables, as well as figures, that follow the APA format can be found throughout this book. An example of a qualitative table is included in Table 4.1(1).

# Figures

Any type of illustration other than a table is usually called a figure. A figure can be a chart, graph, photograph, drawing, or some other graphic depiction. Just as with tables, you must carefully consider how to use a figure. A well-prepared and well-presented figure can show a great deal of information. Figures sometimes take time to produce. However, programs like Excel also allow you to make some figures in the form of different types of graphs.

Like tables, you must make sure that a figure supplements the text and does not simply duplicate it. Further, you need to consider what type of figure ought to be included and how elaborate it ought to be. The figure should convey essential facts and be easily read, easily understood, and carefully prepared. Several guidelines that pertain to tables also pertain to figures:

*Table 4.1(1)*   *Focus Group Themes: Barrriers and Supports to Physical Activity (adapted from Royce, Sharpe, Greaney, Neff, Ainsworth, & Henderson, 2003)*

| Themes | Dimensions | Illustrative Examples & Comments |
|---|---|---|
| What does physical activity mean? | Structured physical activity | • Aerobics, weightlifting, StairMaster, swimming, exercising at the senior center<br>• Mall walking<br>• Basketball, baseball, golfing, softball, volleyball, tennis<br>• Horseback riding<br>• Boating and water skiing<br>• Martial arts<br>• Bicycle riding, hiking, fishing, hunting and processing the game, roller skating, swimming in home pool, line dancing<br>• Go-cart racing |
| | Unstructured physical activity | • "I don't like bending over and touching my toes 20 times. I do not find that fulfilling. But bending over to pull a weed I don't mind doing it. So, I find I have to think of ways, things to do so I will be active, things that are productive."<br>• Vacuuming<br>• Washing windows<br>• Climbing stairs<br>• Mowing and competing with neighbors to see who has the best lawn<br>• Washing the car and restoring autos<br>• Shopping (of all kinds)<br>• Leisurely walking—with dog, to get mail<br>• "Keeping up with the kids and grandkids."<br>• "Playing soccer with my son and taking him to basketball practice. Running back-and-forth for everything from my mother to my husband, son, daughter all day."<br>• Coaching children's athletic teams<br>• Dancing in the living room |
| | Occupational activity | • "Some people get exercise from working in the factories." |

1. Put table number (in Arabic numbers) and title at the top of the figure.

2. Indicate on the figure itself (either at the bottom or with the title) the source of the data, if it is not directly from your research or evaluation data.

3. Use notes in the form of superscript letters if you need to explain anything further about the table. You can put a superscript letter next to a heading and then explain its meaning under the figure.

4. For figures that have data cases, always include the number of respondents at the bottom of the table by indicating N = (the number).

Figures in the form of graphs are a popular way to display visual data. Graphs show data in pictorial form, but also have the advantage of showing relationships. The most commonly used are line graphs, bar graphs (also called column graphs), and pie graphs or charts.

## Line Graphs

Line graphs are the most useful for showing trends in relationships between two variables. Generally the shape of the curve is more important than the precise value of any given point. The following guidelines suggested by Robinson (1985) are useful when constructing line graphs:

1. Label both axes in direction of increase, generally with the independent variable on the horizontal axis and the dependent variable on the vertical axis.

2. Avoid using a legend or key if possible—label the curve directly.

3. Adjust scale for ease of reading. If the graph is too big when zero is used at the intersection of the vertical and horizontal axis, you can use a double slash mark to show how numbers were skipped for a large interval on either of the axes.

4. Make data curves easy to identify.

Figure 4.1(2) shows an example of a basic line graph.

## Bar Graphs

Bar graphs or charts, and a variation called histographs, are used to show quantitative relationships. Technically speaking, if the bars are vertical, they may be called column graphs. If they are horizontal, they are usually called bar graphs. An example of data appropriate for a bar graph would be the number of participants in six different recreation programs in 1 year. Robinson (1985) suggested the following guidelines for bar graphs:

1. Be sure to make it easy to distinguish the bars by using width or shading.

2. Label the graph clearly.

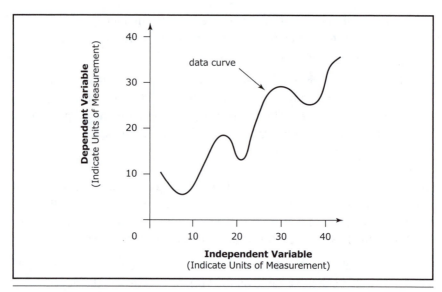

***Figure 4.1(2)*** *Example of a Basic Line Graph*

3. Choose between vertical or horizontal bars logically. For example, use vertical bars for quantities we think of vertically, i.e., temperature) and horizontal bars for ones we think of horizontally (i.e., distance).

Figure 4.1(3) provides an example of a bar graph.

## Pie Graphs

Pie graphs or pie charts are useful for showing the relative proportions to the whole. They are sometimes called 100% graphs because they show how 100% of something is distributed. Expenditures for budgets are often shown pictorially in pie charts. Sometimes the precise quantities are difficult to see when displayed as a pie graph, so it is best to use five or fewer categories. Shading or using color also makes the graphs easier to understand. The following suggestions are useful when constructing pie graphs (Robinson, 1985):

1. Arrange the segments clockwise in order of size with the largest at 12 o'clock.

2. Place labels within the segments if possible.

3. Avoid making the reader rotate the page.

4. Include percentage for each segment, if space permits.

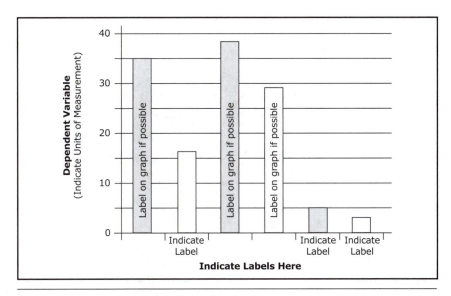

*Figure 4.1(3)*  *Example of a Generic Bar Graph*

Figure 4.1(4) shows an example of a generic pie chart.

## Other Types of Visual Images

Graphs are the major type of figures that you will likely use in your evaluation and research reports, but you might also consider drawings or pictures, depending upon the topic that is addressed. The "rules" for these types of figures are the same as for other figures and tables. They must be necessary, simple, and easy to read. They should be labeled appropriately and should be keyed to the text. All figures should be numbered consecutively. You should also consider how easily drawings and photographs will reproduce if more than one copy of a report is needed.

# From Ideas to Reality

Some people find the development of visual images to be fun to do after the data have been collected and analyzed. Graphics offer an opportunity for the evaluator or researcher to be creative, as many possibilities exist for how to visually portray ideas and data. As people read a report, some will find that the tables and figures are the most interesting part of the report, because they allow the reader to make interpretations about the data. Whatever the case, you should consider the possibility of using tables and

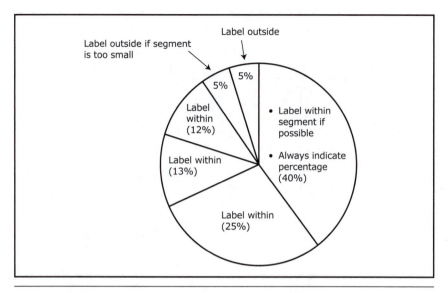

***Figure 4.1(4)*** *Example of a Generic Pie Graph*

figures when they are appropriate in any report. We would emphasize, however, that your tables and figures should always be simple, uncluttered, and easily understood. They can add greatly to the readability of the findings from a project.

Now that you have studied this chapter, you should be able to:
- Explain the differences between different types of visual images
- Prepare an appropriate graphic given data results
- Demonstrate how visual images link to text information

# 4.2 Developing Conclusions and Recommendations: The Grand Finale

Drawing conclusions is an ongoing process throughout an evaluation or research project, but a point comes when the conclusions and recommendations must be finalized and written. For qualitative data, the process of analysis is the process of drawing conclusions. For quantitative data, however, statistics and probabilities are only numbers until the evaluator interprets them in the form of conclusions.

Evaluation does not occur if judgments in the form of conclusions are not made. Similarly, research data are worthless unless they provide conclusions and connections to help understand the body of knowledge better. The evaluator's responsibility is to base judgments on the data that are available. Although some conclusions may result in self-evident recommendations, the effective evaluator will explain the recommendations that evolve from conclusions. Sometimes recommendations are made to keep the program, policy, or whatever is being evaluated the same, while other times they result in specific suggestions about improvement, change, or even termination. In research, recommendations may focus on how the results might apply to practice or how future research should be conducted. Whatever the case, you need to have confidence in what is concluded and offered as recommendations.

How easy or how difficult conclusions and recommendations are to write will depend to a great extent on the type of project and the desires of the stakeholders in the evaluation process. As the amount of data available increases, generally the number of alternatives that can be addressed in conclusions and recommendations also increases. However, the most important guideline to follow in drawing conclusions is to make sure they are consistent with the criteria you set at the beginning. The conclusions should answer your evaluation or research questions. Thus, the criteria established and the evidence collected should result in a framework for developing conclusions and offering the best course of action.

You will need to organize your data to discuss your findings so you can draw conclusions. As noted in the previous chapter, developing visual presentations is a good way to organize data, but you will also need to discuss them in a narrative form in the report. By using the narrative and visuals, you will tell the story about your project. You will report statistics and $p$ values in the findings. You will show qualitative data by actually using quotes and anecdotes to interpret the results. In other words, findings or results are the data summaries portrayed either through narrative and tables/figures if the data are quantitative, or through the summaries of descriptive and quoted material from qualitative data. From the findings, then, it will be necessary to develop the "bottom line," including essentially what the overall conclusions are and what action needs to be taken to address those conclusions.

# Writing Conclusions

Conclusions follow directly from the findings and are used to summarize what has been learned as a result of the project. The conclusions should relate *directly* to the criteria or research questions of the project. In a report, which will be discussed in the next chapter, the conclusions section follows immediately after the findings or results section. No new evidence or findings are presented in the conclusions that have not been presented previously.

Several aspects should be considered when writing conclusions. Some of the important qualities are concision, accuracy, relevancy, and reflection of the purposes and findings. Several key points to keep in mind. First of all, conclusions must be made. Do not leave conclusions up to the reader to interpret. You should not expect the reader to have to make his or her own judgments based on the findings in an evaluation project or research study. Conclusions are an essential part of the evaluation/research process. Involving others in an organization when writing conclusions may be useful so that they understand what the data say and what the results might mean. These individuals may also be helpful in providing additional ways to interpret the data.

Second, present conclusions with the best possible justification for why they were made. Draw conclusions from evidence and make recommendations from conclusions, but do not overextend either. No conclusion should ever exist that does not have explicit data as the basis for it. Although often difficult, try to keep personal biases out of the conclusions. The conclusions should be a summary of what the findings mean that have already been presented.

Finally, keep in mind that conclusions are not difficult to make if the criteria are clear, the evaluation questions are explicitly stated, and the data are reliable and valid. If the study has not been adequately designed, conclusions are difficult to make in actuality and may raise ethical issues.

# Making Recommendations

Recommendations are the proposed courses of action to be followed based on the conclusions. Recommendations in evaluation projects relate to what needs to be done. Recommendations in research project often include how the data might be applied in practice or how the research should be done differently next time. The recommendations and conclusions should be closely linked such that the recommendations appear as an inevitable outcome of the conclusions. They are the finale to the project and follow from the study's findings and conclusions. Many evaluators often stop short of making recommendations, even though the purpose of evaluations is to determine the worth or value of something so that action can be taken. Although the findings should speak for themselves, a good evaluator will need to interpret the data and make specific judgments in the form of recommendations.

Several aspects should be kept in mind when writing recommendations, particularly for an evaluation project. Recommendations must relate directly to the criteria and the conclusions. Don't stray off to tangentially related topics in developing recommendations. You must keep in mind the purpose of the project. Judgments should be made based on the best information available, even though sometimes this information is not perfect. Indeterminacy always exists in any evaluation project, but as the evaluator you simply have to acknowledge anything that might be less than ideal for a given situation. People are continually making judgments anyway, so you might as well state them formally as recommendations so that they are less likely to be misunderstood. Not to make a recommendation or a judgment is to make the suggestion that everything is fine concerning whatever aspect of an organization you're evaluating.

Some people have a hard time differentiating between conclusions and recommendations. Conclusions state an interpretation of the findings, whereas recommendations are specific, tactical proposals for action that eliminate, replace, or augment current actions to steer a program, person, policy, place, or participant into preferred directions. Recommendations may provide examples, call for further evaluation and more information, suggest an allocation of resources, advocate offering the same services to others, propose reordered priorities or changes in policy or program, or may rank program strengths or deficiencies according to their importance or seriousness. As you can see, recommendations may take a number of directions. Table 4.2(1) shows an example of conclusions and recommendations resulting from conducting an evaluation project.

*Table 4.2* *Example of Conclusions and Recommendations (material adapted from a class evaluation report by Lara Pietrafesa, Kim Boyette, and Tonya Bryan)*

This project was an evaluation of satisfaction with the Student Recreation Center Aerobics Program at the University of North Carolina at Chapel Hill. Data were collected using the triangulated methods of questionnaires to participants, interviews with instructors, and observations of randomly selected classes.

**Conclusions:**
1. Participants and instructors were generally satisfied with the aerobics program as indicated by the high marks given to the facilities and equipment.
2. Participants had high satisfaction with the instruction and the total workouts that they were able to achieve.
3. Instructors were satisfied with the management of the classes and the teaching schedules that they were assigned.
4. Concerns were expressed by both participants and instructors concerning the large class sizes, the number of classes offered, and the scheduling of the classes.

**Recommendations:**
1. The Student Recreation Center should continue to maintain the high quality of the facilities and equipment and the communication that exists between management and the instructors.
2. More classes need to be offered at different times during the day. No classes are offered in midafternoon or after 8:30 p.m., so these times might be appropriate to consider as new class times. Offering more classes should cut down on the classes that are presently overcrowded and might make the offerings more convenient to student schedules.

The evaluator, as well as the users or stakeholders, should keep in mind that recommendations are given to guide future directions. They are suggestions based on what the evaluator saw in conducting the evaluation project. The use of recommendations is another issue that must be considered by those who have the power to make changes, and using recommendations will be discussed later in this unit. Not all recommendations can be addressed, but stakeholders should at least know the possibilities for changes that are offered through recommendations.

The evaluator might wish to consider who should be involved in making recommendations. Just as with conclusions, involving others who will be affected by possible recommendations is a good strategy. If you, for example, talk to program staff that may know parts of an organization better yourself, these staff may be most helpful. If staff is involved at every step of the evaluation and especially in drawing up recommendations, then they are more likely to become invested and use evaluation results.

In making recommendations, the evaluator should also consider the organization's willingness/ability to make changes. Recommendations that are impossible to carry out because of insufficient resources may cast doubt on the ability of the evaluator to do his/her job. If you only have hunches about possibilities for changes, make sure you say those ideas are hunches rather than presenting them as specific recommendations.

You could use words such as "The manager might consider developing a written maintenance schedule for the park trails." The bottom line is the recommendations ought to be realistic and practical for implementation possibilities. For research studies, recommendations may be made for practice, but they also may be made regarding further research needed.

The end result is that conclusions and recommendations offer judgments about gathering more data, making a change, raising an issue, leaving things as they are, contributing to the body of knowledge, or a combination of these possibilities. In making recommendations, the evaluator or researcher must have confidence that the evaluation project or research study was well done and that judgments are based on sound data.

# From Ideas to Reality

Writing conclusions and recommendations is the final process in interpreting the data and making judgments about an evaluation or research project. These conclusions and recommendations are usually brief, concise, and to the point. When you have reached the point of writing conclusions and recommendations and are able to address the criteria that you have been using throughout the project, you have reached the "grand finale" of the evaluation. Sometimes conclusions and recommendations are easy to write. Other times you will have to work to figure out what your findings or results mean. If you have done a good job of planning the project and collecting data, the conclusions and recommendations should become obvious once the data are analyzed.

Now that you have studied this chapter, you should be able to:
- Describe the differences between conclusions and recommendations
- Write conclusions and the subsequent recommendations from project findings

## 4.3 Report Writing: Saving a Paper Trail

Every evaluation or research project should result in a written report. The length and nature of the written reports may differ depending on the project, but something should be written even if it is only an executive summary. Research often results in a written document in the form of a thesis and/or a publication in a research journal that might have a broad base of readers.

The report serves as a written record of what you did and what you learned. You may think you will remember the conclusions, but writing ensures that you will have that information available when needed in the future. Without something written, in time you will have difficulty remembering what was done and the recommendations that were made. Usually regular activities like staff evaluations have a summary written that can be placed in an individual's personnel file. The purpose of this chapter is to describe what goes into an evaluation report and to provide a brief summary of how a research publication may be similar or different.

The evaluation report may range from a full report to a "Reader's Digest" condensed version to an executive summary. The report length and type will depend on the agency, the extent of the project, and how the information will be shared. The extent of the report needs to be negotiated between the evaluator and agency at the beginning of the project. Regardless of the extent or nature of the report, as an evaluator you will want to strive for technical detail and excellence. Reports should be comprehensive in addressing your criteria, well-organized, and clearly written. Regardless of the time, financial, and physical resources or constraints, you should not shortcut the preparation of the final written report.

Your report should provide a clear picture of the evaluation process and answer the questions or criteria posed. It should tell who, what, when, why, where, and how, just as your proposal/initial report did when you planned the project. In the final report, however, these responses should be precise and concise. And, of course, the report must contain your judgments in the form of conclusions and recommendations. The formal report consists of several components that will be discussed in detail: cover; executive summary; table of contents; the body of the report that includes introduction, methods, findings, conclusions and recommendations; and appendices.

# Cover

The cover is not necessarily the most important aspect from the evaluator's standpoint, but often it is the first thing that the evaluation report reader will see. If a cover is used, it should be designed with thought because it gives the first impression. It need not be fancy but should include the title of the evaluation project, who was evaluated, names of evaluators, for whom the report was prepared, dates of the evaluation, and date of the report. If a formal cover is not used, this same information should appear at the top of the report.

Depending on the relationship of the evaluator to the agency, the report might be sent under a cover letter or a cover letter might be one of the first pages. The cover letter simply transmits the report from the evaluator to the organization. The cover letter states that the report is completed and offers any other general information that ought to be considered by the agency or the reader in reading and understanding the conclusions and recommendations.

# Executive Summary (Abstract)

Evaluation reports typically include an executive summary, sometimes called simply a summary or an abstract. The summary usually comprises about a page, or less than 500 words, with the most important points of the entire project described. Sometimes the extent of a report *is* the executive summary. Most people will read the executive summary and then decide whether to read the rest of the report. In other cases, the summary may be the only part read, as some people will simply not have time to read an entire report. Nevertheless, you need to include whatever is required by the sponsoring agency so that your executive summary is clearly documented.

The summary almost always appears first, before the main text. It includes a statement of the purpose, how the project was conducted, and the main conclusions and recommendations.

The executive summary is written in nontechnical terms. It is usually written to be accessible to a wide audience. In many cases, the full evaluation report will not be distributed widely within an organization, but the executive summary might be shared with a number of people who can then get the full report if they want further details. In that way, the executive summary should be able to "stand on its own."

Ironically, even though the executive summary goes first, it must be written carefully *after* the rest of the report is completed. Nothing should appear in the executive summary that is not carefully described in the main part of the report. The executive summary is the condensed version of the most important aspects of the report. Table 4.3(1) shows an example of a well-done, short executive summary.

# Table of Contents

Depending on the length of the report, you may or may not need a table of contents. Often this list of topic areas of the evaluation sections is helpful to the reader in finding a particular topic. If a report is presented electronically, the table of contents can be an outline that allows the reader to easily move from section to section.

If subheadings are used, these should be listed in the table of contents and indented appropriately to show the level of the headings. If tables and figures are used, you may want to list the tables and figures by title and page number immediately following the table of contents, as was done for this textbook. Obviously, the table of contents, like the executive summary, cannot be completed until the main body of the report is written, even though it is placed at the beginning of the report.

---

*Table 4.3(1)   Example of an Executive Summary (adapted from the work evaluation project of students Cathy Mitchell, Tonya Sampson, and Charlene Hardin)*

---

The Qualifying Tournament at the University of North Carolina at Chapel Hill (UNC-CH) for the Intramural Big Four Tournament was the focus of this evaluation. The purpose of the evaluation was to improve the qualifying tournament at UNC-CH with a specific focus on determining the reason for low participation and analyzing the currently used methods of advertising. Three methods were used for data collection: captains of teams that participated in the qualifying tournament received a questionnaire during the tournament, captains of regular season teams that did not participate received a telephone interview, and the directors of the intramural programs at the Big Four universities involved (Wake Forest, Duke, North Carolina State University, and University of North Carolina-Chapel Hill) were personally interviewed. Two major conclusions were drawn. First, the majority of regular season captains did not know about the qualifying tournament or they would have considered participating. Second, very little advertising was done at UNC-CH to inform potential participants of the qualifying tournament. The evaluators recommend that the following methods of advertising be considered in the future: use the student newspaper to make announcements, put banners around campus, send flyers to residence halls and fraternities/sororities as well as post them on campus, and set up a table in the "pit" to provide information to interested persons. The evaluators also suggest that the organizers of the Big Four Tournament consider automatically sending regular season champions for each activity to the tournament. In the event that a team or individual cannot attend, then a qualifying tournament should be held.

# Introduction to the Project

The introduction is the first of the four sections that are typically included in the body of an evaluation report. Each of these sections should begin with a brief overview about the project and what will be covered in that section. In any of the sections, subheadings should be used liberally as they help the reader to follow the report. Subheadings, however, are provided for the readers' convenience and should not preclude the writer using transition sentences between subheading topics. In a good report, subheadings should be able to be removed without disrupting the smooth flow of the report.

The introduction to the main report sets the scene and provides a context, tells the purpose of the project evaluation, and describes the characteristics of the agency or the units evaluated. Depending on the criteria, the introduction might refer to an organizational chart to show information about the organization and may explicate the purpose or mission of the organization. Program goals and objectives might be presented, as well as a bit of history if the reader is unfamiliar with the background of an organization or a project.

The introduction also describes the design procedures, including the evaluation model used, the timing, and a justification for why the study was undertaken. You should describe any restrictions that were imposed or encountered in doing the project. Stating the evaluation process briefly and providing a general time line is helpful.

The specific criteria that were examined and the evaluation questions that you addressed are the most important aspects of the introduction. If these questions are made specific at the beginning, the conclusions can be addressed as answers later in the report, and the reader will be able to understand why the project was undertaken.

# Methods Section

The methods section contains details about the procedures used for data collection and analysis, the development or selection of instruments, and the details of sampling including composition, size, and time periods. The methods should relate directly to the criteria identified. The connections between the method(s) chosen and the evaluation questions should be evident. Any examples of questionnaires, checklists, or interview schedules should be put into the appendix with a note in the narrative saying, for example, "In Appendix A is a copy of the questionnaire used."

Any limitations or problems that existed in data collection or analysis should be noted in this methods section. The methods should be specific enough that if someone wanted to do a similar evaluation project, they could read the methods section and be able to replicate the project. They should also be able to see how you dealt with trustworthiness (i.e., reliability and validity) in data collection and analysis. The strengths and weaknesses of methods used should also be justified and noted briefly.

# Findings

The findings section is where the results are presented. In most reports, this section is the longest section. The findings may include qualitative or quantitative analyses. If triangulated methods or data sources are used, all results from the methods or sources should be mentioned in this section.

A description of the respondents usually is presented first in the findings section of a program evaluation, although sometimes this information might be included in the methods section when the sample is described. This demographic information provides the reader with background about who comprised the sample. Organizing this section in relation to the specific criteria or the evaluation questions raised is often useful. In the case of a goal-free evaluation, the findings section should provide a structure for organizing the results that will evolve as data are collected. The use of tables and figures, described in Chapter 4.1, are usually helpful in presenting the findings. In addition, the analysis of patterns, themes, tendencies, trends, and categories should be made clear in this section. All the data should be presented here that are relevant to the project. No additional data findings should be introduced outside of this section.

# Conclusions and Recommendations

The conclusions and the recommendations are the final section of the body of the report and should naturally link to the criteria identified and the findings. The conclusions will show the relationships of the findings to the evaluation criteria. The recommendations address the positive and negative aspects of the findings and propose courses for action. Possible and/or desired recommendations for change or improvement should be stated, along with possible suggestions for future evaluations. A summary of how to write conclusions and recommendations was presented in Chapter 4.2.

# Appendices

The appendices of an evaluation or research report will include any material that is too detailed or technical to be considered in the regular report. Information that might be in the appendices includes: organizational charts, instruments, instructions to subjects, human subject approval forms for research projects, tables of data if too large for the findings section, and copies of correspondence. Few people ever read appendices, but they will look at them if any questions arise, so this information needs to be included.

Sometimes additional information is included in an appendix, such as the cost of a project or a detailed summary of evaluation procedures. Do not, however, include anything in the appendices that has not been referred to in the text. The text should indicate why and where each appendix exists. Similarly, the appendices should be given page numbers and labeled with A, B, C, and so on to enable the reader to find them easily and reduce potential confusion with the Arabic numbering of tables and figures.

Table 4.3(2) gives a summary outline of the order that information should appear in an evaluation report.

# General Observations about Evaluation Report Writing

The evaluation project report should be readable and free of academic jargon. You may know a lot about evaluation, methods, and statistics, but your audience may not. Therefore, you should make the evaluation report as simple and as straightforward as possible, with simple explanations if they are needed. The data in an evaluation project should do the impressing, not a fancy writing style. Don't write to impress, write to communicate. Further, the report should show what occurred in the project in a straightforward way.

People write in different ways. Some people find using a detailed outline to be helpful. Others like to start with lead sentences or develop tables and figures first. Some people like to write the findings first and then fill in the other parts of the report. It doesn't matter where you start writing a report. You just have to end up with a final product that tells the evaluation story.

For some people, writing the report is a delightful experience once all the other hard work of data collection, analysis, and interpretation is done. Other people will struggle with writing. As stated before, the better the criteria and data collection and analysis, the easier the report should

*Table 4.3(2) Outline for a Written Report*

```
                        Cover
                        Cover Letter (optional)
                        Executive Summary
                        Table of Contents including Appendices
                        List of Figures/Tables (optional)
                        Introduction
                            Purpose
                            Setting
                            Models/Design/Theoretical Framework
                            Criteria Measured
                        Methods
                            Procedure
                            Sampling
                            Statistics or Analysis Used
                        Findings
                            Results of Analysis
                            Tables and Figures
                        Conclusions
                        Recommendations
                        Appendices
```

be to write. Writing, however, requires a fair amount of effort. You will likely have to write several drafts before the report is complete. Some people find it helpful to write for a while and then set the report aside and come back to it in a day or two with fresh eyes. Writing is a personal experience, so you have to decide what is best for you. Be sure, however, to give yourself adequate time to write the report, as it is not easy to organize and complete at the last minute. You will also need adequate time to proofread your report and double-check to make sure your executive summary is consistent with other elements of the report.

Keep in mind that you can't include everything in the evaluation report. You will have to think carefully about what to address and what data you will supply. A fine line exists between too little and too much data in an evaluation report, but you will need to try to find that compromise. Having others in an organization look at the report before it is finalized to get their reactions to the information that is included may be useful. It is paramount, however, to keep your criteria in front of you as you write so you don't go into any unnecessary tangents.

Sometimes rather than writing a full report, you may want to use a summary sheet for a particular project. The executive summary may be a basis for this summary, but you may want to go into a bit more detail concerning the conclusions that you draw.

If a short summary is used instead of a full report, it should include: name of activity/event, place of activity/event, participants (characteristics and number), strengths of program, weaknesses of program, and recommended changes. A series of these short reports would provide a good paper trail that may help in planning future evaluation projects.

Describing how to write a research report or thesis in detail is beyond the scope of this book. Your university will have specific guidelines for writing an honors thesis or a Master's thesis. Guidelines for particular journals are usually included in those journals or are available from the journal's website. A research article includes the same four dimensions of the evaluation report—introduction, methods, findings, and conclusions. In addition, it includes a literature review and a section at the end that describes the recommendations for application of the conclusions and recommendations for theory and for future research. The other "rules" for good writing generally apply to writing research articles for publication, although these articles may be more detailed than most evaluation reports. The focus on the connections between theory as criteria for research, the data collection and analysis, and the results and conclusions are similar regardless of whether an evaluation or research project is undertaken.

## From Ideas to Reality

The final report is the composite of all your work on an evaluation or research project. You will want to make it readable and usable. As outlined in this chapter, an evaluation report should contain several standard components, but you can be creative within that report as long as the information is communicated clearly. In writing a research article, the writing style and organization should fit the guidelines of the journal where the article will be sent. Before any project is begun, determine what the final report will resemble and then work on the components of the report as you move along. Writing the evaluation report or research article can be exciting and fun because it is the tangible evidence of all the hard work that you have done on a project.

Now that you have studied this chapter, you should be able to:
- Outline the components that comprise an evaluation report or a research article
- Given a report, write an executive summary from the report
- Assemble a report or article as a result of having developed criteria, collected data, and interpreted the findings

## 4.4 Oral Presentations: Telling the Tale

Along with a written report for an evaluation project or for a thesis or published article, often an oral report or presentation is also given. In the long run, the oral report may be the most effective way to get the information to people. Many people will not take the time to read an entire written report but they will listen to a presentation. The same principles that apply to any good evaluation oral report also apply to a research presentation.

The oral report will vary greatly and may be long or short, formal or informal, and addressed to technical or general audiences. The same principles of the written report also mirror an oral presentation regarding the format. A written or oral report will have an introduction, methods, findings, and conclusions and recommendations sections. Many times in an oral report, however, you will not have much time, so you must be selective with the material that you present.

Several basic principles should govern any type of oral presentation:
- Present your material in terms of your purpose and audience
- Make important points stand out
- State the points as simply as you can

As you begin to develop the oral presentation you will need to ask questions. What sort of people will make up the audience? What will be their primary concerns? Should you focus on the whole project or just a portion of it? Keep in mind that for most people, listening carefully is harder than reading carefully. As a listener, if you miss a point in a speech, you can't go back to it as you could if you were reading. Therefore, as a speaker you must be careful to grab and hold the audience. You must try to make the report interesting and easy to follow.

In writing a report, you can write an executive summary for the nontechnical audience. In a speech, however, you can't give a two-part speech and ask some people not to listen to portions of the presentation. Thus, you have to carefully consider what you will discuss and keep the presentation at the general audience level. You have to figure out the target audience and write the presentation aimed at them. How much do they know now? How technically sophisticated are they about the content of the evaluation as well as evaluation procedures? What will they do with the information given to them?

Most speeches either inform or persuade. In an evaluation report, you are presenting a summary with recommendations so you are attempting to both inform and persuade. You are, in a sense, selling your ideas. You want to present the material carefully, honestly, and as truthfully as you analyzed it. If you believe in the trustworthiness of your evaluation project, it will be difficult to present the material in any other way.

## Planning the Oral Presentation

Knowing whether the audience will have the report in front of them or whether they will have read it previously is important. Think about what two or three questions would be uppermost in their minds. What do they most want to know? From this information, you can begin to prepare the presentation by writing an outline. Like the written report, an oral report is a matter of selecting and organizing information on the basis of the purpose of the project and your analysis of the audience. Keep in mind that you have to think of your time limits. The presentation speech needs to have a beginning, middle, and end. In the presentation, you should always tell the audience what you are going to tell them, tell them, and then tell them what you told them.

Time limits are important. For every minute a speaker runs over her/his allotted time, the more hostile an audience can get. People talk too long for two reasons: they haven't planned their presentation, and/or they haven't practiced and don't realize how long it takes to cover a point. Good organization is more important in an oral report than a written one. You will not be able to cover everything. Plan the presentation, however, so you can shorten it if needed, or go into more detail if time allows. Usually a question time accompanies the presentation so people can ask for clarification or expansion of points if you do not cover something in detail that interested them.

You will also need to choose a mode of delivery. Speaking from memory is not recommended. Speaking word for word from the actual written report can result in not talking to the audience. Speaking from notes is the best way to assure a conversation with the audience. Also, always keep in mind that your audience is listening as well as possibly reading a PowerPoint presentation.

The introduction, which includes your purpose and process (methods), sets the stage. Most audiences will listen carefully for 60 seconds at the beginning of a talk. They then decide what to do next. If the topic and/or presentation are interesting, they will continue to "tune in." The bottom line is that you have to get their attention and then keep it.

The body has the substance of your talk and usually includes a brief description of the procedures used and some of the major evaluation findings. The conclusion of the presentation will include your conclusions and recommendations or "calls for action."

In making the oral presentation, keep it simple. Concentrate on the overall picture and stick to the basics. Just as you would use subheadings, use verbal cues to make clear to the audience the pattern of what you say. Use words like "for example" and highlight your conclusions and/or recommendations with numbers like first, second, third. It is usually best to limit the use of math and numbers in a speech or else explain what it is you are doing. Visual aids such as slides and PowerPoints can also help you get your message across, but present those visuals in a clear, simple way.

## Using Visual Aids

Think about how visual aids might be helpful. In a short presentation, however, don't try to use too many slides. For 10 minutes about 10 visual aids would be enough. A rule of thumb is usually one slide per minute of talking. Make sure the audience can easily see the aids. If your presentation is less than 10 minutes, your time may be better spent in talking than showing visuals, although a handout with the main points is usually helpful.

You may want to use flip charts which are portable, require no special equipment, do not require a dark room, and allow for spontaneity. Flip charts, however, are usually not good for large audiences because they cannot be seen easily in the back of a room.

PowerPoint presentations are commonly used and are effective with large or small audiences. Slides in the form of PowerPoint presentations are portable, versatile, and can include photos, graphs, and/or charts. Slides, however, take advanced preparation, require a slightly darkened room, and can provide a distraction if they are too elaborate. Moreover, they are easy to abuse and must be simple with *big* print. The use of too many "bells and whistles," while entertaining, can detract from the important content of your presentation. You must remember to coordinate your visuals with your speech.

Handouts are useful for detailed or complex material, especially statistical examples. They can also be used to cover content you may not be able to get across in a speech or that you wish the audience to carry away with them. Only pass out handouts ahead of time that you are going to use in your speech; otherwise the audience will read them instead of listening to you. If handouts are a backup, give them out at the end of the presentation. Differentiate handouts with different colors of paper if you have several for people to examine during your presentation.

Props can be effective attention-getters, but they must be large enough to be seen by the whole audience. Passing an item around is not a good substitute for a large prop.

The bottom line is to make visual aids big, simple, and clear so their meaning can be grasped quickly. When people are looking at the visual aid, they are not listening to you. Try to keep distraction of visual aids to a minimum by practicing with the aids. Practice using them when practicing your speech. Try to get the audience to shift its attention naturally. Be sure the audience can see the aids. Point to and emphasize major aspects on the screen.

## Giving the Presentation

The delivery of an oral presentation takes practice. Do not expect to do it perfectly the first time. Learn from your mistakes. With competence comes a feeling of being in control of the situation. When you feel in control, you will feel more comfortable in the situation. Practice ahead of time, preferably to someone else, but at least practice out loud. Evaluate the presentation and work to improve it. Don't practice until the speech sounds canned, but do go over it two or three times.

When giving the actual presentation, dress appropriately for the setting. Avoid anything flamboyant or extreme that would detract your audience's attention. The four most common voice errors made are talking too softly, too fast, without expression, or using vocalized pauses (e.g., "uh," "ok," "now," "you know," "I mean"). Practice avoiding these errors. Also, use your eyes to connect with the audience—their body language will tell you how the presentation is going. Maintaining frequent eye contact is essential to a good speech.

Ninety percent of the audience's perception of how good your presentation is will be determined by the attitude you project. You need to project an attitude of competence and confidence. Remember that you are the expert on this topic. Show enthusiasm for the evaluation project. Treat the audience with respect and courtesy, and they will respond in kind. Watch your time limits. Use a watch.

After a presentation, time is usually allowed for questions. In answering questions, repeat the question so all can hear, especially if you are in a large room. This repeating of the question will also give you a moment to gather your thoughts and make sure that you understand what the questioner is asking. If you don't know the answer, say so. Unexpected questions often offer interesting perspectives. Don't get into a long discussion or argument with one member of the audience. Other people will get bored. Invite that person to talk further with you afterward.

Presenting an oral report after completing a project is the frosting on the cake. After all the work you have done, you will want to share your results with an audience who is interested. It will be up to you, however, to make sure that your presentation is as interesting as your project conclusions.

# From Ideas to Reality

It isn't possible to include a videotape along with this book to show an example of a good presentation, but most of us have had numerous experiences with listening to presentations. The advice suggested in this chapter should be useful to consider, but it is also important to draw on our own personal experience about what you have liked and not liked about other presentations. You can learn a great deal by observing others and adopting the strengths of their modes of communication. The prerequisite for a good presentation, however, will always be having something important to say, which is a result of all the hard work that was put into developing the criteria, evidence, and judgment for an evaluation or research project.

Now that you have studied this chapter, you should be able to:
- Give a presentation that describes the results of an evaluation project
- Evaluate another presentation in terms of its strengths and weaknesses
- Choose visuals that will be appropriate for the presentation that you are giving

# 4.5  Evaluating Projects and Studies: Pitfalls and Problems

The process of evaluating anything is a continuous one. As we noted early in this book, intuitive evaluation is almost always happening in people's lives. However, as goofy as it might sound, we also need to evaluate our own evaluation and research efforts. If things don't go as planned, the information obtained may be helpful to avoid future mistakes and to improve skills. Even if you feel the project was successful, it is often useful to pause to reflect at least intuitively, if not systematically, on what went well.

Now that the major topics related to criteria, data (evidence), and judgment regarding evaluation and research projects have been covered, a few words of summary about how to evaluate systems, individual evaluation projects, and research may be appropriate. For any undertaking, a professional should always consider what was done well and what could have been improved. In this next to last chapter, we offer some notes on what to consider in evaluating evaluation and research, whether it is your own or someone else's. We will also identify several common pitfalls that can get in the way of doing evaluation. This summary will likely sound familiar as most of these points have been addressed elsewhere in the text, but we would like to try to pull together the underlying themes one last time.

## The Process of Evaluation and Research

Evaluating or researching anything is not easy, especially when it is approached in a formal, systematic way. You must be confident, first of all, that an evaluation system or project can make a difference in an organization and that research can contribute to the body of knowledge. Some people refer to this as the "so what?" question. Further, you have to recognize that some people are fearful of evaluations, so you must make sure that receptivity to what you are doing exists. Some people are afraid of criticism, and evaluation has the potential for offering criticism, but hopefully it can be offered in a constructive way. Some people have little faith in evaluations, because they have been through them before and they did little good or the recommendations were never carried out.

Political pressures also exist. Fears and biases can affect any project and the evaluator ought to know that they may exist. You should make sure that you are in agreement with the stakeholders and decision makers about what is to be evaluated. For example, if the Park and Recreation

Commission thinks that the entire youth sports program ought to be evaluated, but as Athletic Director you think only the youth basketball program needs to be examined, you will have to do some negotiation concerning what the evaluation will entail. If you are not aware of the political pressures, you may become discouraged during the course of the evaluation process. Further, research can also be political, so some of these same concerns may be raised. All of these concerns need to be taken into account in undertaking a project and evaluating its success.

An evaluator or researcher needs to go into an evaluation or research project with all good intentions and an open mind. Each undertaking will be different, so you can't use the same old method or instrument in every case. Organizations that have good objectives or standards to follow will likely be able to do evaluations easier than those organizations that do not. Where objectives do not exist, you will have to write your own or rely on other models. Evaluators as well as researchers will also need to work with the resource and time constraints that are often built into projects. Sometimes nothing can be done about time and money constraints, but in some cases doing *no* evaluation is better than doing one that is poorly designed or that collects data that are too limited or even the wrong data. Even though determining criteria, using models, and determining types of data are not always exciting, these design steps are crucial in setting up a good project.

For a project or study to be successful, you must select good methods and measurement tools. Measuring some criteria can be difficult. You must be aware of this possibility in undertaking a project and not promise more than you can deliver. In some areas of leisure services, no assessment tools have been created yet. You may need to develop instruments to address the criteria for particular projects. Developing instruments is not a bad situation, but it will take an additional amount of effort. A lack of standardized instruments exists in the field of recreation services because most professionals have not been particularly oriented toward measurement and statistics. We do not suggest that you have to use sophisticated statistics in evaluation projects, but you do need to know what statistics are appropriate, given particular situations, and how to be sure that instruments are reliable and valid. If you want to know, for example, whether differences exist between girls and boys in your program, you need to be able to make those conclusions based on the use of inferential statistics.

# Gremlins to Avoid

In conducting any project, potential problems will always exist. Table 4.5(1) provides some guidelines to assist in developing evaluation systems as well as individual evaluation and research projects. You should also be aware of some of the downfalls or gremlins that commonly occur in doing any type of systematic inquiry:

- Make sure you have the skills and knowledge necessary to do the type of project needed or research desired. If not, get help or get someone else to do the evaluation.
- Be clear about the purpose of the project. Make sure stakeholders are also clear about those purposes as well.
- From an administrative point of view, make sure the expense of a project in terms of time and effort is comparable to the value received from doing the inquiry. This cost-benefit may be difficult to measure, but the concept should be kept in mind.
- For an evaluation system in an organization, consider how both internal and external evaluators can be used from time to time.

*Table 4.5*  *Guidelines for Evaluation Systems, Evaluation Projects, and Research*

| Type | Guidelines |
|---|---|
| Evaluation Systems | • Make data appropriate to criteria<br>• Rebut evaluation fears<br>• Get receptivity within the organization<br>• Use both external and internal evaluators<br>• Institute a systematic process<br>• Be aware of political pressures<br>• Counter possible measurement problems |
| Evaluation Projects | • Conclusions and recommendations should reflect data<br>• Determine evaluation criteria carefully<br>• Checking trustworthiness of instruments<br>• Collect data carefully<br>• Have a clear evaluation purpose<br>• Develop the necessary competencies to be an evaluator<br>• Write a clear, concise evaluation report<br>• Make the evaluation project timely and on time<br>• Use sound instrument design<br>• Select an appropriate sample<br>• Use statistics and data analysis properly |
| Research Studies | • Use sound theory<br>• Thoroughly review the literature<br>• Make research questions or hypothesis clear<br>• Collect and analyze data carefully and appropriately<br>• Tie the theory to data findings<br>• Determine the "so what?" of the study<br>• Provide recommendations for application and future research |

Using only one or the other has some drawbacks. In setting up a system, consider how you might use both.

- Remember that evaluation does not only occur at the end of something (summative) but may occur as an assessment or as a formative evaluation.
- Try not to allow bias, prejudice, preconceived perceptions, or friendship to influence the evaluation or research outcomes. Further, do not let the whims of the administration prevent you from doing the type of project that you think needs to be done.
- Make sure you go into an evaluation understanding thoroughly the organization and its limitations. This suggestion may pertain more if you are an external evaluator, but it should be considered in all situations and contexts.
- Select and use evaluation research methods and measurement instruments that are specifically related to the criteria. To avoid this gremlin, you must spend time at the beginning of a project carefully planning what you will do.
- In conducting projects, think about the logical timing of the project. Keep in mind when it can best be done within an agency and when people involved are most likely to be receptive to data collection as well as the reporting of conclusions and recommendations.
- Continually think about how the criteria, evidence, and judgment phases of the project fit together. Each succeeding component should be a natural outgrowth of what has gone before.
- Collect data carefully. Careless collection of data results when the wrong instrument and poorly written questions that are inappropriate to respondents are used.
- Although much has already been covered about instrument design, keep in mind that a well-written instrument is necessary to avoid pitfalls related to reliability and validity. In addition, consider the reading level of a questionnaire, so you do not bias the sample toward higher educated groups.
- When doing any evaluation or research using quantitative data, keep in mind issues related to randomization, maturation, and history.
- Consider sample selection carefully so that you are not biased. In addition, think carefully how you will motivate people to participate. Before you begin to collect data, think about the size of the sample, its representativeness, and the desired response rate.

- When doing projects be aware of the possibility of the Hawthorne effect, whereby people will act differently just because you are paying attention to them.
- Data analysis should be considered before a project is begun. The statistics or qualitative analysis to be used need to be determined early on.
- In using statistics where you will address statistical significance, you must be able to determine how much difference makes a difference. Small differences may be statistically significant with a large population but they may not mean anything. As an evaluator or researcher, you must be able to decide what the statistics mean.
- Make conclusions and recommendations based only on the data that you collect from the project. Do not claim more than you have evidence to support.
- Make sure you address all the results from an evaluation, not just those aspects that are positive. You may have to handle negative results carefully, but you also may have an ethical responsibility to make sure they are addressed. Be careful that you don't discount any findings.
- Be open to finding unexpected results as you conduct a project. The real value of some evaluation and research projects is what you learn that you didn't expect.
- Write a concise, complete, well-planned evaluation report. Unless you are able to communicate the results of a study, the evaluation itself will do little good. This report also requires that you write specific recommendations.
- Get results disseminated as soon as possible after an evaluation project is completed. Nothing kills the enthusiasm for an evaluation like having it drag on for months or even years.

## Thoughts about Research Projects

Most of the principles noted apply to both research and evaluation projects. The audience for research studies is often broader than for evaluation projects. Further, other researchers often are most interested in the body of knowledge, although practitioners certainly will be interested in applied research as well.

When a research study is submitted to publication, it is sometimes sent to a "juried" journal. To be juried means that peers (i.e., usually other researchers) review the work and comment about its relevance, rigor, and presentation style. Different journals will have different guidelines, but generally the evaluation criteria for such articles include significance, contribution, content, rigor, and writing style. The paper must make a contribution to the literature and the development of a body of knowledge. The data must be collected and analyzed appropriately so the reader sees the trustworthiness of what she or he reads. In addition, the paper needs to be written in a manner that is understandable and in conformity with the publication's guidelines (e.g., American Psychological Association; APA). A researcher writing the results for publication in a juried journal should read the guidelines of the journal and follow them carefully. Some topics are better suited for some journals than others.

Articles for publications are generally submitted to an editor, often electronically, with several copies included. The editor may send the paper to an associate editor, who has expertise in the topic of the article. This associate editor will generally ask one to three other individuals to review the paper and make an evaluation. This process may take two to three months. A decision to accept, accept with minor revisions, resubmit with major revisions, or reject is generally made. Writers are encouraged to resubmit if that is an option, paying close attention to the recommendations that are made. A recreation professional's obligation is to make sure that she or he contributes to the body of knowledge and this contribution is best done through good research and efforts to get that research published.

# From Ideas to Reality

Problems and pitfalls will occur in all projects and studies, but they are worth considering as you embark on doing projects that are usable and that will result in enlightened decision making. Successful evaluation and research projects will require careful planning and hard work, but the rewards and benefits will be there for those professionals who understand the value of evaluation and research in all areas of leisure services. Many topics reviewed in this chapter have been covered in more detail elsewhere in this textbook. Evaluation and research skills require a lifetime to learn. As authors of this book, we have conducted many evaluation and research projects. Each time we learn something new. Sometimes we learn from our mistakes, and sometimes we learn because something worked really well. Evaluation and research are always challenging, and that is what makes them interesting and useful.

Now that you have studied this chapter, you should be able to:
- Summarize how to avoid problems in conducting an evaluation or research project
- Evaluate your own studies as well as those of others to make sure they are trustworthy

## 4.6 Using Evaluations and Research for Decision Making: The Beginning

The best evaluation or research criteria and data collection will be useless unless the conclusions and recommendations are applied in some way for decision making or to contribute to the body of knowledge. When a project comes to an end, it really marks the beginning of making decisions and of conducting future studies. The purpose of any evaluation research is to get information for action. Depending whether you are an internal or external evaluator, you may have a different stake in what action occurs. Nevertheless, if an evaluation is to be done as more than just an application of research methods, it needs to be used. You can use several strategies to make sure that the evaluation or research is used.

These strategies are not just done at the end of the project but must be considered throughout the project and after it is over. When offering suggestions for changes in an organization, those people (staff or participants) directly affected by the changes should be consulted and should be involved in making recommendations. This involvement is not always possible but should be considered.

The recommendations you propose are a starting point for action. This action can be applied to any of the five Ps. You can always suggest several types of actions: evaluate more, change something, take no further action, or terminate something. An agency also has the prerogative to ignore the recommendations, but hopefully this does not occur unless the benefits and consequences of the recommendations have been carefully considered. For any evaluation project, the potential exists for implementing findings, considering the findings for implementation, implementing changes, or accepting the findings but taking no action. You might ask if an evaluation project is successful if recommendations are:

- Implemented in total?
- Implemented in part?
- Considered but rejected?
- Not implemented but other changes made?
- Not implemented but other nonrelated changes made?
- Not implemented, no changes made?
- Not implemented and evaluation findings challenged or rejected?

No specific answers exist to these questions, but an evaluator must consider what they imply. According to Farrell & Lundegren (1987), evaluators may experience some resistance to recommendations if the organization is more fixated on survival rather than change. Some organizations don't want to rock the boat, have hidden political issues, ingrained staff conventions, and/or staff with inadequate skills and competencies to make necessary changes. You can do little about some of these factors, except know that they exist and try to design the evaluation project keeping those considerations in mind.

In general, a successful evaluation or research project might be defined in many ways. Utilization might be defined as serious consideration of the results in making decisions, whether the actual recommendations are actually instituted or whether future researchers follow your suggestions. Utilization also occurs when the results are actually applied to a situation or to previous literature. When you have spent much time and effort working on an evaluation project, you would hope that at least some of your recommendations are used and/or implemented.

## Conducting Projects to Influence Their Use

Theobald (1979) noted many years ago (but it is still true today) that evaluations run two major risks: (1) a technical failure in research design, and (2) political barriers in terms of how a study will be received. This textbook has been about designing technically appropriate and trustworthy projects. Sometimes recommendations are not used because the project is done poorly or in a mediocre fashion and the findings do not seem trustworthy.

Potential political barriers may be more difficult to address. Potential users of evaluations should be identified early and you should find out what they want to get from a project. Administrators need to be informed and involved in the process because these individuals generally will be responsible for providing resources for implementing the recommendations. The prompt completion and early release of results is often another way to encourage use.

As an evaluator or researcher you should *not* undertake a project if you are sure the results will have no effect on decisions, if the results will not contribute to the body of knowledge, or if you believe an organization is not interested in change. Don't undertake any project unless a high probability of producing valid, precise, and applicable information exists and the results can be made conceptually clear to program administrators, managers, other researchers, students, or practitioners. Otherwise, a project is a waste of time and resources.

Although writing reports has already been discussed at length, the use of any study may be dependent on how a report is written and presented. Effective methods of presentation of findings and dissemination of information using clarity and attractiveness, spelled-out recommendations, summary sheets, and addressing advocates of the recommendations will be essential if evaluations are to be used. The report, however, can be written in a variety of styles depending on the audience. Sometimes your audience, for example, will understand the common jargon you use. Other times they may not. Jargon free studies are usually easiest to read, as are studies that use an active voice. "We suggest" rather than "it is suggested" or "we found positive results" rather than "there were positive results" are examples of using an active voice and writing more concisely.

# Encouraging Evaluation Use

Once a project is completed and reported, several plans might be offered to communicate the recommendations both inside and outside the organization. First, it may help to call a staff meeting and discuss the recommendations and their implications. Meeting with individual staff to discuss the results may also be useful and appropriate.

Second, participants might be consulted. Sometimes the program participants can make sure that their recommendations are considered, as can colleagues and co-workers who understand the importance of conducting the evaluation.

Third, the organization's decision makers will need to reevaluate their goals and objectives to see if they are realistic in light of the evaluation recommendations. The Board of Directors or a Parks and Recreation Commission may be the appropriate people to involve. Once possible recommendations to address are determined, then a list of priorities must be set and a timeline for making changes developed. Often more recommendations are made than can be handled at any one time. Some of the less expensive and complex items can be addressed immediately, while others may take more planning. Budgets and other resources may also need to be tied to the plans.

Fourth, the evaluator must not expect that all recommendations for change can be made. Sometimes it is a matter of priority or identifying the relative importance of different recommendations. Time lag may also result with recommendations. Some recommendations take a few weeks or months to implement while others may take years. Sometimes you must impress upon people the value of moving slowly toward some kinds of change. Further, sometimes the recommendations may result in greater change or more changes than an organization actually wants. Thus, in making recommendations that have the potential to be used, the evaluator may find it is better when only moderate changes are suggested and only a few important suggestions are made rather than extensive recommendations.

Fifth, keep in mind that in some situations, the conclusions from a project may be negative. It is important to carefully consider what negative evaluations or results mean. One of the problems with some evaluation methods, like experiments, is they don't tell why something happened. The evaluator must carefully examine what results mean before offering recommendations about a program. The same is true with evaluations that show no difference occurred or show mixed results. As was discussed earlier, no difference may not be sufficient reason to eliminate a program, but it may mean that the recommendation is for further evaluation or research using a different method. If the results of a project are unclear, you may want to do further work.

Finally, additional suggestions to encourage the implementation of evaluation recommendations include encouraging positive attitudes about evaluations in staff and decision makers. The focus of evaluations should be on what they tell us that can improve the delivery of recreation services, rather than just a summary of good news or bad news. Evaluators will need to help people see the connections between findings of evaluations and what is going on in an organization. Helping staff and decision makers develop positive attitudes about evaluation and research, however, should not occur only at the end of the project, but throughout the design, data collection, and judgment phases.

# From Ideas to Reality

The most likely way that results will be used is if a trustworthy evaluation or research project has been undertaken and if you have drawn specific conclusions and recommendations that can be feasibly considered or implemented. Evaluation and research projects are sometimes not used when people are afraid to go out on a limb and draw conclusions or make recommendations. In this case, a gap exists between findings and clear courses for future action. The implications of making changes, particularly within organizations, however, are not always obvious. If the evaluator or researcher does not make judgments in the form of conclusions and recommendations, decision makers in agencies may not realize the ways that systematic inquiry can help them improve. We have offered a number of ways to think about how evaluations can be used, but we must emphasize that facilitating use is a process that has its origins when a project is

# Appendix A

## Table of Random Numbers

| | | | | | | | | | | | |
|---|---|---|---|---|---|---|---|---|---|---|---|
| 10480 | 15011 | 01536 | 02011 | 81647 | 91646 | 69179 | 14194 | 62590 | 36207 | 20969 | 99570 | 91292 | 90700 |
| 22368 | 46573 | 25595 | 58393 | 30995 | 89198 | 27982 | 53402 | 93965 | 34095 | 52666 | 19174 | 39615 | 99505 |
| 24130 | 48360 | 22527 | 97265 | 76393 | 64809 | 15179 | 24830 | 49340 | 32081 | 30680 | 19655 | 63348 | 58629 |
| 42167 | 93093 | 06243 | 61680 | 07853 | 16376 | 39440 | 53537 | 71341 | 57004 | 00849 | 74917 | 97758 | 16379 |
| 37570 | 39975 | 18137 | 16656 | 06121 | 91782 | 60468 | 81305 | 49684 | 60672 | 14110 | 06927 | 01263 | 54613 |

| 77921 | 06907 | 11008 | 42751 | 27756 | 53498 | 18602 | 70659 | 90655 | 15053 | 21916 | 81825 | 44394 | 42880 |
| 99562 | 72905 | 56420 | 69994 | 98872 | 31016 | 71194 | 18738 | 44013 | 48840 | 63213 | 21069 | 10634 | 12952 |
| 96301 | 91977 | 05463 | 07972 | 18876 | 20922 | 94595 | 56869 | 69014 | 60045 | 18425 | 84903 | 42508 | 32307 |
| 89579 | 14342 | 63661 | 10281 | 17453 | 18103 | 57740 | 84378 | 25331 | 12566 | 58678 | 44947 | 05585 | 56941 |
| 85475 | 36857 | 53342 | 53988 | 53060 | 59533 | 38867 | 62300 | 08158 | 17983 | 16439 | 11458 | 18593 | 64952 |

| 28918 | 69578 | 88231 | 33276 | 70997 | 79936 | 56865 | 05859 | 90106 | 31595 | 01547 | 85590 | 91610 | 78188 |
| 63553 | 40961 | 48265 | 03427 | 49626 | 69445 | 18663 | 72695 | 52180 | 20847 | 12234 | 90511 | 33703 | 90322 |
| 09429 | 93969 | 52636 | 92737 | 88974 | 33488 | 36320 | 17617 | 30015 | 08272 | 84115 | 27156 | 30613 | 74952 |
| 10365 | 61129 | 87529 | 85689 | 48237 | 52267 | 67689 | 93394 | 01511 | 26358 | 85104 | 20285 | 29975 | 89868 |
| 07119 | 97336 | 71048 | 08178 | 77233 | 13916 | 47564 | 81056 | 97735 | 85977 | 29372 | 74461 | 28551 | 90707 |

| 51085 | 12765 | 51821 | 51259 | 77452 | 16308 | 60756 | 92144 | 49442 | 53900 | 70960 | 63990 | 75601 | 40719 |
| 02368 | 21382 | 52404 | 60268 | 89398 | 19885 | 55322 | 44819 | 01188 | 65255 | 64835 | 44919 | 05944 | 55157 |
| 01011 | 54092 | 33362 | 94904 | 31273 | 04146 | 18594 | 29852 | 71585 | 85030 | 51132 | 01915 | 92747 | 64951 |
| 52162 | 53916 | 46369 | 58586 | 23216 | 14513 | 83149 | 98736 | 23495 | 63250 | 93738 | 17752 | 35156 | 35749 |
| 07056 | 97628 | 33787 | 09998 | 42698 | 06691 | 76988 | 13602 | 51851 | 46104 | 89916 | 19509 | 25625 | 58104 |

| 48663 | 91245 | 85828 | 14346 | 09172 | 30168 | 90229 | 04734 | 59193 | 22178 | 30421 | 61666 | 99904 | 32812 |
| 54164 | 58492 | 22421 | 74103 | 47070 | 25306 | 76468 | 26384 | 58151 | 06646 | 21524 | 15227 | 96909 | 44592 |
| 32639 | 32363 | 05597 | 24200 | 13363 | 38005 | 94342 | 28728 | 35806 | 06912 | 17012 | 64161 | 18296 | 22851 |
| 29334 | 27001 | 87637 | 87308 | 58731 | 00256 | 45834 | 15398 | 46557 | 41135 | 10367 | 07684 | 36188 | 18510 |
| 02488 | 33062 | 28834 | 07351 | 19731 | 92420 | 60952 | 61280 | 50001 | 67658 | 32586 | 86679 | 50720 | 94953 |

| 81525 | 72295 | 04839 | 96423 | 24878 | 82651 | 66566 | 14778 | 76797 | 14780 | 13300 | 87074 | 79666 | 95725 |
| 29676 | 20591 | 68086 | 26432 | 46901 | 20829 | 89768 | 81536 | 86645 | 12659 | 92259 | 57102 | 80428 | 25280 |
| 00742 | 57392 | 39064 | 66432 | 84683 | 40027 | 32832 | 61362 | 98947 | 96067 | 64760 | 64584 | 96096 | 98253 |
| 05366 | 04213 | 25669 | 26422 | 44407 | 44048 | 37937 | 63904 | 45766 | 66134 | 75470 | 66520 | 34693 | 90449 |
| 91921 | 26418 | 64117 | 94305 | 26766 | 25940 | 39972 | 22209 | 71500 | 64568 | 91402 | 42416 | 07844 | 69618 |

| 00582 | 04711 | 87917 | 77341 | 42206 | 35126 | 74087 | 99547 | 81817 | 42607 | 43808 | 76655 | 62028 | 76630 |
| 00725 | 69884 | 62797 | 56170 | 86324 | 88072 | 76222 | 36086 | 84637 | 93161 | 76038 | 65855 | 77919 | 88006 |
| 69011 | 65795 | 95876 | 55293 | 18988 | 27354 | 26585 | 08615 | 40801 | 59920 | 29841 | 80150 | 12777 | 48501 |
| 25976 | 57948 | 29888 | 88604 | 67917 | 48708 | 18912 | 82271 | 65424 | 69774 | 33611 | 54262 | 85963 | 03547 |
| 09763 | 83473 | 73577 | 12908 | 30883 | 18317 | 28290 | 35797 | 05998 | 41688 | 34952 | 37888 | 38917 | 88050 |

| 91567 | 42595 | 27958 | 30134 | 04024 | 86385 | 29880 | 99730 | 55536 | 84855 | 29080 | 09250 | 79656 | 73211 |
| 17955 | 56349 | 90999 | 49127 | 20044 | 59931 | 06115 | 20542 | 18059 | 02008 | 73708 | 83517 | 36103 | 42791 |
| 46503 | 18584 | 18845 | 49618 | 02304 | 51038 | 20655 | 58727 | 28168 | 15475 | 56942 | 53389 | 20562 | 87338 |
| 92157 | 89634 | 94824 | 78171 | 84610 | 82834 | 09922 | 25417 | 44137 | 48413 | 25555 | 21246 | 35509 | 20468 |
| 14577 | 62765 | 35605 | 81263 | 39667 | 47358 | 56873 | 56307 | 61607 | 49518 | 89656 | 20103 | 77490 | 18062 |

| 98427 | 07523 | 33362 | 64270 | 01638 | 92477 | 66969 | 98420 | 04880 | 45585 | 46565 | 04102 | 46880 | 45709 |
| 34914 | 63976 | 88720 | 82765 | 34476 | 17032 | 87589 | 40836 | 32427 | 70002 | 70663 | 88863 | 77775 | 69348 |
| 70060 | 28277 | 39475 | 46473 | 23219 | 53416 | 94970 | 25832 | 69975 | 94884 | 19661 | 72828 | 00102 | 66794 |
| 53976 | 54914 | 06990 | 67245 | 68350 | 82948 | 11398 | 42878 | 80287 | 88267 | 47363 | 46634 | 06541 | 97809 |
| 76072 | 29515 | 40980 | 07391 | 58745 | 25774 | 22987 | 80059 | 39911 | 96189 | 41151 | 14222 | 60697 | 59583 |

# References

American Camp Association. (2007a). *Accreditation process guide.* Monterey, CA: Healthy Learning.

American Camp Association. (2007b). *Creating positive youth outcomes.* Monterey, CA: Healthy Learning.

American Camp Association. (2008). *Designing quality youth programs.* Monterey, CA: Healthy Learning.

American Psychological Association. (2001). *Publication manual of the American Psychological Association* (5th ed.). Washington, DC: APA.

Anderson, D. H., & Schneider, I. E. (1993). Using the Delphi process to identify significant recreation research-based innovations. *Journal of Park and Recreation Administration, 11*(1), 25–36.

Babbie, E. (2006). *The practice of social research* (11th ed.). Florence, KY: Cengage Learning.

Baldwin, C. K., Caldwell, L. L., & Witt, P. A. (2005). Deliberate programming with logic models: From theory to outcomes. In P. A. Witt & L. L. Caldwell (Eds.), *Recreation and youth development* (pp. 219–239). State College, PA: Venture Publishing, Inc.

Bennett, C. F. (1982). *Reflective appraisal of program (RAP): An approach to studying clientele-perceived results of Cooperative Extension programs.* Ithaca, NY: Cornell University.

Burlingame, J., & Blaschko, T. M. (1997). *Assessment tools for recreational therapy* (2nd ed.) Ravensdale, WA: Idyll Arbor.

Campbell, D., & Stanley, J. (1963). *Experimental and quasi-experimental designs for research.* Chicago: Rand McNally.

Colorado Trust, The. (2007). *The importance of culture in evaluation.* Retrieved on December 16, 2008, from http://www.coloradotrust.org.

Connolly, P. (1982). Evaluation's critical role in agency accountability. *Parks & Recreation, 17*(2), 34–36.

Corbin, J., & Strauss, A. (2008). *Basics of qualitative research: Techniques and procedures for developing grounded theory* (3rd ed.). Thousand Oaks, CA: Sage Publications.

Crompton, J. L. (1985). *Needs assessment: Taking the pulse of the public recreation client.* College Station, TX: Texas A & M University.

Crompton, J. L., & Tian-Cole, S. (1999). What response rate can be expected from questionnaire surveys that address park and recreation issues? *Journal of Park and Recreation Administration, 17*(2), 60–72.

Csikszentmihalyi, M. (1975). *Beyond boredom and anxiety.* San Francisco, CA: Jossey-Bass.

Dattilo, J. (1988). Assessing music preferences of persons with severe disabilities. *Therapeutic Recreation Journal, 22*(2), 12–23.

Delbecq, A., Van de Ven, A., & Gustafson, D. H. (1975). *Group techniques for program planning: A guide to nominal group and Delphi processes.* Glenview, IL: Scott Foresman.

Dillman, D. A., Smith, J. D., & Christian, L. M. (2009). *Internet, mail, and mixed-mode surveys: The tailored design method* (3rd ed.). Hoboken, NJ: Wiley.

Dunn, J. K. (1987). Establishing reliability and validity in evaluation instruments. *Journal of Park and Recreation Administration, 5*(4), 61–70.

Ellis, G. D., & Witt, P. (1982). Evaluation by design. *Parks & Recreation, 17*(2), 40–43.

Ellis, G. D., & Williams, D. R. (1987). The impending renaissance in leisure service evaluation. *Journal of Park and Recreation Administration, 5*(4), 17–29.

Farrell, P., & Lundegren, H. N. (1987). Designing and objectives-oriented evaluation and translating results into action. *Journal of Park and Recreation Administration, 5*(4), 84–93.

Ferguson, D. D. (1983). Assessment interviewing techniques: A useful tool in developing individual program plans. *Therapeutic Recreation Journal, 17*(2), 16–22.

Fletcher, J. E., & King, M. (1993). Use of voter surveys to plan bond campaigns for parks and recreation. *Journal of Park and Recreation Administration, 11*(2), 17–27.

Geertz, C. (1983). Thick description: Toward an interpretive theory of culture. In R. M. Emerson (Ed.), *Contemporary field research* (pp. 37–59). Boston: Little, Brown.

Girl Scouts of the USA. (2000). *Tool kit for measuring outcomes of Girl Scout resident camp.* New York: GSUSA.

Glover, R. B, & Glover, J. (1981, November). Appraising performance—Some alternatives to the sandwich approach. *Parks & Recreation*, 27–28.

Gorin, S., Hooper, C., Dyson, C., & Cabral, C. (2008). Ethical challenges in conducting research with hard to reach families. *Child Abuse Review, 17*(4), 275–287.

Guba, E. G., & Lincoln, Y. S. (1981). *Effective evaluation.* San Francisco, CA: Jossey-Bass.

Hale, R. (1990). *MYSTAT: Statistical applications.* Cambridge, MA: Course Technology, Inc.

Halle, J. W., Boyer, T. E., & Ashton-Shaeffer, C. (1991). Social validation as a program evaluation measure. *Therapeutic Recreation Journal, 25*(3), 29–43.

Henderson, K. A. (1988). Are volunteers worth their weight in gold? *Parks & Recreation, 23*(11), 40–43.

Henderson, K. A. (2006). *Dimensions of choice: Qualitative approaches to parks, recreation, tourism, sport, and leisure research.* State College, PA: Venture Publishing, Inc.

Henderson, K. A., Bialeschki, M. D., Thurber, C., Whitaker, L., & Scanlin, M. (2007). Intentional youth development through camp experiences. *Camping Magazine, 79*(5), 6–8. (correction p. 71 in 79(6)).

Henderson, K. A., Presley, J., & Bialeschki, M. D. (2004). Theory and leisure research: Reflections from the editors. *Leisure Sciences, 26*(4), 411–426.

Hollenhorst, S., Olson, D., & Fortney, R. (1992). Use of importance-performance analysis to evaluate state park cabins: The case of the West Virginia State Park System. *Journal of Park and Recreation Administration, 10*(1), 1–11.

Howe, C. Z. (1980). Models of evaluating public recreation programs: What the literature shows. *Leisure Today/Journal of Physical Education and Recreation, 50*(10), 36–38.

Howe, C. Z., & Carpenter, G. M. (1985). *Programming leisure experiences: A cyclical approach.* Englewood Cliffs, NJ: Prentice-Hall.

Howe, C. Z., & Keller, M. J. (1988). The use of triangulation as an evaluation technique: Illustrations from regional symposia in therapeutic recreation. *Therapeutic Recreation Journal, 22*(1), 36–45.

Hudson, S. (1988). *How to conduct community needs assessment surveys in public parks and recreation.* Columbus, OH: Publishing Horizons, Inc.

Impara, J. C., & Plake, B. C. (Eds.). (1998). *The thirteenth mental measurements yearbook.* Lincoln, NE: Buros Institute.

Iso-Ahola, S. (1982). Intrinsic motivation—An overlooked basis for evaluation. *Parks & Recreation, 17*(2), 32–33, 58.

Jacelon, C. S. (2007). Older adults' participation in research. *Nurse Researcher, 14*(4), 64–73.

Kellogg, W. K. Foundation. (2001). *Logic model development guide.* Battle Creek, MI: Author.

Kraus, R., & Allen, L. (1987). *Research and evaluation in recreation, parks, and leisure studies.* Columbus, OH: Publishing Horizons, Inc.

Krejcie, R. V., & Morgan, D. W. (1970). Determining sample size for research activities. *Educational and Psychological Measurement, 30,* 607–610.

Krueger, R. A., & Casey, M. A. (2009). *Focus groups: A practical guide for applied research* (4th ed.). Thousand Oaks, CA: Sage Publications.

Lankford, S., & DeGraaf, D. (1992). Strengths, weaknesses, opportunities, and threats in morale, welfare, and recreation organizations: Challenges of the 1990s. *Journal of Park and Recreation Administration, 10*(1), 31–45.

Lincoln, Y. S., & Guba, E. G. (1985). *Naturalistic inquiry.* Beverly Hills, CA: Sage Publications.

Loftus, G. R., & Loftus, E. F. (1982). *Essence of statistics.* Monterey, CA: Brooks/Cole Publishing Co.

Lundegren, H. M., & Farrell, P. (1985). *Evaluation for leisure service managers.* Philadelphia, PA: Saunders College Publishing.

MacKay, K. J., & Crompton, J. L. (1990). Measuring the quality of recreation services. *Journal of Park and Recreation Administration, 8*(3), 47–56.

Malik, P. B., Ashton-Shaeffer, C., & Kleiber, D. A. (1991). Interviewing young adults with mental retardation: A seldom used research method. *Therapeutic Recreation Journal, 25*(1), 60–73.

McKenzie, T. L. (2006). *SOPLAY (System for Observing Plan and Leisure Activity in Youth): Description and procedures manual.* San Diego, CA: San Diego State University.

Michigan State University. (1976). *Survey research for community recreation services.* Research Report 291. East Lansing: Michigan State University Agricultural Experiment Station.

Mohr, L. B. (1988). *Impact analysis for program evaluation.* Chicago, IL: The Dorsey Press.

Norusis, M. J. (1983). *Introductory statistics guide.* Chicago, IL: SPSS, Inc.

Orthner, D. K., Smith, S., & Wright, D. (1986). Measuring program needs. *Evaluation and Program Planning, 9,* 199–207.

Patton, M. Q. (1978). *Utilization-focused evaluation.* Beverly Hills, CA: Sage Publications.

Patton, M. Q. (1980a). Making methods choices. *Evaluation and Program Planning, 3,* 219–228.

Patton, M. Q. (1980b). *Qualitative evaluation methods.* Beverly Hills, CA: Sage Publications.

Posavac, E. J., & Carey, R. G. (1992). *Program evaluation: Methods and case studies.* Englewood Cliffs, NJ: Prentice Hall.

Research Spectrum, The (2001). Available at: http://www.researchspectrum.com.

Riley, B., & Wright, S. (1990). Establishing quality assurance monitors for the evaluation of therapeutic recreation service. *Therapeutic Recreation Journal, 24*(2), 25–39.

Robinson, P. A. (1985) *Fundamentals of technical writing.* Boston, MA: Houghton Mifflin.

Rossman, J. R. (1982, June). Evaluate programs by measuring participant satisfactions. *Parks & Recreation,* 33–35.

Royce, S. W., Sharpe, P. A., Greaney, M. L., Neff, L. J., Ainsworth, B. E., & Henderson, K. A. (2003). Conceptualizing barriers and supports for physical activity: A qualitative assessment. *International Journal of Health Promotion and Education, 41*(2), 49–56.

Salkind, N. J. (1991). *Exploring research.* New York: Macmillan.

Scriven, M. (1967). The methodology of evaluation. In R. W. Tyler, R. M. Gagne, & M. Scriven, *Perspectives of curriculum evaluation,* (pp. 39–83). Chicago, IL: Rand McNally.

Search Institute. (1996). Developmental assets. Available at: http://www.search-institute.org.

Sengstock, M. C., & Hwalek, M. (1999). Issues to be considered in evaluating programs for children and youth. *New Designs in Youth Development, 15*(2), 8–11.

Shafer, R. L., & Moeller, G. (1987). Know how to word your questionnaire. *Parks & Recreation, 22*(10), 48–52.

Siegenthaler, K. L. (1994). Importance-performance analysis: Application to senior programs evaluation. *Journal of Park and Recreation Administration, 12*(3), 57–70.

Smith, M. F. (1989). *Evaluability assessment: A practical approach.* Boston, MA: Kiuwer Academic Publishers.

Stumbo, N. J. (1983). Systematic observation as a research tool for assessing client behavior. *Therapeutic Recreation Journal, 17*(4), 53–63.

Stumbo, N. J. (1991). Selected assessment resources: A review of instruments and references. *Annual in Therapeutic Recreation, 2,* 8–24.

Taylor, S. J., & Bogdan, R. (1984). *Introduction to qualitative research methods: The search for meaning* (2nd ed.). New York, NY: Wiley.

Theobald, W. (1979). Evaluation of recreation and park programs. New York: John Wiley & Sons.

Theobald, W. (1987). Historical antecedents of evaluation in leisure programs and services. *Journal of Park and Recreation Administration, 5*(4), 1–9.

Thurber, C., Schuler, L., Scanlin, M., & Henderson, K. (2007). Youth development outcomes of the camp experience: Evidence for multidimensional growth. *Journal of Youth and Adolescence, 36,* 241–254.

Tinsley, H. E. A. (1984). Limitations, explanations, aspirations: A confession of fallibility and a promise to strive for perfection. *Journal of Leisure Research, 16*(2), 93–98.

Webb, E. J., Campbell, D. T., Schwartz, R. D., & Sechrest, L. (1966). *Unobtrusive measures: Nonreactive research in the social sciences.* Chicago, IL: Rand McNally & Company.

Weiss, C. H. (1975). Interviewing in evaluation research. In E. L. Struening & M. Guttentag (Eds.), *Handbook of evaluation research.* Beverly Hills, CA: Sage Publications.

Wicks, B. E., Backman, K. F., Allen, J., & Van Blaricom, D. (1993). Geographic Information Systems (GIS): A tool for marketing, managing, and planning municipal park systems. *Journal of Park and Recreation Administration, 11*(1), 9–23.

Wright, B. A., Duray, N., & Goodale, T. L. (1992). Assessing perceptions of recreation center service quality: An application of recent advancements in service quality research. *Journal of Park and Recreation Administration, 10*(3), 33–47.

Yin, R. K. (2003). *Case study research: Design and methods.* Thousand Oaks, CA: Sage Publications.

# Glossary of Terms

*a priori:* the determination ahead of time of processes or procedures.

**accountability:** a relative term that describes the capability of an organization or program to justify or explain the activities and services it provides.

**accreditation:** the process of assuring that an organization has met specific standards set by a professional or an accrediting body.

**achievement tests:** tests to show what an individual has learned.

**American Camp Association (ACA):** an organization that sets standards for organized camping in the United States.

**American Psychological Association (APA):** an organization that provides (among many services) a manual of style guidelines for research and report writing.

**analysis of variance (ANOVA):** parametric statistic used to measure the differences between three or more group means.

**anonymity:** no one knows the identity of the participants.

**appendices:** the supportive material included with a thesis or report that includes additional information about the sample, instrument, and/or analyses.

**archives:** written records or documents.

**assessment:** the examination of needs and interests that provides the foundation for further planning—the "what should be" related to the needs and interests.

**attitude tests:** tests that measure the opinions or beliefs of the test-taker about an object, person, or event. They usually refer to some internal state of mind or set of beliefs that are stable over time.

**audit trail:** the process of documenting how data were collected and analyzed in a qualitative study.

**axial coding:** the second step after open coding that organizes the open codes into themes.

**benefits:** positive outcomes.

**benchmarking:** a standard of operation that an organization can use to compare itself to an average or to other agencies.

**best practices:** an aspect of an agency, process, or system this is considered as a model for excellence.

**between-method triangulation:** the use of two or more methods to measure the same phenomena—also called mixed methods or mixed modes.

**bivariate:** the examination of the relationship of two variables.

**black box model:** the goal-free approach to evaluation.

**body:** the major part of an evaluation report that includes the introduction, methods, findings, and conclusions/recommendations.

**case:** the unit or individual involved in a study.

**case study:** an intensive investigation of a unit such as an individual, a group, or an organization generally with a focus on process and explanation.

**central tendency:** the measures of mean, median, and mode.

**chi-square:** a nonparametric statistical analysis of two categorical variables.

**close-ended questions:** questions asked that provide specific options as answers.

**code numbers:** the numbers used to identify individuals for purposes of keeping track of who responded and did not respond to a questionnaire.

**codebook:** the written information that tells how coding has been done for a measurement instrument.

**code sheet:** a compilation or spreadsheet showing all the data or records for the cases examined in a study.

**coding:** the numeric assignment of a value to a variable from quantitative data and the word or phrase assignment of a name to an idea from qualitative data.

**Commission on Accreditation of Rehabilitation Facilities (CARF):** the national accrediting body for rehabilitation programs.

**competencies:** the abilities, skills, and knowledge one has to undertake a task.

**complementariness:** how a set of results obtained from different data sets or methods enrich each other.

**conclusions:** a summary of the major points learned in an evaluation or research project.

**concurrent or criterion-related validity:** a form of internal reliability that asks whether the scores on a particular instrument correlate with scores on another instrument.

**confidentiality:** the identities of the participants responding are known by the evaluator but s/he does not share that information.

**congruence:** similarity or consistency found in using two or more methods or data sets.

**consensus:** overall agreement.

**constant comparison:** a systematic method for recording, coding, and analyzing qualitative data that includes comparisons among cases, groups, and themes.

**content analysis:** a process used in analyzing documents, records, transcribed conversations, letters, or anything in a textual form.

**content validity:** the contents of the theoretical expectations that one wishes to measure.

**continuous data:** data that can be measured along a continuum and that have an infinite number of possible values.

**control group:** the group in an experimental design that does not receive an intervention or treatment.

**conversational interview (also called an unstructured interview):** an interview form in which no questions are predetermined but emerge as the interviewer and interviewee begin to converse.

**correlation:** measures of association.

**cost-benefit analysis:** relating the costs of a program or an operation to the benefits realized as expressed in dollar figures.

**cost-effectiveness analysis:** a ratio of the costs of a program or service to the revenue generated.

**Council on Accreditation (COA):** the National Recreation and Park Association body that assesses through standards the quality of university curricula in recreation-related areas.

**Council on Accreditation of Park and Recreation Agencies (CAPRA):** the National Recreation and Park Association body that assesses through standards the quality of community park and recreation organizations.

**cover:** the physical paper that surrounds an evaluation report and gives the information about the title, authors, and organization.

**cover sheet:** the letter sent with an questionnaire or with a final report to explain what the project is/was about and why it is important.

**covert:** when something is hidden or not known.

**credibility:** a quality measure of the internal validity or how well something measures what it is supposed to measure.

**criteria:** the standards or the ideals upon which something is evaluated or studied.

**criterion-referenced evaluation:** measurement based on a level of performance.

**data display:** a form of data reduction where information is assembled to aid in interpreting themes that emerge from qualitative data.

**data reduction:** the process of coding and examining data for analysis.

**debriefing:** the process of discussing and informing participants of the results of a project.

**deductive theory/analysis:** examining something by going from narrow perspectives to derive conclusions from reasoning—in systematic inquiry going from theory to hypotheses to observations to confirmation.

**delphi studies:** a technique that seeks to draw conclusions based on the consensus established from experts about a particular topic.

**demographics:** population characteristics of a group of people such as age, state of birth, race, or gender.

**dependability:** the consistency or reliability of an instrument to measure the same results time after time.

**dependent variable:** the variable that is assumed to have been caused by or related to another (independent) variable.

**descriptive/evocative designs:** investigative methods used to determine existing conditions by analyzing data for purposes of explanation or comparison; compare with **experimental designs.**

**descriptive statistics:** univariate measures used to characterize data.

**discrete data:** noncontinuous finite numbers that have no in-between measurements.

**econometrics:** any process that involves an analysis of how economic aspects affect an organization.

**economic impact:** the amount of revenue activity generated in an area due to a particular event such as a festival or due to tourist trades.

**effect size:** a statistic used along with statistical significance to show the magnitude of differences between groups.

**effectiveness:** the end results or the impact.

**efficiency:** the relationship between inputs and outputs.

**emic:** ideas expressed by the respondents that are shown as quotes or anecdotes.

**empirical data:** any data that can be observed.

**enlightened decision making:** using systematic inquiry to make the best and most informed decisions concerning the value or worth of something.

**enumeration:** a qualitative data analysis procedure that counts the number of occurrences.

**ethics:** the philosophical basis for determining right and wrong.

**etic:** interpretations of the researcher concerning the meanings of ideas expressed by respondents.

**evaluation:** the systematic collection and analysis of data to address some criteria to make judgments about the worth or improvement of something; making decisions based on identified criteria and supporting evidence.

**evaluation process:** the steps undertaken in doing an evaluation project that include broadly establishing criteria, collecting and analyzing data, and making judgments (conclusions and recommendations) from the results.

**evaluation project:** the specific study undertaken to determine the worth or value of some aspect of the five Ps.

**evaluation report:** the written or oral report that summarizes the evaluation project.

**evaluation research:** the process used to collect and analyze data or evidence.

**evaluation system:** a process for determining and addressing the evaluation needs of an organization related to the five Ps of program, participants, personnel, policy, and place.

**evaluator:** the individual or individuals conducting the evaluation.

**evidence:** the data that are collected and analyzed in an evaluation project.

**evidence-based practice:** a decision-making process that integrates the best available research, professional expertise, and participant characteristics.

**Excel:** a spreadsheet program that can be used to organize and analyze quantitative data.

**executive summary:** an abstract (usually ranging from 100–500 words) that states information about an evaluation or research process and what was found in conducting the project.

**experimental designs:** investigative methods used to assure control in the collection of data; compare with **descriptive/evocative designs.**

**Expert Judgment:** the use of professionals who have expertise or training to enable them to make evaluations.

**external evaluator:** someone such as a consultant who evaluates from outside and is not employed full-time by the organization.

**external validity:** how well the results of a measurement can be generalized to similar situations.

**face validity:** a common term used to describe whether an instrument measures the contents it is supposed to measure.

**field test:** a "practice" run for a study that focuses on sampling procedures and administration processes.

**five Ps:** the components that might be evaluated within a recreation organization (personnel, places, policy, program, participants).

**focus groups:** a particular form of group interviews, where individuals within a group are asked to respond and discuss particular criteria or issues.

**follow-up contact:** a second or third encounter with an individual, usually in the form of a phone call or postcard/letter to request that they respond to a survey.

**follow-up questions:** similar to probes. They are asked in a interview to encourage people to give additional information.

**formal evaluation:** the systematic evaluation undertaken where specific criteria are set, data are collected, and judgments made.

**formative evaluation:** the systematic examination of the steps in the development and implementation of some aspect of the five Ps. It is usually related to some aspect of the program or organizational process and occurs during an activity.

**frequency counts:** the number of times a behavior occurs.

**Friedman Analysis of Variance:** a nonparametric test used for repeated measures.

**full participant:** an individual who participates fully in a group but is also doing an observation as a method of evaluation.

**goal:** general statement about an organization and its programs that evolves from the organization's purpose or mission.

**goal-attainment:** a model of evaluation where pre-established goals and objectives are used to measure outcomes.

**goal-free:** a model of evaluation that examines a unit irrespective of the goals and objectives—also known as the Black Box Model.

**grounded comparison:** a term coined in this book to describe how qualitative data may be analyzed using a combination of grounded theory and constant comparison.

**grounded theory:** a process of coding and analyzing qualitative data that results in emerging or inductive theory and theorizing.

**Hawthorne Effect:** idea that the presence of evaluators may affect responses.

**hypothesis:** the questions or hunches, based on theory, derived concerning the possible outcomes of a research project.

**impact evaluation:** another term for program evaluation that refers to whether or not interventions produced the intended effects or outcomes.

**importance-performance:** a research technique that is used to quantify customer satisfaction by combining measures of importance and satisfaction/opinions about the performance of an organization.

**independent variable:** a variable that is stable and not influenced by another (dependent) variable.

**in-depth Interviews:** personal interviews that cover a range of topics in which the interviewee is asked to talk, given open-ended questions.

**inductive theory/analysis:** examining something in an open-ended and exploratory way, including thinking beyond current knowledge toward the unknown—in systematic inquiry going from observations to patterns to tentative hypotheses to theory.

**Inferential Statistics:** measures used to compare variables or to predict future behavior.

**Informal Evaluation:** intuitive unstructured approaches to making decisions.

**informed consent:** a person's permission to participate in an evaluation or research project.

**inputs:** the resources available and expended in an organization.

**Institutional Review Boards (IRB):** the policing organizations that make sure the privacy and rights of individuals are not violated when they participate in research.

**inter-observer reliability (also known as inter-rater reliability):** a measure of the consistency of agreement from rater and rater.

**inter-rater reliability (also known as inter-observer reliability):** a measure of the consistency of agreement from rater and rater.

**internal evaluator:** someone who evaluates some aspect of the five Ps who is a member of the organization.

**internal validity:** how well an instrument measures what it is supposed to measure for a particular project.

**interpretation:** the process of analyzing data to determine what they mean.

**interpretive:** a worldview that suggests the world can be viewed from multiple perspectives and truths.

**interval data:** data put into ordered categories that have meaningful size differences between the data points.

**interval sampling:** choosing predesignated periods of time for doing sampling.

**interview guide (also called a semi-structured interview):** A list of the topics to be covered in an interview. They include no particular sequence or specific wording.

**interview schedule:** the list of questions asked in an interview.

**interviewer bias:** the potential prejudice, inadvertent leading, or unconscious judgment that may exist in conducting an interview.

**intuition:** the internal sense about something.

**Intuitive Judgment:** a pseudo-model of evaluation that allows an individual to evaluate based on gut-level feelings about some aspect of the five Ps.

**Joint Commission on Accreditation of Healthcare Organizations (JCAHO):** the organization that sets standards of evaluation and accreditation for hospitals.

**judgment:** the determination of the value or worth of something based on the evidence collected from previously determined criteria. It should be the outcome of data collection and analysis.

**KASA:** a level of program evaluation that includes the measurement of Knowledge, Attitudes, Skills, and Aspirations.

**key informants:** People who provide more in-depth information than regular respondents.

**Kruskal-Wallis:** a nonparametric test used to examine the differences in means between two or more groups.

**latency recording:** a measure of the time elapsed between a cue and when a behavior occurs.

**leisure programming cycle:** the process of conducting needs assessments, setting objectives, planning programs, implementing programs, evaluating, and making revisions for the next program.

**leisure services or delivery systems:** human service organizations and enterprises that provide recreation, leisure, and/or educational services to improve the quality of life of individuals within the society. These may be therapeutic, private, not-for-profit, public, or commercial organizations.

**Likert scales:** used in a particular kind of close-ended question that uses a scaling system usually going from "strongly disagree" to "strongly agree."

**Logic Model:** a picture showing how program components should lead to program outcomes.

**Mann-Whitney:** a nonparametric statistic used to determine differences in rankings on some variable.

**matrix:** a visual picture that shows the relationship of data.

**mean:** the average for a variable.

**measurement instrument:** a tool, usually in the form of a questionnaire or test, used to gather data.

**measurement:** the collection of information or the gathering of data, usually quantitative.

**median:** a descriptive statistic of the point at which half the scores lie above and half lie below.

**methods:** the established procedures used to collect data.

**mixed modes (also known as triangulation):** more than one data set or method used to get information.

**missing data:** information that is not reported by an individual on a questionnaire. The missing data may be due to an oversight or because the individual did not want to answer a question.

**mode:** the most common response to a variable.

**multiplier:** a number used in econometric studies to show the potential that a dollar has to be spent and re-spent in a community

**multivariate:** the examination of the relationship of more than two variables.

**National Recreation and Park Association (NRPA):** the professional association of individuals employed in park and recreation organizations.

**negative evidence:** qualitative data that is opposite or contradictory to the major points that are being uncovered.

**nominal data:** categorical data that define a distinct group and have no relative numeric value such as male/female or yes/no.

**nominal group technique (NGT):** a collective decision-making technique used to do assessments and strategic planning.

**nonparametric:** statistics based on assumptions of a nonnormal distribution that usually include smaller sample sizes.

**nonprobability sampling:** the sampling strategy used to select people in some way that is not based on an equal potential for being selected.

**nonreactive:** unobtrusive observation by not interacting with people.

**nonrespondents:** those individuals who are asked to participate but fail to respond to a survey.

**nonresponse bias:** the error that might exist in a survey because some people respond and some people do not and what the differences might be.

**nonsampling error:** the biases that exist due to who responds to a survey.

**norm-referenced evaluations:** measurement based on the relative position of a person or things in relation to each other using the same measuring tool.

**normal distribution:** the way that scores occur.

**open coding:** the process of identifying the ideas or concepts in qualitative data and giving them names.

**open-ended questions:** questions asked that do not provide options for answers.

**oral histories:** in-depth interviews conducted that explore the entire life of an individual.

**ordered responses:** responses to a question that have a logical order associated with the way that the responses are listed.

**ordinal data:** data that are ranked and indicate how each measure relates to another measure.

**outcomes:** the results, impact, or effect of something.

**outlier:** responses that occur way outside the normal distribution.

**outputs:** the activities undertaken by an organization to impact outcomes.

**overt:** when something is known.

**paper-and-pencil tests:** measurement instruments that are given for individuals to administer to themselves.

**paradigm:** a worldview that describes how one thinks about data and how systematic inquiry should be done.

**parametric:** statistics based on the assumption of normal distribution and randomized groups.

**partially close-ended questions:** questions asked that provide fixed responses but allow the respondent to add his/her additional responses if the existing options are not appropriate.

**participant:** the individuals who receive the services of a recreation-related organization. These may be clients, consumers, players, or anyone otherwise involved in programs and activities in communities, organizations, or in institutions.

**Pearson's correlation:** a parametric statistic used to measure the relationship between two variables.

**peer program review:** a process used in Therapeutic Recreation in which professionals review and evaluate one another's programs.

**people involvement:** the number and characteristics of individuals who participate in a program.

**performance appraisal (also known as performance evaluation):** the process of personnel evaluation.

**personality tests:** tests that relate to a variety of characteristics of an individual.

**personnel evaluation (also known as performance appraisal):** the evaluation of staff.

**personnel:** all staff that work for pay or without pay (volunteers) within a recreation-related organization.

**physical evidence:** traces from the past that provide information.

**pilot study:** a "practice" run for an instrument or a project that gives the evaluator preliminary information about reliability, validity, and usability of a measurement.

**politics:** the personal and collective beliefs that exist.

**population:** all the people who might comprise a delineated group.

**positivism:** a worldview that suggests facts and truths can be found and articulated.

**post-positivism:** a perspective closely aligned with positivism but that allows for creativity in data collection and the interpretation of results.

**posttest:** the measurement given to an individual or group after an intervention is over or time has passed.

**practice change:** the personal adoption and application of new ideas.

**predictive validity:** the ability of an instrument to predict some behavior.

**preordinate:** pre-established goals and objectives used to measure outcomes.

**pretest:** the measurement given to an individual or group at the beginning or before some intervention is completed.

**probability sampling:** the sampling strategy that allows everyone within a group to have an equal opportunity of being selected.

**probes:** the questions asked in interviews to encourage people to give additional information. These include questions like, "Can you give me an example?" "Can you tell me more?" or "How did you feel?"

**Professional Judgment:** a model of evaluation using expert opinions to determine the worth or value of a program.

**program:** all of the activities, instruction, competition, and events that are planned by a leisure service organization.

**program audit:** an accountability term used to quantify the services rendered

**qualitative:** data that appear in the form of words.

**quality assurance (QA):** the process used in healthcare organizations as well as other organizations to assure that certain standards are being met.

**quality control:** assuring that the highest standards of practice are maintained.

**quantitative:** data that appear in the form of numbers.

**quasi-experiments:** those methods that do not meet the strict requirement of an experiment (random samples, control groups, and pre-testing).

**random digit dialing:** a sampling method used for phone interviews where prefixes and numbers are randomly dialed to contact respondents.

**randomization:** the process of assigning people randomly to groups when an experimental design is used.

**range:** the difference between the highest and lowest scores.

**rapport:** establishing a trusting relationships between two individuals or between an individual and a group.

**ratio data:** the most sophisticated level of data in which a true zero point is calculated.

**reactions:** the degree of interest, likes and dislikes, satisfactions, motivations, appeal, and perceived benefits that people attribute to a program.

**recode:** to change a code by collapsing data.

**recommendations:** the proposed courses of action to be followed based upon the conclusions drawn.

**record:** the listing of all the information from an individual or a case.

**reliability:** the determination of whether a measure consistently conveys the same meaning—it is also called stability, dependability, replicability, or consistency.

**reliability correlation or coefficient:** a statistic that tells how likely an instrument is to measure consistently.

**research:** the systematic collection and analysis of data to answer a theoretical question and to contribute to a body of knowledge.

**response rate (also known as return rate):** the percentage of responses to a survey based on the actual number returned divided by the number spent.

**responsive evaluation:** paying attention to the use of the evaluation by addressing the evaluation needs and interests of stakeholders such as administrators, boards, funding agencies, staff, or participants.

**responsive evaluation (also known as utilization-focus evaluation):** the active approach to evaluation that starts by finding out what the key decision makers expect from an evaluation and then determining how to conduct the evaluation.

**return rate (also known as response rate):** the percentage of responses to a survey based on the actual number returned divided by the number spent.

**sample:** a representation of a total population.

**sampling:** the process of drawing a representative selection of respondents from the population.

**sampling error:** the amount of statistical error that might exist because you can't or don't always sample correctly

**saturation:** used in theoretical sampling to indicate a point where no new theoretical data are evident and data collection can stop.

**scientific method:** the formal process used in research whereby research questions/hypotheses are generated, data collected, and results related back to original questions/theories.

**selective coding:** process of integrating axial codes to develop explanations of the results or theorizing.

**self-check:** the process of examining oneself in relation to making evaluation decisions.

**semantic differentials:** a particular kind of close-ended question that includes a list of bipolar adjectives that the respondent chooses.

**semi-structured interview (also known as an interview guide):** A list of the topics to be covered in an interview. They include no particular sequence or specific wording but are all covered at some point in the interview.

**service quality:** a technique used to measure the dimensions of consumer expectations and perceptions.

**sign test:** a nonparametric statistic used to determine differences when the data are categorical.

**single subject technique:** a way to evaluate the effect of interventions on an individual participant or client.

**skewness:** a measure of the symmetry of a distribution.

**snowball sampling:** using an initial sample of people and then getting those individuals to suggest others who might fit the criteria for the sample.

**social desirability:** the possibility that a respondent may answer a questionnaire based on what she or he perceives to be the socially acceptable answer or the "right" answer.

**sociometrics:** a technique used to analyze how individuals within groups relate to one another.

**SOPLAY and SOPARC:** systems for data collection used to examine physical activity.

**Spearman correlation:** a nonparametric statistic used to measure the relationship between two variables.

**staged questions:** questions asked in such a way that one must respond to one question in order to know which question to answer next.

**standard deviation:** the measure of dispersion or how closely data group around a mean.

**standardized interview (also known as a structured interview):** An interview form that includes the exact wording and sequencing of questions as they are asked to each individual participating in a study or project.

**standardized tests:** tests designed and modified by a process that results in reliability, validity and specified instructions for administration and interpreting the results.

**standards:** predetermined criteria used to evaluate how an organization functions.

**statistical packages:** software developed to assist in statistical analysis.

**statistical significance:** the unlikeliness that differences between groups are a result of chance.

**structured interview (also known as a standardized interview ):** An interview form that includes the exact wording and sequencing of questions as they are asked to each individual participating in a study or project.

**summative evaluation:** the systematic terminal examination of the impact and effectiveness of a program. It usually occurs at the end of something.

**surveys:** the category of methods that asks people directly about some criteria. Surveys may be done using questionnaires or interviews.

**systematic inquiry:** the process of using evaluation and/or research to improve something or add to the body of knowledge.

**systems approach:** a model of evaluation that focuses on processes and on determining whether an organization is successful under a given set of conditions.

*t*-**tests:** parametric statistic used to measure the difference between two group means.

**theoretical sampling:** a sampling strategy used to collect qualitative data where people are interviewed/observed based on the data gathered until a saturation point is reached when no further new themes are being uncovered.

**theory:** a systematic structure for giving order and insight to what has been observed—an explanation.

**thick description:** a way of writing qualitative data that includes both the evaluator's and the respondents' perspective.

**time sampling:** Spot checking based on a plan for doing observations

**transferability:** the qualitative equivalent to external validity or how well the results of a measurement can be generalized to other situations.

**triangulation (also known as mixed modes):** collecting data for an evaluation project by using more than one method, source of data, or evaluator.

**trilogy:** three of something. The focus of evaluation is on criteria, evidence, and judgment.

**trustworthiness:** the quality of the data collected that assures that errors in interpretation are not made. The term is usually used to refer to qualitative data but may be appropriate for quantitative data as well.

**type I error:** a belief that two groups are different when in fact they are the same.

**type II error:** a belief that two groups are the same when in fact they are different.

**univariate:** the examination of the distribution of cases on only one variable.

**unobtrusive methods:** observing, recording, and analyzing human behavior in a situation where interaction with people generally does not occur and where people are unaware that their behavior is being observed or recorded.

**unordered responses:** responses that have no specific order related to the way they are portrayed.

**unstructured interview (also known as conversational guide):** an interview form in which no questions are predetermined but they emerge as the interviewer and interviewee begin to converse.

**usability:** how effectively and efficiently an instrument is administered and analyzed.

**utilization-focused evaluation (also known as responsive evaluation):** the active approach to evaluation that starts by finding out what the key decision makers expect from an evaluation and then determines how to conduct the evaluation.

**validity:** the determination of whether a measure does what it says it does. This term is also associated with meaning, relevance, credibility, and transferability.

**variable:** a name associated with values that have logical groupings of characteristics. A variable might be state of birth that would have all the states in the U.S. as possible values.

**variance:** a dispersion measure that describes the extent to which scores differ from one another.

**visual analysis:** using graphics as data that are generally content analyzed in some way.

**visual maps:** a method for graphically showing the relationship of concepts in qualitative analysis.

**Wilcoxon:** a nonparametric test used to determine the relationship when the dependent variable has more than two values ranked.

**within-method triangulation:** the collection of both qualitative and quantitative data using the same method.

**worldview:** the philosophy from which each of us views the world, including broad assumptions about data and how projects should be undertaken. This term is also referred to as a paradigm.

# Index

# Other Books by Venture Publishing, Inc.

Facilitation Techniques in Therapeutic Recreation
  by John Dattilo
File o' Fun: A Recreation Planner for Games & Activities, Third Edition
  by Jane Harris Ericson and Diane Ruth Albright
The Game and Play Leader's Handbook: Facilitating Fun and Positive Interaction, Revised Edition
  by Bill Michaelis and John M. O'Connell
The Game Finder—A Leader's Guide to Great Activities
  by Annette C. Moore
Getting People Involved in Life and Activities: Effective Motivating Techniques
  by Jeanne Adams
Hands On! Children's Activities for Fairs, Festivals, and Special Events
  by Karen L. Ramey
Health Promotion for Mind, Body, and Spirit
  by Suzanne Fitzsimmons and Linda L. Buettner
In Search of the Starfish: Creating a Caring Environment
  by Mary Hart, Karen Primm, and Kathy Cranisky
Inclusion: Including People With Disabilities in Parks and Recreation Opportunities
  by Lynn Anderson and Carla Brown Kress
Inclusive Leisure Services: Responding to the Rights of People with Disabilities, Second Edition
  by John Dattilo
Internships in Recreation and Leisure Services: A Practical Guide for Students, Fourth Edition
  by Edward E. Seagle, Jr. and Ralph W. Smith
Interpretation of Cultural and Natural Resources, Second Edition
  by Douglas M. Knudson, Ted T. Cable, and Larry Beck
Intervention Activities for At-Risk Youth
  by Norma J. Stumbo
Introduction to Outdoor Recreation: Providing and Managing Resource Based Opportunities
  by Roger L. Moore and B.L. Driver
Introduction to Recreation and Leisure Services, Eighth Edition
  by Karla A. Henderson, M. Deborah Bialeschki, John L. Hemingway, Jan S. Hodges, Beth D. Kivel, and H. Douglas Sessoms
Introduction to Therapeutic Recreation: U.S. and Canadian Perspectives
  by Kenneth Mobily and Lisa Ostiguy
Introduction to Writing Goals and Objectives: A Manual for Recreation Therapy Students and Entry-Level Professionals
  by Suzanne Melcher
Leadership and Administration of Outdoor Pursuits, Third Edition
  by James Blanchard, Michael Strong, and Phyllis Ford
Leadership in Leisure Services: Making a Difference, Third Edition
  by Debra J. Jordan

Leisure and Leisure Services in the 21st Century: Toward Mid Century
  by Geoffrey Godbey
The Leisure Diagnostic Battery Computer Software (CD)
  by Peter A. Witt, Gary Ellis, and Mark A. Widmer
Leisure Education I: A Manual of Activities and Resources, Second Edition
  by Norma J. Stumbo
Leisure Education II: More Activities and Resources, Second Edition
  by Norma J. Stumbo
Leisure Education III: More Goal-Oriented Activities
  by Norma J. Stumbo
Leisure Education IV: Activities for Individuals with Substance Addictions
  by Norma J. Stumbo
Leisure Education Program Planning: A Systematic Approach, Third Edition
  by John Dattilo
Leisure for Canadians
  edited by Ron McCarville and Kelly MacKay
Leisure Studies: Prospects for the Twenty-First Century
  edited by Edgar L. Jackson and Thomas L. Burton
Leisure in Your Life: New Perspectives
  by Geoffrey Godbey
Making a Difference in Academic Life: A Handbook for Park, Recreation, and Tourism Educators
  and Graduate Students
  edited by Dan Dustin and Tom Goodale
Managing to Optimize the Beneficial Outcomes of Leisure
  edited by B. L. Driver
Marketing in Leisure and Tourism: Reaching New Heights
  by Patricia Click Janes
The Melody Lingers On: A Complete Music Activities Program for Older Adults
  by Bill Messenger
More Than a Game: A New Focus on Senior Activity Services
  by Brenda Corbett
The Multiple Values of Wilderness
  by H. Ken Cordell, John C. Bergstrom, and J.M. Bowker
N.E.S.T. Approach: Dementia Practice Guidelines for Disturbing Behaviors
  by Linda L. Buettner and Suzanne Fitzsimmons
The Organizational Basis of Leisure Participation: A Motivational Exploration
  by Robert A. Stebbins
Outdoor Recreation for 21st Century America
  by H. Ken Cordell
Outdoor Recreation Management: Theory and Application, Third Edition
  by Alan Jubenville and Ben Twight

Parks for Life: Moving the Goal Posts, Changing the Rules, and Expanding the Field
   by Will LaPage
The Pivotal Role of Leisure Education: Finding Personal Fulfillment in This Century
      edited by Elie Cohen-Gewerc and Robert A. Stebbins
Planning and Organizing Group Activities in Social Recreation
      by John V. Valentine
Planning Areas and Facilities for Sport and Recreation: Predesign Process, Principles, and Strategies
      by Jack A. Harper
Planning Parks for People, Second Edition
      by John Hultsman, Richard L. Cottrell, and Wendy Z. Hultsman
Programming for Parks, Recreation, and Leisure Services: A Servant Leadership Approach, Third Edition
      by Donald G. DeGraaf, Debra J. Jordan, and Kathy H. DeGraaf
Puttin' on the Skits: Plays for Adults in Managed Care
      by Jean Vetter
Recreation and Leisure: Issues in an Era of Change, Third Edition
      edited by Thomas Goodale and Peter A. Witt
Recreation and Youth Development
      by Peter A. Witt and Linda L. Caldwell
Recreation for Older Adults: Individual and Group Activities
      by Judith A. Elliott and Jerold E. Elliott
Recreation Program Planning Manual for Older Adults
      by Karen Kindrachuk
Recreation Programming and Activities for Older Adults
      by Jerold E. Elliott and Judith A. Sorg-Elliott
Reference Manual for Writing Rehabilitation Therapy Treatment Plans
      by Penny Hogberg and Mary Johnson
Service Living: Building Community through Public Parks and Recreation
      by Doug Wellman, Dan Dustin, Karla Henderson, and Roger Moore
Simple Expressions: Creative and Therapeutic Arts for the Elderly in Long-Term Care Facilities
      by Vicki Parsons
A Social Psychology of Leisure
      by Roger C. Mannell and Douglas A. Kleiber
Special Events and Festivals: How to Organize, Plan, and Implement
      by Angie Prosser and Ashli Rutledge
Survey Research and Analysis: Applications in Parks, Recreation, and Human Dimensions
      by Jerry Vaske
Taking the Initiative: Activities to Enhance Effectiveness and Promote Fun
      by J. P. Witman
Therapeutic Recreation and the Nature of Disabilities
      by Kenneth E. Mobily and Richard D. MacNeil

Therapeutic Recreation: Cases and Exercises, Second Edition
    by Barbara C. Wilhite and M. Jean Keller
Therapeutic Recreation in Health Promotion and Rehabilitation
    by John Shank and Catherine Coyle
Therapeutic Recreation in the Nursing Home
    by Linda Buettner and Shelley L. Martin
Therapeutic Recreation Programming: Theory and Practice
    by Charles Sylvester, Judith E. Voelkl, and Gary D. Ellis
Therapeutic Recreation Protocol for Treatment of Substance Addictions
    by Rozanne W. Faulkner
The Therapeutic Recreation Stress Management Primer
    by Cynthia Mascott
The Therapeutic Value of Creative Writing
    by Paul M. Spicer
Traditions: Improving Quality of Life in Caregiving
    by Janelle Sellick
Trivia by the Dozen: Encouraging Interaction and Reminiscence in Managed Care
    by Jean Vetter